Queer Cities,
Queer Cultures

Queer Cities, Queer Cultures

Europe Since 1945

Edited by
Matt Cook
and
Jennifer V. Evans

B L O O M S B U R Y
LONDON • NEW DELHI • NEW YORK • SYDNEY

Bloomsbury Academic

An imprint of Bloomsbury Publishing Plc

50 Bedford Square	1385 Broadway
London	New York
WC1B 3DP	NY 10018
UK	USA

www.bloomsbury.com

Bloomsbury is a registered trade mark of Bloomsbury Publishing Plc

First published 2014

British Library Cataloguing-in-Publication Data
A catalogue record for this book is available from the British Library.

ISBN: HB: 978-1-4411-4190-3
PB: 978-1-4411-5930-4
ePDF: 978-1-4411-4840-7
ePub: 978-1-4411-1166-1

Library of Congress Cataloging-in-Publication Data
Queer cities, queer cultures: Europe since 1945/edited by Jennifer V. Evans, Matt Cook.
pages cm
Includes bibliographical references and index.
ISBN 978-1-4411-4190-3 (hardback: alkaline paper) – ISBN 978-1-4411-5930-4 (paperback: alkaline paper) – ISBN 978-1-4411-4840-7 (epdf) – ISBN 978-1-4411-1166-1 (ePub)
1. Homosexuality–Europe–History. 2. Gays–Europe–History. 3. Gays–Europe–Social conditions. 4. Gays–Political activity–Europe–History. 5. Homophobia–Europe–History.
I. Evans, Jennifer V., 1970- editor of compilation. II. Cook, Matt, editor of compilation.
HQ76.3.E8Q415 2014
306.76′6094–dc23
2013048257

Typeset by Deanta Global Publishing Services, Chennai, India
Printed and bound in India

This volume is dedicated with much love to
Jason Bennett
and
Ben Tooke

CONTENTS

ACKNOWLEDGEMENTS

We first conceived this book in 2008 as the first of a series of conversations made possible by the generous support of our home institutions. Birkbeck, University of London, supported Matt's research trip to Berlin where Jen was conducting research of her own. Over the years that followed, Carleton University has funded numerous follow-up trips to London and Brighton, which allowed the conversation to deepen and continue. We have had the great good fortune of working with a wonderful group of contributors, who responded swiftly and with good humour at each request for information or revision. We owe them huge thanks for their patience, and for their fascinating insights into the queer worlds they bring to life in their chapters. Our editors at Continuum, Emma Goode and before her Rhodri Mogford and Michael Greenwood, have been a pleasure to work with throughout the entire process. Jane Freeland and Emmanuel Hogg at Carleton helped us in innumerable ways as we drew the final manuscript together. Thanks too to Grishma Fredric for shepherding it through the final process. Our partners and children Jason, Gwen, Gillian, Ben, Jaya and Chetan have, as ever, provided welcome diversion along the way.

Writing is as much a personal as a communal affair. We have learnt so much from each other these last few years about collaboration, friendship and commitment to a common cause. It has been a rewarding experience on all levels.

CONTRIBUTORS

Tom Boellstorff

Tom Boellstorff is professor in the Department of Anthropology at the University of California, Irvine; from 2007 to 2012 he was editor-in-chief of *American Anthropologist*. His publications include *The Gay Archipelago, A Coincidence of Desires, Coming of Age in Second Life* and (as co-author) *Ethnography and Virtual Worlds: a Handbook of Method*.

Richard Cleminson

Richard Cleminson is reader in the history of sexuality at the University of Leeds. He has published on the history of male homosexuality in Spain, hermaphroditism in Iberia and the history of anarchism and sexuality.

Matt Cook

Matt Cook is senior lecturer in history and gender studies at Birkbeck, University of London, director of the Raphael Samuel History Centre, and an editor of *History Workshop Journal*. He is author of *London and the Culture of Homosexuality, 1885–1914 (2003)* and *Queer Domesticities: homosexuality and home life in twentieth century London (2014)*; lead author and editor of *A Gay History of Britain (2007)* and co-editor of *Queer 1950s (2012, with Heike Bauer)*.

Rosa Maria Medina Doménech

Rosa Medina Doménech is a senior lecturer in the History of Science Department, University of Granada (Spain). Her latest research has focused on the Spanish culture of love in the most repressive years of Francoism (Ciencia y sabiduría del amor: una historia cultural del franquismo, 1940–60, Iberoamericana/Vervuert, 2013). She is currently working on the intersection of the history of emotions and sexuality, centring on the history of subjectivity and gender in the Spanish sixties.

Peter Edelberg

Peter Edelberg is a historian and postdoctoral fellow at the University of Copenhagen. He took the PhD degree in 2011. He has published on the history of sexuality and gender, the Second World War and historiography.

Fatima El-Tayeb

Fatima El-Tayeb is associate professor of literature and ethnic studies and associate director of Critical Gender Studies at the University of California, San Diego. She is the author of two books, *European Others. Queering Ethnicity in Postnational Europe* (University of Minnesota Press, 2011) and *Schwarze Deutsche. Rasse und nationale Identität, 1890–1933 (Black Germans. Race and National Identity, 1890–1933, Campus 2001)*, as well as of numerous articles on the interactions of race, gender, sexuality and nation. Before coming to the United States, she lived in Germany and the Netherlands, where she was active in black feminist, migrant and queer of colour organizations. She is also co-author of the movie Alles wird gut/ Everything will be fine (Germany 1997).

Jennifer Evans

Jennifer Evans is associate professor of modern European history at Carleton University in Ottawa Canada, where she currently serves as graduate director. She is the author of *Life Among the Ruins. Cityscape and Sexuality in Cold War Berlin* (2011) in addition to articles in the *American Historical Review, German History, and the Journal of the History of Sexuality* on post-1945 German queer history. She is currently at work on a special theme issue of *German History*, due out in 2016, on 'Queering German History'.

Dan Healey

Dan Healey is professor of modern Russian history at the University of Oxford. He is the author of the first book-length study of the queer history of modern Russia *(Homosexual Desire in Revolutionary Russia: The Regulation of Sexual and Gender Dissent*, [Chicago: University of Chicago Press, 2001]), and many other publications on gender and sexuality in Russia.

Gert Hekma

Gert Hekma teaches gay and lesbian studies, and sexuality and gender studies at the Department of Sociology and Anthropology, University of Amsterdam. His research is on the sociology and history of homo/sexuality. His present work is on the sexual revolution of the 1960s.

Roman Kuhar

Roman Kuhar is an associate professor of sociology at the University of Ljubljana and researcher at the Peace Institute in Ljubljana. He is the author of several books, including *Media Construction of Homosexuality* (2003), co-author (with A. Švab) of *The Unbearable Comfort of Privacy* (2005) and co-editor (with J. Takács) of *Beyond The Pink Curtain: Everyday life of LGBT people in Eastern Europe* (2007) and *Doing Families: Gay and Lesbian Family Practices* (2011).

Dimitris Papanikolaou

Dimitris Papanikolaou is a university lecturer in Modern Greek and a Fellow of St Cross College, Oxford University. He is the author of *Singing Poets: Literature and Popular Music in France and Greece* (Oxford: Legende, 2007) and has had articles published in *New Cinemas, Byzantine and Modern Greek Studies and the Journal of Modern Greek Studies.*

Ralph Poole

Ralph J. Poole is professor of American studies at Salzburg University, Austria. He taught at the University of Munich, Germany, and at Fatih University in Istanbul, Turkey. He was also visiting scholar at the Center for Advanced Studies in Theater Arts at the CUNY. His publications include books on the Avant-Garde tradition in American theatre and on satirical and autoethnographical 'cannibal' texts, a co-edited anthology on the American melodrama from the eighteenth century to the present, and a collection of essays on 'dangerous masculinities'.

Antu Sorainen

Antu Sorainen is a postdoctoral research fellow at the Academy of Finland. She published a book on lesbian trials in Finland, journal articles on queer legal history, edited an issue on the queer 'field' (SQS 1/2011), and co-edited a book on the concept of Sittlichkeit (2011). Her current research concerns queering kinship through will-writing.

Judit Takács

Judit Takács graduated in history, Hungarian Language and Literature and Cultural Anthropology at ELTE, Budapest, and completed an MA in social sciences at the University of Amsterdam. She holds a PhD in sociology and works as a senior research fellow at the Institute of Sociology, CSS, Hungarian Academy of Sciences.

Florence Tamagne

Florence Tamagne is associate professor in contemporary history at the University of Lille 3. She has published in *English History of Homosexuality in Europe: Berlin, London, Paris, 1919–39* (Algora Pub., 2004) and notably contributed to R. Aldrich (ed.), *Gay Life and Culture* (Universe, 2006) and G. Hekma (ed.), *A Cultural History of Sexuality in the Modern Age* (Berg, 2011). She is currently working on rock music, youth cultures and politics in France, Britain and Germany (1950s–80s).

Isabel Vélez

Isabel E. Vélez is an independent scholar. She earned a BA in women's studies from Yale University, and is ABD in the History of Consciousness Program at the University of California, Santa Cruz.

Introduction

Matt Cook and Jennifer Evans

(Dis)ordering queer Europe

We began our conversation about queer European cities in London in 2008 at a conference on the 'Queer 1950s'.[1] It continued during a visit to an exhibition of Herbert Tobias' photography at Berlin's Museum of Modern Art – the Berlinische Galerie – the following year. Our respective research interests in these two cities, in the urban and national contexts of queer lives in that first full post-war decade, and in the significance of art and representation in couching those lives gave us pause for considerable thought.[2] Berlin and London were both deeply scarred by war; they were both iconic or infamous in terms of their queer pasts; and they were both associated with each other in the lives and imaginations of numerous queer people. If divided by conflict and in part by the cold war that followed, they also saw burgeoning countercultural connections in the 1960s and 1970s, influences from the United States in terms of commodified and radical gay subcultures, and then also wider political union which made a pitch for common European values – embracing latterly LGBT (Lesbian, gay, bisexual and transgender) rights and equalities.[3]

What these two cities had in common leapt out at us, and yet what we also observed was that these urban contexts produced and framed different understandings and experiences of queer identity and subculture. These differences had to do with national histories, the law, geographical situation, histories of Empire and in turn of immigration, cultures of home and socialization, and mythologies and stories associated with each city. They troubled presumptions about common European cultures of sexuality and offered us the scope for a comparative study of European urban queer lives as a way of thinking about the vicissitudes of identification and experience.[4] We wanted to deploy a queer approach to the past and to these urban spaces which started from the presumption that sexual identities were not fixed and were deeply contextual in terms of both space and time. We thus sought to investigate the differences made by the experience of dictatorship,

communism, capitalism and liberal or social democratic traditions. And we
also sought to consider the impact of the scale and reach of different cities;
of transnational ideas about gay causation, sociability and radicalism; of
geographical situation; of the denomination 'Latin' or 'Germanic', 'Eastern'
or 'Northern' European; and latterly of the internet. All such variables
and many more have an impact on the way in which sex and desire are
understood, experienced and associated with particular identities in urban
contexts.[5] Questions abounded for us about the amorphous nature of Europe
and how it changed shape depending on whether we talked geographically,
politically, historically or in terms of the Eurovision Song Contest. Who was
central, marginal or exempt from these different configurations and what
did that mean for queer urban lives in those contexts?

In raising these issues and asking these questions we felt we had a reasonable
critical engagement. But as we laid out plans for the collection and invited
scholars and activists to contribute, our blind spots – perhaps especially
as two Anglophone editors – emerged. We had assumed, for example, that
1945 was a good start date, a significant shared reference point for our
collection to launch from. However, as the chapters that follow vividly
show, other dates proved as significant. For Istanbul, it was the creation
of the modern Turkish state in 1923; for Madrid and Barcelona, the end
of the civil war in 1936; for Moscow, Stalin's death in 1953; for Ljubljana,
Slovenian independence in 1990; for Helsinki, Finland's accession to the
European Union in 1991. And of course, even when traumas like World War
II were shared between nations, the impact was differently felt – Berlin, Paris
and London each suffered quite distinctly.

We realized too that these disparate moments of national transition and
crisis had very particular and often unexpected impacts on queer urban
lives. There was not always greater tolerance of difference in the move to
social democracy and some missed the multifaceted urban countercultures
that sometimes existed under more draconian regimes. Other histories also
intersected: for the Finnish, ideas of masculinity were historically formed in
contrast to the supposedly emasculated Swedes. Antu Sorainen suggests in
her chapter that this had an impact on Helsinki's queer life. Its particular
histories of war and labour, meanwhile, meant that the working class Kallio
area of the city was disproportionately female for long periods leading to
intense networks of support and intimacy between women. Our contributors
on Amsterdam (Gert Hekma), London (Matt Cook) and Paris (Florence
Tamagne) suggest how patterns and histories of migration to these cities
have brought into sharp focus the limits of gay or homosexual identities and
the inclusions and exclusions they enact. Their accounts – together with the
closing reflection by Fatima El-Tayeb – demand a reconsideration of smug
assumptions about the value of coming out or of a visible and permanently
situated gay scene. They suggest the need to think in more expansive terms
in order to uncover the investments in different but intersecting identities
and identifications. In other words, as Laura Doan tells us, we need to think

carefully and contextually about the ways 'desire' was understood and so also experienced.[6] Such approaches to the past are underpinned by an academic and theoretical appropriation of queer – one which was to the fore as we conceptualized this volume. Yet what becomes clear in the chapters that follow is that queer does not only signify an approach to thinking about sexuality and the complex ways in which people have understood themselves over time. To some it is also a valuable umbrella synonymous with LGBT or a label which signals an identity that is more radical than those other categories. The filmmaker Derek Jarman, for example, claimed queer over gay – the former encapsulating for him the anger, urgency and radicalism needed in the context of the AIDS crisis. Others use it (ourselves included) to refer both to those LGBT identities that have become well established since the 1970s and also to men and women who before and after that time may not have claimed or associated with them but were yet involved in emotional and intimate relationships with members of the same sex. Queer in this way might accommodate individuals who 'disturb' categories that have become conventional.[7] To yet others, queer is a more troublesome term: for some older anglophone men and women it belongs in the mouths of homophobes and has been hard to reclaim; for others the idea of stable identification – of being 'gay' or 'lesbian' – was and is appealing and also politically useful. It can be easier to fight for rights and equalities for a defined group of lesbians and gays than an amorphous band of queers. The former categorization can also more readily link to an international struggle. Queer can, meanwhile, seem rarified or trendy, better suited to the hallowed halls of academe or in the youth-oriented and increasingly commercialized 'scene'. The challenge for us as editors and you as readers, then, is to hold onto these various meanings and associations and to know also that the authors have chosen and used their terminology deliberately and in ways which evoke particular traditions, histories and affiliations. It is a sensitivity to these multiple threads and the way they together evoke diverse experience and identifications which in our eyes makes this collection part of a queer project.

Finally, queer can speak metaphorically to the unexpected, multiple, diverse and sometimes downright ambiguous outcomes we found in the different urban settings explored in this volume. The language used and also the varying temporal anchors and intersecting histories we have been discussing highlight very different national and urban traumas and associated repressions. These did not create a uniform set of experiences or possibilities for the queer people who lived in these places, spaces and moments in time. Yet lives were also lived within the broader shared contexts of the cold war, of the threat of nuclear conflict, of international protest movements, of the political and economic unification of a growing number of European nations (from the six nations in the European Economic Community of 1958 to the 28 in the European Union of today), of Americanization and consumerism, of changing possibilities for travel, movement and leisure, and of transnational media and virtual networks.[8] These and other factors have been unevenly understood and experienced, but they cannot be neatly allotted to particular nations and cities. They instead leaven the local and particular with some shared if differently inflected reference points.

Our initial organization of this book – into cities that were 'Liberal', 'Iconic', 'Under Dictatorship' 'Out in the Cold', 'On the Borders' – soon fell apart in light of all this. If this initial structure was meant questioningly and with scepticism, it still carried with it too many presumptions. We found that the chapters as they were submitted sat uncomfortably wherever we placed them. Cities under dictatorship did not only see repression but also different kinds of queer expression Richard Cleminson, Rosa María Medina Doménech and Isabel Vélez show in relation to lesbian subcultures in Barcelona before the death of dictator General Franco. 'Liberal' and 'iconic' cities sometimes witnessed a narrowing of perception and experience as Gert Hekma suggests in relation to Amsterdam. Istanbul might seem on the edge geographically, but in the way Ralph J. Poole conjures the city here, it is thematically central to the collection in terms of highlighting especially vividly the kinds of border crossings and hybridities that feature in each of the other chapters. Cities we had placed in separate sections showed surprising similarities and for reasons we hadn't anticipated. Roman Kuhar demonstrates how Ljubljana gained some of its character and some distinctiveness to queer culture by being, like Istanbul, on geographical crossroads, in its case 'of Slavic, Germanic and Latin cultures'. The Slovenian capital (one of our cities initially 'Out in the Cold') resonated in unexpected ways with Helsinki (one of our 'liberal' cities). The fact they were the largest cities in their respective countries but relatively small in pan-European terms provided scope for unanticipated points of comparison, not least in the absence and then much sought after sense of permanent queer space. In terms of the actual pace of change, there were more surprises again as Barcelona, Madrid and Moscow (Dan Healey) came into alignment. In the particularly close relationship of urban and national history, these Spanish cities also spoke to Budapest (Judit Takács) and Ljubljana. Berlin, London and Athens (Dimitris Papanikolaou), on the other hand, were linked by a sense of disjunction from a wider national story. In other words, none of the cities discussed here was or is univocal – there were different scenes to be part of and experiences to be had at different times or in parallel at the same time. All this goes to show what Phil Hubbard's recent work documents most vividly – that the relationship between cities and sexuality is dynamic and changing. The former are not merely the stage or background for sexual activity, identity and communities, but, as the chapters ahead attest, are active agents in their very constitution.[9]

If the differences between places are evident, taken together the chapters also suggest important similarities between all these cities. The authors describe resonant changes over time such that intergenerational sex has become taboo, the nature of prostitution has shifted, equality in coupledom has come to be primary and gay and lesbian scenes have become more commercialized (though enduringly male dominated in terms of visibility and spatial tangibility). There are also shared socio-economic and cultural reasons why men and women, gays and lesbians, find themselves limited and enabled in their cities in particular ways. Interestingly, each of the contributors – including the two of us – seems to have felt a pull towards the present and a need to explain the queer coordinates of the different cities now. Indeed the chapters perhaps cohere in the production of a history of the queer urban present – riffing on French philosopher Michel Foucault's genealogical project in which he sought meanings of the present through investigations of the past. The queer challenge, Doan reminds us, is to do this without simply reading the present and present understandings onto past moments; and to take the past on its own terms even as we seek out some explanation in it for what happened next. Each author is troubled by contemporary situations – by individualism, by ongoing violence and by economic disparity and dwindling resources in the context of heightened aspiration and expectations. They are each sceptical about fantasies of shared European values, including sexual emancipation, and show who gets left out of such narratives and how unevenly putatively shared values have been taken up socially, culturally and politically in different national and urban contexts. History, they each demonstrate in different ways, is an important tool in understanding the emergence of these fantasies and in finding inconvenient lives, practices and communities that have been excluded or marginalized. Investigating the queer past has become a strategy in disorientating the present.

In short, the criteria which informed our initial organization paled as other resonances and dissonances emerged and criss-crossed the contributions. And so we abandoned our initial schema and instead decided to present the chapters in alphabetical order by author – a random criterion, which we hope allows the chapters to speak to each other more freely.

Imagining and reimagining the queer city

Methodologically as well as conceptually, this book is also quite queer in the sense of being non-normative. In various interesting ways, it is not a typical edited volume. It comes not as the result of the collective imaginings of a conference but through email exchanges and conversations sometimes with scholars we have not even met. We were thinking and discussing in ways which, as Tom Boellstorff suggests in his postscript on queer cities, are indicative of the new forms of relationality enabled by the internet age. These have been taken up by gays, lesbians and queer-identified people all across today's Europe. Not all (or even most) of our contributors are historians – we have contributors from history of science, anthropology, sociology, Hispanic studies, gender and sexuality, and literary studies. Some have tenured permanent positions in their universities; others have not. Some have been activists, insiders and witnesses to the urban queer cultures they focus upon. Others write as outsiders to the cities they describe. We have a gender split and our contributors range in age. None of these factors trumps others, but they do inflect the kinds of stories that they tell and the particular investment in the histories they recount. The book is a testament to the usefulness and richness of hybridity and interdisciplinarity.

Varied too are the sources. Some chapters are more rooted in the materiality of the city streets and the way that space has changed and been used over time – as tracked through maps, press reports and police records in Peter Edelberg's piece on Copenhagen, for example. Others pivot on city space as it is remembered in oral history testimonies and autoethnography (London, Helsinki) or written in literature and imagined on film (Madrid, Barcelona, Budapest, Istanbul). These various renditions can suggest the ways in which individuals live in and engage with their cities – and also signal how others might perceive them. The refurbishment and reopening of some of Istanbul's hamams is part of a reinvention and reincorporation in the present of past cultures idealized through memory and representation. Barcelona has become a totem for trans subculture in part through the way film-maker Pedro Almodóvar and others have conjured the city's counterculture. Reading the collection as a whole, we see the importance of nostalgia and of temporal markers (pre- and post-certain pivotal events like those detailed earlier) in the way the city is experienced queerly now – as better, worse, more constraining, liberating or transgressive, as more or less sexy.[10]

Across the book we thus see different ways of getting at the recent histories of particular queer urban cultures. Different sources give different kinds of access to everyday lives, opening out understandings of some at the expense of others. The volume does not aim and cannot hope to be comprehensive, not least because there is no easy A–Z (or LGBTQ) of identity. Often there is a defiance or evasion of categorization – among the male prostitutes in Copenhagen and in Amsterdam in the 1950s and 1960s for example. People invariably have multiple identifications which meet and intersect in different ways and bring different realms of safety or danger, comfort or discomfort into play. Tamagne suggests that queer Arabic men can feel out of place in the gay Marais and often find social composure on the edge of the Parisian centre. Queer nodes of contact, she shows, do not always conform to expectations. Although the Marais and, in London, Soho, hold firm in our imagination as explicitly queer areas, when we take into account the unique subjective experiences of Arab Parisian queers and the changing ethnic and economic diversity of neighbourhoods like Notting Hill and Brixton in London, we can't help but see that race mediates how queerness is lived, expressed and indeed often remembered.[11] Generally, unacknowledged ideas about whiteness and nationhood are significant in the way queer individuals perceive and experience their sense of urban belonging or displacement.

Despite our best intentions to problematize and question fixed identity categories, what emerges as often in the chapters that follow is the significance of homosexual, gay, lesbian or dyke identity to individuals as they forged a sense of self and place in their different urban contexts. This gave some people a sense of rootedness and a position from which to organize their own individual or collective opposition to the status quo. There is and was yet something seemingly more ineffable and fluid in aspects of the sub- and countercultures to which these men and women belonged. If queer has been theorized since the 1990s as a state of being at odds with fixity and definition, this often emerges in relation to place rather than people in this collection.[12] Often, individuals and groups seemed to seek firm ground through identity categories like gay or lesbian and find affirmation for them in specifically gay-nominated places like bars, clubs and cafés. Yet the city as a whole can be more equivocal and sometimes incorporates places where the strategic denial of identity might be helpful or where homosex takes place without it being the mark of a fixed sense of identity. The sexual identities we now take to be self-evident can thus sometimes be hard to locate in the shifting and multivalent cultures of the city. This is perhaps especially true for women and trans people: repeatedly here we witness the way in which visible, public and subcultural spaces have been identified most clearly with gay men. Several cities have witnessed the time-honoured struggle for an autonomous lesbian bar culture amidst more established gay male scenes.[13]

Queer maps

The collection shows that the meanings of city space are not made solely by the builders and shapers of the urban environment. Cities are made in the everyday machinations of people's lives. In simple, oft-repeated quotidian acts, people lay claim to the spaces around them and invest in them personal and collective meanings – making them, so the geographers say, into places.[14] Urban historians and historians of sexuality in particular have described the pursuit of pleasure amidst the danger of regulation and sometimes outright hatred that have mediated everyday encounters and attachments.[15] This, they suggest, has helped forge places of adventure as well as leisure, belonging and community, like-mindedness and identity in uneven urban landscapes. Cities have in this way often had a uniquely liberating effect for queer identified people despite pressing urban dangers, and there has been a deeply constitutive relationship between queer citizens and city spaces.[16] How spaces are used and sometimes co-opted changes depending on the actors involved, the historical conditions at play at a particular moment, and the evolving relationships between and among diversely connected groups. Through use, governance, different mappings and stories, myths, tall tales and gossip, places take on layers of meaning and are thoroughly imbued with the past and with expectations and assumptions passed from one generation to the next. People thus often live their lives within diverse and overlaid conceptions of the city. State and local government might rely on firmly drawn physical maps of the city to identify and police its queer citizens. Businesses seeking out the pink pound might meanwhile map out a wholly different view of the city by charting queer consumer trends and laying claim to a certain street corner as especially economically viable. At the same time, a trans streetworker might find the same space appealing for different though similarly entrepreneurial reasons. These various mappings are gendered, classed and inflected by sexuality, and while they might be dangerous to one person or group, they might be liberating to another. In Budapest and Athens, courts and police services are known to have generated extensive pink lists of homosexual offenders, mapping the city along an axis of moral regulation and social control. Yet as we see in Copenhagen, these same modes of regulation might be mobilized in different ways. Even in an age of illegality, Edelberg shows, homophile men solicited the support of police and their maps and lists for protection against blackmailing rent boys. In Ljubljana, Kuhar avers that the support of politicians against anti-Pride thugs is heartening even if it might not be completely altruistic. Space, in other words, is best understandable when we recognize its functional, historical and associative meanings for the widest array of audiences, contemporary as well as historical. The trick is to do so mindfully, in full recognition of the intricate, often imperceptible, and seemingly contradictory processes at work.

A city's meaning is not solely dependent upon narratives from the inside – from Moscovites, Parisien(nes) or Ljubljanians. Some cities are iconic – with meaning for inhabitants and outsiders which transcend the local. And as geographer Doreen Massey has argued, for some cities more than others, feelings of attachment and belonging are invariably inflected by transnational forces, some percolating within the city itself, others wafting in from afar via the media, along tourist networks, or with the circulation of international capital.[17] We see this at work here. Queers in Athens and Amsterdam looked to Paris as the apex of cultural modernity. Many others focused their gaze on imperial and Weimar Berlin as a source of inspiration for queer history and place making, whether in the guise of Magnus Hirschfeld's legal reform campaigns or in the lore of the city's vibrant bar and café scene. In their contributions, Roman Kuhar and Judit Takács show that this fascination with the city on the Spree extended over the 1945 divide and was further nurtured by subcultural pathways that linked socialist countries behind the Iron Curtain to East and West Berlin queer scenes. Even after the fall of the wall and the reconstitution of Berlin as a world city, Jennifer Evans shows in her analysis of the monument erected to gays and lesbians just how emblematic a place it remains for an international audience wanting to memorialize Nazi persecution as a touchstone of international queer suffering and human rights abuses. Berlin continues to hold a certain mystique subculturally and as an example of lessons only unevenly learnt.

Repression, progression and hybridization

Much of this volume explores local-level practices as a way of providing insight into the pervasive use of identity in the post-1945 period. National-level debates yet also serve as excellent barometers of the tenacity of the gay/straight binary over more overtly-queer projects intent on denaturalizing experience. The Berlin memorial caused controversy in the planning stages because activists and historians thought exclusively in terms of male versus female victimization. While this had a foundation in Nazi jurisprudence insofar as the regime explicitly targeted gay men over lesbians, this meant that in the original formulation of the memorial there was no room to differentiate between forms and practices of gender expression. Victimization was instead linked explicitly to identity as if it was the sole mark and category of experience. Gender may have played a mediating role in how a national community of suffering was represented in Germany, but in causing significant retrenchment into existing single-sex spheres and rubbing salt into long-festering wounds, the planned memorial foreclosed on an opportunity to incorporate the experiences of those on the margins of community, notably trans and genderqueer citizens past and present. In Spain – similarly struggling with vestiges of a fascist past – feminist, trans and queer activists in Madrid and Barcelona appear to have been more successful in finding ways to queer oppositionality. Where cracks appear in the pavement, as it were, is in the commodified scene of tourism, where business and state entrepreneurs turn to convenient stereotypes to reproduce rigid and hierarchical – not to mention heteronormative – understandings of gender, identity and desire. It can suggest an unproblematic liberalism. In Barcelona and Madrid, as in Berlin, much cultural and actual capital was invested in promoting Spain's liberal moorings as one of the most tolerant countries in Europe. There was a much touted sense of improvement and progress in all this, which however welcome also served to exclude some people and pasts and erased complex conjunctions of identities, communities and ways of being in the world which didn't fit a contained and sanitized version of LGBT life.

Celebrations of toleration are important responses not just to historic examples of state repression but also to everyday acts of violence that continue to haunt queer life across Europe. But the twenty-first century appearance of openness, several of our contributors observe, is still a fallacy. Europeans remain enamoured with the fantasy of the mobile, borderless, European citizen who moves easily between cities and spaces within them.[18] This relates to a further fantasy of a tolerant Europe, risen from the ashes of World War II and the uneven transitions to democracy that ensued. Underpinning both of these is a narrative of progression in terms of sexual citizenship linked to European liberalization. As this collection shows, this is more myth than reality. For many, there can be no true refuge in the imagined post-national city, not at least for those still coded as eternally provincial and backward, whose behaviours, attitudes and actions fall short of this cosmopolitan ideal. If there is a depressing reproduction of outsiderness in this, the queer urban polyphony described across this collection also textures bland pan-urban and transnational imaginings. Everyday attempts to reconstitute city space and encode it as queer has had a galvanizing effect on alternative community formations, as the example from the working-class and anarchist parts of Helsinki shows quite clearly. These provide an unstable yet welcoming ground for community formation of a variety of sorts – a less commodified vision of queer cosmopolitanism perhaps. This, our contributors suggest, need not hinge on so-called western values. In Moscow and Ljubljana, long-held Slavic traditions mingled with western ones in the queer scene and experience. These have been attended by violence and reprisal, yet this mixing has also given distinctive shape and meaning to localized queer practices. In Turkey, an abiding 'western' pulse has not foreclosed on the possibility for Muslim cultural practices – practices which might sometimes be deemed rather queer. In other words, a truly queer Europe requires ways of looking for hybridization, not merely in the form of peaceful coexistence but in terms of what El-Tayeb describes as the creolization of traditions, understandings, practices and ways of socializing and of conducting relationships. Looking across the 12 European cities in this volume (we would have loved to have included more) reveals a melding and intersection of the local and particular with transnational and international concerns and conceptions. We find, in the end and as a result, no way of conjuring a typical queer European city. This may seem like a curiously unstable foundation upon which to build a volume on queer European cities. It is, however, perhaps truer to people's everyday urban queer lives to look to complex and intersecting identifications, identities, places and spaces. It is relatedly perhaps truer to queer European cities to see them as perpetual works in progress rather than a *fait accompli*.

Notes

1 The basis for an edited collection: Bauer, H. and M. Cook (eds) (2012), *Queer 1950s: Rethinking Sexuality in the Postwar Years*. Basingstoke: Palgrave.

2 Cook, M. (2003), *London and the Culture of Homosexuality, 1885-1914*. Cambridge: Cambridge University Press; Evans, J. V. (2011), *Life among the Ruins: Cityscape and Sexuality in Cold War Berlin*. New York: Palgrave Macmillan.

3 Bunzl, M. (2004), *Symptoms of Modernity: Jews and Queers in Late-Twentieth Century Vienna*. Berkeley: University of California Press; Halperin, D. M. (2011), *How to Be Gay*. Madison: University of Wisconsin Press; Stryker, S. (2008), *Transgender History*. Berkeley: Seal Press.

4 El-Tayeb, F. (2011), *European Others: Queering Ethnicity in Postnational Europe*. Minneapolis: University of Minnesota Press.

5 Hubbard, P. (2012), *Cities and Sexualities*. London: Routledge.

6　Doan, L. (2013), *Disturbing Practices: History, Sexuality, and Women's Experience of Modern War*. Chicago: University of Chicago Press.

7　To draw on the title of Laura Doan's recent intervention in queer history writing and making. Doan, L. (2013), *Disturbing Practices*.

8　Berghof, H. and T. Kühne (2013), *Globalizing Beauty: Consumerism and Body Aesthetics in the Twentieth Century*. New York: Palgrave Macmillan; Herzog, D. (2011), *Sexuality in Europe: A Twentieth-Century History*. Cambridge: Cambridge University Press; Mazower, M. (2000), *Dark Continent: Europe's 20th Century*. New York: Vintage; Mort, F. (1996), *Cultures of Consumption: Masculinities and Social Space in Late 20th Century Britain*. New York: Routledge; Puar, J. (2007), *Terrorist Assemblages: Homonationalism in Queer Times*. Durham: Duke University Press; Suri, J. (2005), *Power and Protest: Global Revolution and the Rise of Détente*. Cambridge, MA: Harvard University Press.

9　Hubbard (2012), ch. 1.

10　Boym, S. (2002), *The Future of Nostalgia*. New York: Basic Books.

11　Ferguson, R. (2003), *Aberration in Black: Toward a Queer of Color Critique*. Minneapolis: University of Minnesota Press.

12　See the articles in the special issue of *Social Text* edited by Eng, D., J. Halberstam and J. Munoz (2005), 'What's queer about queer studies now', 23(3–4) (Fall–Winter), *Social Text*.

13　Bell, D. and G. Valentine (1995), *Mapping Desire: Geographies of Sexualities*. New York: Routledge; Higgs, D. (1999), *Queer Sites: Gay Urban Histories Since 1600*. New York: Routledge; Retter, Y., A-M. Bouthillette and B. G. Ingram (1997), *Queers in Space: Communities, Public Places, Sites of Resistance*. Seattle: Bay Press.

14　Bech, H. (1997), *When Men Meet. Homosexuality and Modernity*. Chicago: University of Chicago Press; de Certeau, M. (1984), *The Practice of Everyday Life*. Berkeley: University of California; Johnston, L. and R. Longhurst (2009), *Space, Place and Sex. Geographies of Sexualities*. Lanham: Rowman and Littlefield Publishers; Massey, D. B. (2005), *For Space*. Thousand Oaks: Sage.

15　Bunzl (2004); Cook (2003); Evans (2011); Houlbrook, M. (2005), *Queer London: Perils and Pleasures in the Sexual Metropolis*. Chicago: University of Chicago Press; Mort, F. (2010), *Capital Affairs: London and the Making of a Permissive Society*. New Haven: Yale University Press; Tamagne, F. (2004), *A History of Homosexuality in Europe: Berlin, London, Paris 1919-39*. New York: Algora.

16　Cook (2003); Hubbard (2012); Houlbrook (2005).

17　Massey, D. (1991), 'A global sense of place', *Marxism Today*, 38, 24–9.

18　Downing, L. and R. Gillett (2011), *Queer in Europe*. Farnham: Ashgate.

Further reading

Bech, H. (1997), *When Men Meet: Homosexuality and Modernity*. Chicago: Chicago University Press.

Bell, D. and G. Valentine (eds) (1995), *Mapping Desire*. London: Routledge.

Doan, L. (2013), *Disturbing Practices: History, Sexuality, and Women's Experience of Modern War*. Chicago: University of Chicago Press.

Downing, L. and R. Gillett (eds) (2011), *Queer in Europe*. Franham: Ashgate.

El-Tayeb, F. (2011), *European Others: Queering Ethnicity in Postnational Europe*. Minneapolis: University of Minnesota Press.

Hemmings, C. (2002), *Bisexual Spaces: A Geography of Sexuality and Gender*. London: Routledge.

Herzog, D. (2011), *Sexuality in Europe: A Twentieth Century History*. Cambridge: Cambridge University Press.

Higgs, D. (1999), *Queer Sites: Gay Urban Histories Since 1600*. London: Routledge.

Hubbard, P. (2012), *Cities and Sexualities*. London: Routledge.

Johnston, L. and R. Longhurst (2010), *Space, Place, and Sex: Geographies of Sexualities*. Lanham: Rowman.

Retter, Y., A-M. Bouthillette and B. Ingram (1997), *Queers in Space: Communities, Public Spaces, Sites of Resistance*. Seattle: Bay Press.

Tamagne, F. (2004), *A History of Homosexuality in Europe: Berlin, London and Paris, 1919–1939*. New York: Algora.

Pasts

1

The queer margins of Spanish cities, 1939–2010

Richard Cleminson, Rosa María Medina Doménech and Isabel Vélez

"Hablar en voz baja es hablar, pero solo para los que disponen de un oído alerta" [To speak quietly is to speak, but only for those who possess a sharp sense of hearing],

JUAN GIL-ALBERT, *HERACLÉS. SOBRE UNA MANERA DE SER*.[1]

Introduction

The return of political democracy and peace in most European countries would, particularly from the 1950s onwards, mean changes in sexual behaviour, new sexual identities, a transformation of the position of women in society and, even, incipient changes in attitudes towards homosexuality.[2] In Spain, where the dictatorship of General Francisco Franco had been consolidated at the end of the three-year civil war in 1939, these changes were slow to come or difficult to perceive. Despite this, and while Madrid and Barcelona were not Berlin, London or Paris, the chapter will illustrate how queer life did survive under the dictatorship and will trace some aspects of its more open presence in the post-dictatorship city.

For the defeated of the Spanish civil war – republicans, socialists, regional nationalists and anarchists, among others – the end of authoritarian regimes elsewhere rekindled the hope that the Allies would continue their advance beyond the Pyrenees and finally depose the pro-Axis General Franco. Such a hope was, however, quickly dashed. Franco remained in power, the 1940s were viciously repressive and the dictator was to become 'rehabilitated' in the 1950s as the 'sentinel of the West' in the fight against communism as US military bases were installed on Spanish soil and Spain 'came in from the cold'. Although the regime underwent a certain degree of change over Franco's nearly 40 years in power and despite the fact that it was not monolithically repressive and was contested by multiple forms of more or less clandestine resistance, the defeat of open democratic and progressive politics in Spain was confirmed until 1975, the year of the death of the *Generalísimo* or *Caudillo*, as he preferred to be called. Spain, a country where the vanquished in the civil war suffered the destruction of their social and political dreams through incarceration, death, internal or external exile, saw the institutionalization of traditional mores under the banner of 'National Catholicism', driven by strong fascistic rituals encouraged by the Spanish *Falange* especially in the early years of the regime.

For Francoism, with its notion of natural hierarchies, idealized ruralism, sharp social divisions between men and women and education in accordance with the 'National Spirit', all former leftist political parties and trade unions, along with 'rational', that is, non-religious thought, were considered part of the legacy of the 'anti-Spain', locked in combat with the true values of 'Spanishness' or *hispanidad*. For the ideologues of the regime, women had to be confined to the domestic sphere as 'angels of the hearth'.[3] Hegemonic masculinity, with the male elevated as the breadwinner and head of family and with violence legitimized as a political tool, meant that 'effeminacy' was decried as having ruined Spain and brought moral pollution to society. So strong was the association between masculine decadence and national decline that one of the cabal of generals who pronounced against the Republic, Queipo de Llano, declared in a radio address on 25 July 1936 in Seville as the full force of political repression rained down on the city, 'People of Seville! I do not have to wish you courage because I already know of your valour. Finally, if any invert or effeminate should proffer any insult or alarmist judgement against our glorious national movement, I say you should kill him like a dog'.[4]

The politics of the ousted Republic (1931–39) was seen by the regime as a betrayal of the essence of Spain: the application of an imported European form of politics inappropriate to Spain's historical roots and present needs. Given the flowering of sexual freedoms and the consolidation of a limited but diverse visible queer culture in the 1930s,[5] Francoism reserved a special place for the city as a site of moral contagion, a fount of political, social and sexual transgression. Early on in the dictatorship, regime-acolyte and psychiatrist, Dr Antonio Vallejo Nágera, wrote of the necessity to psychically cleanse the Spanish city and to eliminate the perversion entailed by the loose morals of the Republic;[6] within this context, the new regime presented the opportunity to impose a rapid programme of cultural and religious 'sanitization' and homogeneity, an endeavour extended beyond the metropole to Spain's remaining colonial outposts.[7] Although such an association between city and decadence is neither unique to Spain nor to authoritarian regimes (democratic countries were also concerned with 'deviancy' in the city), what was unusual about the Spanish case in post-war Europe was the intensity of this association and the exterminating measures taken against 'undesirables'. The resulting physical and symbolic annihilation of the incipient predominantly male gay culture born during the republican period was trenchant; at least for a time, those who practised alternative sexualities were forced underground, into prison camps or exiled.

Given such an apparently bleak panorama, the task of how to 'read' the queer subject, whose desire and sensibility must be expressed in a coded way is particularly problematic.[8] How can we trace not only what Richard Sennett has termed the 'suffering body', the body that was deemed unhealthy, non-normative or foreign and its pain historically,[9] but also the murmurings of resistance and queer life lived out despite a harshly repressive regime either as a discrete form of continuity with a remembered past or as new flowerings of same-sex desire? Perhaps Gil-Albert's words cited in the epigraph to this chapter are suggestive in this sense. We need to listen attentively to silences and quiet utterances; we need to accept the need to disrupt our own contemporary expectations regarding definitions, identities and evidence for queer existence. We need, in many respects, to read 'against the grain', identifying evidence that may be less easy to find and certainly less 'robust' than traditional historiography may suppose.[10] In order to approach this task, we will do well not only to consider how what Michael Warner has termed 'regimes of the normal' operated under Francoism, but also to question what our present notions of 'diversity' include – and exclude – and revise our typologies of 'queer' to uncover expressions that are not located in our own notions of the strange, unusual, shocking, eccentric or extravagant.[11] In this way, more hidden, or at least differently expressed queer lives that do not necessarily follow other western or northern European models may come to light. Such 'local orderings' can generate different perspectives within any given regime of knowledge/power; they can also open up the doors to different kinds of histories and can illuminate traces of other subjectivities.

Longevity, memories and strategies of resistance

Memories of previous patterns of existence, established traces of queer presences and the longevity of certain localities in Spanish cities known for their queer life served as strategies of resistance or survival in the early years after the civil war, whose devastating effects – personal, political, economic and infrastructural – cannot be underestimated.[12] Often these spaces were located in the Spanish cities in the pre-war period, especially in the capital, Madrid; sometimes they were found in other cities such as Barcelona,[13] San Sebastian or Cadiz and, less so, in rural areas.[14] It was the larger city, nevertheless, that acted as a magnet for gay lives in the past, as it does in the present, while at the same time, as we have seen, constituting a focus for those regimes reactive towards homosexuality. This dialectical relationship between threat and opportunity means that, as Julie Abraham puts it, 'To denounce the city is still to denounce homosexuality, and to denounce homosexuality is still to denounce the city. . . . To embrace homosexuality, then, is still to embrace the city, and to embrace the city is still to embrace homosexuality'.[15] It is this dialectical relationship that will enable us to explore in this chapter the multiple configurations of queer life in Spanish cities, the ways in which these connect with other marginalities, such as the lives of immigrants and other 'outsiders' in the neo-liberal world, and from a perspective that examines how such subjectivities are mutually dependent, we suggest the interconnections, solidarities and tensions between all these figures of exclusion.

The thriving gay cultures at the end of the nineteenth century in Madrid and Barcelona were memories,[16] if that, by the 1940s, but we should not assume that as a consequence of the repressiveness of the regime all gay culture had been completely obliterated. Queer life and queer (parts of) cities were also made by the availability of spaces outside of these cities and in their vicinities, which enabled queer experience to continue and consolidate itself. Sitges, on the coast near Barcelona, enjoyed relative freedom as a tourist centre and attractive venue for both national and foreign gays from at least the 1950s, permitted by the regime's twin desire to earn foreign money and to present a patina of openness on the international stage. Another space was Ibiza, an island that also allowed Spaniards a taste of the kind of freedoms that most other Europeans enjoyed at the time, away from the drab, uniform and asphyxiating life on the mainland.[17] In addition to the more overt presence of gay men and lesbians, on a more furtive level, Punta del Verde, near Cadiz, was renowned as a meeting point for men in the 1940s and 1950s,[18] and certain products, for example, the 'Lola' cigarette brand, were recognized among the initiated as signs of being gay.[19] Such examples suggest more than an incipient gay culture. The apparent paradoxical observation made by one contemporary writer that despite the repression, in Barcelona 'Se podía vivir una vida gay llenísima en los años 50' [You could live gay life to the full in the 1950s], requires an explanation.[20] This apparent paradox continued into the 1960s in Barcelona, a period documented photographically by Joan Colom, who recorded a full range of local figures in the Raval area of the city, including male prostitutes.[21]

In order to navigate this 'double condition', as Raymond Williams called it,[22] whereby the city encapsulated the potential for the maintenance *and* production of secrecy, our approach in this chapter will be threefold while not aiming to be all inclusive or to provide an exhaustive history of queer experience in Spanish cities in the space of one short chapter. First, we discuss the relation between fiction and fact, between novelization and lived experience, as a device in the construction of queer memory. Second, we look at some specific expressions of queer life – the geography of queer space in Madrid and Barcelona. Third, we discuss the intersections between democratization, rights, citizenship and tourism in the early twenty-first century as instances where queer has become a positive commodity to be traded by municipal and national authorities and gays alike. Such a quality is often in contrast to other, perhaps non-sexualized subjectivities, such as the racial 'other' or the recently-arrived immigrant population.

The novelization/fictionalization of the queer past

In discussing queer Spanish cities, it is not our aim to present a simple hierarchy of 'evidence' whereby the existence of places of gay sociability, demonstrations or police arrests takes precedence over memories and memoirs, desires and expressed hopes.[23] As Mark Turner has pointed out when writing about London, 'Fact and fiction blur here. As they always are wont to do, and much of the material [used in his book] requires us, at the very least, to interrogate our definitions of "evidence" when it comes to marginalized, often hidden, urban practices from the past'.[24] This is our cue to examine some examples of recent novelization and fictionalization of queerness in Spain, where queer lives may not be the main component of stories but are woven into broader narratives, often with transnational backdrops. These 'fictions' may enable us to disinter past realities and invite us to re-think the past in different ways; they should not be dismissed as 'mere fictions' or opposed simply to supposed 'facts'.[25] Neither should we think of such representations as constituting mere 'paradoxes' or 'contradictions' under authoritarian regimes, but instead as an opportunity to examine the extent to which particular categories of representation (hetero/homo, man/woman, black/white) as fixed identities are rendered significant and how they come about in the first place.[26] Such a precarious presence suggests that a simplistic positioning of 'in' or 'out' under a particular regime needs to be revised in favour of seeing how queer performs the work of 'becoming' rather than already being. As Robert Young has argued: 'External or internal, this division into same and other is less a site of contradiction and conflict than culture's founding possibility. . . . [C]ulture is always a dialectical process, inscribing and expelling its own alterity'.[27] In novels populated by queer characters we see not a lack of queer community in the city but instead a fragile one inhabited by instances of resistance.[28]

There has been a recent small proliferation of novels in English on the Spanish Civil War and the ensuing Franco dictatorship, both written originally in English and translated from the Spanish or Catalan.[29] These novels connect with the recent process of the 'recuperation of historical memory' in Spain, a process that gathered strength in the years immediately preceding the passing of the 2007 'Law of Historical Memory' and which aims to provide justice for the victims of repression in the civil war and the dictatorship.[30] While queer experience has not been a central concern of either this literary trend or the recent legislation on historical memory,[31] the fiction thus produced has occasionally represented queer lives as part of post-civil war experience eking out an existence between repression, self-knowledge and self-affirmation. It can also be argued that this literature connects with a broader process of 'normalization' of queerness culturally and socially, in the legislative field and in society more broadly.[32]

Aly Monroe's *The Maze of Cadiz* depicts a homosexual character as a protagonist caught between social mores, criminality and homosexuality in the 1930s and by doing so not only re-inscribes the attractiveness of this city as a place of intrigue and sensual possibilities, but also serves to reconnect Cadiz with its own past and an established gay presence.[33] But it is the extremely successful *La sombra del viento* [The Shadow of the Wind] by Carlos Ruiz Zafón that more convincingly integrates a gay character into the thread of a novel and most carefully illustrates the subtleties and dangers of gay existence in a city, in this case Barcelona, under the Franco regime.[34] Among the many characters populating a depressed post-war Barcelona is Don Federico, the neighbourhood clock seller, who, despite the restrictions of the period, was probably 'el hombre más educado y cortés de todo el hemisferio occidental' [the most educated and polite man of the whole western hemisphere]. However, he was known for other qualities of a supposedly less decorous nature: 'su predilección erótica por efebos musculados del lumpen más viril' [his erotic preference for muscled ephebes of the most virile lumpen type] as well as certain transvestite tendencies. He liked to imitate the 'queen of the pasodoble', Estrellita Castro. Despite a certain degree of respect and tolerance from his neighbours (a historic tolerance in Spain, in some milieus, of the folkloric 'mariquita' or 'nancy boy' with all the latter's connotations), these three qualities were to incite the wrath of a corrupt former police officer who has Don Federico beaten and detained for a few nights in the local police station. The camp nature of Federico (his 'pluma'), his condition as an invert and 'maricón' (queer) and his continuing desire to occasionally dress up as a Pharaoh queen, all illustrate the difficulties – but also the pleasures – of being gay in Barcelona in the post-war period.[35]

Given the restrictions operating on gay life, despite the more generally open nature of the Second Republic, many Spanish men and women left the country to live freer lives abroad or to escape persecution. This transnational dimension of queer experience, visually evident in films but present in novels too, has permitted the evocation of homosexuality in various ways that intersect with the repressiveness of the Franco regime. The emigration of the gay character abroad to escape to more liberal climes is a common motif clearly present in Spain from the 1920s through to the historical novels of today.[36] The escape to London in the semi-autobiographical novel *Todos los parques no son un paraíso* by the former priest Antonio Roig Roselló, first published in 1977, posits the many contrasts between Spain and Britain at the time. The more recent *The Olive Groves of Belchite* by Elena Moya, published in English, Spanish and Catalan versions, is an example of the recent desire to recover the past and to denounce the sexual restrictions of Francoism, in this case suffered by the author herself, partly expressed through one of the novel's protagonists.[37]

In visual terms, 'Amar en tiempos revueltos' [Love in Turbulent Times], initiated in 2005, was perhaps the remarkably successful Spanish television series, which most disrupted the straightforward association between Francoism and sexual repression. The series depicted in soap opera form life and love over several decades, beginning at the outset of the civil war in 1936 and running up to 1957, in the middle of the Franco period. What has surprised viewers is the representation of a more heterodox Spanish society in contrast to the perceived monolithic nature of Francoism and its effectiveness as a totalitarian regime in crushing any sign of modernity or diversity in daily life. Such a 'fictional' perspective is linked to a renewal of the value of historical evidence, leading to the argument that despite the extremely repressive nature of the regime, there were institutional and ideological fissures that made the dictatorship far from being monolithic. Without denying or playing down the very real effects of repression for most Spaniards' daily lives, such work has also suggested that resistance, in a diversity of forms, was widespread, although often silent and invisible to the regime, as well as, to some extent, to some historians looking for traditional forms of resistance.[38] The depiction of Ana and Teresa as lovers in the 1952–53 chapters of 'Amar en tiempos revueltos' does, however, as in all literary and filmic creation, raise the question of the accuracy of the representation.[39] Even though from our present historical memory, their – almost out – lesbian love seems to be impossible and a result of the literary imagination, some eye witnesses of the time also refer to noticeable lesbian lives. Richard Wright observed 'Lesbian women living their quiet, secluded lives within the shadows of cathedrals where they go to confess and make their atonements',[40] providing an exotic anti-modern and ultra-Catholic vision of the country 'out of the occidental orbit'. Others, however, such as the Dutch photographer Cas Oorthuys, observed women in the 1950s as products of the tentative modernity being experienced in the city.[41] The depiction of a kind of 'historical present' in 'Amar en tiempos revueltos' does, then, coincide with the imagery, and therefore the life, of some Spanish women at the time.

The series owes its success, no doubt, to its ability to represent complex social relationships without sidelining the poverty and repressiveness of the dictatorship in its focus on daily lives in a district of Madrid characterized by a diverse socio-economic population. The relationship between Ana and Teresa would certainly qualify as a more hidden one within the in/out division, suggested by authors in other contexts,[42] and probably corresponds to most Spanish lesbians' experience at the time. Ana is rich, powerful and well educated and identifies herself as a woman who loves another woman rather than as a lesbian. She is recently widowed and owns her own home. Teresa, by contrast, is less aware of her desires, denies her homosexuality, is from a lower socio-economic group and feels guilty for betraying her husband, whom she also apparently loves. Ana encourages her to seek out personal and work-related development and this partial lifting of restrictions shows how both women are products of the tentative modernity being experienced in Madrid in the 1950s. In one love scene, the backdrop is formed by a rich array of consumer products and this encourages the viewer to see the women's love not as archaic but decidedly modern with the emphasis placed on women's ability to choose who they love.[43] The couple also frequent cafeterias and restaurants, they use taxis and both work in the business world, Ana being the owner of a department store. The modernity of these women's past would have likely corresponded to the post-civil war model inhabited by real-life couples such as that of one of the founders of the anarchist Mujeres Libres organization, Lucía Sánchez Saornil, who sought refuge in Valencia at the end of the war with her partner América Barroso. The life of anonymity in Sánchez and Barroso's case, however, is more associated with a political awareness consolidated by defeat than by the 'in' of the women in the television series.[44] Other women, such as the poet Carmen Conde, who was married to the poet Antonio Oliver Belmás but was also in love with Amanda Junquera, attest to the more hidden or 'in' lives of lesbian love and have become disputed figures in subsequent recuperations of queer historical memory.[45] Only later was Conde's desire for this other woman recognized in the obituaries that followed her death. Such models were not the only option available, however, and several (possibly less political or 'educated') lesbian women developed a presence even under Francoism.[46] In the more permissive district of the Eixample in Barcelona, in the cabaret world, under cover of darkness, the semi-clandestine nature of these spaces afforded some women a limited 'out' existence under the regime.

This section explores same-sex love under the Franco regime and has argued that part of the process of historical recuperation of this queer sexuality can be achieved by fictional and filmic representation in the present, widening of the memory of sexual diversity during the dictatorship. By means of these brief outlines, we can see that even under Francoism the ways in which women could experience homoerotic desire were diverse. The provision of historical evidence of queer sexuality under the dictatorship has hardly yet begun. There is, of course, a large amount of work to be done, not least with respect to female friendships and diverse masculinities in the women's *Sección Femenina*,[47] and, as part of a project to rehabilitate the memory of space in the city, an examination of the significance of boarding schools, gymnasiums, schoolyards and the incense-heavy airs of Catholic colleges, which may all give up their secret lesbian lives in due course.[48] The imaginary and transgressive maps of queerness as represented in the (straight) male protagonist of Ventura Pons' film, *Barcelona (Un mapa)* (2007), played by José María Pou, guides the direction of queer historians working through the shaded streets of past queer geographies. One of the characters, employed as a delivery boy in Barcelona under the dictatorship, carried a street map with the 'dark side' of streets shaded by pencil partly to avoid the heat of the sun but also to be able to inhabit the shadows as a means of 'passing' in a repressive city. To this end, he also rubbed out the Passeig de Gràcia on his map, the artery which runs through Barcelona and by which the victorious Nationalist troops entered the city in January 1939.

The geography of queer space

There is a small plaque in Barcelona's central area of the Ciutadella that commemorates the murder by neo-Nazi skinheads of Sonia Rescalvo, a transwoman, in 1991.[49] Four homeless people were beaten in the same attack. The city of Seville also harboured an expressive and radical queer culture as witnessed by the life and struggle of the transanarchist Rosa Pazos, also murdered in July 2008.[50] In a different way from the examples discussed in the previous section, when such spaces pass from the virtual geography of memory to the physical landscape as memorials (places of memory), the city facilitates the act of recollection for a community and more broadly for society in general.[51]

Setting such memories in place in a city's queerscape, locating them physically, can certainly lead to an entrenchment, a reification of one act over another, perhaps less well-known or publicized act. But it can also liberate the communal memory from the burden of recalling, providing the mental space for analysing the act being recalled, and using it symbolically. It is appropriate that this kind of mental place-marker should exist in Barcelona. Certainly, it can exist in any city, or town, or even hamlet, in Spain and in many other places. But that it should do so in Barcelona helps ground and locate a city that, in the queer imaginary, holds important sway as a harbinger of change, and as the grounds where radicalization finds a narrative home. Two recent films highlight this condition.

Popular visual culture has used Barcelona as a particularly transqueer city, or a city where trans and queer people experience a prominent presence. The most obvious exponent of this use is Pedro Almodóvar's *Todo sobre mi madre* (All About My Mother, 1999). The trans character Agrado is perhaps the most articulate exponent of the cost/value relationship between the body, identity and the spaces it can inhabit. Her monologue is, arguably, the highlight of the film and assertion *par excellence* of these connections. Another more subtle, yet arguably very powerful moment of cinematic transqueer Barcelona presence occurs in the Oscar-winning movie *Milk*. When Harvey Milk meets a young Cleve Jones in the street and tries to convince him to join his political action, Jones declines, alleging no further interest at the moment than an upcoming trip to Europe. In a determining moment in the film, Jones returns from his European trip radicalized after having witnessed a 'riot' in Barcelona, where the 'drag queens' in full regalia were fighting the police, while blood flowed on the streets.[52] In a description reminiscent of the Stonewall riots, Jones marks the moment as a transformative experience for the power of queerness, of the image of the most marginalized and transgressive people standing up to a powerfully repressive state apparatus, and fighting to win. Whether this conversation actually took place or not, whether the actual Cleve Jones felt this was a radicalizing moment for him, the film certainly, and poignantly, makes it so. It is possible to read this as an attempt at providing a 'Stonewall-like' moment to explain Jones's change of heart; or perhaps, as a more intelligent way of historically locating Milk's actions, in light of a more international moment of global change and political transformation. In all likelihood, the riots alluded to were those of the 1st and 8th of February 1976 protests that demanded political amnesty. These political actions and others that followed in Barcelona and other Spanish cities were the political expression of local, community-based organizations seeking democratization and justice in the aftermath of Franco's death. At a macro-political level, these demands were met with the profound transformation of the legal, administrative and political structure of the Spanish state during the so-called transition to democracy. At a more local level, these base communities became the roots of the eventual 'associative strategy' or 'third sector' strategy for securing social justice that developed over the intervening decades.[53]

The political space that opened up for these 'third sector' actors has been financed in powerful ways by municipal governments. It is outside the scope of this chapter to offer a political analysis of these strategies, although LGBTQ tourism is one vector within this process that we discuss below. It is important to consider how these city-/municipality-based funding strategies have helped to provide stable, legitimate global working spaces for transqueers. From 4 to 6 June 2009, Barcelona hosted the 'First Annual International Congress on Gender Identity and Human Rights'. Financed by the Barcelona municipal government, and other governmental and non-governmental sources, the Congress brought together transmen/women from 67 countries in order to create both a set of documents addressed to governmental and non-governmental actors regarding the realities, needs and desires of the trans community, and, perhaps more importantly, a network of international transactivists willing to continue to document, analyse and create an archive of useful knowledge on how to change laws and practices that have an impact on transqueer human rights. The global nature of the conference belies its locational dynamics. Taken in conjunction with the imagery produced by the queer demos in the late 1970s in the central Ramblas boulevard in the city, which have gained iconic status,[54] the use of the past as a constant backdrop to the present has meant that Barcelona has, perhaps not by design, but certainly by choice, become a repository of transqueer history, action and identity.

In Madrid, from Chueca to Lavapiés:
The post-colonial city queers the queers

One of the most notable transformations of the Spanish city in the past 30 years has been the growing influx of immigrants. From a country of net migrants, Spain has become home to a large number of new arrivals. In fact, Spain can 'in recent years boast of one of the most accelerated rates of immigration growth in the world'.[55] This experience has brought to the fore a new sense of space and of relations in the social and physical environs, especially in neighbourhoods that bear the highest numbers of immigrants in the country. And this not only in relation to questions of integration or inclusion, but also, and most importantly, in how the experiences of border crossing, belonging and legality (those who have papers and those who don't) are discussed and used as models for activist engagement.

The case of the historical working-class Lavapiés quarter is especially instructive. While Chueca has gained pride of place as the queer barrio of Madrid, Lavapiés nevertheless also has a claim to queer history. Some of the oldest lesbian bars in Madrid, for example, 'Medea', are located in this neighbourhood.[56] As far back as the fourteenth and fifteenth centuries, the area of Lavapiés was a blending space, as well as a borderland of sorts. At that time, it was the junction of a *judería* (Jewish quarter), an Arab barrio, and a nearby wall that separated these areas from the rest of the Christian city.[57] Later on, it became a locus of internal migration, and eventually of international immigration. Building on this mixed past, from the early '80s onwards, queer bars and locales began to appear in and around the central plaza that gives its name to the neighbourhood.

The Lavapiés of the twenty-first century has become an amalgam of immigrants, lifelong locals, activists who work outside the margins of 'the system' and other various social agents. Their attempts at creating, maintaining and refashioning a community have yielded some changes and some challenges. An important actor in the neighbourhood is Eskalera Karakola, an 'occupied' building that was taken over in 1996 by a women's collective. In this space, various women's groups, organized under the larger 'umbrella' of Eskalera – and of the Red de Lavapiés, a group of community activists that seek to develop alternative spaces for social and political action in the neighbourhood – came together in order to respond to a variety of concerns. Their organizational strategies and purposes were not aimed at social assistance, but rather at 'intellectual and political demands'.[58] Although they had to move from their original occupied house, they have relocated and maintained a vital presence in the neighbourhood as a space where a practical and critical feminism can be brought to bear on the material and political challenges of women in the barrio, and on the discursivity and practices of patriarchal power systems.

In a recent activity, designed to coincide with Pride events that, in 2010, were dedicated to the struggles for transexual rights and freedoms, one of Eskalera's groups staged a discussion and produced a manifesto that was countersigned by a large number of feminist groups. The roundtable debate, entitled 'Transfeminismo desde la otra orilla' [Transfeminism from the other shore], produced a manifesto that serves as a map as well as an archive. In it, the writers highlight the political and material connections between crossing (national) borders, and crossing (gender) borders. Relying on feminism as a common political and theoretical base, they fashion two separate yet intertwined identities, 'transfeministxs' and 'transfronterizxs', positions that are meant to reflect the common experiences of disenfranchisement, and the critical response to such, that accrues to border-crossers.[59] This perspective also lays claim to the city space as a borderland space, where by virtue of attempting to formulate a liberatory citizenship, transfeminists, transfronterizxs, or those who are both, can make evident these connections, and begin to respond to the ideologies that motivate the state apparatus in ways more in accord with their own interests.

In the context of Eskalera Karakola and Lavapiés, it becomes evident that the notion of border crossing, and inappropriate otherness that is represented both by immigrants and transqueers have common political roots, and that the political, disciplinary and discursive practices that seek to regulate and control the border crossings have a common origin. In fact, the demand of 'papers for everyone' has a special echo in the lives of transqueers who are often paperless as if they were stateless.

From inappropriate bodies to exemplars of the new tourism

The inappropriateness of the sexually, geographically and legally peripheral bodies of the immigrant and queer populations of historic Madrid quarters such as Lavapiés can, through a process of commodification and re-signification, nevertheless become central to regulation, integration and city living. Or at least some of them can. In 'Genderbashing', Viviane Namaste cites the work of Canadian sociologist Dorothy Smith arguing that governments regulate bodies and space through (legal) texts.[60] This position is true of the Spanish model of granting rights, and also of responding to the absences in these rights. The text and the power of textual representation become a primary product of both the State and various social actors in the act of claiming rights.

In a queer context, a trio of nationwide laws has come to symbolize the extending of human and social rights to queer collectives. The 'gay marriage law' (2005), the 'Transexual rights law' (2007) and the 'Law of asylum' (2009) have become powerful national and international symbols of the advancement of what constitutional scholars often call 'fourth-generation' rights. These texts have, if very unevenly, begun to take into positive consideration queer identities as a basis for claiming political and human rights. Nevertheless, these laws operate within the constraints of a legal system that still relies on natural law in its argumentations and on judges not trained in sensitivity to queer issues. The exclusions of such laws, or at least some of the less progressive assumptions on which they are based, are echoed in socio-economic terms in the new forms of queer tourism and overt consumption that Spain is currently experiencing.

Tourism became crucial to the Franco regime from the 1960s both for reasons of international legitimacy and the earning of hard cash, propitiating city spaces of sexual permissiveness for queer lives. The most recent decade has seen the growth of a new kind of tourism, whose campaigns reproduce gender stereotypes as well as reinforcing class divisions and elitist access. In 2009, a tourism campaign specifically addressed to women was launched. It reinforced the notion of Spain as a 'laboratory of sexual freedoms', as Lucas (Raquel) Platero has suggested.[61] Spain, in newspaper reports, would be the 'most tolerant country in Europe', the country 'where legally everything is possible', a liberal, modern and democratic nation which 'had thrown off any suspicion of Roman Catholic views on same-sex couples'.[62] This particular campaign was directed towards lesbian women who desired to have children and, in Alicante, offered 'a wedding, insemination and a week's roasting in the sun'. Such a tourist package placed Spain, 'thanks to its flexible legislation . . . at the top of favourite tourist destinations'. The week's holiday was based on the biologistic assumption that (lesbian) women's desires were less overtly in tune with the more expressive sexuality of gay men and more fundamentally linked to maternity mediated by technological innovation: two Madrid women who had used the service believed that 'The offer is very attractive because they let you be peacefully, as if on holiday, and at the same time, you come back home pregnant. You do the follow-up in your own town'. For international couples, however, this follow-up could be highly problematic in terms of a lack of (inter)national legal recognition of such new forms of maternity.[63]

Gay men were not left out of this new development. Building on the emblematic past enjoyed by Barcelona as the first city to come out on the streets in favour of gay rights in the new democracy in 1977, the city was, after Amsterdam, the second most favoured gay destination. With Madrid, the Catalan city accounts for half the businesses trading under the rainbow. The courting of gay male 'Dinkies', who spend up to 47 per cent of their income on travel and leisure,[64] is envisaged as part of a 'spectacular' increase in trade in this area. This is a different kind of tourism from the variety offered to women in Alicante: from a seat at the Eurogames (some 6000 LGBTQ sportspeople), to the promotion of Sitges as the clubbing heaven of the coast where lesbians seem not to have a place,[65] to the Pink Corner in the Barcelona International Tourism Salon in 2009, lesbians rarely get a look in.[66] Another variation of this model has been the inauguration of residences for national and foreign gay couples to retire to, especially in areas traditionally strong in gay tourism.[67]

Conclusion

This chapter on Madrid and other queer cities in Spain has not attempted a triumphalist 'coming of age' story of LGBTQ communities from the repression of the Franco era to the 'liberation' of the twenty-first century. It has not concentrated on the formation and cultural cache of Chueca or the vibrant gay scene of Barcelona. Instead, it has tried to evaluate critically what Bowker has termed 'local orderings' with a view to signalling the multiple places where queer has been evoked at some point along the 'in/out' scale, made visible or lived out as a marginal experience against the backdrop of political regimes that were/are not monolithically dictatorial and repressive or uniquely progressive and democratic. The chapter has also problematized the relationship between 'fact' and 'fiction' and the usefulness in re-thinking queer histories provided by other evidence, including novels, memories and films as a means of writing a nuanced form of history that is sensitive to the creation of new depictions of queerness and queer subjectivity in our present. It has also suggested that such local orderings betray certain exclusions within these sources given the fact that diversity inside the margins has still not been fully accomplished in Spanish cities. Gender inequalities are still at work in social environments such as tourism, a social space that also suffers from the marginalization of transgender and aged queers, and which promotes gender differences, whereby Barcelona is promoted as a 'cool' gay male place to visit, and the 'pro-maternal' Valencia is ideal for lesbians seeking insemination and a family. In this way, the 'usefulness' of some expressions of queer to legitimize the democratic project is contrasted with the edginess surrounding the incorporation into the physical and legal landscape of new immigrant communities, often deemed dangerous or disruptive for social cohesion within a spectacular and commodified model of human relations.

In this sense, queering the city may not be the province of LGBTQs alone; more 'problematic' categories, unruly in their incorporation into cities and sometimes both queer and immigrant, pose challenges to the new legal frameworks for same-sex marriage, intimacy and, in some cases, physical survival. The model of gay-themed vacations, public consumption and high visibility of especially gay men in television series and programmes remains 'another country' for many at the queer margins of today's Spanish cities. Some of those who have benefitted from same-sex marriage legislation or the new gender equality law forget or ignore the fact that these laws were introduced at the same time that the Spanish Socialist Party (PSOE) hardened its restrictions on immigration, increased expulsions and presided over a period during which police forces were given quotas of immigrants to locate and remove from the country.[68] Such limitations invite us to cast a critical eye over the rainbow colours that flap in the wind at so many events and that hang from so many town halls. Are the flags becoming more two-tone, exalting youth and money, rather than reflecting a truly diverse set of lifestyles, desires and political and economic circumstances? Is the future to be driven by the less and less openly camp gay male who possesses ever greater purchasing power? Is this the kind of 'queerification' that we desire for our cities? The Spanish case shows how individual cities and localities are coming out of the closet to promote gay tourism; the result, however, may be an exquisitely designed model whose dimensions are rather exclusive and restrictive. In this chapter, using queerness as an analytical tool to analyse marginalization, we have connected different figures of exclusion in our Spanish cities. This fruitful use of queerness helps us to go beyond triumphalist readings of gay life and invites us to build new forms of solidarity in our urban lives.

Notes

1   Juan Gil-Albert, *Heraclés. Sobre una manera de ser,* Madrid: Akal, 1987, p. 7. This discussion of homosexuality, presented as a "Hommage to Plato", was originally written in 1955 but had to wait more than twenty years to be published.

2   A good overview of these changes is provided in Herzog, D. (2001), *Sexuality in Europe: A Twentieth-Century History*. Cambridge: Cambridge University Press.

3   For the historical background to the notion in the medieval and early modern periods, see Aldaraca, B. A. (1991), *El ángel del hogar: Galdós and the Ideology of Domesticity in Spain*. Chapel Hill: Dept. of Romance Languages, University of North Carolina. For a brief outline of the situation of women before Francoism and a discussion of changes to come after 1939, see Graham, H. (1995), 'Women and social change', in H. Graham and J. Labanyi (eds), *Spanish Cultural Studies*. Oxford/New York: Oxford University Press, pp. 99–115. On the resistance of women to heteronormativity under the Franco period, see Osborne, R. (ed.) (2013), *Mujeres bajo sospecha: Memoria y sexualidad (1930–1980)*. Madrid: Editorial Fundamentos, and, Medina Doménech, R. M. (2013), *Ciencia y sabiduría del amor. Una historia cultural del franquismo, 1940–1960*. Madrid/Frankfurt: Iberoamericana/Vervuert. More generally, see Nash, M. (2013), *Represión, resistencias, memoria. Las mujeres bajo la dictadura franquista*. Comares: Granada.

4   Speech cited in Reig Tapia, A. (1990), *Violencia y terror. Estudios sobre la guerra civil española*. Madrid: Akal Universitaria, p. 56. Queipo also promised that if any rightists who supported the insurrection were killed by the left, he would kill ten for every dead rightist. If the guilty leftists were already dead, he would disinter their bodies and 'kill them again'. On the relation between masculinity, violence and the consolidation of Franco's regime, see Vincent, M. (1999), 'The Martyrs and the saints: Masculinity and the construction of the Francoist crusade', *History Workshop Journal*, 47, 68–98.

5   See, for example, Zubiaurre, M. (2012), *Cultures of the Erotic in Spain, 1898–1939*. Nashville: Vanderbilt University Press.

6   Vázquez García, F. and A. Moreno Mengíbar (2004), *Historia de la prostitución en Andalucía*. Seville: Fundación José Manuel Lara, p. 244. Vallejo expressed this desire in his book *Higienización psíquica de las grandes urbes* [The Sanitization of the Great Cities] (1941).

7   In respect of (Spanish) Equatorial Guinea, see Medina-Doménech, R. M. (2009), 'Scientific technologies of national identity as colonial legacies: Extracting the Spanish nation from equatorial Guinea', *Social Studies of Science*, 39(1), 81–112.

8   Bleys, R. C. (1996), *The Geography of Perversion: Male-to-male Sexual Behaviour outside the West and the Ethnographic Imagination 1750–1918*. London/New York: Cassell, p. 11. Bleys notes that this question of legibility is rendered by Eve K. Sedgwick as the 'epistemology of the closet', by Lee Edelman as 'homographesis' and by J. Stockinger as 'homotextuality'.

9   Sennett, R. (1996), *Flesh and Stone: The body and the City in Western Civilization*. London: Faber and Faber, pp. 82–6 and *passim*.

10 See Medina Doménech, R. M. (2012), 'Sentir la historia. Propuestas para una agenda de investigación feminista en la historia de las emociones', *Arenal*, 19(1), 161–99.

11 We draw here on the work by Bowker, G. C. (2000), 'Biodiversity datadiversity', *Social Studies of Science*, 30(5), 643–83. For 'regimes of the normal', see Warner, M. (1993), 'Introduction', in *Fear of a Queer Planet: Queer Politics and Social Theory*. Minneapolis/London: University of Minnesota Press, pp. vii–xxxi (xxvi).

12 An example: in the years 1939–45, some 200,000 Spaniards starved to death as a result of the poverty entailed by the war and the economic and social measures of the new regime. See Cazorla Sánchez, A. (2010), *Fear and Progress: Ordinary Lives in Franco's Spain, 1939–1975*. Chichester: Wiley-Blackwell, p. 9.

13 An example would be the placing of a wreath of roses by a group of men known as 'Las Carolinas' on the site of the demolished urinal in 1934 (Trujillo Barbadillo, G. (2009), *Deseo y Resistencia (1977-2007). Treinta años de movilización lesbiana en el estado español*. Madrid: Egales, p. 61, n. 54). The original story was recounted in Jean Genet's *The Thief's Journal*.

14 The tendency to assume that all queer life worth noting carries on in cities alone has, to some degree, been rectified. Although useful, comments such as Henning Bech's in his (1997), *When Men Meet: Homosexuality and Modernity*. Cambridge: Polity Press, p. 98, according to which 'The city is the social world proper of the homosexual, his life space; it is no use objecting that lots of homosexuals have lived in the country', cannot no longer be taken as read. Despite recognizing that gay lives make the city and that the city makes gay lives, Houlbrook, M. (2005), *Queer London: Perils and Pleasures in the Sexual Metropolis, 1918–1957*. London/Chicago: University of Chicago Press, has been critical of the city focus (pp. 4–6).

15   See Abraham, J. (2009), *Metropolitan Lovers: The Homosexuality of Cities*. Minneapolis/London: University of Minnesota Press, pp. xiv and xv. The racial and class dimensions, however, can be lost in such evaluations. See Rushbrook, D. (2002), 'Cities, queer space, and the cosmopolitan tourist', *GLQ: A Journal of Lesbian and Gay Studies*, 8(1–2), 183–206.

16   On this subculture among men, see Cleminson, R. and F. Vázquez García (2009), *'Los Invisibles': A History of Male Homosexuality in Spain, 1850–1939*. Cardiff: University of Wales Press, pp. 220–9.

17   See the descriptions of life in Ibiza from the 1950s in Rafael Azcona, *Los europeos*, published outside of the country by the Librairie des Éditions Espagnoles in Paris in 1960. We draw on the 2006 edition published by Tusquets (Barcelona). In this account, lesbian couples are mentioned in addition to the 'queer bashing' of gay men (pp. 112, 150, 183–5).

18   On Punta del Verde, see Moreno Mengíbar and Vázquez García, *Historia de la prostitución en Andalucía*, p. 251.

19   Guasch, O. (1991), *La sociedad rosa*. Barcelona: Anagrama, p. 73, n. 1.

20   Arnalte, A. (2003), *Redada de Violetas. La represión de los homosexuales durante el franquismo*. Madrid: La Esfera de los Libros, p. 271, quoting Luis Antonio de Villena's observations.

21   Some of these images can be seen in the collection, with prologue by José Cela, C. (1964), *Izas, rabizas y colipoterras*. Barcelona: Editorial Lumen.

22   Abraham (2009), p. 42, referring to Williams' (1985), *The Country and the City*.

23   The category 'evidence' and 'experience' have long been critiqued. See Wallach Scott, J. (1991), 'The evidence of experience', *Critical Inquiry*, 17(4), 773–97.

24   Turner, M. W. (2003), *Backward Glances: Cruising the Queer Streets of New York and London*. London: Reaktion Books, p. 8.

25   The relationship between fiction and fact and their inherence in the past and the present is explored sensitively in Bravmann, S. (1997), *Queer Fictions of the Past: History, Culture, and Difference*. Cambridge: Cambridge University Press.

26   Wallach Scott (1991), p. 400.

27   Young, R. J. C. (1995), *Colonial Desire: Hybridity in Theory, Culture and Race*. London: Routledge, p. 30.

28   Cf. the comments made by G. Chauncey in 'The policed: Gay men's strategies of everyday resistance in times square', in B. Beemyn (ed.) (1997), *Creating a Place for Ourselves: Lesbian, Gay, and Bisexual Community Histories*. London: Routledge, pp. 9–25.

29   Three examples originally written in English include Samson, C. J. (2006), *Winter in Madrid*. Basingstoke/Oxford: Pan Macmillan; Boling, D. (2008), *Guernica*. London: Picador; Hislop, V. (2008), *The Return*. London: Headline Review.

30   For the letter of the Law, see http://www.boe.es/g/es/bases_datos/doc.php ?coleccion=iberlex&id=2007/22296. For a discussion of its contents and implications, see the special issue of the *Journal of Spanish Cultural Studies*,

9(2), 2008, 'The politics of memory in contemporary spain', and Richards, M. (2006), 'Between memory and history: Social relationships and ways of remembering the Spanish civil war', *International Journal of Iberian Studies*, 19(1), 85–94.

31 The Law seeks to compensate for persecution, violence or loss of human rights as a result of political or ideological reasons in general and as a result of cultural, linguistic or sexual orientation options in particular (see p. 53411). As a result of campaigning by the Spanish LGBTQ Federation and the Asociación de Ex-Presos Sociales, new legislation has approved financial compensation for incarceration arising out of the Francoist legislation of 1954 and 1970 that substantially criminalized male homosexuality.

32 For the letter of the 2005 law on same-sex civil marriage see the Official State Bulletin at http://www.boe.es/boe/dias/2005/08/08/pdfs/A27817-27822.pdf.

33 Monroe, A. (2008), *The Maze of Cadiz*. London: John Murray. On the historical presence of homosexuality and, to some degree, tolerance for the same in Cadiz, see F. Vázquez García (2013), 'Homosexualidad y crisis del 98: La invención de Cádiz como moderna "Sodoma"', forthcoming in J-L. Guereña (ed.), *Repenser les sexualités*. Tours: Presse de l'Université François-Rabelais.

34 Ruiz Zafón, C. (2001), *La sombra del viento*. Barcelona: Planeta; (2004), *The Shadow of the Wind*, trans. L. Graves, London: Weidenfeld & Nicolson.

35 Ruiz Zafón (2001), pp. 41–2; pp. 164–5; p. 573.

36 See Hernández-Catá, A. (1929), *El Angel de Sodoma*. Madrid: Mundo Latino (second edition), in which the protagonist escapes to Paris, aims to meet a man in a tryst, cannot bear his own homosexuality and throws himself under a train to his death.

37 Moya declared recently that 'Como mujer, lesbiana y periodista he sufrido el franquismo, sus consecuencias' [As a woman, a lesbian and a journalist I have suffered under Francoism and the consequences brought about by it]. See the interview at http://foros.universogay.com/mensaje-entrevista-elena-moya-autora-de-los-olivos-de-belchite.html (consulted 24 January 2011).

38 Gracia, J. (2004), *La resistencia silenciosa. Fascismo y cultura en España*. Barcelona: Editorial Anagrama.

39 This debate can be seen with respect, for example, to Guillermo del Toro's 'Pan's Labyrinth'. See Smith, P. J. (2007), 'El laberinto del fauno', *Film Quarterly*, 60(4), 4–9, and, Vivancos, A. (2012), 'Malevolent fathers and rebellious daughters: National oedipal narratives and political erasures in El laberinto del fauno (2006)', *Bulletin of Spanish Studies*, 89(6), 877–93.

40 Wright, R. (2002) [1957], *Pagan Spain*. Jackson, MS: Banner Books, p. 221.

41 See http://www.apeuropeos.org/madrid-mayo-1955-cas-oorthuys/ (consulted 25 September 2013).

42 Cf. Fuss, D. (1991), *Inside/Out: Lesbian Theories, Gay Theories*. London: Routledge.

43 Medina Doménech (2013), pp. 145–259.

44. A very brief mention is made of Mujeres Libres founder Lucía Sánchez Saornil's lesbianism in Ackelsberg, M. A. (2005) [1991], *Free Women of Spain: Anarchism and the Struggle for the Emancipation of Women*. Oakland, West Virginia/Edinburgh: AK Press, p. 172 and in Nash, M. (1995), *Defying Male Civilization: Women in the Spanish Civil War*. Denver: Arden Press, p. 92. The article by Sanfeliu Gimeno, L., 'Lucía Sánchez Saornil; una vida y una obra alternativas a la sociedad de su tiempo', is more extensive on this point and can be viewed at http://www.feministas.org/IMG/pdf/Mesa_memoria_franquismo-_Lucia_Sanchez_Saornil.pdf (consulted 17 December 2010).

45 See Simonis, A. (2009), *Yo no soy ésa que tú te imaginas: el lesbianismo en la narrativa española del siglo XX a través de sus estereotipos*. Alicante: Centro de Estudios sobre la Mujer, Universidad de Alicante, esp. ch. 2.

46 See Albarracín Soto, M. (2008), 'Libreras y tebeos: las voces de las lesbianas mayores', in R. Platero Méndez (ed.), *Lesbianas: discursos y representaciones*. Barcelona: Melusina, pp. 191–212.

47 Rosón Villena, M. (2013), 'Contramodelo a la feminidad burguesa: Construcciones visuales del poder en la Sección Femenina de Falange', in Osborne (ed.) (2013), pp. 293–309.

48 Cf. the comments of R. (Lucas) Platero on the occasion of the seminar on 'Memory and Sexuality of Women under Francoism' in April 2010 whereby a 70-year-old woman after the seminar arranged to meet Platero near the school where her first love with other girls took place. For a brief presentation of the colloquium with an interview of Platero, see http://uned.estudiasocial.net/seminario-uned-memoria-y-sexualidad-de-la-mujeres-bajo-el-franquismo/.

49 Cía, B. (1994), '310 años de cárcel para siete "skins" por asesinar a un travestido en Barcelona', *El País*, 14 July, p. 4.

50 http://www.cnt.es/noticias/la-anarquista-rosa-pazos-ha-sido-asesinada (consulted 24 January 2011).

51 Hertz, B-S., E. Eisenberg and L. Maya Knauer (1997), 'Queer spaces in New York city: Places of struggle/places of strength', in G. B. Ingram, A-M. Bouthillette and Y. Retter (eds), *Queers in Space: Communities, Public Places, Sites of Resistance*. Seattle: Bay press, pp. 356–70 (p. 358). A comparison can be made to Paul Harfleet's Pansy Project, the planting of a pansy at sites of homophobic abuse in the United Kingdom.

52 Cleve Jones would eventually become Milk's protégé and an activist in his own right, organizing the AIDS Memorial Quilt and other queer actions in his many years of activism in the United States.

53 Gómez, M. (2006), 'El barrio de Lavapiés, laboratorio de interculturalidad', *Dissidences: Hispanic Journal of Theory and Criticism*, 2(1), http://www.dissidences.org/Lavapies.html (last accessed 24 June 2011).

54 The classic image which is often reproduced is that of gays, lesbians and trans figures demonstrating against the 'Law of Social Dangerousness' used against homosexuals from 1970 onwards. This law was slowly dismantled and eventually revoked in 1995. See the front cover of Benito Eres Rigueira, J. and C. Villagrasa Alcaide (eds) (2008), *Homosexuals i transsexuals: Els*

altres represaliats i discriminats del franquisme, des de la memòria històrica. Barcelona: Edicions Bellaterra, for a typical image.

55 Suárez Navaz, L. et al. (2007), 'El Estado y las luchas de los sin papeles en España: ¿Una extensión de la ciudadanía?', in L. Suárez Navaz et al. (eds), *Las luchas de los sin papeles y la extensión de la ciudadanía. Perspectivas críticas desde Europa y Estados Unidos.* Madrid: Editorial Traficantes de Sueños, p. 185.

56 García, Y. (2007), 'Más allá de Chueca: Lavapiés y La Latina, nuevos barrios gays de Madrid', at adn.es (online), 4 June, http://www.adn.es/impresa/ madrid/20070604/NWS-0044-Chueca-alla.html (accessed 22 November 2010).

57 Gómez (2006).

58 Ibid.

59 The words 'transfeministxs' and 'transfronterizxs' are written with the 'x' here instead of the masculine 'o' or feminine 'a' in order to maintain gender neutrality, a device commonly used by radical movements. In many respects, such movements draw on the contestatory politics of *mestiza* practice as proposed by Anzaldúa, G. (1991), *Borderlands – La Frontera: The New Mestiza.* San Francisco: Aunt Lute Books. For the relation between 'effective' protest and 'affective', that is, caring and solidarity-based practice, see Shukaitis, S. (2011), 'Nobody knows what an insurgent body can do: Questions for affective resistance', in J. Heckert and R. Cleminson (eds), *Anarchism and Sexuality: Ethics, Relationships and Power.* Abingdon: Routledge, pp. 45–66; for discussion of the 'feminist research and organizing collective', Precarias a la deriva, which emerged out of the Eskalera, see pp. 53–60.

60 Namaste, V. K. (2006), 'Genderbashing: Sexuality, gender and the regulation of public space', in S. Stryker and S. Whittle (eds), *The Transgender Studies Reader.* London: Routledge, pp. 584–600 (p. 585), citing Smith, D. (1987), *The Everyday World as Problematic: A Feminist Sociology.* Toronto: University of Toronto Press, p. 17.

61 Platero Méndez, R. (2009), 'La construcción del sujeto lésbico en el estado español', *Regiones, Suplemento de Antropología*, 39, pp. 11–17.

62 Ortiz, A. M. and J. Gómez (n.d.), 'El paquete turístico de la España ZP', *El Mundo, Suplemento Crónica* 626, http://www.elmundo.es/suplementos/ cronica/2009/626/1245535215.html (accessed 30 July 2010).

63 All quotations from ibid.

64 'A la caza del turismo gay' (2009), http://www.youtube.com/watch?v=-feMv PvcOf4&feature=youtube_gdata (accessed 1 August 2011).

65 Gay Sitges Paradise (2008), http://www.youtube.com/watch?v=4_6Hnoy WASU&feature=youtube_gdata (accessed 26 January 2011).

66 http://www.elconfidencial.com/sociedad/ciudades-espanolas-salen-armario-captar-turistas-20090824.html.

67 Munárriz, A. (2009), 'Primer edificio de viviendas sólo para gays', *El Público*, 22 September, http://www.publico.es/espana/254011/primer/edificio/ viviendas/solo/gays (accessed 1 July 2010). The campaigner Jordi Petit has

noted recently that equality in residences generally is a pending issue. See his comments in Bonet, N. (2007), '30 años de orgullo gay en Barcelona', http:// www.20minutos.es/noticia/247894/0/orgullo/gay/barcelona/, 15 June (accessed 2 August 2010). More generally, for Madrid as a (mainly male) gay travel and tourist destination, see Giorgi, G. (2002), 'Madrid En Tránsito: Travelers, visibility, and gay identity', *GLQ: A Journal of Lesbian and Gay Studies*, 8(1–2), 57–79.

68 The juxtaposition of these developments has been emphasized by many analysts. See, for example, Pérez-Sánchez, G. (2010), 'Transnational conversations in migration, queer, and   studies: Multimedia stories', *Revista Canadiense de Estudios Hispánicos*, 35(1), 163–84 (with thanks to Francisco Molina Artaloytia for bringing this article to our attention).

Further reading

Houlbrook, M. (2005), *Queer London: Perils and Pleasures in the Sexual Metropolis, 1918-1957*. Chicago: University of Chicago Press.

Medina Doménech, R. M. (2013), *Ciencia y sabiduría del amor: Una historia cultural del franquismo, 1940–1960*. Frankfurt: Iberoamericana/Vervuert.

Platero, R. (Lucas) (ed.) (2012), *Intersecciones: Cuerpos y sexualidades en la encrucijada*. Barcelona: Bellaterra.

Sáez, J. and P. Vidarte (eds) (2005), *Teoría queer. Políticas bolleras, maricas, trans, mestizas*. Madrid: Egales.

Trujillo, G. (2008), *Deseo y Resistencia. Treinta años de movilización lesbiana en el Estado español*. Madrid: Egales.

2

Capital stories: Local
lives in queer London

Matt Cook

There is a story of gay London since the war which I want to rehearse briefly. It somewhat contextualizes but also eludes the lives and experiences of the three men whom I discuss in the main body of the chapter and who elaborate other overlapping and separate queer mappings of the capital, and show how the shifting ground of the past gets used unevenly in the present. The story goes like this. For men in the 1950s and early 1960s, there were the private member clubs for a 'respectable' middle-class set and some rougher bars known for trade (rent boys). There were working class 'dilly boys' at Piccadilly Circus and the 'normal' lads you might still find in one of the city's legendary cottages (public toilets). The threat of arrest was omnipresent and high-profile prosecutions exposed those cottages, Mayfair flats and queer networks linking the metropolis to stately country retreats.[1] Soon, though, the partial legalization of homosexuality in 1967, the reverberations of the Civil Rights movement in the United States, student protest in Paris and Women's Liberation changed the tenor of queer life of the city – not least in the invocation to pride and visibility. The Gay Liberation Front met for the first time in 1970; Pride marched in 1972; Bang!, London's first big American style club, opened its doors on Charing Cross Road in the mid-decade. There were, it seemed, more experiments in living, sex, drugs, art, performance, film and literature in the city. A gay press made it easier to find gay flat shares, gay bars and gay services in the capital and began to suggest more fully the commercial potential of the pink pound.[2]

From 1981, the capital consistently had the highest incidence of HIV and AIDS in the country. Gay Londoners and their friends and families experienced a period of terrible loss and grief and shifting patterns of daily life. The latter might now involve hospital, doctor, and home visits, as well as a recalibration of sex and social lives. This took place in the context of Margaret Thatcher's censorious conservative government and also a wider homophobic backlash in the press and (opinion polls suggested) among a wider public.[3] The Greater London Council under Ken Livingstone between 1981 and 1984 and some of the labour-controlled London boroughs (Islington, Hackney and Lambeth most famously) attempted a fight back by pushing an equal opportunities agenda in their service provision.[4] Gay pride marches in London at the end of the decade attracted tens of thousands – especially after the passing of the hated Section 28 in 1988, which prevented local authorities from 'promot[ing]' the acceptability of homosexuality in schools and libraries. The ensuing pride march was headed by Welsh miners, showing support in turn after a gay and lesbian group based in London had campaigned for them during the miners' strike of the mid-eighties.

If gay men were commonly linked with the left in what had become a determinedly politicized identity,[5] there was a parallel, sometimes overlapping, and certainly growing media association in the 1990s of gay men with fashion and style, with loft-style living and with gentrification of certain areas of the city.[6] In the 1990s, many gay Londoners began to feel less embattled as attitudes shifted. The final years of the decade and the early years of the new century saw legal change in the direction of 'equality' (rather than sexual and social revolution).[7] There was greater visibility on TV and film, and in more self-confident gay villages in Soho and Vauxhall especially. A hipster metrosexual scene around Hoxton and Shoreditch later gained ground on the back in part of a local arts and gallery scene there. The census of 2001 suggested that the London borough of Islington had the second highest proportion of declared residential gay couples in the country (at 2.26% of the population). It was second only to the city of Brighton and Hove (at 2.67%), an hour out of London to the south and to many a seaside extension of London's gay and lesbian pleasures.[8] The Registry Office of the London borough of Westminster (which includes Soho) just missed being the first in the country to conduct its 1000th civil partnership in September 2006. Brighton and Hove again won out by a week. Civil partnership celebrations often brought families of origin and families of choice together in new circumstances, reflecting what some experienced as a more convivial and live-and-let-live urban culture.[9] Others felt a palpable loss of gay community, a depolitization which unhitched gay from left wing politics, and an accession to neo-liberal individualism and consumer culture.[10] The internet, meanwhile, brought a new virtual dimension to socializing and cruising for sex, radically shifting London's gay and queer culture once more.[11]

This particular account of gay London, with its dates and geography, is important in understanding gay life in the capital and identifying reference points which most of the men I've interviewed over the last few years mentioned or were surely familiar with. It suggests a shared history, a coming together and a consolidation of 'community': an equivocal success story.[12] It is a story on the whole of things 'getting better' and one that focused on commercial and public demonstrations of gay socializing, pride and protest – those activities where identity and community become most visible and can seem most palpable. Gathering those oral histories has, meanwhile, alerted me to the way each of the Londoners I talked to inhabited this but also rather different cities. They remembered supposedly repressive eras with some nostalgia and excitement, and found 'the world we had won' (as Jeffrey Weeks has it) hard.[13] Queer men have had to find a sense of composure within various intersecting and conflicting myths, narratives and life trajectories – including big historical markers, community pleasures and tragedies, and personal, intimate experiences and memories. By identifying themselves as camp, queer, homosexual or gay in the period since 1945, my interviewees certainly plugged into networks of other men, into ideas about distinguishing characteristics, propensities and cultures, and into subcultural knowledge of places and 'scenes' in the city. But in their testimonies they also indicate the multiple dimensions of identity and identification, and the complicated ways in which their understandings of their desires were entwined with the material, economic, cultural and social circumstances of their urban lives, the streets or areas where they lived, their proximity to or distance from family, the money they had and the jobs they did, their relationship status, health, age and much more besides.[14]

I want to give some sense of this complexity through snapshots of three men's lives. Alan was born in 1932 and came to London in the early 1950s, did various office and service sector jobs while living in and around Notting Hill in central west London and then in middle and older age in Hackney to the east. He died in 2011. Michael was born in 1942 and brought up between the homes of his aunt and parents in Islington and Stamford Hill. He enjoyed a career in advertising and then the arts and something of the 1960s swing. Photographer Ajamu X was born in 1964, arrived in Brixton in the late eighties and has lived and worked there ever since. As I discuss these men – and some few others in passing – I suggest the significance of the story I told at the outset in their everyday lives or else as a reference point, anchor or something to react against. These men indicate some aspects of change over time which runs through that story. Through these testimonies I suggest too, though, how the local and particular, how memories and distant associations, and how intersecting identifications, interests and passions modulate and fracture homogenizing assumptions about gay identity and the gay city and scene.[15] Crucially, I don't see any of these men as representative or typical or more important than other men I interviewed or indeed anyone else. Neither are the places they lived and remembered especially significant or necessarily more significant than other places in the capital's queer histories. Their value is that they are indicative of a complexity I think is important to hold on to when we think about queer life in London – a complexity which certainly touches established places and histories but is not bound by them; which involves remembered and hoped for London as well as the one that was being lived in the here and now.

Alan[16]

Alan (1932–2011) contacted me after I made a call to an older gay men's group in London, and I interviewed him in 2010 in the common room of his sheltered accommodation in Hackney, east London. He reminisced chiefly about Notting Hill in the 1950s. He had moved there from his working-class family in Portsmouth (in England's south-west), after accompanying his mother from there to Paddington Station in the late 1940s and experiencing the queer draw of the city. 'When I went outside I saw all these black guys walking up and down, I thought to myself "hello this is another world." That's what made me come to London. I wanted to get away from Portsmouth, it was very dreary dull; I was beginning to feel the urge I think!' Alan's first employer (Hall's Telephones) found him accommodation on Harrow Road with a Mrs Valentine – 'a wonderful woman', widowed in the war and caring now for her son and daughter alone. 'She knew I was gay, everyone knew I was gay. . . . I was camp and all the rest of it and I was just out and out gay'. Alan would take lovers home ('I know more about you than you think I do', she told him), and if he was not in, Mrs Valentine would let them wait in his room. Alan encountered something that I came across frequently in interviewees' memories of London in the immediate post-war years – a sense of live-and-let-live toleration and even active support in the crowded inner-London bedsitterlands of Notting Hill, Paddington, Islington, Pimlico and St Pancras. This nuances the broader narrative about the intolerance and repression of the 1950s. In these areas and others, Victorian and Edwardian terraced housing had been divided and subdivided into flats and bedsits as middle class residents increasingly moved to the new more spacious suburbs roughly from the 1930s onwards. While bedsitter and boarding house living came more broadly to suggest singleness, loneliness, a rupture from family and also proximity to the dangers of the city, Alan and other queer men found comradeship with each other and also with landladies, landlords and other tenants.[17]

Alan left Mrs Valentine's to live with two successive boyfriends, before being chucked out by the last and finding a place to live with Flora Macdonald – 'the matriarch' of the Notting Hill queer community in the mid-1950s. 'She was quite eccentric, looked like cat weasel, hair and all ragged beard and god knows what else, rattled along the road with her bike and he was like the contact for people' for sex and places to stay. 'She knew everybody and she gave [girls] names to a lot of them'; Alan was 'Nelly Bagwash'. Flora put Alan up for 3 months, and in that period would sometimes go out to cut the hedge at 11 p.m.; 'that was the time they would come out of the shebeens [or illegal bars]. You would get the black guys coming down the road . . . she'd bow in front of them and say "hello sexy"'. When Alan walked past her into the house on one occasion and went to bed, Flora guided one of these men in afterwards. 'The next thing I knew there was this guy stark naked . . . he jumped into bed and that was that! Good night Diane!' Flora and Alan seem to have associated black men with 'a classic stereotype of a natural, spontaneous sexuality',[18] which was not (in Alan's view) codified and categorized like his own and other white camp men in his network. This was a transitional period in British sexual cultures when it was still just possible to sleep with men and women and have a claim on 'normality' (not least through a repudiation of effeminacy). This complicates presumptions (then and since) about a singular and separate minority of defined homosexual men.[19] For those like Alan who embraced a singular sexual identity yet largely desired men who did not, there were repercussions for the way they lived in this city. There was certainly a deep and often enduring affection between Alan and his lovers. Girlfriends, marriage and children nevertheless took precedence in terms of where those lovers lived and the frequency with which they were able to see their boyfriend. Alan saw his relationships as necessarily temporary. 'They all got married', he said, 'every one of them'. In response to this Alan suggested the need for resourcefulness in his urban life which relied on mobility and the ability to move on. Alan moved from Flora's place to a flat of his own. His landlady there disapproved of his new black boyfriend, and 'I said "that's it, moonlight flit."' 'It was easy, very easy' to find places to stay he said (though his anecdote signals the trouble black men – queer, normal or neither – were having finding accommodation in the city at this time).

Alan described queer, drug, prostitution and Afro-Caribbean counter cultures coming together in the bedsits, flats, streets, shebeens and cafes of Notting Hill in the 1950s and 1960s. It seemed, he said, 'to gel' and was 'very supportive'. The black guys 'knew our camp names' and 'a lot of the landladies . . . were on the game'. 'I remember walking down the road one day when there were police cars around and all that', he said. 'This girl was running past me, saw me with my hair and goodness knows what else, grabbed hold of me by the arm, dragged me down the steps of a basement in through the door . . . and there I was staying the night with all these prostitutes around me . . . running around in their blinkin' bras and knickers'. Pre-internet and pre-gay press, the cogency and tangibility of neighbourhood and neighbourhood networks were perhaps especially significant for men like Alan.[20] 'We used to have parties [in flats and houses] in the 1960s', he said. 'We used to have three big parties a year and we used to tell people when we would have the next one; all these people would turn up. It was wonderful. We didn't have technology like today, but we got speakers around the walls, connected together – sound coming from different directions'. Though new queer venues with small dance floors like the Candy Bar in Soho opened in the sixties, Alan and these other party-goers perhaps found more licence on a domestic party circuit.

Alan joined the Campaign for Homosexual Equality (CHE) in the early 1970s. The local group was part of his social circuit and he DJ-ed for them as well as for the Gay Liberation Front (in a not infrequent – though infrequently described – cross-over between the groups). At one event in a west London church hall, 'in came the blinking GLF. God, dear me, they were all in drag. Dancing on pews – trust them!', he said laughing. He seemed to relish this, just as he relished being with a colleague when he was working in the canteen at insurers Lloyds of London during this period: 'Rose was in her 50s; very very camp; I think she was meant to be a woman . . . [in the canteen] she was dancing . . . singing . . . slapping the lettuce on the plates. Oh wonderful times! Lloyds', said Alan, 'was another gay community . . . very camp it was. A lot of the underwriters were gay'.

The West End didn't feature in Alan's social life, as our overarching narrative at the outset suggested it might. 'I think the nearest [I got] was Speaker's Corner' – a place where he went to listen to CHE speakers. Neither did he find much of a social scene in Hackney – where he moved in the mid-1970s for a place to live after a relationship break up. 'There was some gay community going on [in the 1980s]', he said. 'There were three gay pubs in Kingsland Road; there was a lesbian pub in Stoke Newington High Street, which is now a Tesco. . . . I used to go to them at one time, which wasn't too bad, but they all closed down. There has been nothing since but the isolation I feel in Hackney'. For Alan, what was key was what was local and accessible, a tangible sense of community and belonging on his doorstep or in his workplace. In his sheltered accommodation 'they all know I'm gay and they are all very friendly, we have a laugh and a joke. But it's not the same thing', he said; 'I should be with my own'.

Alan contrasted Notting Hill in the 1950s with the Portsmouth of his youth and with the Hackney of his middle and older age. Through this he articulated the dullness of life in Portsmouth (long past its queer heyday in the early twentieth century) and the loneliness and sense of insecurity he felt in east London. Talking about Notting Hill was in part a way of explaining what felt wrong to him about being gay in these other places.[21] The day I interviewed Alan, he had been watching *Tales of the City* – the adaptation of the first of Armistead Maupin novel about a boarding house in San Francisco in the 1970s. 'It did remind me of my time in Notting Hill', he said.

Alan's feeling of support, safety, fun and adventure in Notting Hill during the 1950s and 1960s supersede other ways that he might have talked about life in the area in this period. Aside from the brief reference to the racist landlady, he did not mention everyday racism and Teddy Boy animosity and attacks which culminated in racial riots of 1958 and gave the area a fresh notoriety.[22] The absence of those feelings of belonging and safety for him later in Hackney – not least after he was severely beaten up in a homophobic attack – meant that local tensions and socio-economic realities came into sharper focus. They were, of course, also more immediate. 'I do not suffer in silence', he said, 'I went to a meeting last week and [we talked about] what LGBT people would like to find in Hackney, [so that it is] a better place to grow old in . . . I remember way back the Porchester Drag Queen Balls, in Porchester Hall in Queensway. I thought we could do something [like that] here. I would like to see something like that come back, it is part of gay history'. These regular balls ran from the late 1960s to the mid-1980s and were highlights of the trans calendar. What Alan described in his search for community was a desire to bind such pasts into the present, to recoup a sense of a queer London to which he felt he could belong. Part of the sadness for him was that that milieu had shifted: the particular countercultures and countercultural cross-overs he enjoyed were no longer part of street and home life in gentrified Notting Hill or for that matter Hackney. More broadly, his particular queer identification and way of being queer was perhaps no longer so readily anchored in particular places and scenes in the city. Yvonne Sinclair, who has compiled a website with images of drag balls and events of the 1970s and early 1980s, writes: 'It's sad to think that all this has now been lost; all the gaiety and exuberance of those times and these venues are now just memories'.[23]

Alan reminds us that age and generation are centrally at stake in the way the queer city and particular areas within it are experienced as embracing or alienating, as enabling or disabling. Alan had heard that Hoxton and Shoreditch 'had become very arty', but though he mentioned it as an area that might resonate with his experience of Notting Hill, he didn't engage with what was a younger scene. The city and areas within it changed over this half-century, but so did Alan: he was perceived and perceived himself differently at different moments. Feelings of belonging and safety in the city shifted too in consequence.

Michael[24]

Michael came of age in the early 1960s having been born and bought up in London between the homes of his parents, grandparents and aunt. He was not an incomer to the city as Alan had been and describes a sense of rootedness there and the importance of that to him – tracing his ancestry in the city back to Huguenot immigrants from France in the seventeenth century. Relations are knitted into Michael's account of his life in London with some resentment (for mother and sister) and also with enduring allegiance and a sense of responsibility (for his aunt and nieces and nephew). Michael's parents had an unhappy marriage and led 'a double life' through much of the 1950s, modelling domestic unity to his father's Ford motor company employers and telling Michael not to let on about their disharmony to school friends. They finally divorced when Michael was in his late teens. In an era when outward respectability was at a premium for many, double lives were not only a feature of queer experience. This also perhaps led Michael in the opposite direction: his avowed bisexuality in the 1960s was not something he kept secret, even though pre-1970 that did not mean the same thing as being 'out' in a post gay liberationist sense.

At 18 he moved in with a (straight) school friend in Bayswater just adjacent to Hyde Park. 'We paid a pittance and it was a fabulous flat . . . you could live in central London relatively cheaply [in the 1960s]', he said. Throughout that decade and much of the two that followed, parts of central London remained affordable prior to and during an uneven process of gentrification. This allowed artists, students, and others without much money to make a home there. Filmmaker Derek Jarman, for example, lived in warehouses along the South Bank in the 1960s and 1970s for virtually nothing in a period when counterculture 'spread and entrenched itself . . . often in the empty spaces that economic change or decline had opened up in the run-down inner cit[y]'.[25] The suburbs where his parents lived were, Jarman felt, determinedly straight and represented convention, casting the centre in a more bohemian and dissident light. This conceptual urban split informed Michael's conception of the city too.[26] During this period Michael saw director Federico Fellini's *La Dolce Vita* in an arts cinema in Edgware Road. That film, together with an invitation from the brother of a close school friend and new friendships with two Italians in London, drew him to Rome and a lifelong affinity with the city. 'This was the place for me', he said. Gay life felt much easier for him there and in Paris and Amsterdam – cities he also visited frequently in the 1960s. 'You could often spot gay men on the Friday night ferry to Holland', he said, while cheap flights to Paris from a small airport in Kent allowed him to go 19 times in one year. These cities represented and offered a greater sense of freedom and possibility to Michael and were an antidote to aspects of queer life in London. His experience of the latter was sometimes tarnished by suspicion, the risk of arrest and blackmail, and a restricted sense of openness. 'You even had to go abroad to get a gay listings of London. You couldn't find one at home', he said. If risks haunted those other European cities too and if discretion was surely needed there as in London for many, these things were less keenly felt by a weekender from another country. Michael's queer map thus extended and still extends well beyond London and links into these and other cities where friendships were forged and to which lovers moved. This queer Europeanism has a history. Queer and usually wealthy or privileged Englishmen had frequently turned to the continent in the preceding half century and more.[27] But this accelerated post war in a growing trend for gay weekending – facilitated latterly by the deregulation of the European air industry in 1992 and the resulting advance of cheap airlines like Easyjet (from 1995).

Michael lived in Rome for 18 months, returning at 21 because his mother was terminally ill and his aunt very sick. He took a caring role with her – 'I always thought I owed her', he said. There was not the rupture from family that Alan and others experienced and there was a continuity in such relationships. Michael's aunt had long paid for him to go to the opera, to classical music, and had bought him a membership to the National Film Theatre, fostering these passions in him. The opera house, other music venues, and the NFT were and continue to be an important part of his map of the city. Michael didn't associate this in interview with a queer sensibility as others have done, however, but rather with that family link.[28] Places in the city that at face value have queer resonances might be valued for quite other reasons.

While Alan described the significance of local community in London, Michael was more wide ranging not only in his reach beyond the city but also in the way he moved around within it. He talked of unofficial queer sex venues – of the Biograph (or Biogrope as it was known) Cinema at Victoria and an old Jewish theatre in the East End, which for a short period showed porn films to packed houses of men who had heard about the place by word of mouth (it was closed down after a police raid on a night Michael couldn't go). Michael felt the homoerotics of the city streets in this period too (the backward glances and shop-window lingering) and describes a cottaging circuit on the Circle Line of the Underground. 'You used to buy a ticket and every Circle Line station had a loo'. He earned enough to run a car and to be part of a 'car circuit' in which men drove out of central London to cruising grounds distant from the underground network (to parts of Hampstead Heath, for example). Though he knew there were risks associated with such activity, he also felt that in the sixties 'it was easy and relatively safe'. Contrary to the broader story of progressive liberalism, it was in the following decade that he heard of more muggings and attacks on gay people – possibly because a more overt gay subculture made gay men (in his words) 'easy prey'; possibly also because a new gay press drew attention to assaults that might previously have gone unnoticed or unreported. What Michael marks out – like Alan – is a shifting sense of safety and possibility in the city streets, and perhaps unexpectedly a greater feeling of security for him prior to – rather than after – the change in the law in 1967 which partially legalized sex between men. Another interviewee, on the other hand, having had a brush with the law in the 1950s, remained nervous until then: it was only in 1967 that Rex and his partner bought a double bed and had it delivered to their East Dulwich home after 15 years together. They worried even then about the police and about the judgement of neighbours. 'It was a hell of a statement to make', he said.[29]

Michael recalls parties and gatherings in houses which were different from the ones Alan remembers or which another interviewee, Angus, enjoyed with young hippies, punk, musicians and artists in the late 1960s and early 1970s (and which he credits in part with politicizing him). Some parties Michael went to in that same period were attended by younger and older men who, he says, were quite predatory. 'There were these older [privileged] men . . . who had these lock ins' to prevent younger guests escaping (their clutches or with their possessions perhaps – either way there could be on both sides suspicion and a sense of danger). For some of the younger men – who weren't necessarily gay – there were 'business opportunities [and] holiday trips'. As in the earlier decade, it wasn't only homosexual men who partook in London's queer life. If 1950s and early 1960s sociology suggested isolated men who in the words of one 'st[oo]d apart',[30] this was not the story that emerged through Michael and other interviewees' narratives. They describe more wide-ranging everyday social and sexual contact. The queer urban scene as Michael remembers it involved cross-generational patronage and also class mobility which, he felt, waned from the 1970s as the gay scene became bigger and more anonymous. 'You could cross the class barriers if you were gay in London forty or fifty years ago'. 'The gay scene was much smaller then', he explained, 'and if you could be trusted to be discrete and not to blackmail you could be invited to parties and to dinner' – and sometimes four or five times a week (a figure he compares to the four or five times a year for him in more recent years). Michael thus described a close domestic social circuit forged in the context of wariness and danger but which yet brought new opportunities for some.

If the GLF was a key marker in the narrative I outlined at the start and was in some ways personally important to Alan, for Michael at 27 and in full-time work, it was peripheral. He went on the first pride march through central London in 1972, but was 'on the fringe, mainly because of my lifestyle; I was very busy at work'. Instead, he described 'a massive shift' ushered in by the new American style clubs – Bang! and later Heaven. They were as important in stories of visibility and growing confidence to some gay men as the GLF was to others,[31] and became the new focus of Michael's social life after the 'little dives that came and went' in Sloane Square, Soho, Covent Garden and Victoria – 'places with tiny dance floors where you would be separated if you danced too close to another man, and where there was always an elderly woman in attendance!' The new clubs were, he said, 'like a damn bursting'.

Like Alan and Angus, Michael lived in the late 1960s and early 1970s in Notting Hill, but then and following his subsequent move to Islington (and in with a long-term boyfriend), it was not counterculture but a commercial scene which drew him. This was a scene which from the 1970s increasingly focused on Soho and the West End (as Earls Court, further west gained a more niche clone and leather reputation). The 1970s represented for Michael a narrow window of particular freedom and possibility: after partial legalization, and with the GLF and the new club scene, yet before AIDS. The disease, he said, 'changed London's social and sexual culture'. Included in Michael's weekly circuit in the 1980s were now visits to 'buddies' allocated by the Terrence Higgins Trust (the first and largest AIDS charity in the United Kingdom) and to the London Lighthouse – the AIDS hospice and respite centre in Ladbroke Grove, adjacent to Notting Hill, which opened in 1986 despite local protest.[32] One of the things he remembers through this period is encountering diverse men living in widely different circumstances. The disease opened lives and networks to others in the most tragic of circumstances and necessitated new and urgent forms of community in the city. These for Angus became more exclusively gay. He experienced sexual and social boundary crossings in his London life in the 1970s, but saw straight male and some female friends 'running scared' in the early 1980s. This was the moment when Angus' circle became more exclusively gay. If the bigger story associates such exclusivity with identity politics in the early 1970s, for Angus it was connected to the devastating onset of AIDS.

Michael moved from advertising to a job in the arts in 1980s and also suffered a period of ill health. This led him not only to reassess both his social life and some friendships, but also to recognize some strong ongoing bonds – with his nieces and with former boyfriends and colleagues. Michael's queer London had changed – the 'scene' became less important as he grew older. It also felt less accessible and approachable to him. He observed (like Alan) that many of the city's local gay bars (three in Islington, where he lived) closed in the late 1990s and early 2000s as commercial gay life became ever more consolidated in the West End and in Vauxhall. The venues there are for him too crowded and there is not the sense of ease in striking up conversation that he experienced in earlier years. He still seeks a sense of community, though, and that is why he attends the older men's gay group which Alan also went to. For Michael, this was one of the few men-only spaces where it was possible to chat without obligation or presumptions about a sexual motive. It forged a new form of supportive community, and the group was well represented at Alan's funeral in 2011. Yet if Michael and Alan shared this space in older age, the London of their younger years were markedly different – inflected by different investments in the capital, different living circumstances, different occupations, different levels of income, and a different sense of mobility and perhaps belonging. If they came together as 70 and 80 year olds respectively, the 10-year age gap between them may also have seemed more of a gulf in the 1960s and 1970s.

Ajamu X[33]

Ajamu moved to Brixton, south London in 1987 at the age of 23. He had been living in Leeds with a girlfriend before coming to London and attending the first black gay men's conference in Islington in 1987. Soon after he moved with a friend into a council-owned short-life property managed by the Brixton Housing Co-op. It had no bath and so Ajamu used the bathroom of a friend living in one of the converted flats that had formerly been part of a gay squatting community between 1973 and 1983.[34] Ajamu became active in the co-op, forging friendships with members of the gay subgroup as well as with activists and journalists working on the radical anti-racist monthly *Race Today*, which had offices in the same building. He describes his artistic, black and gay identities, and his politics, developing in relation to each other partly through the physical proximity of these organizations, people and places – and his easy movement between them.

Ajamu talks about feeling anchored in Brixton by a number of factors. First by the housing co-op and the history of the immediate area – including that of the gay squatting community, of the radical women's and black press, and also of an underground black queer scene with local cruising spots and an illegal shebeen run in the 1970s by bisexual black artist Pearl Alcock in Railton Road. Pearl's was also discussed by some of the (almost exclusively white) squatters. 'There I was', said Paul, an Australian squatter, 'a terrified little white boy being sensually samba'd around by a gorgeous black man who of course was having great fun mocking me and, at the end of the basement room, Pearl was ensconced with her little record player playing 45s, seeming so much like some African queen'.[35] Cultural stories about blackness and about a fantasized Africa shaped Paul's experience and memories of Pearl's bar. It was given a different inflection in the black queer history Ajamu recounted as he guided me around Brixton's and a geography invisible to me until then. Pearl's was not in Ajamu's account an exotic 'other' place but one of the very few places in Brixton which comfortably accommodated black queer men in the 1970s.

Secondly, Ajamu suggested the significance to his sense of belonging in Brixton of an alternative and more mixed commercial gay scene locally, which he experienced directly as it emerged in the early 1990s. He remembers black gay nights at the Fridge nightclub and Substation South, for example. Finally, Ajamu noted the lasting local impact of the Greater London Council's work with artists, and gay and minority ethnic groups under Livingstone's leadership between 1981 and 1984 and Lambeth Council's status throughout the 1980s as one of London's so-called loony left local councils.[36] Ajamu said that Brixton (which sits within Lambeth), 'shaped my politics'; it attracted 'outsiderness': 'if you are black and gay they merge in Brixton'. There is a muted echo of this in the testimony of gentrifiers in the 1990s who moved to the area not only for 'bargain Victoriana' but also for 'new urban experiences' associated with Brixton's multiculturalism and countercultural reputation.[37] One of the women interviewed in a comparison of three gentrified areas of south London in the late 1990s valued Brixton's 'very diverse population' more than the reputation of local schools (a draw to incomers to the other south London areas). 'We don't stick out here as two women living together', she said. Another remarked that 'the best thing about living here is that it's an open community. . . . There's no norm'.[38]

There is a marked hybridity in the way Ajamu has lived out his queer life in Brixton and London,[39] and this does not quite map onto wider perceptions of what 'gay' looks like in the city. He describes a certain invisibility as a black gay man in Brixton because of perceptions of what gay was and still is conceived to be and which I touched on at the outset. White and more effeminate friends get more trouble than he ever has, he said. By the same token, doormen have been suspicious of Ajamu trying to get into gay bars and clubs in the West End. 'Do you know what kind of club this is?' they asked; 'in Brixton I have never had this kind of problem'.

Ajamu moved into a smaller co-op flat share in 1992. From there he ran parties for the Black Breakfast Club and the Black Perverts Network. For the latter, he explained as we sat in the flat's main room: 'where you're sat now this was the chillout area, kitchen was bar area, downstairs was sex area'. He put on photographic exhibitions of his work in the main room (renamed the Parlour Gallery for that purpose) and used the same space as part of a HIV testing campaign, and to develop a black gay history archive, rukus! (now held by the London Metropolitan Archives and one of a number of LGBT collections in archives across London – including at Bishopsgate Institute and London School of Economics – which form a further queer urban and historically inflected network).

Concepts and experiences of family – or origin and choice – are significant too in the way Ajamu thinks about his flat and its place in Brixton. There are reciprocal visits with his family of origin in Huddersfield, Yorkshire (northern England). His mother arrived at his current flat insisting he get net curtains – a hallmark of a respectability that is important to her and, Ajamu suggests, first-generation Afro-Caribbean immigrants more broadly. His family of origin continue to use his given name, Carlton, when he goes back. Ajamu is a name and identity he associates specifically with his life in London and his political, artistic and queer identities there. These names and identities are not mutually exclusive, though, and he described in the interview how he holds them together. Of his family of choice Ajamu notes that 'with the black gay community [we have] kind of adoptive sons [to] look out for . . . [we're known as] dad, or grandma, we create a family frame of reference. The black community do this. I'm not sure about other communities'. Ajamu talks of his 'daughters' who live in Brixton, Streatham, and 'one [who] lives in the States now'. 'They spend time, come here and cook, so daughters might turn up: "hi mum how you are doing?" and just come and cook'. His home is an easy part of their queer urban circuit. 'I was walking down Brixton escalator the other day and one of my granddaughter's came up and said "how are you doing Grandma?"' This relates for him to a specific sense of solidarity forged through black and gay identifications and reflects and reproduces caring roles he sees as characteristic of the wider Afro-Caribbean community.[40] We might also observe something similar in Alan's camp world in the 1950s in which, for example, he was taken in by the older queer Notting Hill matriarch, Flora.

The fusion of influences from the preceding years come together in Ajamu's flat, and like the earlier squats, it had and continues to have several functions in Ajamu's sexual, artistic, social, familial, cultural and political life. He differentiates this from the commercial scene in Soho, which helped put London on the international gay tourist map in the 1990s and which is such a prominent feature of the capital's gay history. Here Ajamu felt objectified and the area was associated for him with a different incarnation of gay identity to the one he felt comfortable with and which mapped onto Brixton rather the city centre. The extent to which each of my interviewees formulate their sense of queer or gay self-hood and community in the city in partial opposition to other formations associated with other places and also other times is striking. This is not to say these scenes were mutually exclusive: though in the 1990s I associated with Duckie at the Vauxhall Tavern (that enduring performance and dance 'alternative' to the West End), I actually went to Soho as often: it was near work and later near home too.

Ajamu sees his generation and the particular artistic and political milieu he moved into in Brixton as different from the lives of his younger 'daughters' and 'granddaughters'. 'I'm in my 40s and am probably artistic and leftfield. . . . Friends in their 20s – as far as they are concerned the battle has been won. . . . My younger friends have their own apartments, they don't live co-operatively; while I live in an independent house I am still part of a community. . . . [My] younger friends live in individual units'. Ajamu, like Alan and Michael before him, identifies changes in urban queer life within his life course. He and the others also suggest how frequently we measure others in the present through the prism of our memories of past social forms, places and people. In this way, queer London is never only of its moment, but is understood, assessed and experienced through a tacking back and forth across time, drawing earlier experiences and ideas into the present with varying degrees of joy, nostalgia, relief, regret and grief.

I didn't interview Ajamu's younger friends and so haven't accrued a sense of where their urban community lies. What is certain, though, is that feelings of community arise at different times and in different places in the city, can be fleeting or enduring and can be encompassing or just a part, perhaps a small part, of daily life.[41] My interviewees were often right in observing the demise of the communal forms in the city that they had enjoyed, but that doesn't mean that other newer queer communities didn't coalesce subsequently there. For those of earlier generations, these may be harder to see because they are formed in a different light, in different places, and in different ways (most obviously the internet). So, while by the 1980s many of the squatters in Brixton felt that they had lost something from their heyday in the 1970s, a different configuration of circumstances allowed for the development of another, differently formulated, differently valuable, differently politicized sense of community. This has held Ajamu in the area for 25 years.

Conclusion

The Guildhall in the City of London was built in the mid-fifteenth century on the site of what was the largest Roman amphitheatre in Britain. Remnants of that amphitheatre can still be seen in the basement of the building, while upstairs is the historic Guildhall itself with an adjoining art gallery displaying paintings associated with London's history and most especially the pomp of the City's mayors and visiting dignitaries. In February 2013, the London Metropolitan Archive convened its 10th Annual LGBT history conference here, coinciding with the annual LGBT History Month celebrations. Both signalled and showcased a resurgence in historical consciousness among LGBT groups and individuals. A profusion of community history projects were presented at the conference – on the Pink Singers, on gay British Asian experience, on gay Brighton, Bristol and Manchester, and the Campaign for Homosexual Equality (CHE). The conference proceedings took place in the astonishing Guildhall itself, speakers and participants flanked by pictures of visiting royals in some of the worst 1970s fashions imaginable. Viewed in the context of this particular conference, our Royals seemed especially camp. The day ended with a private view of Ajamu's photographic exhibition 'Fierce' – his portrait series of Black British born queer men and women under 35. They were hung in the central gallery – adjacent to others hung with very different art indeed. There was a sense of this place being queered, as others had been over previous years through casual everyday actions or through self-consciousness activism.

The multifaceted projects showcased at the conference, the different faces in Ajamu's exhibition of black queer men and women, and the queering of the Guildhall suggest some of the problems and possibilities of charting the history of queer London since the war. There are loosely shared coordinates – knowledge of the same queer and queered places, of moments of collective celebration and grief, of urban icons like Oscar Wilde or Quentin Crisp and the paths they trod. But we negotiate and respond to these things in distinctive ways, value some over others, and draw other people and places into the mix. We find ourselves either identifying or not identifying with them because of other imperatives in our lives associated with our jobs, income and aspirations; with proximity to or distance from family; with being an insider or incomer to the city; with being white, being black, being politicized or not; having faith or not; with having children or not. My queer London in the first part of this century included playgrounds and parks in and around Stoke Newington, north London, as I was looking after my kids. While they were playing on the swings, I'd sometimes spot the other gay parent – not so very hard to find in that area as it happened, and in a period marked by greater visibility and broadening possibilities for lesbian and gay parenting, including – from 2002 – adoption. The children's secondary school marks LGBT history month with a special concert. The school is now also part of the way I map the capital somewhat queerly.

This profusion of queer stories and mappings of London does not wholly displace the narrative I opened this chapter with. I've suggested that that story resonates with the testimonies I've gathered – providing points, places and moments of identification and dis-identification. Some defined themselves in relation to recent or more distant urban histories, finding composure through one of those 'touches across time' (as literary scholar Caroline Dinshaw has it).[42] The writer and playwright Neil Bartlett, for example orientated himself in London in the 1980s in part by exploring the contours of the queer city a century earlier.[43] The loss of urban queer scenes like those of 1950s and 1960s Notting Hill was meanwhile sad for Alan and made the queer city in later years a little lonely and disorientating for him. Changes are rarely decisive and memories and residues of the past unevenly affect the way the men I interviewed engaged with new scenarios and places. When we look askance, take our cues from everyday lives and memories, or take the cultural temperature from the (supposed) margins, we don't find a homogenous, singular and collectively comprehended gay London. We find instead an altogether queerer city.

Notes

1   On these points see especially: Higgins, P. (1996), *Heterosexual Dictatorship: Male Homosexuality in Postwar Britain*. London: Fourth Estate; Houlbrook, M. (2005), *Queer London: Perils and Pleasures in the Sexual Metropolis, 1918–1957*. Chicago: University of Chicago Press; Cook, M. (ed.) (2007), *A Gay History of Britain: Love and Sex Between Men Since the Middle Ages*. Oxford: Greenwood World, ch. 5.

2   On these points see: Cook (2007), ch. 6.

3   Watney, S. (1986), *Policing Desire: Pornography, AIDS and the Media*. London: Comedia; Cook (2007), ch. 6.

4   Cooper, D. (1992), 'Off the banner and onto the agenda: The emergence of a new municipal lesbian and gay politics, 1979–1986', *Critical Social Policy*, 36, 20–39.

5   Robinson, L. (2007), *Gay Men and the Left in Post-War Britain: How the Personal Got Political*. Manchester: Manchester University Press.

6   Butler, T. and G. Robson (2001), 'Social change, gentrification and neighbourhood change in London: A comparison of three areas of south London', *Urban Studies*, 38, 2145–62.

7   From 1997 foreign partners of lesbians and gays were given immigration rights on the same basis as straight couples, and from 2000 gays and lesbians were allowed to serve in the military. The age of consent was equalized at 16 in 2001 and joint and step adoption by gay and lesbians introduced in 2002. Section 28 was repealed in 2003 and discrimination in employment on the basis of sexual orientation outlawed in the same year. Civil Partnerships for gay and lesbians were introduced in 2005; marriage in 2014.

8 Both figures are likely to be significantly lower than the actual numbers. Duncan, S. and D. Smith (June 2006), *Individuation versus the Geography of 'New' Families*. London: South Bank University, http://www.lsbu.ac.uk/ahs/downloads/families/familieswp19.pdf.

9 Weeks, J. (2007), *The World We Have Won: The Remaking of Erotic and Intimate Life*. London: Routledge, ch. 7.

10 Penn, D. (2002), 'The New Heteronormativity: The sexual politics of neo-liberalism', in Russ Castronon (ed.), *Materializing Democracy: Towards a Revitalised Cultural Politics*. Durham: Duke University Press.

11 Cocks, H. (2009), *Classified: The Secret History of the Personal Column*. London: Random House Books, 183; Weeks (2007), p. 160.

12 For a queer problematization of lesbian and gay community history and community building through history see: Herring, S. (2007), *Queering the Underworld: Slumming, Literature, and the Undoing of Lesbian and Gay History*. Chicago: University of Chicago Press.

13 Weeks (2007).

14 On this point see: Bravmann, S. (1997), *Queer Fictions of the Past: History, Culture, and Difference*. Cambridge: Cambridge University Press, p. 127.

15 On this approach to history and the past see especially: Samuel, R. and P. Thompson (1990), *The Myths We Live By*. London: Routledge.

16 This section draws in part on chapter 5 of: Cook, M. (2014), *Queer Domesticities: Homosexuality and Home Life in Twentieth Century London*. Basingstoke: Palgrave Macmillan. All quotes are from my interview with Alan in June 2010.

17 White, J. (2001), *London in the Twentieth Century: A City and Its People*. London: Viking, p. 95; Mort, F. (2010), *Capital Affairs: London and the Making of the Permissive Society*. New Haven: Yale University Press, p. 109; Cook (2014), sec. III. On the associations of London bedsits see: Armstrong, M. (2011), 'A Room in Chelsea: Quentin crisp at home', *Visual Culture in Britain*, 12(2), 155–69.

18 Weeks (2007), p. 46; Mort (2010), pp. 132–6.

19 On this point see: Waters, C. and M. Houlbrook (2006), '*The Heart in Exile*: Detachment and Desire in 1950s London', *History Workshop Journal*, 62 (Autumn), 142–63.

20 See: Holmes, C. (2005), *The Other Notting Hill*. Studley: Brewin.

21 On the comparative dimensions of memory see: Hirsch, M. and V. Smith (2002), 'Feminism and Cultural Memory: An introduction', *Signs*, 28(1) (Fall), 1–1912.

22 Miles, R. (1984), 'The Riots of 1958: Notes on the ideological construction of "race relations" as a political issue in Britain', *Immigrants and Minorities*, 3(3), 252–75.

23 See: http://www.yvonnesinclair.co.uk/ (consulted 26 March 2013).

24 All quotes from Michael are taken from my interview with him in July 2011 and a later conversation in April 2013 after he reviewed an early draft of this piece.

25 Beckett, A. (2009), *When the Lights Went Out: Britain in the Seventies*. London: Faber, p. 245.

26 For more on this conceptual divide see: Dines, M. (2009), *Gay Suburban Narratives in British and American Film and Fiction: Homecoming Queens*. Basingstoke: Palgrave Macmillan; Jarman, D. (1991), *Modern Nature: The Journals of Derek Jarman*. London: Century, pp. 192, 196; Hodge, S. (1995), 'No Fags Out There: Gay men, identity and suburbia', *Journal of Interdisciplinary Gender Studies*, 1(1), 41–8; Giles, J. (2004), *The Parlour and the Suburb: Domestic Identities, Class, Femininity and Modernity*. Oxford: Berg.

27 See, for example: Aldrich, R. (1993), *The Seduction of the Mediterranean: Writing, Art and Homosexual Fantasy*. London: Routledge.

28 On this point see: Dyer, R. (2001), *Culture of Queers*. London: Routledge; Halperin, D. M. (2012), *How to Be Gay*. Cambridge, MA: Harvard University Press.

29 Rex, interview, 2010.

30 See: Rees, J. T. (ed.) (1955), *They Stand Apart. A Critical Survey of the Problems of Homosexuality*. London: Heinemann.

31 On this point see: Burton, P. (1985), *Parallel Lives*. London: GMP.

32 'Protest at AIDS hostel', *Evening Standard*, 14 August 1986.

33 This section draws in part on chapter 7 of: Cook (2014). Citation is taken from my interview with Ajamu X in May 2011.

34 See: Cook, M. (2011), '"Gay Times": Identity, locality, memory, and the Brixton squats in 1970's London', *Journal of Twentieth Century British History*, 24(1), (2013): 84–109.

35 Peter in a letter to Ian Townson, 17 January 1997. Ian Townson Collection, Hall Carpenter Archive, London School of Economics.

36 Cooper (1992).

37 Butler and Robson (2001), p. 2156.

38 Ibid.

39 Gilroy, P. (2004), *After Empire: Melancholia or Convivial Culture?* London: Routledge.

40 This is something Mary Chamberlain observes in relation to familial dynamics in the West Indies. Chamberlain, M. (1998), 'Brothers and Sisters, Uncles and Aunts: A lateral perspective on Caribbean families', in S. Silva and C. Smart (eds), *The New Family?* Thousand Oaks: Sage.

41 On such fluctuations in experiences of community see: Stockton, K. B. (2006), *Beautiful Bottom, Beautiful Shame: Where 'Black' Meets 'Queer'*. Durham: Duke University Press, Introduction.

42 Dinshaw, C. (1999), *Getting Medieval: Sexualities and Communities, Pre- and Postmodern*. Durham: Duke University Press.

43 Bartlett, N. (1987), *Who Was that Man? A Present for Mr Oscar Wilde*. London: Serpent's Tale.

Further reading

Cook, M. (ed.) (2007), *A Gay History of Britain: Love and Sex Between Men Since the Middle Ages*. Oxford: Greenwood World.

—(2014), *Queer Domesticities: Homosexuality and Home Life in Twentieth Century London*. Basingstoke: Palgrave Macmillan.

Cooper, D. (1992), 'Off the Banner and onto the Agenda: The emergence of a new municipal lesbian and gay politics, 1979–1986', *Critical Social Policy*, 36, 20–39.

Gardiner, J. (2003), *From the Closet to the Silver Screen: Women at the Gateways Club 1945–1985*. London: Pandora.

Higgins, P. (1996), *Heterosexual Dictatorship: Male Homosexuality in Postwar Britain*. London: Fourth Estate.

Hornsey, R. (2010), *The Spiv and the Architect: Unruly Life in Postwar London*. Minneapolis: University of Minnesota Press.

Houlbrook, M. (2005), *Queer London: Perils and Pleasures in the Sexual Metropolis, 1918-1957*. Chicago: University of Chicago Press.

Jennings, R. (2007), *A Lesbian History of Britain: Love and Sex Between Women Since 1500*. London: Greenwood.

Jivani, A. (1997), *It's Not Unusual: A History of Lesbian and Gay Britain in the Twentieth Century*. Bloomington: Indiana University Press.

Mort, F. (2010), *Capital Affairs: London and the Making of the Permissive Society*. New Haven: Yale University Press.

Power, L. (1995), *No Bath But Plenty of Bubbles: Stories from the London Gay Liberation Front, 1970–73*. London: Cassel.

Robinson, L. (2007), *Gay Men and the Left in Post-War Britain: How the Personal Got Political*. Manchester: Manchester University Press.

Waters, C. and M. Houlbrook (2006), '*The Heart in Exile*: Detachment and desire in 1950s London', *History Workshop Journal*, 62 (Autumn), 142–63.

3

The queer road to *Frisind*: Copenhagen 1945–2012

Peter Edelberg

In 1989, the first legally recognized male couple in the world, Axel and Eigil Axgil, hit newspaper front pages all over the world. Having been together for nearly 40 years and being two prominent homophile activists, fellow activists had asked them to be among the first couples to enter into a 'registered partnership' as it was called. The two elderly men kissing in a carriage in front of Copenhagen City Hall reinforced the idea that this was what gays and lesbians had always wanted, and finally justice had prevailed. The pictures cemented the idea of Danish *frisind*, which more or less means liberal-mindedness. The idea of 1989 as the year of justice for homosexuals and of Danish *frisind* has perhaps been retold too many times and thus has become too one-sided and unnuanced. The traditional story is a liberal one – with stable identity categories and an overall sense of progress. While not completely wrong, this story can be usefully complicated and queered by acknowledging differing subjectivities, discontinuities in experience over time, and the role of discipline and surveillance in the creation of contemporary gay subjects. I take this queerer perspective in this chapter by presenting a mapping of (mainly male) queer Copenhagen in the period from 1945 to the present with special focus on male prostitution. I trace the major changes in legal frameworks as well as analysing how the queer scene shifted, and I argue that the fundamental change in queer life has been in subjectivities rather than circumstances. Even though the social context has changed dramatically, what queer men want has changed even more. This leads us to rethink the relationship between liberation and normalization and to question the story that takes us from oppression to freedom over the course of the post-war period or sets the Stonewall riots of 1969 and the advent of ideas of Queer Nationhood and Queer Theory in the early 1990s as pivotal moments in Danish queer history. We need to take different periods on their own terms: the queer subject of the 1950s was not the same as that of later decades; possibilities have simultaneously widened and narrowed. The subcultural scenes of the 1950s accommodated a range of legal and illegal acts and desires, feeding a diversity of queer practices and identities. In later decades, I show, the queer subject was more disciplined, but was freer from legal limits and prohibitions.

Bar life

We know little about Copenhagen's gay culture in the inter-war period. A few of Copenhagen's homosexual bars can be traced back to the time before World War I (Bycaféen – today Cancan – and Centralhjørnet, for example), but we don't know anything about the clientele until much later. A pamphlet from 1910 described a bar in Jorck's Passage, where 'young lads' with 'disgusting inclinations' and 'older folk of obviously degenerated demeanour' were said to meet.[1] In 1924, the Supreme Court disbanded the homosexual social club, Nekkab, which had existed since 1919. Later in the 1920s, police allowed homosexual bars to exist – although they kept them under surveillance. An article from 1925 in the scandal-mongering magazine *Illustreret Kriminal-Tidende* apparently written by a homosexual man under the name 'Lydia' describes a couple of homosexual cafés in Copenhagen where the ambience was 'tasteful and noble'.[2] Other bars had a more shadowy character. A police observation report described the bar Hansa in Badstuestræde frequented by 'homosexualists' (of both sexes), 'piss house boys', female prostitutes with their pimps, criminals and other 'scum of the city'.[3]

These are the first clues for historians to an organized homosexual scene in Copenhagen. Before that time there were no bars, clubs, organizations, magazines or the like. We know that so-called pederasts had met in private circles from the first quarter of the nineteenth century, and that a certain park was used as a meeting spot since the second half of the same century (Ørsted's Park is still a main cruising area for gay men in Copenhagen). Homosexual city life in the late nineteenth and early twentieth centuries was mostly a street affair. Homosexual men and 'normal' teenage boys benefitted from each other sexually, economically and socially.[4] In 1930, a new Penal Code decriminalized sodomy but set the age of consent for homosexual conduct at 18, whereas for heterosexual conduct it was 15. The Code also criminalized male prostitutes, whereas female prostitution was legal as long as the woman had some kind of ordinary job as well. The decriminalization seems to have gone relatively unnoticed by homosexuals as well as the rest of the public, but had major significance as it set the tone of the debate on 'the homosexual question' in decades to come.

After World War II, a network of homosexual bars/restaurants blossomed in Copenhagen in the streets around Nikolaj Square, known as the Minefield, and the streets around Larsbjørnsstræde, known as the Ditch. In the period 1945–68, we know of Mandalay (today Men's Bar), Kiki, Bjørnen, and Cancan in Larsbjørnsstræde, Cosy Bar, Masken Bar, and Heidelberg in Studiestræde, Fortuna in Fortunstræde, Bellman's Basement in Nikolaj Square, Admiralkroen in Boldhusgade, Apollo Bar in Vestergade, Bycaféen and Centralhjørnet in Lavendelstræde and Café Intime in Frederiksberg. Although frequently visited by plain-clothed police officers, no reports or accounts after World War II mention bar raids or harassment of legal socializing.

The police observation reports give us a glimpse of the atmosphere in these bars. A report on Bellman's Basement from February 1951 mentions 40 male and 2 female guests, almost exclusively homosexual: 'None of the guests took offence when a male couple was caressing each other, and the chance of getting "engaged" in this place is big'.[5] In the same restaurant 5 months later, the observer notes that apart from the pianist, the two male waiters and the woman behind the bar, the guests were 'from all levels of society. All age groups are apparently represented among the guests'. A homosexual man described the place:

> The Bellman Basement was more "posh" than the other places. It was a long room, and you had to walk up some steps and open the door and just take a view of the crowd. . . . After you had been there, you hurried over to Fortuna – which was more unrestrained. Someone sat there and pounded on a piano – he was called the Beetroot. There was also someone named Eva, a man who sang.[6]

The police noted that Apollo Bar was frequented by 'American negroes', 'sailors of all nationalities', 'prostitute women from the Larsbjørnsstræde neighbourhood', 'Danish soldiers', 'typical homosexuals', 'office clerks', homosexual women 'wearing long trousers and jacket' – all entertained by 'the giant waitress Viola'.[7] Overall, these descriptions show that there were rich opportunities for frequenting homosexual bars. There was dancing, music, flirting and good chance of meeting a likeminded person. The diversity of the scene is noteworthy, and the fact that the police did not harass the bars as long as minors were not present made Copenhagen quite exceptional in an international context.

The homosexual bars were not exclusively filled with homosexuals. One man described his evenings in Cancan, accompanied by a male friend, as well as his girlfriend, in 1960:

> My friend Thor, who like me was on apprentice salary, abused the "interest" from the gays when we went to a gay bar, where we knew with near certainty that we would be treated to a beer by one of the gays. We

did not pretend to be sexually interested, our abuse did not go further than a beer. Of course my girlfriend Lillian heard about these visits, and she followed the daily debate on gay culture. So she became curious, and we decided to visit a gay bar, so she could see for herself.[8]

The diverse clientele in the gay bars show that instead of imagining a closed closet, we should imagine a walk-in closet with a broad crowd of different genders, nationalities, social classes, sexualities, occupations and gender expressions. Pre-Stonewall homosexual life in the city allowed border crossings – before such supposed transgressions became fashionably queer.

Street life

To understand the extent of queer life in its many forms, we must follow the queers out of the bars and into the streets, which were still a widely popular arena for queer encounters. In public restrooms, backyard toilets, and parks men had encounters, some one-off, others developing into ongoing sexual relations, relations based on monetary exchange, or lifelong partnerships. A homosexual life might include some or all of these at different times. Sex in toilets or in parks could be a supplement to picking up a man in a bar. A homosexual man recounts that by the end of the 1940s 'either you found someone in the street, in a piss house, or in one of the restaurants. . . . It was not just one-night stands. Sometimes it developed into a friendship that could last 8 days, or perhaps a month or more'.[9] It was illegal to display 'indecent behavior or encourage immorality'[10] – punishable with a fine or a prohibition against coming near certain places for a specified period. This man recounts that he was twice forbidden to go near the toilet at City Hall Square, even though he had done nothing 'indecent' except for being there for 'too long'.

According to a letter about homosexual crime from the chief of the Vice Squad to the Department of Justice in 1960, more than 10,000 men had 'in later years' (probably from 1950 to 1960) been implicated in cases regarding public encounters of sexual conduct with a minor or male prostitution.[11] This constitutes about 2.9 per cent of the male adult population in Copenhagen at the time. 'Criminal homosexuality', as it was termed, was a considerable part of city life, and not something only homosexuals indulged in. From February 1951 to August 1952, the police arrested 589 men who had behaved 'indecently' in public rest rooms. The interrogations revealed that 152 were identified as homosexual, 88 bisexual and 208 heterosexual (the police thought 67 of these were rent boys).[12] The possibilities for sexual encounters were going on in a world of mixed sexualities.

In a police report regarding male prostitution, a man was interrogated about a meeting in a backyard. He explained that one evening in March

1964 he had sought out the Larsbjørnsstræde neighbourhood 'where he knew there were small bars, visited by so-called "pullers"'. (Rent boys are in Danish called 'trækkerdrenge' literally translated 'pulling boys'.) That evening he noticed a marine soldier 'who had placed himself', and seeing the marine the man became sexually aroused. He placed himself next to the marine, said 'Good evening', and gave him a cigarette. The marine said that he was short of money, and the man promised him two tenners (about 27 Euros in today's prices):

> [The man] . . . walked first into the backyard that was rather dark, and shortly after the marine followed. He walked over to the accused . . . and [the man] caressed the marine's shoulders and embraced him. Then he unbuttoned the marine's trousers down below and manipulated the marine's member. . . . Suddenly [the man] felt disgust at the act and pushed the marine away.[13]

The marine got his two tenners and the man hurried out though the doorway, where he was arrested and later convicted for buying the favours of a prostitute. In another case from 1952, a 40-year-old man was convicted for a sexual encounter with a 13-year-old boy in a public restroom. The man had gone to the restroom for a homosexual encounter, and in the walls between the cabins there was a big hole. Later the man explained to the police that the boy in the other cabin had peeked through the hole and shown interest, whereas the boy explained that the man had initiated the talk although he himself had been curious, willing and not resistant.[14] The stories illustrate how encounters in restrooms and backyards could unfold, whether they ended up in arrest or, more commonly, in each going his or her own way. They also alert us to aspects of the homosexual scene which are worth further exploration, namely intergenerational encounters and the exchange of money.

The age spectrum was quite wide in the homosexual subculture. Police Inspector Jens Jersild found that of 145 young men arrested in 1953 for prostitution, 22 per cent were under 18 years of age the first time they had accepted money for sexual favours, 48 per cent were between 18 and 21 years and 30 per cent over 21.[15] In my own investigation of 79 court cases against men convicted during the years 1961–65 for using a male prostitute, the latter were between 14 and 20 years old.[16] Another study by Jersild from 1964 showed that out of 1298 boys, who in the period from 1950 to 1960 had been accosted by men subsequently convicted of sex or indecency with a minor, about a third were under 11 years old, about a third 12 to 14 years old and about a third 15 to 17 years old.[17] While 'rent boys' (who we should rather call young men who consciously sought out public toilets, street corners and bars for transactional relations) formed part of the homosexual scene, not every case of indecency or sex with a male minor can reasonably be blamed on 'the homosexuals'. These figures nevertheless indicate the age spectrum in homosexual street life since the illegal encounters occurred in the same places as other homosexual encounters – in streets and alleys and around homosexual bars. A study Jersild cited, where 340 boys under 18 years, who had been removed from home due to male prostitution, shows that about a third had made contact with men 'under private circumstances' (including semi-private circumstances, such as youth and sports associations), about a third in streets, parks or restrooms, and about a third in or around 'homosexual bars or the like'.[18] The courts defined transactions of sex and money as prostitution, but the convicted usually said the money was an innocent present in relation to sex. Either way, both young and older men were a significant part of post-war homosexual subculture. In the period 1945–65, 745 young men were convicted for male prostitution. There were other cases, of course, in which charges were dropped (this was typical) or which the police didn't discover. Having arrested 60 'male prostitutes' in 1959, the Copenhagen Police suggested the number they could have apprehended was 600.[19]

We must imagine a queer Copenhagen, with certain junctions: streets, alleys, squares, restrooms and parks, as well as bars, restaurants, ballrooms and organizations. This mobile topography shifted when a bar was closed, a toilet hired a guard or the police intensified patrolling of certain streets and squares. It is a less tidy picture than has traditionally been presented, and it involved multiple border-crossings: between child and adult, private and public, relations of affection and of prostitution, between the wealthy and the poor, the upper and lower class. Borders between economic and cultural classes were also challenged. Recognizing this allows us to understand some of the changes that the subculture underwent in subsequent years, not least in becoming less subcultural.

Lifelong relationships

Toilet-sex and encounters in streets and alleys could be for a single night, but might also develop into lasting relationships. A gay man recounts an evening in January 1963 when he was a teenager, and it snowed heavily:

> ... when I was left at City Hall Square, I actually had to go to the restroom and went to the underground restrooms. By chance I looked at a guy, standing to the right of me. He had blue hair and was pretty outrageously dressed, clad in leather. I was so fascinated by him. . . . He was obviously also interested in me, so we walked around the city in the snow. . . . He comes over to me and asks: "Tell me, are you up for anything?" I say: "For what thing?" "Can we go to your place or mine?", he then asks. So we went home to Ulrik, as he was called. . . . He was 20 at that time and I was 16.[20]

They moved in together and stayed together until Ulrik's death in 2002. In October 1963, the author Martin Elmer also met the love of his life, Erik, at a late night at Cosy Bar. 'Although Erik and I were together almost every other day the following weeks, it was not until November, during a weekend stay . . . in Northern Zealand that we spent the first night together', wrote Elmer, who often attacked frivolous gays and saw himself as a respectable homophile. He insisted that 'sexual relations' was a 'surrogate for the real thing', namely 'the love life of homophiles'.[21] The story of how Axel Johannes Lundahl Madsen and Eigil Axel Eskildsen met each other is well known. It was at an evening organized by the Association of 1948 (of which more later). They were engaged in 1950, and took the self-invented surname Axgil as a sign of their commitment.

Such accounts show that the homosexual world included both lifelong commitment and deeply felt romance and that such relationships could be initiated anywhere. We should not presume that they were in a separate category from briefer encounters. All three couples relate how their lifelong commitments were not monogamous, and their relationships were, for them and others, supplemented by other encounters. 'If someone offered me a delicious dish', said Axgil, 'I did not decline. Especially if Eigil allowed it'.[22]

Just as lifelong relationships and quick encounters could overlap, deep-felt romantic relationships could easily fall within the criminal category. Martin Elmer was 33 years old when he met Erik at Cosy Bar, 12 days after Erik's 21st birthday. Two weeks prior to this, Elmer could have come under suspicion of buying a rent boy, just as Ulrik, in spite of his own young age, in principle committed a crime by taking a 16 year old home. A series of interviews with homosexuals from 1961 revealed that 30 per cent had broken the law by having relations with men under 18 after they had turned 18 themselves.[23] The numbers indicate that a considerable number of homosexuals crossed the legal boundaries – even though the majority did not.

Associational life

Until 1948, men with a sexual interest in men could only meet in bars, streets, restrooms or in private circles. But with the organization of a national union of homosexuals of both genders, these opportunities widened dramatically. The Association of 1948 was founded on Bonfire Night, 23 June 1948 by a small circle of homosexuals with Axel J. Lundahl Madsen in the centre. The mission of the Association was, according to the first regulations

> through personal acquaintance and correspondence to make connections and create a free association of people, who feel solidarity with other fellow human beings with the same position regarding homo- and bisexual problems, and support and help them if they are in difficulties.[24]

Initially, the Association was a social club rather than a political organization. It was not until 20 years later that political lobbying become central to its activities. The Association quickly became popular, and in 1950 it had somewhere between 1,000 and 1,400 members, of whom 60 per cent lived in Copenhagen and about 20 per cent were lesbians. People between 18 and 21 years old were only allowed as an exception and persons under 18 were prohibited from attending any gathering.

The police in the major cities, Copenhagen, Aarhus and Odense, followed this development with deep concern, but although they frequently interviewed members and those staffing club nights, they found very little which could reasonably be considered criminal. The Association followed a strategy of presenting themselves to the police as if what they were doing was the most natural thing in the world. They invited the officers to the theatre nights and to the balls they held. Dismayed officers reported that

> after the show . . . we watched the "party" for about half an hour. There were around 100 participants, among which about 10 women. The party was decent and unapproachable, but it was a rather shocking sight, when almost all the gentlemen, when a pianist began to play, jumped up and danced with each other, and simply repulsive to watch older, chubby gentlemen dancing with young lads. As we . . . realized everyone was aware of us, we left.[25]

The demands of the Association for civil rights and their cooperative strategy towards the police bore fruit in 1950. The Association's chair sent an official letter to the Copenhagen Police Department, complaining that his members had been harassed by young men in the street, and that some had 'directly offering themselves to our members . . . for money'.[26] The chair was well aware that the police were suspicious that the Association was a cover for prostitution, and took the opportunity to notify them that harassment and male prostitution were actually the responsibility of the authorities. The officers turned up and safeguarded the following party as requested. The open strategy suggested that the Association felt they had nothing to hide, and also presumed that homophile citizens had the same rights to protection as all others.

The Association blossomed in the 1950s. It had local sections in Copenhagen, Odense and Aalborg, and later in Norway and Sweden (which subsequently became independent). In March 1950, to take just one example, the Copenhagen section held club nights on Wednesdays and Saturdays, and in addition 14 special events, such as art or literary evenings, women's evenings and dance nights. Later that year the section expanded to three regular nights a week, and planned an extra evening for a special artistic circle and a dancing course for members.[27] From 1949, the Association published the magazine, *Vennen* [The Friend], which had articles about the situation of homosexuals in society, poems, short stories, scientific articles on sexuality, contact adverts, international homosexual news, literature reviews, letters to the editor, erotic and romantic drawings, photographs and much more. The writers in *Vennen* began using the term 'homophile' instead of homosexual to underline that homophilia was about emotions rather than sex, just as homosexuals were called 'our emotional fellows'. The magazine trumpeted the message that homophiles were born that way, and thereby had as much right to be as everybody else.

The differences between associational life on the one hand and street and bar life on the other are significant. The Association was built on the idea of an affiliation between individuals, based on an inborn and shared feeling, different from 'the normals'. Street and bar life was, as we have seen, not limited to homosexuals, or homophiles, but was based on transactions and relations between men who might or might not consider themselves homosexual. You did not need a membership card to street and bar life, as you did for the Association. Just as sexualities were fluid in street and bar life, the age spectrum was not limited to what was legal. The public character of the Association meanwhile meant the stipulation of an age limit of 21. It was typical for homophile organizations at the time to distance themselves from prostitution and corruption of minors and to adopt what the historian Julian Jackson calls 'the politics of dignity'.[28] These differences mark an important shift in homosexual city life. As the homosexuals came out of the shadows, demanded equal rights and came to public notice, they had to conform to the rules of society regarding sexual relations. This shift did not happen abruptly, but was a long process from 1948 to the middle of the 1970s.

Even though the Association stood in formal opposition to the illegal part of bar and street life, this was not clear-cut in practice. The question of 'boy lovers' was discussed in an issue of *Vennen* in 1949, where 'paedophiles' were presented as one of three types of homosexuals: the 'inverts' (feminine), the 'paedophiles' and the 'ordinary homosexuals'. These types were presented as three aspects of the same homosexuality, and the paedophiles were called 'the most genuine homosexuals' because of their supposed immunity towards women. Paedophiles were painted in the colours of ancient Greek ideals, and the piece said that they could 'throughout their lives sacrifice themselves for a younger heterosexual friend'.[29] This article was praised in the following issues, and the editors proudly made the point that the Association seemed able to include and create fellowship between all these types.

In 1955, police finally cracked down on the Association, exposing several leading members and many others as having slept with minors. This so-called Great Pornography Affair saw about 280 men convicted for sleeping with minors, and the leading company dealing in male erotica convicted for distribution of pornography. The Association suffered deeply and in a massive loss of confidence, membership dropped from about 1600 to 62.[30] Many of the cases showed that Association life was not separate from life in the streets.

Oppression

Homosexuals encountered many forms of oppression in the period 1945–65. A national survey in 1947 showed that a majority of the population saw consensual homosexual sex between adults as the worst or next worst on a list of crimes including murder, rape and burglary. However, homosexual sex was the only item on the list which was not, in fact, a crime at the time.[31] Apart from the negative attitude expressed in the survey, homosexuals encountered different forms of harassment, exclusion, violence, theft and blackmail, including – prior to 1970 – from rent boys. Some homosexuals felt driven to suicide. There was injustice in the face of the law too. As we saw earlier, there was an unequal age of consent. The legal age for homosexual sex was 18 years from 1933 to 1976, but 15 for heterosexuality. Between 1961 and 1965, homosexuals could be punished for buying sex from men who were under 21 years of age. There were no such limits on hetero-sexual prostitution. Many homosexuals felt the police were unduly harsh on public sex.

As I have suggested, the Association initially had an active and cooperative relationship with the police – in spite of the latter's negative attitude. In the very first issue of *Vennen* in 1949, under the headline 'The Police are also protecting us', was an interview with a public prosecutor. He encouraged homosexuals to report all blackmailers and the editor applauded him 'for his good will and outspokenness'.[32] In the early 1950s, as the police intensified patrolling of homosexuals, *Vennen* sharpened its pen against them, however. In an article of April 1953, Axel J. Lundahl Madsen praised the chief of the Vice Squad, Jens Jersild, but heavily criticized other officers in the department for having 'written some of the most deceiving reports on homosexuals'.[33]

Many were highly critical of the police orders on a considerable number of homosexuals to abstain from visiting certain places. In 1955, Lundahl Madsen criticized the unreasonable way the police had treated a young man who had been given such an order. The young man had met an acquaintance within the zone in which he was prohibited from 'standing still or walking back and forth'. Two officers saw the brief encounter, and took him to the City Court for violation of the order.[34] Many felt hunted by the police.

The articles in *Vennen* and the complaints in police archives indicate that organized homosexuals did not accept what they saw as unjust treatment by the authorities. The tone became increasingly harsh up to 1955, where the conflict between the police and the Association exploded in the Great Pornography Affair. Lundahl Madsen and Helmer Fogedgaard wrote furious articles against the measures the police and the authorities had taken. Fogedgaard compared it to the persecution of the Jews and wrote that 'we want this cursed nanny mentality, that is being maintained with our money, to go to Hell'.[35] When the police arrested Fogedgaard during the affair, he wrote enraged accounts of police incompetence and injustice, describing how an individual was powerless when the system had its mind set on convicting him. The Association helped individual members in their complaints against the police and the courts, and also wrote general letters to the authorities. From the early 1960s, the *Activist Group Vennen* was launched and added its voice to protests. Though little attention had been given to homosexual voices in the period 1945–60, from this point on many people started listening – because of debate on the so-called Ugly Law.

The Ugly Law

The official response to the panic of the 1950s came in 1961. The Secretary of Justice had a proposal on his desk to raise the age of consent for homosexuals from 18 to 21. He disregarded this, and instead he took up a proposal to criminalize men or women who paid for homosexual sex with an under 21-year-old in cash or commodities. Whereas public opinion had been almost unanimous in the 1950s in criticizing homosexuals, the measure caused a split. 'Discrimination of a minority' became a new slogan for progressive psychiatrists, several MPs, centre-left wing newspapers, out homosexuals and leading intellectuals. It is not clear why this change in opinion happened, but it was probably part of a rising new left wing opinion against conformism and discrimination. Several leading voices who defended homosexuals, called it 'Denmark's negro problem', indicating that they saw it as a larger debate around discrimination of minorities worldwide. The day after the new addition to the Penal Code was passed in Parliament, a leading newspaper criticized it under the heading 'An ugly law', stating that it would lead to blackmail and crime. The criticism of the law continued for 5 years until its repeal.

This repeal was celebrated as a major triumph for homosexual rights and tolerance of diversity. But a closer look at the 5 years the law was in force reveals a more complicated picture. Surveillance, patrolling and disciplining of the homosexual subculture reached an unprecedented scale. In the journal of the Vice Squad, we can see that from 1959 to 1965 around 1,000 men were arrested, fined or warned each year for homosexual offences (that is public sexual acts, having sex with a minor, or paying a boy under 21 for sex). However, only 79 men were convicted under the new measure.

The cases brought under the Ugly Law give us a glimpse of a homosexual culture in which the exchange of cigarettes, money, food, shelter, affection, sexual favours and glances between adult men and teenagers were integrated, accepted and fetishized. Most homosexual prostitution during this period was convicted under the law that prohibited sex with minors, which carried heavier penalties. The Ugly Law cases allow us to look at homosexual prostitution cases on the borderline between legal and illegal homosexual encounters. The typical encounter might go as follows. A marine soldier around 18 years would turn up at certain street corners where 'a uniform was worth its weight in gold', as the rumour went among the soldiers. There he would meet a homosexual man of around 40, and eventually they would go home to the man's apartment and have drinks, food, and sex. The price was on average 23 DKK (the equivalent of 30 Euros in today's prices).

The homosexual men who were caught did not regard their actions as paying for sex. For them, the money was a small token of gratitude, money for the bus home, money for breakfast, money for a cab or the like. Usually, they were convicted anyway since the boy would state to the police that he would not have done it but for the money, thus proving in the eyes of the court that it was indeed prostitution and not a 'sympathy affair' as the opposite term had it. However, looking through the case files, we might suggest something more complex than a simple dichotomy of prostitution versus sympathy affairs. According to the new prostitution law, an explicit or implicit promise of money was crucial for the court to convict a man for buying prostitution. In several cases, the accused man argued insistently that there had been no promise of money, neither explicitly nor implicitly. To counter this argument, the court argued that any man who went to a gay bar or a known prostitution haunt, knew that any boy under 21 expected money. This line of argument was usually successful in court. In one case, a man met a boy in the Latin Quarter and they went home and had sex – no money was exchanged. Questioned by the police, the boy admitted that he entertained the thought of getting money, but having such a good night, and being bisexual himself, he had forgot about it. The man was convicted anyway since he ought to have known that picking up a boy, in that neighbourhood, at that time at night, with no prior conversation equalled an implicit promise of money.

Another case brought a different outcome, even though money did indeed change hands. In September 1963, a 20-year old marine met a homosexual in the Latin Quarter in the notorious bar/restaurant Mandalay, and they agreed to meet again the following week. The week after, they went to the man's place and had sex. The next morning the marine asked for money and was given it. Both evenings the man bought food and beers for the marine at Mandalay. These conditions seemed perfect for a conviction, but the man was acquitted since 'they have been at a restaurant together', and waited for sex until the second date. In other words, this constituted a 'sympathy affair'. Thus, we see that the police did not so much patrol prostitution as redefine it. Certain places, certain inequalities, certain ways of meeting that were prevalent in the homosexual subculture were dubbed prostitution, while other ostensibly quite similar scenarios were not. It came down to the intentions behind the money, and the way it was exchanged, not the money per se.

In 1964, Jersild published *The Pedophiles: Child Lovers*.[36] In the book, Jersild speculated from his vast statistical material, that there was a clear-cut distinction between homosexuals and paedophiles. Looking back at the period, Jersild's thesis does not seem convincing. The homosexual subculture and the prostitution subculture went on in the exact same spaces. In the homosexual magazines, homosexuals never denied that many homosexuals slept with underage partners, instead it was claimed that it was the boys, who seduced the older men, not vice versa. The hypocrisy of differing laws governing heterosexual and homosexual sex was pointed out. The mainstream homosexual erotic magazines were full of nude boys, both before and after puberty. The concept of the paedophile had not been introduced into Danish discourse before this time. A few psychoanalytically interested people knew it, but it was not used in the press, in police records, in psychiatric reports, or in magazines. In the reviews of Jersild's new book, the reviewers underscored that 'Jersild wants to introduce a new word into the Danish language',[37] and Jersild explained that he hoped that the concept of the paedophile could help to clear the 'normal homosexuals' from charges of unlawfulness. Homosexual men did not attain rights because they had always been respectable. Rather, rights came with increased discipline. There was thus, both carrot and stick in the changes that came to gay lifestyles and behaviours.

Jersild's thesis turned out to be a self-fulfilling prophecy. After the repeal of the Ugly Law, discrimination became the new issue for the centre-left, and male prostitution was legalized on the same terms as heterosexual prostitution. Following this almost total legalization, one would expect homosexual prostitution to boom in the late 1960s and early 1970s. But instead, official investigations concluded that it was as good as gone.[38]

The consequences of the Ugly Law

Instead of viewing the repeal of the Ugly Law as a return to status quo, we must review the profound change reflected in criminal statistics and the disappearance of rent boys. During the 1960s, homosexual crime dropped steadily and reached a historically low level in the 1970s. It has subsequently dropped even further. Simultaneously, the rent boys disappeared. In other words, the Ugly Law worked. The police had managed to dismantle the social spaces where homosexual, intergenerational, transactional relationships flourished. Furthermore, it seems that homosexuals had taken on the idea of equality as the measure of acceptable sexual relations; equality in age, in sexuality, and in status. The reward was the status as citizens – citizens who should be treated with respect and had the right to equality under the law. Those who could not conform to the new order of things were increasingly seen as within that new category of paedophiles.

The debate on the Ugly Law centred on issues of 'discrimination' and 'equality'. They gave homosexuals a final push out of the closet. This was a change from the 1950s 'containment doctrine' towards homosexuality. In the late 1960s and the 1970s, organized homosexuality was politicized to a much higher degree than ever before. It was thus not the Stonewall riots that were pivotal in Denmark, but rather 1965 and the introduction and repeal of the Ugly Law. The law had the effect of producing a new kind of homosexual subject, a new homosexual world and a new public consciousness of homosexuality.

The 1970s

The process of loosening laws around sexuality that had been going on since the 1930s, accelerated in the 1960s and 1970s: the introduction of 'the pill' and access to birth control counselling for girls from the age of 15 (1966), decriminalization of pornography (1969), free access to abortion (1973), obligatory sexual education in schools (1970), abolition of the Copenhagen Vice Squad (1971) and equal age of consent for homo- and heterosexuals (1976). The rising generation of homosexuals faced a new world. They no longer felt obligated to hide from public view. 'Coming out' became an obvious – if still controversial – thing to do. The Association of 1948 was renamed the National Union of Homophiles, and later Homophiles was exchanged for Gays and Lesbians, endorsing the new openness and direct approach of the 1970s. Beside the National Union, a Gay Liberation Front sprang up in 1971 (the same year as in the United Kingdom), and campaigned through activist zaps – on several occasions posing as girl drum majorettes in full skirts and big beards and prancing through the main streets of several cities singing 'Willy! Willy! Wauw, wauw, wauw!'[39] A Lesbian Front created in 1974 allied with the new feminist movement, also focused on these kinds of activities, on inwards consciousness raising and on developing a critique of what both movements saw as a patriarchal, homophobic capitalist society.[40]

Many of the homosexual cafés and bars continued as before, and new modern discos came along. PAN Disco, run by the National Union, became an institution and an entry point for young people into gay and lesbian life in Copenhagen. Bar life was usually gender mixed, with only a few bars being men or women only. Despite clashes of ideology and vocabulary, on the whole cooperation was the norm between gays and lesbians and between old and new homosexual movements. With the increased focus on identity politics and 'coming out', the homosexual scene became a scene for gays and lesbians, rather than the broad range of queers we saw in the 1950s.

AIDS, equal rights and homogenizing

In the early 1980s, Denmark had the highest AIDS incidence per inhabitant among European countries. This incidence grew and peaked in 1993 and has been declining since.[41] However, the Danish authorities did not turn to new oppressive measures, such as Section 28 in the United Kingdom or the ban on gay saunas in Sweden. Instead, nationwide campaigns were launched to inform the population that HIV was a threat to homo- and heterosexuals alike. In schools, newspapers and on TV, the message was spread that condom and lubricant use was the best way to avoid infection. The National Union worked closely with health authorities to ensure that campaigns did not turn homophobic.[42]

The teenage rent boys reappeared briefly in the 1980s – perhaps due to rising unemployment and general social hardship. Reports suggest that they were a much smaller group than in the 1950s, much more marginalized from mainstream society and no longer an integrated part of the gay scene, but perhaps catering to the small paedophile grouping. Paedophiles were increasingly segregated from the gay scene in both discourse and practice, and were increasingly demonized as awareness of child sexual exploitation grew in the 1980s and 1990s. The rent boy of the late twentieth century seems much more to be a symptom of poverty than his mid-century counterpart who usually had food and shelter. AIDS and city redevelopment destroyed the last remnants of the rent boy scene in the 1990s, and rent boys have not been seen in the streets of Copenhagen since 1999. Homosexual relationships involving monetary exchange is happening on the internet, and yet even there the few studies done seem to indicate an experimental fringe phenomenon rather than dynamics involving exploitation or poverty.[43]

At the same time as the AIDS crisis, parliament was working on improving the situation of homosexuals in society. The outcome of this work was the law on civil unions for gays and lesbians in 1989. The law secured homosexuals the same rights as married couples, except the right to adoption, insemination, and church weddings. These exceptions have been overturned gradually, and the centre-left government introduced gender neutral marriage laws in 2012, beginning an era where gays and lesbians have all the civil rights heterosexuals have.

Although queer theory and activism did reach Copenhagen, it was mostly an academic discussion. Just as Stonewall took on a different meaning in a Danish context, because Danish gays, lesbians, and transsexuals did not experience the same oppression and police harassment as in New York, queer activism made little sense in a country where the authorities openly supported gay and lesbian rights and the health authorities launched nationwide campaigns on HIV and AIDS. Historically, the struggles for gay and lesbian rights were as often with the authorities as against them. Queerness in Denmark today is discussed among gender and sexuality scholars, as well as art and literature critics, but it is not associated with a significant political movement. The cultural dynamics of the western world seem to demand that political innovations that appear in the United States be imported to Europe. Such innovations are nevertheless reinvented in different national and urban contexts, and the queer phenomenon has simply not caught on in the general Danish LGBT public.

Today, issues regarding homosexuality have become mainstream. Traditionally, the left wing has secured homosexuals equal rights, and the younger generation of politicians on the right is no longer opposed. Only details in law are left to work for in Denmark. Gay and lesbian activists are today increasingly focusing on hate crimes and social discrimination, aided by many sympathetic politicians at all levels. Recently, the National Union changed its name (again) to LGBT Denmark, writing transgender rights into their charter.

The sociologist, Henning Bech has argued that heterosexuals have increasingly taken over aspects of homosexual lifestyle, including serial monogamy, kinky sex, bar life, and self-styling as a sexual being. Consequently, Bech argued, the homosexual disappears as a social category, a problem, or a distinct species. This 'homo-genizing' and 'disappearance of the modern homosexual' is indeed notable in contemporary gay and lesbian culture.[44] In the new millennium access to information about different sexualities, porn sites catering to all tastes, as well as dating sites that reveal the gay or lesbian next door, have eased entry into a gay or lesbian life. Straight couples seem to have little problem with going to a gay bar, just as gays and lesbians do not feel they have to belong to a 'subculture' that is hardly subcultural any more.

Being gay or lesbian does not carry the connotations of social tragedy or drama that it did for previous generations. Today, gay social life ranges from small queer parties to grand-scale events like the World OutGames in 2009 or the annual Gay Pride Parade – all in addition to traditional gay bar and now internet cruising. An important innovation of the twenty-first century has been the inclusion of ethnic minorities into the gay scene. The group Sabaah, run by and for LGBTs of other ethnic background than white Danish, has done pioneering work, welcoming people of all backgrounds to their parties and giving minority LGBT people a safe space while at the same time avoiding a separatism that could enhance segregation. Homophobia, while still in existence and occasionally violent, is not *comme il faut* in public in Denmark. The homophobes now occupy the margins and grey areas of society – those places where homosexuals used to hide: the dark alley at night, the private gathering, the small circle of friends in the know.

Liberation or normalization?

This cheerful story of the liberation of gays and lesbians in Denmark sounds like a cover-up for normalization, and to some degree it is. However, we rather need to realize that the homosexual subject has changed profoundly during the twentieth century. Michel Foucault wrote that 'homosexuality is not a form of desire, but something desirable'.[45] The form as well as the longings and ideals of homosexuals have changed. The queer man of the 1950s, who may or may not have identified himself as homosexual and longed to meet straight young men in the streets after a night at the gay bar, was not the same as the 1970s gay activist who wanted sexual revolution and complete frankness about sexuality. Today, these subjectivities are shadows of the past as today's gays and lesbians differ little from their heterosexual counterparts.

Thus, liberation and normalization become two sides of the same coin. With equal rights and inclusion into mainstream society, some parts of former gay and lesbian culture were left behind. We should not forget the disciplining process that was a prerequisite for including homosexuals into society. The sidelining of paedophilia and transactional relationships was crucial for creating a gay subject who could be seen as acceptable – and this did not happen 'by itself'. These discontinuities should warn us against seeing 'gay liberation' as a straight process, so to speak, and make us realize that what gays and lesbians want today is not necessarily what their forebears wanted or desired. The perpetual reinterpretation of what makes homosexuality desirable continues to change the field we are trying to describe. Indeed sweeping words like liberation or normalization may not be accurate; perhaps, we should turn to concepts like the increase and/or limitation of social possibilities, and the shifts in tastes and dreams.

Frisind has made life easier for homosexuals in Denmark in the twenty-first century, and has perhaps erased entrenched presumptions about the homosexual type. The road to liberal-mindedness has been twisted and unpredictable. Gay marriage in church is not 'the end of history', but hopefully the beginning of something new where we can focus less on who is odd and who is normal. History teaches us that instead of fixing the 'true' form of homosexuality we should look at why it is so desirable for so many people. And take it from there.

Notes

1 Lützen, K. (1998), *Byen Tæmmes: Kernefamilie, sociale reformer og velgørenhed i 1800-tallets København.* Copenhagen: Hans Reitzels Forlag, p. 409.

2 *Illustreret Kriminal-Tidende* (1925), no. 32, p. 7.

3 National Archives in Copenhagen, Copenhagen Police, 3. inspectorate, section B. *Vice Squads observation reports on restaurants etc. (Hansa).*

4 von Rosen, W. (1993), *Månens Kulør: Studier i dansk bøssehistorie 1628-1912.* Copenhagen: Rhodos.

5 National Archives in Copenhagen, Copenhagen Police, 3. inspectorate, section B. *Vice Squads observation reports on restaurants etc. (Bellman-kælderen).*

6 Account by Ejnar, born ca. 1931 in Bech, H. (1989), *Mellem Mænd.* Copenhagen: Tiderne Skifter, p. 70.

7 National Archives in Copenhagen, Copenhagen Police, 3. inspectorate, section B. *Vice Squads observation reports on restaurants etc. (Apollo Bar).*

8   Account by Arrow Ross, born 1939, private correspondence, May 2011.

9   Account by Gregers, born ca. 1932, in Bech (1989), p. 90.

10 *Police Regulation of 1913, §9.*

11 National Archives in Copenhagen. Department of Justice. Legal Section, no. 71/1959, box 2. *Letter from Jens Jersild to Nordskov Nielsen, 7 November, 1960.*

12 National Archives in Copenhagen, Copenhagen Police. *Complaint Cases 448/1951.*

13 National Archives of Copenhagen. Copenhagen City Court 5.107/1964.

14 National Archives of Copenhagen. Copenhagen City Court 10.323/1962.

15 Jersild, J. (1953), *Den Mandlige Prostitution: Årsager, omfang, følger.* Copenhagen: Dansk Videnskabs Forlag, p. 75.

16 Edelberg, P. (2012), *Storbyen Trækker: Homoseksualitet, prostitution og pornografi i Danmark 1945–1976.* Copenhagen: DJØF's Forlag.

17 Jersild, J. (1964), *De Pædofile: Børneelskere.* Copenhagen: Nyt Nordisk Forlag, p. 124.

18 Ibid., p. 131.

19 National Archives in Copenhagen. Justice Department. Legal section 177/60, packet 1. *Letter from the Defence Secretary to the Justice Secretary, Apr. 12, 1965.*

20 Account by Henning in Jens Vesterlund, *Ud af usynligheden: Ældre homoseksuelles livshistorier.* Copenhagen: Frydenlund, p. 111.

21 Elmer, M. (1987), *Erik min elskede.* Aalborg: Kirskovs Forlag, pp. 31–3.

22 Interview with Axel Axgil, *Out & About*, July 2009, p. 14.

23 Christensen, A. (1961), *Et seksuelt mindretal.* Copenhagen: Hans Reitzels Forlag, p. 111.

24 National Archives in Copenhagen. Department of Trade, Industry and Shipping. 118-2-49. *Regulations for the Association of 1948.*

25 National Archives in Copenhagen. Department of Trade, Industry and Shipping. 118-2-49. *Police rapport, Oct. 9, 1950.*

26 National Archives in Copenhagen. Department of Trade, Industry and Shipping. 118-2-49. *Letter from the Association of 1948 to Police Station 4, Aug. 26, 1950.*

27 *Vennen*, March and July 1950.

28 Jackson, J. (2009), *Living in Arcadia: Homosexuality, Politics, and Morality in France from the Liberation to AIDS.* Chicago: University of Chicago Press, p. 125.

29 *Vennen* (1949), no. 6, pp. 81–3.

30 von Rosen, W. (1999), 'Pornografiaffæren i 1955' in *Zink*, no. 4.

31 Norseng, Per (1966), *Lov og Rett – oppfatninger og innstillinger.* Oslo: Institutt for rettssociologi og forvaltningslære, p. vi.

32 *Vennen*, January 1949, p. 5.

33 *Vennen*, April 1953, p. 62.

34 *Vennen*, January 1955, p. 12.

35 *Vennen*, April 1955, p. 119.

36 Jersild (1964). The book was in Danish, and came out in an abbreviated English version in 1967. See the list of further reading.

37 *Ekstra Bladet*, 10 April 1964.

38 For a thorough discussion of the career, cases and effects of the ugly law, see Edelberg (2012).

39 Omann, S. (2011), *Virkelige Hændelser fra et Liv ved Fronten*. Copenhagen: Forlaget Wanda.

40 Lützen, K. (1986), *Hvad hjertet begærer: Kvinders Kærlighed til Kvinder 1825–1985*. Copenhagen: Tiderne Skifter, p. 294.

41 Smith, E. (2003), 'HIV/AIDS surveillance in Denmark: The challenges ahead', *JAIDS: Journal of Acquired Immune Deficiency Syndromes*, 32, 33–8.

42 Fouchard, J., B. Hansen and H. Mikkelsen (2005), *Bøssepesten: Historien om aids-bekæmpelsen blandt bøsser i Danmark 1981–1996*. Copenhagen: Borgen.

43 Jacobsen, D. V. (2009), *Trækkerdreng eller 'bare dreng'*. Thesis, Aalborg University; Lautrup, C. and J. Heindorf (2003), *Mandlig Prostitution*. Copenhagen: Videns- og Formidlingscenter for Socialt Udsatte.

44 Bech, H. (1997), *When Men Meet: Homosexuality and Modernity*. Cambridge: Polity Press.

45 Foucault, M. (1997), 'Friendship as a way of life', in Paul Rabinow (ed.), *Ethics: Essential Works of Michel Foucault 1954–1984, vol. 1*. London: Penguin Books, p. 136.

Further reading

In English

Bech, H. (1997), *When Men Meet: Homosexuality and Modernity*. Cambridge: Polity Press.
Jersild, J. (1956), *Boy Prostitution*. Cph.: G.E.C. GAD.
—(1967), *The Normal Homosexual Male Versus the Boy Molester*. Cph.: Nyt Nordisk Forlag Arnold Busck *(Jersild's books are recommended for their historical interest rather than their analysis of homosexuality, pedophilia, and prostitution.)*.
Rydström, J. (2011), *Odd Couples: A History of Gay Marriage in Scandinavia*. Amsterdam: Aksant.
Rydström, J. and K. Mustola (eds) (2007), *Criminally Queer: Homosexuality and Criminal Law in Scandinavia 1842–1999*. Amsterdam: Aksant.

In Danish

Edelberg, P. (2012), *Storbyen Trækker: Homoseksualitet, prostitution og pornografi i Danmark 1945–1976*. Cph.: Djøf's Forlag.

Fouchard, J., B. Hansen and H. Mikkelsen (2005), *Bøssepesten: Historien om aids-bekæmpelsen i Danmark 1981–1996*. Valby: Borgen.

Lundis, B. H. (2012), *Axel Axgil: Kampen for kærligheden*. Cph.: Forlaget Sidespejlet.

Lützen, K. (1986), *Hvad hjertet begærer: Kvinders kærlighed til kvinder 1825–1985*. Cph.: Tiderne Skifter.

von Rosen, W. (1993), *Månens Kulør: Studier i dansk bøssehistorie 1628–1912*. Cph.: Rhodos.

4

Harmless kisses and infinite loops: Making space for queer place in twenty-first century Berlin

Jennifer Evans

As historical geographers have taught us, abstract spaces transform into concrete places – of memory, community, even identity – through a range of overlapping and highly emotional interactions 'from the global to the intimately tiny'.[1] Places are made and remade when the official meanings envisioned in the grand designs of planners, architects and government officials rub up against the everyday tactics of ordinary people forging their own path.[2] When the space in question is imbued with national importance, like a memorial site, existing social cleavages become especially apparent. These are of tremendous help to historians in getting us to think about how the past is mobilized in how we understand and represent present-day concerns. The discord generated in 2006 by an initiative to commemorate LGBT victims of National Socialism provides an interesting case in point. It illustrates the struggle of activists and historians, politicians and city planners – and readers of the international queer media – to forge a space for queer place in contemporary Berlin. By thinking about efforts to build a national LGBT memorial as an exercise in queer place making, I am not suggesting that we think of it simply as an endeavour by and for queer-identified people.[3] To view the memorial debate queerly means analysing the purposes served by identity claims in efforts to come up with suitable com-memorative strategies for the very different forms of suffering experienced by gay men and lesbians at the hands of the Nazis. In its final iteration, the Berlin memorial represents in physical form what Laura Doan has termed 'an ancestral geneology', that is, it became a critically important marker of a common or shared history, in this case, of persecution, as the touchstone of LGBT life the world over.[4] And yet, as this chapter will also show, despite great success in calling attention to past and ongoing prejudice, making identity the focus of such memorialization is perhaps more problematic than it initially appears. The quest to find suitable representational forms that speak to the difference of experience may have the appearance of unifying the community but – as this debate makes clear – it also underscores the fundamental instability of the queer subject, not because it yields to multiple perspectives, but because of the incapacity of the category of the homosexual to effectively contain historical memory on its own.

The acrimony unleashed when several prominent lesbian feminists questioned whether women's experiences of victimization were adequately taken into account in the design specifications quickly breached the local and national press and upon entering cyberspace, it soon circulated as far away as the Australian and American queer media and blogosphere. A testament to how important the city – and Nazi persecution by extension, signified by the symbolism of the Pink Triangle for an international queer community – had become to the construction of Anglo-American queer historical consciousness, the debate confirms Berlin's unique place as a living memorial not only to victims of one of the most heinous regimes of the twentieth century but also to ongoing human rights struggles in the so-called liberal West.[5] When a compromise was finally reached over how best to open up the memorial's mandate so as to better represent the diversity of the LGBT community, the memorial changed from being a marker of historical persecution to a place of mobilization around contemporary concerns. As activists looked back in time to bolster their claims for recognition, their actions had the effect of changing the memorial's orientation from a space of commemoration to a place of consciousness-raising around current struggles. This shift in conceptions of time and purpose shows quite clearly that queer place making in this enigmatic city is multi-perspectival and complex, and deeply important not just to LGBT public memory but also to rights claims on a national and world stage.[6] But it also sheds light on the complicated memorial politics of the early twenty-first century, raising important questions about Berlin's contemporary meaning as a place for diverse claims to history, from identitarian and local to the national and global.

Memorials

Ever since the fall of the Berlin wall, much ink has been spilt on the pernicious role of symbolic spaces in creating the appearance of cohesive identities.[7]

Whether triumphalist commemorations of watershed moments in the birth of a nation or more solemn undertakings, more often than not, memorials are unruly manifestations of intensely selective memories, representing in concrete and stone the experiences and desires of particular groups over others. Memorials struggle to capture multiple and coexisting experiences of marginalization and oppression.[8] And then there are the complex interactions and entanglements behind the impulse to commemorate itself, which are often obfuscated by the projection and appearance of consensus in the rush to unveil a realized design. This is not to conjure the spectre of overzealous lobby groups; changes to the built environment are never benign. As Anthony King suggests in his iconic essay 'Architecture, Capital, and the Globalization of Culture', urban forms 'do not just represent, or reflect social order, they actually constitute much of social and cultural existence'.[9] In places like Berlin, with such a highly fraught and traumatic history, the memorial landscape is particularly tricky. The intensity of building in 1990s Berlin may have created opportunities for large-scale changes to the physical landscape but it also unleashed heated debate as Germans as well as members of the international community contemplated the impact of these alterations on changing perceptions of past crimes.[10]

Despite the appearance of acceptance after the fact, commemorative cultural practices are by their nature highly fraught and in Germany in particular, memorial work of this magnitude is especially contentious, unleashing pages of commentary in daily newspapers and garnering the attention of a wide and interested readership at home and abroad. The decision to construct several memorial sites in the centre of Berlin may have been celebrated as a kind of cultural consensus, but in actuality it was greeted with scepticism on many sides; and not without good reason. As historian James Young put it in a brief to the 1999 parliamentary committee on media and culture, 'no other nation has ever attempted to re-unite itself on the bedrock memory of its crimes or to make commemoration of its crimes the topographical centre of gravity in its capital'.[11] As it became by the late 1990s that the reunified Federal Republic would play a strong role in a consolidating European Union, how it elected to commemorate its past – a past that had touched so many, intimately as well as violently – elicited considerable international interest as well.[12] As Jennifer Jordan has argued, Berlin memorial sites and the debates they unleash may be seen as places of deep significance to German debates about victimization, but they also spoke to European internationalism especially around the issue of human rights.[13] In these ways, Berlin is a city like not many others, one whose cultural symbolism breached borders.

There were several other factors that left indelible marks on the commemorative landscape of twenty-first-century Berlin, which would influence the shape and face of debate over the LGBT memorial. Chief among which was the different memorial tradition in the former German Democratic Republic or GDR, which ceased to exist in 1990. There victimization itself was a thorny issue, as suffering under the Nazis was explicitly linked to ideology, with communists often at the centre of memorial campaigns. This did not stop East German citizens from trying to expand the narrow definition of victim. After two successful wreath-laying exercises, one in Buchenwald in 1983 and another at Ravensbrück a year later, several gay and lesbian groups planned a coordinated effort to coincide with Christopher Street Day (or German Pride) on 30 June 1984.[14] State response was swift. Activists had their photos taken by the East German secret police or Stasi as they attempted to board trains for the two sites. In Sachsenhausen, they were allowed to lay their wreath, but no mention could be made of homosexual victims. Efforts to delimit who could claim victim status may have been undertaken by the Stasi, but they had garnered the support of veterans' organizations and the management of the two camps.[15] Although the GDR no longer stood by the 1990s, queer activists could not help but wonder what remained of these attitudes and how they might mix with the quiet homophobia that still percolated in the West that marginalized the memory of gay persecution in its own way, as a subject still very much under-represented in academic discourse and official commemoration.

From the 1990s onwards, once it was announced that the city would adopt New York architect Peter Eisenman's design for the *Monument to the Murdered Jews of Europe*, each design competition for a new memorial resulted in countless hours of moral and ethical soul-searching. After close to a decade of lobbying for national recognition of Nazi crimes and emboldened by the state's commitment to the construction of Peter Eisenman's memorial, queer activists in Germany felt a glimmer of hope with the 1999 announcement that the Federal Republic was morally obligated 'to commemorate the other victims of National Socialism in appropriate ways'.[16] Buoyed by this decision, the largest national gay rights organization, the Association of Lesbians and Gays (Schwulen- und Lesbenverband or LSVD) built on the actions of earlier initiatives and submitted a formal petition for a queer monument.[17] The red-green majority in the federal parliament (Bundestag) ensured that in 2003 the request would be honoured and within 2 years, the Berlin Senate Administration for Science, Research, and Culture, Urban and Architectural Art (*Senatsverwaltung für Wissenschaft, Forschung und Kultur Kunst im Stadtraum und am Bau*) tendered an open call for design submissions to be vetted first by the LSVD, together with the 'Initiative for the Commemoration of Homosexual Victims' (Initiative 'Der homosexuellen Opfer gedenken'). Of the 127 submissions received from as far away as Tel Aviv, New York and London, they narrowed the field to 26, to be adjudicated by a 11-member prize committee consisting of the Berlin senator for city development, a prominent art historian, several curators and museum directors, two artists, and Günter Dworek, representing the LSVD.[18]

By 2006, it looked as though the city, state and nation was well on its way to honouring homosexual victims of Paragraph 175, the anti-sodomy article of the German Penal Code exploited by Nazis to police the sexual behaviour of male citizens, which resulted in roughly 100,000 arrests and the incarceration of anywhere between 15,000 and 50,000 in jails, prisons and camps where as many as 60 per cent likely died from their treatment there.[19] On the books since the late nineteenth century, the measure was reformed in 1968 in East Germany and 1969 in the Federal Republic, but remained in the criminal code in West Germany with courts even using Nazi-era case files as evidence in post-war trials.[20] The submission from Danish artists Michael Elmgreen and Ingar Dragset was selected in January 2006 precisely because of the way in which its innovative minimalist cube design evoked this enormous sense of grief and alienation. The strikingly simple design, which bore close resemblance to the block-like Stele of the neighbouring Holocaust memorial, included a single-paned glass window, behind which a continuously running black and white film was to play depicting what one journalist termed 'two kissing boys in ironed shirts'. Given that a full third of the population still found 'kissing boys repulsive', this was designed to be art 'at its most provocative'.[21]

Despite a few misgivings about the harsh modernism of the cuboid, which differed quite significantly from other monuments in Cologne, Frankfurt and Amsterdam, the committee seemed to have weathered the storm of public opinion, that is, until that May when noted feminist and editor of *EMMA* magazine, Alice Schwarzer mounted a full-scaled media attack and opened the floodgates of identity politics. Her argument was that women were not just rendered invisible in the current design but were being written out of a shared history of persecution – as the title of the magazine article made plain: 'again, women are forgotten'.[22] In a coordinated article in the leftist *taz* newspaper, caberettist Maren Kroymann reiterated many of the points raised by Schwarzer, most notably that lesbians continue to represent an invisible minority, whose experiences failed then and now to resonate within majority culture. Using legal persecution as the benchmark of victimization, the whole of women's agency and experience during the Third Reich falls away.[23] Furthermore she claimed, in framing the memorial, aesthetically, around men's sexuality, Elmgreen and Dragset simply perpetuate the social isolation of lesbians. They did so both in the name of honouring the victims and critiquing the here and now. Appealing to them as fellow artists, Kroymann argued that 'work with images and symbols' has the potential to make a statement on present injustice as well. The masculine bias was draughted into the very plans themselves. Not only would the proposed memorial fail in its intended purpose of commemorating the dead, if built without alteration, it also threatened to undercut any meaningful effort to confront present-day homophobia. This action on the part of Schwarzer and Kroymann, and all those signatories who by November 2006 had added their names to the petition 'for women in the Homo-Monument', fundamentally changed the terms of engagement. In the 2 years that followed, during which time the memorial was reconceived, redesigned and finally unveiled in the

summer of 2008, activists and opponents clashed over the gender of design
and history, and despite some tough going, managed to shift the focus from
past injustice to present-day politics.

The politics of representation

In the years that followed the *EMMA* action, three things happened: the
history of persecution itself was debated, the question of collective memory
and artistic endeavour was interrogated and finally, a compromise was
reached and aspects of the memorial's design were altered. The debate turned
on a few core issues. Alongside claims of the historic (and ongoing) occlusion
of women from history and history-making (two separate but related things
in the minds of these activists) was the issue of whose task it should be
to undertake commemoration generally, whether the LSVD truly spoke for
all queer groups or whether the historic enmity towards gays and lesbians
was better left to small-scaled actions such as those from the decade before,
many of which witnessed significant participation of women both separate
from and in solidarity with men. Amidst all this, the story of discord and
rising emotions travelled out of Germany and into the pages of gay and
lesbian news media in the United Kingdom, United States and Canada. So
as not to see the project totally derailed and perhaps ensure their relevance
as the premier gay and lesbian organization, the LSVD orchestrated a series
of podium discussions to address the issues swiftly, judiciously and in public.
These, too, were covered extensively by the local Berlin newspapers, by the
national media, and increasingly, by the international lesbian and gay press.
In two of the sessions, the artists were even on hand to defend their design
decisions. In a pointed statement later published on the LSVD website
entitled 'A Portrait is Not Representative', they systematically addressed the
arguments advanced in the *EMMA* article.

They began their commentary by carefully articulating their sympathy
for the claim of marginalization, be it in the art world or on the job site.
Barely a paragraph in, they dropped this conciliatory tone and turned their
sights on what they termed the 'populist attack unleashed by *EMMA*'.
'Why on earth would we want to exclude women? Or transsexuals' they
exclaimed, exasperated by the campaign. Then something interesting
happened. Drawing on aspects of their own aesthetic practice, they put
forward a sophisticated discussion of the gender of oppression. 'Who has
the right to define "the feminine" and "the masculine?"' They suggested
that, according to the *EMMA* line, 'this could be interpreted as a return to
traditional and strongly divided depictions of men and women's lives'. The
decision to fill the memorial's window with a film about two youths kissing
was an attempt to portray 'a vision of intimacy and tenderness' in the face
of rampant homophobia. This image of an 'eternal kiss' was to serve as a
corrective to the sense of alienation and trauma victims suffer, a sentiment

so personal and yet all-encompassing that it 'surpasses representation'. The pain caused by homophobia exceeds words and images, they argued, and so, the artist is left with only gestures towards lived experience. At the same time that they wished to tackle difficult and ongoing societal problems with their work, theirs was not an experiment in verisimilitude. Indeed, on this they were emphatic, going so far to say that 'a picture or portrait can never be a true representation of something'. Accusing the *EMMA* editors of failing to perceive the way they evoked the gender of oppression in their design, in this case, through the image of youthful and ebullient masculine desire as a salve against a violent and homophobic normative masculinity, Elmgreen and Dragset went so far as to claim that they even failed to recognize the echoes of feminist aesthetic tradition in their plan. Countering the notion that the film loop made male sexuality the standard for a generalized gay and lesbian experience, rendering men and men's experience the touchstone for all oppression, they returned to this issue of the strengths and limitations of metaphor in renderings of this sort. In a final exasperated outpouring, they further complicated the picture:

> We ask ourselves, what kind of depiction of men and masculinity do the editors of *EMMA* expect from us? What if we had two feminine boys that might be easily perceived as girls? What about two masculine girls? Would that be allowed? . . . What counts as sexuality and identity should not be controlled by outmoded markers of what is feminine and masculine.[24]

In three single-spaced pages of emotionally inflected prose, Elmgreen and Dragset gave voice to their frustration with what they perceived to be the intellectual rigidity of the *EMMA* editorial position. Despite their effort to justify their design choices on the level of aesthetics, it is clear from their exculpatory tone that there was indeed a disconnect between their artistic vision and any sense of responsibility for audience reaction. It is obvious too that originally at least they were deeply interested in defending their artistic integrity at all costs which they based on what they saw as a keenly resonant awareness of the links between gender, homophobia and power. While they made some good points about the need to think about degrees of gender variance and possible connections to homophobia, this is not a form of 'dis-identification' – of playing off of dominant discourses so as to critique them from within. Rather, in disavowing the representational power of their choice of image – an image, it goes without saying, with a long aesthetic tradition that venerates youth, immanence and beauty as the cornerstone of gay identity – they actually undercut the political power of art.[25] If 'we are in the end all fighting for a diverse and open society', as they claimed in their statement, it does seem curious that they would foreclose any suggestion of revisiting their design given claims that it had a normativizing effect of its own.

A month after Elmgreen and Dragset went public with their position, following a general membership meeting in October 2006, the LSVD posted a resolution on its website calling for the much-hoped for solidarity between gays and lesbians in order to work collectively towards the realization of the memorial's original purpose, to serve as 'a visible statement against intolerance, enmity, and isolation'. This call for solidarity, however, was premised on a condition that the artists' vision of 'an infinite loop of two men kissing' be kept in the final design, both because this was adjudicated by jury – a position underscored a month later in a letter to the organization from the mayor of Berlin Klaus Wowereit[26] – and also because it conformed to the history of persecution more generally, a history that disproportionately affected men. Sensing that such a schism could undermine the entire effort, the LSVD called on the federal authorities, specifically the Minister for Culture and the Berlin Senate, to step up and help find ways to integrate lesbians into the artists' conceptualization.[27]

This action failed to ease tension and simply had the effect of further angering the *EMMA* editorial collective. Under the heading 'Stop the Homo-Monument!' Schwarzer and her supporters referenced the 'patriarchal dominance of the gay men in the movement and the lack of power of lesbians in positions of leadership'.[28] Their voices held resonance beyond the feminist magazine. A special issue of the major LGBT newspaper, *Siegessäule*, showcased opposing positions, with members of the Gay and Lesbian Museum, the Initiative 'Remember the Homosexual NS Victims' and a former board member on the Foundation for Brandenburg State Memorials represented in the opinion piece alongside a single pro-*EMMA* respondent.[29] Although the question of lesbian marginalization seemed to garner minimal support in the gay press, the position had managed to secure the attention of a member of the European Parliament, who sent a letter to the chair of the Federal Cultural Commission recommending action. Having learnt of the artists' reticence to reconceptualizing the piece, representative Gröner underscored that 'there is enough room in the planned memorial site' for both sets of stories. She raised an idea that already had been floating about: the addition of an information sign outlining the shared but different experiences of historical and ongoing persecution, while reminding her federal colleagues that this issue 'had awakened European interest'. For this reason, she pleaded with them to ensure that 'the exclusion of lesbian women' not be allowed to occur.[30] In other words, the issue of representation, memory and diversity, if it hadn't already, now acquired added international resonance.

Part of the problem was that the space where the monument was to be built brought with it a history of its own. As an historian of Berlin gay history noted in an article in a local art magazine, the Tiergarten holds a special place in the story of gay male sociability and persecution. Andreas Pretzel argued that, unlike the location of the Eisenman memorial across the street (which gained notoriety more for its proximity to Hitler's bunker than for any tangible connection to the pre-1945 Jewish community), the Tiergarten 'for homosexuals is a historical and authentic place'.[31] In this

central park, designed in the 1830s by landscape artist Peter Joseph Lenné as
a place of relaxation and respite from the growing city, men had for decades
cruised for anonymous sex along its tree-lined paths. That the park served
as an important node in the city's famously multi-hued sexual geography
was no secret; both the 1923 *Baedeker* travel book and Curt Moreck's 1931
Guide to Depraved Berlin made mention of its allure as a hook-up spot
for gay sex.[32] The Tiergarten before 1933 represented a key part of Berlin's
storied past as an Eldorado for same-sex desiring men. As criminal case files
from the period tell us, the park carried on as a site of sexual contact, only
in the late 1930s and 1940s it was also a place of persecution with many
men fearing being caught out by so-called stool pigeons (*Lockvögel*) – Hitler
Youth specially tasked to lure men with the promise of intergenerational
sex only to denounce them later at the nearby Gestapo and criminal police
precinct.[33]

   This link between sex, space, sociability and persecution had emerged
as a core theme in many of the design submissions, and also formed a vital
part of the lesbian critique of the proposed memorial. Marcel Odenbach
had pitched the idea of a so-called warm lake on the proposed site, complete
with tropical water lilies. This conjoined the notion of 'warmer Brüder' or
warm brothers in English, the derogatory term for same-sex desiring men,
with a flower that symbolized immanent sexuality. Another submission by
Sabrina Cegla, Ingo Vetter and Amit Epstein proposed a 620-metre labyrinth
in artificial baroque style, overlaying the image of cruising, the search for a
life partner, and quest for a way out of persecution. The theme of cruising,
landscape, and desire was also taken up by Piotr Nathan, who planned
to create a stone lake out of six steel walls. The coloured walls would be
lined on the outside with vines. Obfuscated among the greenery was a door
designed to keep at bay the bourgeois conformity lurking on the inside. Katja
Augustin, Jörg Prinz and Carsten Wieworra made it all the way into the final
round with their proposed planting of 100 metres worth of non-indigenous
trees, in whose branches would be placed symbols of love and devotion
alongside the names of well-known gays and lesbians from the period of
Nazi persecution. Another suggestion was for a half circle of stone, playing
off of the Eisenman design and serving as a formal place of reflection and
repose from which to contemplate the history of persecution.

   In Pretzel's estimation, the winning submission by Elmgreen and Dragset
was careful to avoid the all-too-familiar symbology of the ubiquitous pink
triangle. Operating on the level of abstraction, it seemed best suited to
conjure up an emotional response from the imagined visitor through the
proposed film's use of images of intimacy and desire, with a bit of voyeurism
tacked in. Cruising and public sex was left 'where it was' – part of the park's
enduring legacy but not explicitly part of the memorial. A possible problem
with the design, Pretzel conceded, was its refusal to address the hierarchical
nature of victimization, and it was here, he suggested, that the artists may
have opened themselves up to criticism and scorn.[34] And scorn there was.

Alice Schwarzer wanted nothing short of a complete overhaul, since in her estimation the monument was nothing short of 'a ghetto of clichés of male homosexuality'. In a final submission to the magazine, Schwarzer called on Elmgreen and Dragset to rethink their 'homage to toilet sex' (*Klappensex*) since it was a most unfitting contribution to Berlin's memorial landscape. 'An abstract artistic design should be able to speak to both experiences', she argued, citing that over a thousand men and women now called for a 'radical new conceptualization' including members of *Queer Nations*, a newly formed and avowedly queer (as in non-identitarian) organization that had been working behind the scenes to try and find a third way out of the quagmire.[35]

Gendering persecution

There was widespread worry among those in the heritage industry that this fissure between gays and lesbians might grow in size and derail the project altogether. On its webpage, and then downloaded, annotated and sent around to members of the LSVD and *Queer Nations*, the director of the Berlin-Brandenburg State Office of Memorials posted a statement in December 2006 outlining his organization's concern that the issue had gone so far as to 'push the memorialization of homosexual victims of Nazi persecution into the background'. Highlighting the shifting temporal context of commemoration through the course of this debate, Günter Morsch noted that at the same time that Nazi-era persecution was falling out of sight, the memorial was quickly moving away from its original mandate. In embracing a 'more contemporary and future-oriented perspective', it teetered dangerously towards a full-fledged 'political instrumentalization of memory'.[36] In order to avoid just this, the LSVD pulled together several podium discussions to address the issues of representation, space and commemoration. On an evening in mid-January, at the so-called Maneo-Soirée in the ballroom of the Charlottenburg-Wilmersdorf district city hall, Pretzel and Kroymann were joined by an SPD (Socialist Party of Germany) member of federal parliament, the chairperson of the far left party (die Linkspartei or PDS) and the LSVD's Günter Dworek. Moderated by the *taz*'s Jan Feddersen, this evening was designed to provide a public airing of a variety of issues, from the suitability of the Elmgreen and Dragset design to 'a debate that never gets talked about, the possibility of a brotherly or sisterly understanding (*geschwisterliches Verstanden*) of homosexuality'.[37] Although she had participated in a fact-finding colloquium in 2005 that helped launch the design competition, now historian Claudia Schoppmann was unequivocal in condemning the memorial for failing to adequately represent lesbians as victims of historical violence.[38] She cited examples from the research that had gone into her book *Days of Masquerade: Life Stories of Lesbians During the Third Reich*. Lesbians were persecuted by the Nazis, but not in the same manner as men.

Nevertheless, they were frequently targeted as asocial and wore the black triangle in the camps. Because it didn't occur under Paragraph 175, and thus was not a focus of gay and lesbian organizing in the post-war period, it was overlooked and forgotten. This gendering of persecution was even further evidence of the pressing need to revamp the memorial.[39]

As the treatment of gays and lesbians was put under the microscope in the quest to sort out whether the monument in its current form paid adequate tribute to the plight of those who suffered during the Third Reich, the LSVD, the artists themselves, and various activist scholars weighed in on the veracity of Schoppmann's claims. Part of the problem was the murky language of the original 2003 parliamentary decree, which stipulated that the proposed monument must do three things: 'honour the persecuted and killed', 'keep the memory of injustice alive', and serve as 'an ongoing symbol against intolerance, enmity, and the marginalization of gays and lesbians'. At the Manéo-Soirée, Andreas Pretzel drew attention to three myths circulating in the background. These included allegations that the Nazis were themselves gay, that the persecution of gay men represented a kind of 'Homocaust' and the legend of a systematic lesbian persecution on par with gay men. The monument in its current incarnation lent itself to the perpetuation of these myths, he argued. Opponents of the monument were already raising the spectre of queer Nazis. The way the single Stele appears broken off from the Eisenman monument conjures up the idea of homosexual persecution as a derivative of the Holocaust. And the *EMMA* debate certainly traded on the notion of a targeted campaign against lesbians during the Third Reich. Pretzel suggested that these myths, however problematic, formed a core part of contemporary gay and lesbian consciousness. The monument needed to put an end to them once and for all. A way forward might lie with the highly existential experience of viewing the film. Since it could only accommodate a single viewer at a time, it conjured up the feeling of alienation to which both gay men and lesbian might relate. What was needed was an artistic intervention so as to find 'a way to remember lesbians (while) recognizing their specific fate. All this, without evoking the spirit of competition or a sense of equalization'.[40] In order for the memorial to move forward, they required a suitable representational strategy for capturing the shared but different emotional cost of marginalization. What was necessary was a queering of place, a visual strategy that could both encapsulate and go beyond any sense that there was a singularity of experience.

The memorial as media event

From the beginning of its conceptualization to its unveiling, the LGBT memorial was a media event. Lesbian activism had succeeded in opening up a space for greater visibility and by the end of 2007, several prominent

Social Democratic and Green Party politicians joined members of the LSVD and Berlin's queer mayor Klaus Wowerweit to formally request the artists to re-conceptualize the monument's design to speak in some way of lesbian experience. They conceded. The plan was to change the infinite loop of men kissing every 2 years and replace it with a lesbian kiss. For many journalists, to say nothing of Web 2.0 commentators, the compromise was a concession and not a long-term solution.[41] Indeed, many used the unveiling as an opportunity to revisit the dispute. In the *Berliner Zeitung*, the erstwhile daily of communist East Berlin, columnist Gunnar Schupelius doubted very much that the 'kissing men in black and white' would awaken people to remember the violent past. The national *Welt* newspaper saw it differently. 'The memorial, as a piece of public memorial culture, is another example that monuments can also be good art'.[42] For *Die Zeit*, the question whether a kiss was an appropriate symbol of persecution seemed most pressing. According to the *Zeit* reporter, more important still was the fact that this debate forced consideration of the relationship of monuments to the past. In their estimation, it was the interactive nature of the 'Film-Monument' from Elmgreen and Dragset that rendered the past the subject of present and future disputation.

At a cost of roughly 600,000 euros, the memorial was finally unveiled by the federal Minister of Culture Bernd Neumann in a ceremony attended by over 400 people in the spring of 2008. Having seen a televised story relating to the monument's unveiling, 95-year-old Rudolf Brazda decided to make himself known to organizers. One of the last surviving victims of the camps, he was unable to attend the ceremony, but he did attend that year's Pride March, known in Berlin as Christopher Street Day.[43] Gunter Dworek of the LSVD reminded those in attendance that the struggle to realize a memorial was almost two decades long. And there were still signs amidst the celebration that all was not perfect with the commemorations. Despite efforts to hold up the memorial as a symbol of Western tolerance while a sign read that 'in many parts of the world people are still persecuted because of their sexual identity', the artists told the local scene magazine *Zitty* that the federal Minister of Culture actually refused to allow invitations to be imprinted with images of 'the Kiss' – the shorthand term for the infinite loop of kissing men. Other observers noted the absence of Germany's President Horst Köhler, who had been present at the unveiling of the Memorial to the Murdered Jews of Europe.[44]

The memorial was not only of significance to Berlin or German queers. Both the controversy and the unveiling quickly entered the international queer blogosphere through transnational subcultural networks and pathways. Already in 2007, the New York *Gay City News* reported on the cavernous divide between gays and lesbians. In an article by Benjamin Weinthal, the acrimonious falling out was captured in infinite detail and translated for an English-speaking audience. A core feature of the story was the perspective of expat American and Berlin-based activist Jim Baker, who reflected on the differences between queer organizing in the United States and in Germany. 'The lack of coalition building has affected gay and lesbian politics in Germany' to the extent that advocacy is still very male centred.[45] An article in the *Advocate* in 2006 titled 'A Memorial of Our Own' underscored the importance of the Elmgreen and Dragset design to international queer identity politics, while a later article went a step further in placing the Berlin memorial in conversation with other transnational queer commemorative cultures, like those which have resulted in memorials in Amsterdam, Sydney and Tel Aviv.[46] Similarly, positioned in the World News section of the *Gay and Lesbian Times* next to articles on Argentine efforts to legalize same-sex marriage and the Russian ban on blood donation, the memorial's location was described as having great symbolic purchase given its proximity to where decisions were made on the fate of a variety of social and racial outcasts.[47] Even the small Pennsylvania *Erie Gay News* reported on the plans to build a memorial in Berlin, calling special attention to the ongoing stigma German victims experienced after the war.

The queer media engagement with the memorial demonstrates how pivotal the Nazi persecution of German homosexuals was and remained to gays and lesbians abroad.[48] Indeed, almost every article cited its placement in close proximity to the Eisenman memorial as a sign that injustices against gays and lesbians finally had acquired serious treatment in Berlin's memorial landscape. Along the same vein, they referenced that the federal government had sanctioned its construction. What began as a testament to German public memory had transcended the national orbit and was quickly taken up as a symbol of the historic mistreatment of gays and lesbians in many parts of the world. Building the memorial was greeted as an important step forward in recognizing past wrongs, serving as a rallying cry for ongoing struggles. In this way, the building of the memorial in Berlin aided in the materialization of queer memories of suffering, linking the German past to a transnational present. In cyberspace and among the readers of subcultural media, the memorial helped lend shape and form to a universalized set of common queer memories. The events in Berlin conjured up German crime and trauma. But in linking it symbolically to the ongoing battle against marginalization and homophobia, the memories conjured up by the memorial were also taken up by queers across national divides. In seeking to queer place in Berlin, not just in the sense of creating space for a queer memorial, but also in transcending state and nation, the memorial and the international reportage in the queer counterpublic sphere constructed an alternative kind of kinship based around the shared heritage and symbology of Nazi violence and its importance for contemporary queer identity.[49] At the same time, these tensions and the fraught politics of commemoration suggest that queer kinship and solidarity – even in the face of common causes – are not always easy, self-evident, straightforward or successful.

Conclusion

What does this struggle to gender victimhood and representation – and the international interest in how this played out – tell us about the role of history in queer place making in Berlin? To get at this, we need to take seriously the divergent understandings of the past emanating out of the debate and the ways in which the struggle for representation forced an open and frank – if acrimonious – discussion of the rules, structures, and organization of city, rhetorical and memorial space. In bearing witness to past crimes but focusing attention on current struggles, the memorial contributed to bread and butter issues affecting contemporary queers, especially in ongoing and future struggles for legal recognition, a formal apology, remuneration – even for civil union – as an emblem of a time when rights to privacy, personality and self-determination were systematically violated 'in the name of the people?'[50] History was used by these activists to create a coherent meaning of place amidst the shifting terrain of identity politics and invented traditions. The fact that this battle waged in cyberspace and in traditional media, on LGBT blogs in the United States as well as in the various Berlin newspapers tells us that what appears as a localized struggle for a national queer monument quickly breeched these boundaries. In other words, the struggle to realize a HomoMonument, as it was called colloquially, was at once local and global, national and transnational, quotidian and mediatized. Berlin was no longer the building site for a unified German identity, but it quickly became a place of symbolic importance for international human rights struggles.[51] If we are to truly appreciate the role and significance of the memorial in queer place making, we have to think of it as a site claimed by many and instrumentalized by some in the name of community and identity, on a German, European, and global scale. Making space for queer place means looking at how the 'past helps make the present'. But, more importantly, it also means thinking seriously about the unique role played by the city Berlin in a cosmopolitan queer imaginary.[52]

What purpose is served by thinking about the quest to build a monument to the queer victims of Nazism as a politics of place making? Focusing in on the way disparate groups claim and make sense of certain city spaces and the emotions and memories they help call into being sheds light on the role of competing and sometimes overlapping practices and interactions that makes up (even as it troubles) any stable sense of collective memory. Not only does this foreground the messiness of commemorative practices, but it also points to the high degree of emotionality involved in the politics of place making itself. As geographer Nigel Thrift has argued, thinking about claims to space as an inherently relational process is not only methodologically more sound, allowing as it does a way to see place making as having a basis in overlapping, intersectional identities, but it might also make for a more progressive memory politics given the important social, sexual, gender, ethnic, and political orientations, inflections, and implications it makes visible at the core of the memorial process itself.[53] Collective memory is so often 'used, misused, and exploited' by governments and the heritage industry and taken up by average people to give themselves 'a coherent identity, a national narrative, (and) a place in the world'. In view of this tendency, it is doubly important to find ways of keeping it messy, if only to capture the contentiousness of claims making to undermine the power of localist, identitarian and nationalist assertions of neutrality in suggestions that certain spaces bear essential or universal meaning.[54] Instead of reproducing neat yet myopic histories, perhaps a more responsible approach might tackle what Massey refers to as 'the inevitable hybridities at work in the constitution of anywhere'.[55]

Instead of lingering over this battle over definitions of persecution (which pitted gays against feminists and lesbians over whose history should be encapsulated in the monument) as an example of the corrosiveness of identity politics, I have argued it might be more useful to see it as an exercise in place making – the process by which memory and history gel and become fixed in actual material space. Efforts to make the memorial speak to everyday oppressions, those both in Germany and abroad, afforded it a more fixed (though no less problematic) meaning as a site of reflection, pilgrimage and memory. Contemporary Berlin's importance as a site of twenty-first century rights struggles is forged in large part due to its location at the intersection of multi-perspectival (often emotionally-charged) narratives of place. And yet, it is well worth pondering in a future project what is lost as well as gained in the quest to concretize such a vision of queer consciousness in public memory, especially one that – however heroically committed to the present – is rooted in identity politics and disconnected from the past.

Notes

Research for this chapter was provided by the Social Sciences Humanities Research Council of Canada

1 Hague, C. (2005), 'Planning and place identity', in C. Hague and P. Jenkins (eds), *Place Identity, Participation and Planning*. New York: Routledge, p. 4. See also Massey, D. (1995), 'Places and their Pasts', *History Workshop Journal*, 39, 182.

2 Lefebvre, H. (1992), *The Production of Space*. New York: Wiley.

3 Reed, C. (1996), 'Imminent domain. Queer space in the built environment', *Art Journal*, 55(4) (Winter), 64–70.

4 Doan, L. (2013), *Disturbing Practices. History, Sexuality, and Women's Experience of Modern War*. Chicago: University of Chicago Press.

5   Jensen, E. N. (2002), 'The pink triangle and political consciousness: Gays, Lesbians, and the memory of Nazi persecution', *Journal of the History of Sexuality*, 11(1–2), 319–49.

6   See Till, K. E. (2008), 'Artistic and activist memory-work: Approaching place-based practice', *Memory Studies*, 1(1), 99–113.

7   Ladd, B. (1997), *The Ghosts of Berlin: Confronting German History in the Urban Landscape*. Chicago: University of Chicago Press; Halbwachs, M. (1980), *The Collective Memory, 1950*. New York: Harper Colophon Books; Huyssen, A. (2003), *Present Pasts: Urban Palimpsests and the Politics of Memory*. Stanford: Stanford University Press; Jordan, J. A. (2006), *Structures of Memory. Understanding Urban Change in Berlin and Beyond*. Stanford: Stanford University Press; Till, K. E. (2005), *The New Berlin: Memory, Politics, Place*. Minneapolis: University of Minnesota Press; Ward, J. (2011), *Post-Wall Berlin: Borders, Space, and Identity*. Basingstoke: Palgrave Macmillan; Young, J. (2000), *At Memory's Edge: At Memory's Edge: After-Images of the Holocaust in Contemporary Art and Architecture*. New Haven: Yale University Press.

8   Wilke, C. (2013), 'Remembering complexity? Memorials for Nazi victims in Berlin', *The International Journal of Transnational Justice*, 7(1), 1–21.

9   King, A. D. (1990), 'Architecture, capital and the globalization of culture', *Theory, Culture & Society*, 7, 404.

10   Molnar, V. (2010), 'The cultural production of locality: Reclaiming the "European City" in post-wall Berlin', *International Journal of Urban and Regional Research*, 34(2) (June), 281–309.

11   Young, J. (1999), 'Berlin's Holocaust memorial: A report to the Bundestag committee on media and culture, 3 March 1999', *German Politics and Society*, 17(3), 56.

12   Olick, J. and D. Levy (1997), 'Collective memory and cultural constraint: Holocaust myth and rationality in German politics', *American Sociological Review*, 62 (December), 921–36.

13   Jordan (2006), p. 220. See also Markovitz, A. S. and S. Reich (1997), *The German Predicament: Memory and Power in the New Europe*. Ithaca: Cornell University Press.

14   On lesbian commemorative strategies in the GDR see Bryant, D. (2009), 'Queering the antifascist state: Ravensbrück as a site of Lesbian resistance', *Edinburgh German Yearbook 3. Contested Legacies: Constructions of Cultural Heritage in the GDR*. New York: Camden House, pp. 76–89.

15   McLellan, J. (2010), *Love in the Time of Communism: Intimacy and Sexuality in the GDR*. Cambridge: Cambridge University Press, pp. 124–5.

16   Beschluss der Deutschen Bundestages (25 June 1999), www.holocaust-denkmal-berlin.de/index.php?id=44; Christiane Wilke makes the crucial point that there is an important intersectional relationship between victim groups and their efforts to secure national commemoration of their struggles. She argues that many of them attained a measure of moral authority in support of their cause when the state committed to build the Holocaust Memorial. In some instances, they drew direct aesthetic inspiration from the main memorial,

and as such, might be better analysed as part of a common, collective memorial practice. Wilke (2013).

17 Initiative HomoMonument (1999), 'HomoMonument: Eine Republik auf eine selbstgestellte Frage', in *Der homosexuellen NS-Opfer gedenken*. Berlin: Heinrich Böll Stiftung, p. 11.

18 Senatsverwaltung für Wissenschaft, Forschung und Kultur Kunst im Stadtraum und am Bau, 'Entwurf der Auslobung. Gedenkort für die im Nationalsozialismus verfolgten Homosexuellen', 31 May 2005.

19 Lautmann, R. (1981), 'The pink triangle: The homosexual males in concentration camps in Nazi Germany', *Journal of Homosexuality*, 6, 141–60.

20 Evans (2011); Whisnant, C. (2012), *Male Homosexuality in West Germany. Between Persecution and Freedom 1945-1969*. Basingstoke: Palgrave Macmillan.

21 Bisky, J. (27 May 2008), 'Küssende Jungs', *Suddeutsche Zeitung*.

22 'Mal wieder die Frauen vergessen!', *EMMA* (May 2006), http://www.emma.de/hefte/ausgaben-2006/septemberoktober-2006/homo-mahnmal/ (consulted on 18 March 2013).

23 Kroymann, M. (28 August 2006), 'Verschwundene Minderheit', *taz*.

24 Stellungnahme der Künstler (20 September 2006), 'Ein Porträt ist keine Representation', *LSVD-Website*.

25 Munoz, J. (1999), *Disidentifications: Queers Of Color And The Performance Of Politics*. Minneapolis: University of Minnesota Press. On the history of queer aesthetic traditions, see Evans, J. V. (2013), 'Seeing subjectivity: Erotic photography and the optics of desire', *American Historical Review*, 118(2), 430–62.

26 Letter from Klaus Wowereit to the LSVD's director Alexander Zinn dated 13 November 2006.

27 'Resolution – Denkmal für die im Nationalsozialismus verfolgten Homosexuellen – Den preisgekrönten Entwurf verwirklichen', 28 October 2006.

28 'Stoppt das Homo-Mahnmal', *EMMA*, 11/12 October 2006.

29 'Stein des Anstoßes. Um das Homo-Mahnmal ist eine Diskussion entbrannt, weil Lesben sich vom Entwurf nicht repräsentiert fühlen. Die Siegessäule gibt Meinungen Raum', *sieggesäule*, 11 (2006), 8–9.

30 Letter from Member of European Parliament Lissy Gröner to the Representative of the Cultural Committee in the Federal Parliament Monika Griefahn dated 23 November 2006.

31 Pretzel, A. (2006), 'Ein 'Mahnmal Homosxuellenverfolgung', *kunststadt-stadtkunst*, 53, 30.

32 *Baedeker and its Environs: A Guide for Travellers* (1923). Leipzig: Karl Baedeker; Moreck, C. (1931), *Führer Durch das 'lasterhafte' Berlin*. Leipzig: Verlag moderner Stadtführer.

33 See Pretzel, A. and G. Roßbach (eds) (2000), *Wegen der zu erwartenden hohen Strafe: Homosexuellenverfolgung in Berlin, 1933–1945*. Berlin: Rosa Winkel.

34 Pretzel (2006), p. 30.

35 Schwarzer, A. (January 2007), 'Im Getto des Kitsches. Warum der Entwurf für das in Berlin geplante Homo-Mahmal nicht nur politisch ein Skandal ist, sondern auch künstlerisch', *EMMA*.

36 Morsch, Prof Dr G. (15 December 2006), 'Erklärung des Arbeitskreises I der Berlin-Brandenburgischen Gedenkstätten', http://www.gedenkort.de/ps-bbg151206.htm (consulted on 2 April 2013).

37 Leaflet, *MANEO-SOIREE – die Talkrunde: Ein Mahnmal nur für Schwule?* 11.1.07, 20 Uhr, Festsaal des Rathaus Charlottenburg-Wilmersdorf.

38 Schoppmann, C. (2005), 'Im Schatten der Verfolgung: Lesbische Frauen im Nationalsozialismus', *Dokumentation des Auftakt-Kolloquiums zum Kuntswettbewerb 'Gedenkort für die im Nationalsozialismus verfolgten Homosexuellen*. Berlin: Berliner Forum für Geschichte und Gegenwart e.V im Auftrag der Senatsverwaltung für Wissenschaft, Forschung und Kultur, 35–43. See too 'Bericht: MANEO-Soiré: Ein Mahnmal nur für Schwule?' Berlin, 11 January 2007.

39 Schoppmann (1996).

40 Pretzel, A. (11 January 2007), 'Eine Debattenbeitrag zum Streit um den Gedenkort für die im Nationalsozialismus verfolgten Homosexuellen', *MANEO-Soiree* am 11. Januar 2007.

41 See Hannemann, M. (n.d.), 'Streit ums Homosexuelen-Mahnmal. Szenelokalverbot gleich Konzentrationslager?', *Frankfurter Allgemeine Zeitung*http://www.faz.net/aktuell/feuilleton/streit-ums-homosexuellen-mahnmal-szenelokalverbot-gleich-konzentrationslager-1547365.html (consulted on 3 April 2012).

42 Schupelius, G. (13 June 2008), 'Mein Ärger', *Berliner Zeitung*; Luehrs-Kaiser, K. (27 May 2008), 'Zwei Männer und ein schwules Denkmal', *Welt*.

43 Schwab, W. (28/29 June 2008), 'Späte Freude am Mahnmal', *taz*.

44 'Remembering Different Histories: Monument to Homosexual Holocaust Victims Opens in Berlin' (6 June 2006), *Spiegel Online*, http://www.spiegel.de/international/germany/remembering-different-histories-monument-to-homosexual-holocaust-victims-opens-in-berlin-a-555665.html (consulted on 3 April 2013).

45 Weinthal, B. (15 March 2007), 'Berlin's harshly felt divide', *Gay City News*.

46 'A memorial of our own' (28 February 2006), *The Advocate*, 957 and Graham, Adam (7 January 2008), 'A kiss before dying', *The Advocate,* 1010.

47 'Holocaust Gay Memorial Unveiled in Berlin' (5 June 2008), *Gay and Lesbian Times*.

48 Jensen, E. N. (2002), 'Pink triangle and political consciousness' gays, Lesbians, and the memory of Nazi persecution', *The Journal of the History of Sexuality*, 11(1–2) (January/April), 319–49.

49 A similar point is made by Hoang, N. T. (2007) in 'Theorizing queer temporalities. A roundtable discussion', *GLQ: Gay and Lesbian Quarterly*, 13(2/3), 6–7.

50 'In the Name of the People' is the English translation of 'Im Namen des Volkes' which was the title that adorned every court case ledger during the Third Reich.

51 Cochrane, A. (2006), 'Making up meanings in a capital city: Power, memory, and monuments in Berlin', *European Urban and Regional Studies*, 13(1) (January), 24.

52 Massey (1995), p. 187.

53 Thrift, N. (2004), 'Intensities of feeling: Towards a spatial politics of affect', *Geografiska Annaler*, 86 B, 57–78; Wilke (2013). The idea of intersectionality has its origins in Crenshaw, K. (1991), 'Mapping the margins: Intersectionality, identity politics, and violence against women of color', *Stanford Law Review*, 43(6), 1241–99.

54 Said, E. W. (2000), 'Invention, memory, and place', *Critical Inquiry*, 26, 179. James Young makes the point that 'the surest engagement with memory lies in its perpetual irresolution . . . simply the never-to-be-resolved debate over which kind of memory to preserve, how to do it, in whose name, and to what end'. Young, J. E. (1993), *The Texture of Memory: Holocaust Memorials and Meaning*. New Haven: Yale University Press, p. 21.

55 Massey, D. (2004), 'Geographies of responsibility', *Geografiska Annaler*, 86 B (1), p. 7.

Further reading

Downing, L. and R. Gillet (eds) (2011), *Queer in Europe: Contemporary Case Studies*. Burlington, VT: Ashgate Publishing.

Evans, J. V. (2003), 'Bahnhof boys: Policing male prostitution in post-Nazi Berlin', *Journal of the History of Sexuality*, 12(4), 605–36.

—(2011), *Life among the Ruins: Cityscape and Sexuality in Cold War Berlin*. Basingstoke: Palgrave Macmillan.

—(2013), 'Seeing subjectivity: Erotic photography and the optics of desire', *American Historical Review*, 118(2), 430–62.

Herzog, D. (2005), *Sex After Fascism: Memory and Morality in Twentieth-Century Germany*. Princeton: Princeton University Press.

—(2011), *Sexuality in Europe: A Twentieth-Century History*. London: Cambridge University Press.

Hull, I. V. (1996), *Sexuality, State, and Civil Society in Germany, 1700-1815*. Ithaca, NY: Cornell University Press.

McLellan, J. (2011), *Love in the Time of Communism: Intimacy and Sexuality in the GDR*. New York: Cambridge University Press.

Moeller, R. G. (2010), 'Private acts, public anxieties, and the fight to decriminalize male homosexuality in West Germany', *Feminist Studies*, 36(3), 528–52.

Pretzel, A. (2002), *NS-Opfer unter Vorbehalt. Homosexuelle Männer in Berlin nach 1945* Münster: LIT Verlag.

Rowe, D. (2003), *Representing Berlin: Sexuality and the City in Imperial and Weimar Germany*. Burlington, VT: Ashgate.

Sieg, K. (2002), *Ethnic Drag: Performing Race, Nation, Sexuality in West Germany*. Ann Arbor: University of Michigan Press.

Specter, S. (2007), 'Where personal fate turns to public affair: Homosexual scandal and social order in Vienna, 1900-1910', *Austrian History Yearbook*, 38, 15–24.

Whisnant, C. (2012), *Male Homosexuality in West Germany: Between Persecution and Freedom, 1945–69*. Basingstoke: Palgrave Macmillan.

5

From Stalinist pariahs to subjects of 'Managed Democracy': Queers in Moscow 1945 to the present

Dan Healey[1]

Moscow was the capital of a victorious Soviet Union in 1945, and in this era of rapid reconstruction and political complexities, 'queerness' would eventually come under special scrutiny. Wartime contact with 'decadent' Europe threatened to contaminate Soviet 'natural' sexuality at a moment when population losses aroused anxiety. Even more provocatively, after the death of Soviet dictator Joseph Stalin in March 1953, the dismantling of the Gulag forced labour camps threatened to infect society with perversions 'hot-housed' in places of confinement. Law and medicine were mobilized to contain queer sexualities, while 'liberals' and 'conservatives' in the Communist Party would disagree over the need for official sex education. Until the collapse of Communist rule, and of the Soviet Union as multinational empire in 1991, political stalemate arrested the 'sex question'. At the same time, economic and social evolution transformed the experience of queer sexualities, prefiguring the exuberant and anxious approaches to queerness prevalent in Moscow in the early twenty-first century.

The evolution of 'queer' Moscow after 1945 cannot be gauged by the familiar landmarks of Western LGBT history. Under an authoritarian police state there was no legal independent social activism or non-governmental organizing and hence no Russian 'homophile' movement linked to any interwar queer communities. Such solidarities, if they existed, had been disrupted by Stalinist anti-homosexual purges during the 1930s.[2] The Soviet state guarded its monopoly on press, radio and television zealously and operated exceptionally prudish censorship until the late 1980s. Muscovites did not publish their own queer journals until 1990. The year 1968 was not a 'revolutionary' moment in Soviet history, but a year of reaction when the USSR led Warsaw Pact armies to crush the Prague Spring. The year's events stimulated unofficial 'dissident' activism inside the Soviet Union, virtually none of which was 'gay' identified. Police surveillance and persecution of dissidence intensified. There would be no Moscow Stonewall, nor could a Soviet community of self-identified 'gay' people proclaim itself during the 1960s–1970s with demonstrations and pride marches. Feminism was shunned by the political 'dissidents' and found little purchase in an underground intellectual milieu that, for complex historical and ideological reasons, rejected gender as a category of analysis. There was little 'second wave' feminism inside Russia and no 'lesbian separatism'. The HIV/AIDS threat during the 1980s would be perceived and conceived of distinctively by the Soviet medical establishment and media. Moscow in 1989 had a very different history of understanding and living out 'queerness' than that of Europe's western capitals.

The fundamental distinction during the period was the Cold War division of Europe into capitalist and socialist states, into the NATO and Warsaw Pact blocs. The Cold War left its marks on queer Moscow. The USSR led a restive bloc of allies, the socialist 'people's democracies' of East Germany, Poland, Czechoslovakia, Hungary, Romania and Bulgaria. Despite 'sovietization', these countries had diverging histories of regulating queer sexualities, at considerable variance from Russian traditions and Soviet practice. Finally, the primary adversary in the Cold War was the United States, and after Stonewall, Soviet ideologues and gay Russians were compelled to confront the 'Americanization of the homosexual' as a challenge from the opposing ideological camp.

Less provocative but perhaps more pregnant with possibility was the evolution of queer citizenship in the European Union during the 1980s, especially as the last Soviet leader, Mikhail Gorbachev, in office from 1985 to 1991, often spoke of greater engagement with 'our common European home'. The 'political postponement' of queer freedom until the 1990s triggered a sudden and promiscuous downloading of queer ideas in Russian cultural life. At the same time, capitalist transformation brought an explosion of consumerism, including queer cultures, with trends usually set in Moscow, Russia's wealthiest metropolis. The significance of queer freedom in political, economic and social life is the subject of intense debate in Moscow today.

To appreciate the distinctive trajectory of queer Moscow's evolution, I begin by examining the regulation of sexuality in the immediate post-1945 era. After victory in 1945, and after Stalin's death in 1953, surveillance of queer genders and sexualities was renewed and extended, in the wider context of anxieties about social order. The second section explores the complexities of the period of 'political postponement' from 1964 to 1991, when Soviet liberals and conservatives were locked in a frozen conflict over social values, and yet the appeal of the West's 'sexual revolution' challenged all. A final section of this chapter looks at the post-Communist and postmodern era since 1991, when Moscow became the centre of an unprecedented eruption of queer activism and cultural action, and at the same time the focus of new homophobic politics.

After victory, after Stalin

The human losses inflicted in the 1941–45 'Great Patriotic War' confronted the Stalinist leadership with an alarming demographic crisis. Twenty-six million citizens died; of these, 20 million were male, and in both sexes most victims were of reproductive age.[3] Implications for post-war reconstruction and for the strength of the Soviet Army were stark. Even before the war's end, Stalin's eventual successor, Nikita S. Khrushchev, conceived and implemented a series of family policies to replace the population losses as rapidly as possible. Khrushchev's law of 8 July 1944 '[o]n increasing government support for pregnant women' gave single mothers state support for the first time; they had previously depended on alimony from absent fathers. Along with tighter divorce and the 1936 abortion ban, the package led to a surge in post-war single motherhood. Within 10 years, almost 9 million children were being raised by single mothers.[4]

Such a deep population crisis might have triggered anti-homosexual propaganda campaigns, or a spike in arrests under Stalin's anti-sodomy statute of 1934, but the evidence is inconclusive. Little overt animosity explicitly targeting the Soviet queer appeared in the press. The Stalinist habit of silence, acquired in the 1930s, regarding same-sex love prevailed. Nevertheless, it was a constructive silence, with contempt for sexual dissidence in Cold-War-themed journalism, as Erica Lee Fraser has demonstrated.[5] In commentaries on foreign affairs, the national satirical journal *Krokodil* typically portrayed capitalist allies of the United States as feminized, weak and often in queer situations (West German chancellor Konrad Adenauer in drag 'marrying' Uncle Sam, in June 1950, for example). Such images contrasted with representations of the broad-shouldered Soviet Man as he strode away from perverse capitalist blandishments. Fraser argues that these images constructed Soviet masculinity as unproblematically and healthily heterosexual when contrasted with the explicit queering of the capitalist hireling. In post-war cinema too, Soviet heterosexuality was presented as fecund, natural and untroubled by perversion.[6] Queer was an attribute of capitalists and not of the victorious leaders of the world's socialist camp.

Arrests for consensual sodomy between men occurred, but are mostly unrecorded in accessible official documents. The most notorious wartime case took place in late 1944 when the Moscow crooner and superstar Vadim Kozin was charged with sodomy and anti-Soviet statements, and sentenced to the Gulag in 1945. The popular gypsy ballad singer lived indiscreetly, treating young men to dinner and his bed in Moscow's Metropole Hotel, where secret police surveillance was ubiquitous.[7] The accessible record of sodomy convictions is incomplete, but suggests a rising trend in the 5 years after 1945. Still, convictions in the city of Moscow's conventional courts stood at just six for all of 1950. The immediate post-war years were a time of hunger, sickness and hard work; opportunities for sex were slim.[8] I have described elsewhere how queer men met in the 1950s in Moscow's public toilets, parks and bathhouses for sexual encounters, and how private space also afforded opportunities for same-sex love.[9]

We still do not know if secret police actions against homosexuals took place in the late Stalin years. During this period, secret police terror increased, targeting a range of 'counterrevolutionaries' and new 'class enemies'. It seems unlikely that large-scale arrests explicitly for homosexual activity were conducted by the secret police during the post-war years, only because no memoirists or émigré observers recall any mass operations against homosexuals. Gay men would have been collateral victims of the various campaigns against citizens suspected of disloyalty as the Cold War opened, and as Stalin's illness and paranoia advanced.[10]

After Stalin's death in 1953, living conditions improved and official liberalization sanctioned the pursuit of a relatively unmolested private life. The Party under Khrushchev adopted a tutelary approach, steering citizens towards 'communist morality' through public education and social policy reform. Despite the headline trend of official de-Stalinization and political liberality conventionally ascribed to Khrushchev's rule (beginning with his 'secret speech' denouncing Stalin in 1956 and ending with his removal by hardliners led by Leonid I. Brezhnev in October 1964), recent scholarship has noted the regime's nervous responses to the forces unleashed by liberalization, and its search for new methods of control.[11] Decisions about how to treat queer men and women in this period are a heretofore unknown example of renewed authoritarianism during the Khrushchev years.

New evidence shows that concern about homosexuality emerged within, and quickly spread beyond, the Gulag camps and exile settlements, principally located in the remote north and east. From 1953, the Gulag was transferred from secret police management and greatly reduced. Millions were amnestied, and many 'political' prisoners were fully rehabilitated. The release of so many convicts during the mid-1950s triggered a crime wave that alarmed the public, and spawned debates about social order.[12] Gulag doctors and officials worried about the perverse sexual practices that had long been ignored behind barbed wire. Sodomy and male rape were supposedly typical of the criminal subculture of the sex-segregated camps (where more than three quarters of the inmates were male); lesbian relations were also widespread, supposedly principally among the 'criminal' women. The reforming prison service now sought to study and curb perverse sexuality inside the remaining camps, and the state worried about the spread of queer sex in society at large.[13]

As a result, at a time when Moscow jurists were reviewing and abolishing hundreds of Stalin-era statutes at Khrushchev's instigation, the 1934 sodomy ban was reinforced instead. In 1958, a secret directive 'on the strengthening of the struggle against sodomy' issued by the Russian Republic's interior ministry exhorted police to crack down on homosexuality between men.[14] Recorded prosecutions for same-sex relations between men rapidly increased, and the police began routinely monitoring homosexual haunts in parks and public toilets, and used informants threatened with prosecution to incriminate others.[15] Cruising grounds in Moscow acquired notoriety as places where one might be entrapped by a pretty stranger working for the KGB. Yet this was a national strategy, as the 1959 re-arrest of Vadim Kozin in a hotel room with a 16-year-old police decoy, in distant Khabarovsk demonstrated.[16] Male homosexuality remained a crime in Russia until 1993.

While male homosexuals were pursued with new vigour, lesbians, apparently ignored under Stalin, were not criminalized during the Khrushchev era either, but instead subjected to new psychiatric scrutiny. Gulag directors did propose an anti-lesbianism law in 1956, but authorities evidently preferred to deal with lesbians medically behind closed doors, rather than in the open realm of law and courts.[17] Medical 'treatment' of lesbians in the late Soviet decades might entail the prescription of libido-deadening drugs, and compulsory registration as a psychiatric outpatient with unpleasant consequences in daily life.[18] The assignment of the lesbian to medicine coincided with the Khrushchev state's turn to psychiatry to control other forms of dissent, although a direct connection in the thinking of the authorities between sexual and political dissent remains elusive.[19]

The situation for 'free' lesbians in Moscow of these years remains obscure. The privileges of femininity, and the general lack of eligible men, licensed much female intimacy and allowed women to mask same-sex love as conventional friendship. The Moscow actress Faina Ranevskaya (1896–1983) lived in a long partnership with her mentor and lover, the actress Pavla Vulf (1878–1961). After wartime evacuation to Tashkent, they returned to Moscow and lived separately, but took holidays together. Through the 1950s, Ranevskaia nursed Vulf who died in her arms; later she admitted that Vulf had been the only love of her life.[20] Ranevskyia's queer persona reportedly found expression in the faintest of hints: a stirring performance in a Moscow 1945 production of Lillian Hellman's 'The Little Foxes'; her invention of a gender-troubling name for her character 'Lev Margaritovich' in the 1947 comedy film *Vesna* (*Spring*).[21]

Not all lesbian lives during the period were so successful. The poet Anna Barkova (1901–76), survived three periods of imprisonment (1934–39; 1947–56; 1957–65).[22] Her lesbianism was not illegal but her sexuality nevertheless underpinned her conflicted relationship with Soviet power; Barkova's first arrest was for writing an ironic poem about Stalin. Released in 1939, she settled in Moscow province with an ex-prisoner and lover,

Tonia (her surname is unknown) and they survived the war years together, although often quarrelled; Barkova agonized over Tonia in her diary: 'Maybe this is the nature of a decadent orientation: perhaps healthy people never feel this way. But does that mean that they are in the right? . . .. She considered moving to Moscow to live with other female friends; jealous at this betrayal, Tonia denounced Barkova. She was arrested in 1947 and sentenced to 10 years imprisonment for anti-Soviet statements. Released in 1956, she settled with another ex-inmate lover in Ukraine, but they were both re-arrested the following year for writing anti-Soviet material. Barkova was released in 1965, and only fully rehabilitated in 1967, thanks to the intervention of a leading literary liberal, Aleksandr Tvardovskii; but her work was excluded from his journal, *Novyi mir*. In 1967, Barkova settled in a communal flat in Moscow; she insistently re-wrote her diary after each confiscation and left a body of work reflecting on the nature of homosexual desire that remains almost unknown.

Queer solidarities in late-Soviet life

Between 1964 and 1985, under Party leader Leonid I. Brezhnev and two short-lived successors, neo-Stalinists and bureaucrats seeking predictable government curtailed the Khrushchev experiment in 'liberal' de-Stalinization. 'Liberals' given hope in the early 1960s (the so-called *shestidesiatniki*, 'people of the sixties'), and 'conservatives' terrified of losing privileges or of being called to account for their crimes, confronted one another in every sphere of political, social and economic endeavour. Brezhnev mediated with the close assistance of the KGB, normally, in favour of stasis between these camps. Even as political decision-making froze to a halt, economic and social transformation accelerated: by 1965, city dwellers finally outnumbered rural ones for the first time, and Moscow expanded from a dusty metropolis of 4.8 million in 1957 to a global capital of at least 9 million in 1990. Huge new residential districts of concrete apartment towers appeared; they were linked to the historic heart by an impressively efficient Metro. Private car ownership grew, although traffic jams would not appear until the twenty-first century.[23] The pinnacle of Soviet government, industry, arts, sciences and education, Moscow was a magnet for ambition and talent, and queer Soviet citizens were disproportionately motivated among migrants in search of a better life. For sexual and gender dissidents, Moscow offered possibilities and even freedom unmatched elsewhere in the USSR.

Probably the most important factor in creating a sense of opportunity was the expansion of housing as the majority of families were now able to obtain private flats – after decades in communal apartments, shared by multiple households. As new housing complexes sprang up, the prospect of an end to the mutual surveillance of the communal flat held obvious attractions for queers. Moscow got more investment in modernized accommodation than other cities, and yet supply never met demand, with priority given to newlyweds. A new sector of quasi-private, 'cooperative' housing was an expensive alternative available to senior managers and professionals, and some gay men appear to have benefited.[24]

A more likely route for the gay man or lesbian seeking a private apartment in Moscow was to marry heterosexually and join the faster queue of couples entitled to housing. By the 1970s, a 'veritable industry' in marriages of convenience operated in the capital.[25] This 'industry' was not exclusively homosexual; it was the result of internal passport and residency registration barriers, devices introduced to socially engineer the populations of major cities.[26] It was impossible to live legally in Moscow or other 'regime' cities without official permission, granted by an employer, university, or when a resident married a non-resident. Thus, to gain a foothold in the capital, straights *and* queers from the provinces sought sympathetic or credulous Moscow spouses.[27] Russian gays and lesbians married each other too, fully aware of their partners' orientation, in order to jump the housing queue. Fictive marriages also conferred respectability on queer participants, satisfying family curiosity and deflecting official suspicions. Divorce rates soared after relaxations were enacted early in Brezhnev's tenure, and marital breakdown was as much a badge of heterosexuality as an enduring alliance.[28] Soviet queer men (reports do not mention women) also sought to marry foreigners, and leave the USSR permanently. The marital route out of the country could be one of the easiest 'escape routes' for determined queers. During the 1960s–80s obtaining exit visas entailed lengthy paperwork and administrative penalties. Another option, for queers with a Jewish connection, was to seek an exit visa to Israel, but this route came with additional harassment and anti-Semitism.[29]

Not everyone could find private space, and sex in public, which had long played a role in straight and queer intimate life in Moscow, continued to assert itself, particularly for gay men. So too did public courtship and socializing, following traditions established in the late nineteenth century.[30] By the 1970s and 1980s, the principal public meeting places for queer men stretched in an arc around the Kremlin and Red Square, producing a celebrated *marshrut* or 'circuit' for the adventurous.[31] An underground toilet in the Alexander Gardens near the Kremlin Wall and just steps from the busy Lenin Library metro station was a notorious place of assignation. Ten minutes' walk from this public convenience, facilities in GUM department store on Red Square itself, or in the basement of the Central Lenin Museum just off Red Square and directly above the Revolution Square metro, served as the next ports of call. Leaving the museum and crossing Sverdlov Square, one passed a monument of Karl Marx glaring down upon the epicentre of Soviet queerdom: a little garden in front of the Bolshoi Theatre, with its benches facing each other in a circle surrounding a low fountain, forming the northern half of Sverdlov Square. The ensemble was partially shielded from the street by shrubs and gardens. Winter and summer this square – with a plethora of queer nicknames, but commonly known as 'the bald patch' or *Pleshka* – was a popular spot for cruising and socializing.[32]

The *Pleshka* as queer site endured from perhaps the 1930s until the late 1990s when renovation, and then the internet, largely killed it off.[33] That such a visible and central meeting place for queers, in the heart of the capital, lasted so long may seem odd, but the authorities evidently came to tolerate it as a way to monitor a normally secretive minority of non-conformists. Rumours even circulated on the *Pleshka*, evidently attempting to explain the existence of this gathering place, that in the early 1970s, the state had secretly decreed a hiatus in the persecution of homosexuals.[34] Perhaps this was disinformation, circulated by *agents provocateurs*. Official statistics released later show no decrease in prosecutions.[35] Moreover, the clean-up of Moscow's streets before the 1980 summer Olympics, which hit the 'circuit's' gay men as well as prostitutes and the homeless, showed that any such tolerance was conditional.[36]

Continuing the 'circuit' in its arc around the heart of the capital, following Marx Prospect uphill to KGB headquarters on Dzerzhinsky Square, one passed the Children's World department store and side-streets harbouring the Sandunovskie and Central Baths: traditional steam-baths where '[a]s in the toilets, furtive glances and sidelong looks pass between the gay customers, who, having found each other, get acquainted and go elsewhere for consummation.'[37] The busy, well-staffed municipal baths of the capital made it impossible for queer men to colonize them as they had before the Revolution.[38] Later in the 1990s, the 'circuit' extended even farther around the arc, to Staraya Square, where a monument to tsarist Russian victory over the Turks provides a focal point for gay cruising even today.

The 'circuit' of queer spaces surrounding Moscow's heart did not exhaust the city's queer possibilities. A major artery running north from Red Square, Gorky Street, ran into Pushkin Square, popular with all types of nonconformists, and Mayakovsky Square, where lesbians sometimes met. Cruising spots could also be found in Gorky Park, on the south-west fringe of the centre, and farther afield on Lenin Hills, near Moscow State University.[39] There were numerous public toilets used by queer men, near the Kazan Railway Station, on Trubnaya Square near the old State Circus, in Hermitage Park, and on Gogol Boulevard close to a monument to the queer nineteenth century writer Nikolai Gogol.[40] Moreover, late Soviet Man, if he was one of the 15 per cent of householders with a private car in 1985, used it for sexual trysts, although cars were still so rare that no notorious queer parking spots developed in Moscow's suburbs.[41]

At least as striking as the extent of queer men's space in late Soviet Moscow were the audibility of queer language and a new feeling of shared injustice. Queer language, of course, circulated throughout the Soviet Union and it had its roots in the pre-revolutionary homosexual underground, Gulag slang and contemporary criminal and street jargon.[42] Gender inversion was its most enduring characteristic. From at least the nineteenth century, same-sex oriented men used Russian's rich store of gender inflection to refer to self and comrades ironically (so, for example, instead of '*ia poshel*' = 'I went', masculine gender, they used '*ia poshla*', feminine gender). Also popular were feminizing sobriquets; such queeny inversions persisted during the early twentieth century and, with great discretion, during and after the Stalin era.[43] The *Pleshka* and its perverse comradeship seemed to license a degree of linguistic liberty; consider the shock of a friendly heterosexual visitor to the square in the mid-1970s. The writer Alexander Dymov was introduced to the scene there by Alesha, a gay friend. On one early visit, Dymov was present when a friend of Alesha's in a military uniform arrived and addressed them:

> In a high-pitched voice that cracked from time to time, he sang, "My little dears! If only you knew what a cock I've just sucked!" I was shocked on three levels. *Primo*, he was a genuine air force officer in an impeccable uniform, blue epaulettes and gold buttons. *Secundo*, despite the masculine sex of those present, he addressed them as "little dears" [using feminine gender]. *Tertio*, he spoke of himself in the feminine gender . . .[44]

Dymov might have added that to make such a flagrant pronouncement in his presence, someone not known to the speaker, showed confidence in the security of this milieu.

The sensibilities of the *Pleshka's* habitués merit closer attention than they have received. Some, reflecting the intelligentsia prejudice that held open queerness to be criminal, have tended to associate life on the 'circuit' with law-breaking, a lack of education, and the dangers of the Soviet street, dismissing it as hazardous and coarse. They distinguish between intellectual gays who avoided the 'circuit' and working-class queer life on the streets. Intelligent young people supposedly hung around on the 'circuit' only as long as it took to find a partner; once they found one, they abandoned it for the safety of private spaces.[45] There is much truth in this characterization, given the fear of KGB entrapment, and the violence meted out by homophobic gangs, that *Pleshka* stalwarts evidently encountered. However, all was not fear, degradation and empty pleasure-seeking, and the division between stay-at-home educated gays, and rough boys who roamed the streets in search of sex, was never so absolute. Observers noted serious attempts among *Pleshka* denizens to create camaraderie (if not 'community') and to puzzle out the meaning of gay existence in Soviet circumstances.[46] In the early 1970s, the lexicographer Vladimir Kozlovsky interviewed 'Mama Vlada', a man said to be 'the chief homosexual of Moscow', and a member of the 'elite' frequenting the *Pleshka*. In a conversation rich with scabrous wordplay, 'Mama Vlada' argued bitterly against the persecution Russian homosexuals suffer because they were 'nonconformists':

> I don't understand our fucking leaders, who can lock me up and work me over as much as they like, but they will never get me to change. It's

no fault of mine. I was born this way. . . . Oh, if only the authorities up there knew how many celebrated names there are in our ranks. . . . How many of [us there are among] their own KGB, police officers, people in the government, and People's Artists, important cultural figures, award-winners in various fields, scientists, painters, poets.[47]

Repeating apologetics familiar to Russians since before 1917, 'Mama Vlada' argued that Sigmund Freud discovered 'bisexuality' and 'was the first to see in the liberation of humanity from sexual prohibitions the path to spiritual liberation and personal development'. Moreover, 'we have always existed – and what people there have been in our midst: Shakespeare, Tchaikovsky, and Proust . . .' To Kozlovsky, 'Mama Vlada' was a 'major creator of homosexual folklore and mythology', and evidently someone who commanded authority on the *Pleshka*.[48]

A growing solidarity was emerging among queers who met in private apartments, in the closely knit circles of trusted friends (*kruzhki*, singular *kruzhok*) that were ubiquitous in urban society in these years, not confined to homosexuals alone. (Other designations for such groups were *salony/salon,* 'salons', and *tusovka*, 'the scene'.) A gay male Russian-speaking US professor who lived in Moscow for several months in 1979 noted that '[a] strong sense of camaraderie results from the peculiar situation of Soviet gay people, a loyalty and devotion not only to one's lover but also to one's circle of friends (*kruzhok* or *salon*). Most often, gay people meet other gay people through their friends and acquaintances; this is true, of course, outside Russia, but due to the lack of alternatives, it is much more important in Moscow.'[49] A queer New Left visitor from Boston saw in Soviet loyalty to friends and lovers a positive alternative to Western gay life saturated in pornography, consumerism and promiscuity.[50] Dymov, active in illegal publishing (*samizdat*), saw parallels and crossovers in the solidarities between political and sexual dissidents. *Samizdat* relied upon trusted groups to copy (by typewriter) and distribute (by hand) works of banned literature and journalism; he once found himself delivering such material to a gay *kruzhok*.[51] Gay *kruzhki* often circulated whatever reading matter about homosexuality they could obtain.

Significantly for the rise of open gay and lesbian activism in Moscow on the threshold of the 1990s, the queer *kruzhki* of the 1970s–80s developed a sharpened understanding of Soviet homophobia. Virtually all observers commenting on late Soviet gay life mention encounters with charismatic personalities leading their own *kruzhki*, expounding their pet theories of homosexuality, its persecution and prospects.[52] Soviet queers had an increasingly detailed awareness of how Western gay activism was making an impact on the other side of the Iron Curtain, and a sense of how implausible gay liberation might be in the USSR.[53] Some argued that Eastern European people's democracies were more likely to produce a form of queer activism permissible under socialism. As Sasha, a perceptive engineer from

Moscow put it in 1977 when asked if there was any prospect of a Soviet gay movement:

> Definitely not for the foreseeable future. First, we do not have the gay subculture that exists in the West, and it is very difficult to develop the idea of a gay identity, and still less a consciousness of our oppression. Second, even if a group solidarity existed, it would be impossible to organize ourselves, given the political repression. The [Soviet] state has this matter well under control, in contrast, say, to the situation in Poland, for example. And just as a movement for democratic socialism has more chance of emerging in Poland than here, I think that a movement for sexual politics will arise first in one of the people's democracies [rather than here].[54]

Foreign leftist gay activists expressed similar views, even as they made concerted and sometimes daring efforts to establish ties with gay and lesbian 'leaders' in Moscow and Leningrad.[55] The opinion of the Russian-speaking US professor writing in 1980 was pessimistic:

> Soviet society changes with glacial speed; the enormous advances in gay rights during the 1970s in America and western Europe have not begun to happen here, nor are they likely to happen for generations to come. More important, even the small improvements that have occurred are not necessarily permanent. Who knows what will happen after Brezhnev?[56]

There was little or no anticipation of the momentous changes that were about to engulf the Soviet Union's queer citizens.

If same-sex oriented men constituted the most visible element in the diverse strands of queer Moscow life, they were nevertheless not alone. Women who loved women continued to come to self-awareness in isolation, although by the late 1970s there were opportunities to experiment in the underground scene. Elena Gusiatinskaya (born 1946) studied French at the capital's Institute for Foreign Languages. She recalls:

> I sensed my untraditional orientation from a rather early age, in my youth . . . but because in the 1960s this subject was under a total taboo, I did not reflect on it particularly deeply. Since I read foreign languages easily, I had access to a degree of information on the theme. But in general my homosexuality was deeply buried in my subconscious. On one hand, I sensed it, but on the other, I lived a traditional way of life: I got married, I divorced . . .[57]

Another Moscow woman who later gained notoriety as the first Soviet lesbian activist, Evgenia Debrianskaya, also married heterosexually in these years.[58] Olga Krauze was born into a Leningrad professional family in 1953. As a youngster, she wore trousers in the streets and changed into her school dress on the sly. Qualifying as a designer in the late 1970s she was lucky to find a *kruzhok* of gays and lesbians in Leningrad. 'We shuttled back and forth between Moscow and Peter[sburg]. Later I got involved in activism, the underground, mutual aid. I remember very clearly how we organized marriages of convenience with gay men, when they needed saving from prosecution.'[59] Krauze's experience illustrates how artificial it is to divide a history of queer Moscow from that of the Soviet Union's second city, Leningrad. Rail and airfares were very cheap, and shared contacts between the two Russian 'capitals' expanded the circle of trusted friends.[60]

Soviet intersex and trans people emerged from obscurity in this period as a result of the expansion of medical research, centred on Moscow. Professor Aron I. Belkin of Moscow's Institute of Psychiatry, in cooperation with colleagues from the Institute of Experimental Endocrinology, experimented with 'correcting' the sex of intersex persons, and changing the sex of transgender patients. These experts were ignorant of the many Soviet experiments in these areas during the 1920s–1930s, but well versed in Western developments since 1945.[61] In the 15 years after 1961, the endocrinology institute operated on 684 hermaphrodites to 'clarify' their sex, in 71 cases, resulting in a change of passport sex. In the 1970s, many intersex patients were teenagers and adults; there were no standard protocols for treating intersex infants, and local doctors hesitated to intervene. Patients had to journey vast distances to seek advice from Moscow's specialist clinics.[62] Changing the passport sex of a Soviet citizen was apparently harder than 'giving the hermaphrodite an unambiguous sex by means of surgical and hormonal therapy'; despite new regulations introduced in 1974, to change patients' paperwork, doctors had to write dozens of unofficial letters to bureaucrats, falsify medical records, and conduct long-term pastoral relationships with many intersex patients to ensure their successful integration.[63]

Belkin and his colleagues also began sex-change operations during this period. Little is known about these patients and their experience. Igor Kon (1928–2011), the nation's foremost sexologist, noted that the psychiatrist Belkin conducted sex changes without the psychological testing considered standard in the West; there was simply no one he could confidently entrust with the task.[64] Later at the end of the 1990s, surgeons and endocrinologists were well versed in the full range of Western procedures including psychological filtering of prospective patients, and their post-operative pastoral care.[65] As with intersex patients, ordinary Soviet physicians had scant acquaintance with Western medical approaches to the transgendered subject. Some doctors knew about sex change operations and thought they ought to be prescribed for women presenting as lesbians (according to one woman's autobiography published in a queer journal).[66]

Post-communist, Postmodern

In 1985, with the accession of Mikhail S. Gorbachev as leader of the Communist Party, political stasis came to an end. Increasingly bold bids to revitalize the Soviet system flowed from the Kremlin, guided by 'new thinking', 'restructuring' (*perestroika*), 'openness' (*glasnost*), and crucially, 'democracy' as watchwords. The political results – the end of the Cold War (1989), the collapse of Communist rule, the largely peaceful disintegration of the Soviet Union into 15 sovereign states (1991) – are well known. The former socialist bloc abandoned socialist economics and embraced capitalist globalization. The change was seismic, experienced by Russians as liberating, euphoric and deeply unsettling as well.

A discursive 'sexual revolution' accompanied the wider political revolution. With increasing boldness, in the late 1980s, the Soviet media talked openly and explicitly about sex to an audience that was amazed, titillated, shocked and disgusted – and could not, it seems, get enough of it. Glasnost in the realm of sexuality brought stunning media openness to Western ideas and values, frank reflection on the anxieties and joys of ordinary citizens, and even crude attempts to arouse audiences. Sex became of badge of 'post-ness,' post-Sovietness, of life after Communism however it might take shape. All sex became in late Soviet and early post-Soviet culture a credential marking out one's text or product as non- or anti-Soviet, new, fresh and democratic. Homosexuality was publicly acknowledged as one of the social 'problems' that the Soviet system had swept under the carpet. More daringly after 1991 it became a symbol for a spectrum of social and cultural preoccupations (many of them having little to do with queer experience). Yet at the same time, notes of anxiety and fear accompanied these stirrings: HIV/AIDS was a new threat apparently from outside the USSR, and 'non-traditional' sexuality (a label for queer sex that has stuck) was to be blamed.[67]

Moscow was the centre of these developments. However, one should not ignore the vast provincial hinterland in the evolution of post-Communist queer Russia. In political and cultural terms, the late 1980s and the 1990s were a moment of decentralization, when Russia's regions re-discovered their voices. The provinces and republics of the Russian Federation (independent from late 1991 and led by President Boris Yeltsin until 1999) displayed greater confidence and threw up new leaders on the national stage. This was as true in Russia's LGBT culture and politics as in any other field in the 1990s. From 2000, with paramount leader Vladimir V. Putin, a counter-trend towards the re-centralization of power and wealth began, which has not yet run its course. However, the rise of digital technologies and networks has undermined Putin's agenda with significant consequences for queer Russians.

On the eve of Communism's collapse, Soviet queer voices took advantage of democratic politics to speak out with a fresh, uncompromising frankness about homosexuality in the USSR. The first Soviet gay and lesbian magazine, *Tema* (The Theme – a common tag for same-sex love), appeared in December 1989, edited by Roman Kalinin (born 1966) and Vladislav Ortanov (1953–2011), assisted by the politically experienced Debrianskaya, who devised a front-organization to support the publication, the Association of Sexual Minorities (ASM). The ASM hosted several media conferences in Moscow in 1990–91, well attended by Western journalists and soon by Russian ones too; its first, in February 1990, saw *Tema's* associates condemn the persecution of sexual minorities and call for the decriminalization of male homosexuality.[68] Early attempts to develop an organization representing all Soviet lesbians and gays came to nothing, but *Tema* itself galvanized young activists from across the Soviet Union. They had support from international friends, who invited Kalinin to San Francisco in late 1990 on a speaking and fundraising tour. The diminutive blond made an impression on US audiences, and the funds raised went to support a major international conference of gay and lesbian rights, held in Moscow and Leningrad in summer 1991. In June 1991, Kalinin stood in the elections for Russian president as a candidate for the tiny Libertarian Party, and if his chances of winning were non-existent, the media publicized his demands for an end to gay persecution with a degree of bemused curiosity.[69] Activists around *Tema* participated in the public agitation that followed the August 1991 attempted coup against Gorbachev. They printed an extra 4,000 copies of the magazine, with Boris Yeltsin's proclamation denouncing the coup, and distributed them to crowds and soldiers in tanks at the Moscow demonstrations.[70] In retrospect, the small band of activists who gave voice to the demands of homosexuals in the last months of Soviet power now appear braver and more successful than many at the time were prepared to concede. While male homosexuality was still illegal, the KGB still threatening gay men, and when the social taboo against coming out publicly as gay or lesbian remained extremely strong, a core of Moscow radicals dared to organize a campaign for queer rights and to publish their demands in the country's first queer magazine and in the national media.[71]

Decriminalization of gay male sex came soon after, in April 1993, in an omnibus package of laws rushed through the Russian legislature by the Yeltsin administration. The influence of the first generation of queer activists on the legal change was probably very limited. Instead, Russia's 'shock therapy' reformers were keen to enact as much legislation to comply with Council of Europe human rights standards as quickly as possible.[72] When one considers how cooperation broke down later in 1993 between the president (who had a strong popular mandate after the June 1991 election) and the legislature (a holdover from the Soviet regime, packed with Communists), it seems remarkable that the administration managed to get its way on this controversial measure. Nevertheless, the decriminalization of voluntary sodomy between adults was confirmed by legislators in

Russia's first post-Soviet criminal code in 1996–97; a subsequent debate in 2002 about re-criminalization failed to produce a new anti-sodomy law. Two decades after decriminalization, Russia's lawmakers appear to tolerate, if not accept, gay sex as legal, and LGBT citizens as a fact of national life.[73]

Moscow's lesbian and gay activist and cultural groups came and went rapidly during the economically turbulent 1990s. The Moscow Association of Lesbian Literature and Arts, (Russian acronym *MOLLI*), was founded like *Tema* before the Soviet collapse, and carried on until 1995 hosting literary events and supporting the publishing of lesbian writing. Olga Tsertlikh (born 1952) and Liubov Zinovieva (1958) were among its mainstays; *MOLLI's* participants published Russia's first lesbian literary journals *Adel'fe*, *Sofa Safo* and *Ostrov*.[74] United States and EU sponsorship supported safe-sex campaigning groups like the Aesop Centre; and an attempt to establish a national umbrella organization for LGBT activism, the Triangle Centre (*Tsentr Treugol'nik*), opened an office, published a newsletter and held a conference on the rights of LGBT Russians in June 1996. It was attended by 150 activists, most of whom were Moscow-based. Triangle closed when its foreign sponsorship ended the following year.[75]

Another hybrid organization originated in two Moscow scholars' contrasting visions for Russian queer studies. Elena Gusiatinskaya and Viktor Oboin (born 1950) jointly established an archive and library of LGBT materials in an attempt to preserve and analyse the explosion of documentation that appeared from 1990. Oboin, an information scientist, tenaciously chased ephemeral documents from organizations and magazines that emerged and then closed down. He published a newsletter commenting on media homophobia and occasionally positive coverage of queer themes, boldly posting it to every parliamentary deputy and other public figures.[76] Gusiatinskaya, a literary scholar and translator, assembled a library of published LGBT materials (novels, stories, autobiographies, non-fiction) and material about queer themes from the mainstream press. For a time, this collection was housed at the Triangle Centre; when it closed, Gusiatinskaya moved the library to her private flat, and regularly welcomed all those who were interested in reading about queer issues. She facilitated much queer writing, including an impressive anthology of lesbian prose.[77] Oboin moved his extensive document collection to Amsterdam's Homodoc in 2000, and Gusiatinskaya still collaborates with a younger generation of activists.

Most Russian gay men's publishing originated from Moscow during the 1990s. *Tema's* editors fell out, and Ortanov left to set up new projects, including magazines (*RISK*, *ARGO*) and books, eventually agreeing a partnership with Germany's leading gay press Bruno Gmünder. The deal collapsed in the 1998 financial crisis. Another publisher, Dmitry Lychev, produced a successful gay men's magazine, *1/10*, producing 23 issues between 1991 and 1998. Its mix of erotic fiction, news from the gay scenes of Europe and America, and in the pre-internet era, contact ads, guaranteed its longevity. Except for St Petersburg's high-brow literary review *Gay Slaviane!*, Moscow dominated Russia's queer publication market.[78]

For many reasons, this first post-Soviet generation of Moscow activists and entrepreneurs generally failed to found lasting organizations and businesses. Despite decriminalization and democratization, on 'moral grounds' Moscow's city hall denied most of them official registration and thus access to legal personhood; they were condemned to run on a shoe-string from private flats and the corners of host-organizations. The police harassed publishers of erotica and bothersome newsletters; Lychev and Oboin emigrated. During the 1990s, homophobic responses to the new visibility of same-sex love grew louder, and by the turn of the century conservative and nationalist politicians and religious leaders began to mobilize support in parliament and the media against any further 'propaganda for homosexuality' as an acceptable alternative to 'traditional sex'.[79]

The conservative-nationalist turn in Russian politics imposed since 2000 by Vladimir Putin's 'managed democracy' set limits on queer visibility; queers have been confined to the private spheres of commercial space and the internet.[80] However, the managers of democracy underestimated the power of digital media and networking as affluence spread and more Muscovites too young to remember Soviet life come of age. A new generation of queer activists has emerged from this young professional and entrepreneurial class. Most notoriously, the Moscow Gay Pride parades held annually since 2005 have become a flashpoint for dispute between city hall and a group of activists led by a new generation of lawyers and bloggers. (Debrianskaya is one of the few faces from the Soviet spring of the late 1980s who campaigns with them.) City authorities deny the Pride march a permit to function legally, and every year the event ends in beatings and lawsuits as the police shut down the march.[81] Queer activists were visible participants in the December 2011 rallies against vote-rigging in the recent parliamentary elections, carrying signs declaring 'They stole the votes of millions of gay and lesbian families too!' and 'Gays and lesbians against the crooks and thieves'.[82] The June 2013 adoption of a national law banning "propaganda for non-traditional sexual relations" among minors has sharpened state homophobia. The battles still ahead for this young generation of queer Russians are daunting, and yet the distance that Moscow's queers have travelled in the space of a single lifetime inspires respect and hope.

Notes

1   I am grateful to my former colleagues at Reading University for teaching relief that enabled my research and writing, and to Elena Gusiatinskaya and Viktor Oboin, who have taught me so much about queer Russia. I use a simplified form of Russian transliteration in the text; in citations I use the modified Library of Congress system. All translations are the author's own.

2   On pre-war Moscow gay communities, see e.g. my translation of Communist
    Harry Whyte's letter to Stalin in Young, G. (2012), *The Communist Experience
    in the Twentieth Century: A Global History through Sources*. New York and
    Oxford: Oxford University Press, pp. 88–98.

3   Andreev, E. M., L. E. Darskii and T. L. Khar'kova (1993), *Naselenie
    Sovetskogo Soiuza, 1922–1991*. Moscow: Nauka, p. 77.

4   Nakachi, M. (2006), 'Population, politics and reproduction: Late Stalinism
    and its legacy', in Juliane Fürst (ed.), *Late Stalinist Russia: Society between
    Reconstruction and Reinvention*. New York: Routledge, pp. 29–37.

5   Fraser, E. L. (2000), 'Masculinity and the sexual politics of self and other
    in Soviet political cartoons, 1945–1955'. MA thesis, University of British
    Columbia.

6   For example, in the 1949 musical 'Kubanskie kazaki' (The Kuban Cossacks),
    discussed in Healey, D. (2008), '"Untraditional Sex" and the "Simple
    Russian": Nostalgia for Soviet innocence in the polemics of Dilia Enikeeva',
    in T. Lahusen and P. H. Solomon, Jr. (eds), *What Is Soviet Now? Identities,
    Legacies, Memories*. Berlin: Lit Verlag, pp. 184–5.

7   Kozin served 5 years in Magadan in the Far East; Savchenko, B. (2001), *Vadim
    Kozin*. Smolensk: Rusich.

8   On living standards and hygiene, see Filtzer, D. (2010), *The Hazards of
    Urban Life in Late Stalinist Russia: Health, Hygiene, and Living Standards,
    1943–1953*. Cambridge: Cambridge University Press; and Pollock, E. (2010),
    'Real men go to the Banya: Postwar Soviet masculinities and the bathhouse',
    Kritika: Explorations in Russian and Eurasian History, 11(1), 47–76.

9   Healey, D. (1999), 'Moscow', in D. Higgs (ed.), *Queer Sites: Gay Urban
    Histories since 1600*. London: Routledge, pp. 38–9, 51–2, 54, 56. The statistics
    on convictions for 1950 are discussed at ibid., 51. For trials of homosexuals in
    the Soviet countryside in the 1950s, see Healey, D. (2012), 'Comrades, queers,
    and "Oddballs": Sodomy, masculinity, and gendered violence in Leningrad
    province of the 1950s', *Journal of the History of Sexuality*, 21(3), 496–522.

10 On arrests and convictions during the period, see Healey, D. (2001),
    *Homosexual Desire in Revolutionary Russia: The Regulation of Sexual and
    Gender Dissent*. Chicago: University of Chicago Press, pp. 259–63.

11 An excellent guide to the period is Dobson, M. (2009), *Khrushchev's Cold
    Summer: Gulag Returnees, Crime, and the Fate of Reform after Stalin*. Ithaca,
    NY: Cornell University Press; on gender policies, see Ilic, M., S. E. Reid
    and L. Attwood (eds) (2004), *Women in the Khrushchev Era*. Basingstoke:
    Palgrave Macmillan. On private life, see Field, D. A. (2007), *Private Life and
    Communist Morality in Khrushchev's Russia*. New York, Bern and Berlin:
    Peter Lang; and Siegelbaum, L. H. (ed.) (2006a), *Borders of Socialism: Private
    Spheres of Soviet Russia*. New York: Palgrave Macmillan.

12 Dobson (2009), especially chs 4–6.

13 State Archives of the Russian Federation (GARF) *fond* 9414, *opis'* 1, *delo*
    2888 conferences of Gulag medical workers in Kiev, Leningrad, Sverdlovsk
    and Irkutsk in late 1956; ibid., 9414/1/2894 conference of medical workers in
    Gulag prison colonies, Moscow 1958; ibid., 9414/1/2895 conference of penal

medical workers, Leningrad, 1959; ibid., 9414/1a/608 conference of penal camp directors, Moscow, May 1959.

14	The directive is mentioned in GARF 9414/1a/608, pp. 90–1, a speech by one colonel Kashintsev of the interior ministry's prison service, at a Moscow conference of penal camp directors, May 1959. Interior Ministry archives for the 1950s remain classified and the text of the directive is secret. I am indebted to Emily Johnson for discovering this document.

15	Healey (2001), p. 262; police entrapment, see Kozlovskii, V. (1986), *Argo Russkoi Gomoseksual'noi Subkul'tury: Materialy k Izucheniiu*. Benson: Chalidze Publications, pp. 196–9; 'G'. 'The Secret Life of Moscow', *Christopher Street*, June (1980), pp. 15–21. For a trial of two middle-aged men, caught masturbating in a Moscow toilet in the early 1960s, see Feifer, G. (1964), *Justice in Moscow*. London: The Bodley Head, pp. 207–8.

16	On Kozin's 1959 arrest see Boris Savchenko's (2005) introduction to Vadim Kozin, *Prokliatoe Iskusstvo*. Moscow: Vagrius, p. 18.

17	GARF 9414/1/2896/144-144 ob.: correspondence arguing for criminalization of lesbianism, May 1956. On the psychiatric approaches, see Healey (2001), pp. 240–4.

18	Gessen, M. (1994), *The Rights of Lesbians and Gay Men in the Russian Federation*. San Francisco: International Gay and Lesbian Human Rights Commission, pp. 17–18; Healey (2001), p. 244; Sviadoshch, A. M. (1974), *Zhenskaia Seksopatologiia*. Moscow: Meditsina, pp. 165–7.

19	There is still no comprehensive history of Soviet 'psychiatric abuse'; on what is known, see Healey (forthcoming), 'Russian and Soviet Forensic Psychiatry: Troubled and Troubling', *International Journal of Law and Psychiatry*.

20	Kirsanov, V. (2005), *69. Russkie Gei, Lesbiianki, Biseksualy i Transseksualy*. Tver': Ganimed, pp. 296–302.

21	Ibid., p. 302, referring to opinions in Ol'ga Zhuk (1998), *Russkie Amazonki: Istoriia Lesbiiskoi Subkul'tury v Rossii XX vek*. Moscow: Glagol. 'Lev Margaritovich' is a male name, adopted by Ranevskaia's female character after a psychological shock – her abandonment by a lover. The middle name or patronymic 'Margaritovich' (Son-of-Margaret) troubles Russian gender expectations because patronymics are conventionally formed from father's names: Margaritovich is a queer, impossible, patronymic.

22	Kirsanov (2005), pp. 312–22. For translations of Barkova's poems see Kelly, C. (1999), 'Anna Barkova (1901–1976)', in C. D. Tomei (ed.), *Russian Women Writers*. New York: Garland Publishing, pp. 943–56; Vilensky, S. (2001), *Til My Tale Is Told: Women's Memoirs of the Gulag*. London: Virago, pp. 213–20.

23	For statistics see Volodin, A. (1957), *Moskva: Sputnik Turista*. Moscow: Moskovskii rabochii, p. 15; Mawdsley, E. (1991), *Blue Guide: Moscow and Leningrad*. London: A. & C. Black, p. 25. Car ownership: Siegelbaum, L. H. (2006b), 'Cars, cars and more cars: The Faustian bargain of the Brezhnev era', in Lewis H. Siegelbaum (ed.), *Borders of Socialism: Private Spheres of Soviet Russia*. New York: Palgrave Macmillan.

24	For speculation, from a gay Soviet observer, that single homosexuals could buy cooperative flats in Moscow towards the end of the 1970s, see Anon (1980),

'International: Extrait *de Labour Focus on Eastern Europe* (publié à Londres) "Being Gay in Moscou [Sic]"', *Masques: revue des homosexualités*, 5 (Summer), 59–62, at 60; for examples of single gay men owning their own flats from the same period, see 'G'. 'The secret life of Moscow', pp. 18–20.

25 Anon (1980), p. 60.

26 On the origins of the internal passport and registration system, see Shearer, D. R. (2009), *Policing Stalin's Socialism: Repression and Social Order in the Soviet Union, 1924–1953*. New Haven: Yale University Press.

27 On the attraction to Moscow, see 'G'. 'The secret life of Moscow', pp. 20–1.

28 I base these claims on personal observation among friends and contacts in Russia, and on the confidential autobiographies of gay male and lesbian asylum claimants passed to me in the capacity of expert witness. For late Soviet divorce rates, see Juviler, P. H. (1988), 'Cell mutation in Soviet society: The family', in T. L. Thompson and R. Sheldon (eds), *Soviet Society and Culture: Essays in Honor of Vera S. Dunham*. Boulder: Westview Press, pp. 42–3.

29 'G'. 'The secret life of Moscow', pp. 18–20; Dymov, A. (1980), 'Document: Les Homosexuels Russes Coincés Entre La Faucille Et Le Marteau: Homo Sovieticus', *Lui*, fevrier, 92–122, at 104.

30 Healey (2001), pp. 21–49; Healey (1999), pp. 43–9.

31 The 'circuit' undoubtedly varied historically, and seasonally (although one should not discount the Russian hardiness in winter), and the following description relies on a range of sources including 'G,' 'The secret life of Moscow'; Gessen, M. (1990), 'We have no sex: Soviet gays and aids in the era of Glasnost', *Outlook*, 3(1), 42–54, esp. pp. 46–7; Kozlovskii (1986); Dymov (1980), p. 94. The street and landmark names in this section are those in use before 1991 and many have since changed.

32 'Avenue of Sluts', 'Boulevard of Young Gifts', 'Homodrome' (after Hippodrome, racetrack), 'The Zoo', 'Club of Free Emotions', 'Place Pigalle', and 'The Stroke' were some popular labels for the Bolshoi Theatre square; see Kozlovskii (1986), pp. 60, 73.

33 Healey (2001), pp. 216, 339n. 36.

34 Rumours: Anon (1980), p. 59; Dymov (1980), p. 114.

35 The number of convictions for sodomy in the Russian Republic fell within the range of 773 and 883 during the 1970s; Healey (2001), p. 262.

36 The Olympics clean-up is briefly described in 'G'. 'The secret life of Moscow', pp. 15–16.

37 Ibid., p. 16. Side streets nearer the Bolshoi Theatre and also harboured the 'Sadko' and the 'Artistic' cafes that attracted a gay crowd in the late 1970s and early 1980s.

38 Healey (1999), pp. 45, 52; Pollock (2010).

39 Reeves, T. (1973), 'Red & Gay: Oppression East and West', *Fag Rag*, 6 (Fall), 3–6, see 5–6.

40 I am grateful to Viktor Oboin, who took me on a tour of these facilities – or their sites, since the Gogol' Boulevard toilets had long since collapsed, in the

summer of 2000. On Gogol's sexuality, see, Karlinsky, S. (1976), *The Sexual Labyrinth of Nikolai Gogol*. Cambridge, MA: Harvard University Press.

41 Siegelbaum (2006b), p. 96, discusses only heterosexual trysts, but suggestively depicts the Soviet car owner's world as solidly homosocial, and therefore, in my view, not without queer opportunities.

42 Kozlovskii (1986), pp. 6–14.

43 See Healey, D. (2002), 'The disappearance of the Russian Queen, or how the Soviet closet was born', in B. Evans Clements, R. Friedman and D. Healey (eds), *Russian Masculinities in History and Culture*. Basingstoke: Palgrave; Healey, 'Comrades, Queers, and "Oddballs"'.

44 Dymov (1980), p. 94; see also Kozlovskii (1986), p. 18.

45 Gessen (1990) reports such views in an article about Soviet gay life at the end of the 1980s, pp. 46–7.

46 For an argument that 'community' in the Western sense was impossible, see Schluter, D. (2002), *Gay Life in the Former USSR: Fraternity without Community*. New York: Routledge.

47 Kozlovskii (1986), p. 17.

48 Ibid. Appeals to Freudian theory and historical figures, see e.g. Healey (2001), p. 71.

49 'G'. The Secret Life of Moscow', p. 17.

50 Reeves (1973), p. 3.

51 Dymov (1990), p. 114.

52 Reeves (1973), p. 6; 'G'. 'The secret life of Moscow', p. 20; Anon (1980); Dymov (1990), p. 104; Schrijvers, J., A. Hyvönen and R. Härkönen (1984), 'Les Gais De Leningrad', *Gai Pied Hebdo*, 110(10–16 mars), 22–5, at e.g. pp. 24–5.

53 The clearest statements were two Soviet gay 'manifestos': Leningrad's Yury Trifonov's 1977 open letter to Soviet authorities, ignored in Russia but published in the Western gay press; and Moscow's Evgeny Kharitonov's 'Leaflet', celebrating 'our lightweight floral species with our pollen flying who knows where'. See both texts in Moss, K. (ed.) (1996), *Out of the Blue: Russia's Hidden Gay Literature*. San Francisco: Gay Sunshine Press, pp. 224–5, 230–2.

54 Anon (1980), p. 60.

55 For example, a 'Gay Laboratory' in Leningrad operated in 1983–84, and smuggled its manifesto and other materials out to Amsterdam via gay members of the Dutch Communist Party; see Schrijvers, Hyvönen, and Härkönen (1984), 'Les Gais De Leningrad'; note also Reeves (1973).

56 'G'. 'The secret life of Moscow', p. 22.

57 Kirsanov (2005), pp. 396–7.

58 Ibid., pp. 410–12.

59 Ibid., p. 418.

60 For a discussion of Leningrad's alienated underground scenes, see Yurchak, A. (2006), *Everything Was Forever, until It Was No More: The Last Soviet Generation*. Princeton: Princeton University Press.

61 On medical care for intersex patients in the 1920s–30s in Russia, see Healey, D. (2009), *Bolshevik Sexual Forensics: Diagnosing Disorder in the Clinic and Courtroom, 1917–1939*. DeKalb.: Northern Illinois University Press, pp. 134–58; on Soviet sex changes in the 1920s, see Healey (2001), pp. 165–70.

62 Golubeva, I. V. (1980), *Germafroditizm (Klinika, Diagnostika, Lechenie)*. Moscow: Meditsina, pp. 100–1.

63 Ibid., pp. 105–7, 148–50 (quote at 102); Belkin, A. I. (2000), *Tret'ii Pol*. Moscow: Olimp.

64 Kon, I. S. (1997), *Seksual'naia Kul'tura v Rossii: Klubnichka na Berezke*. Moscow: OGI, p. 183.

65 Milanov, N. O., R. T. Adamian and G. I. Kozlov (1999), *Korrektsiia Pola pri Transseksualizme*. Moscow: Kalinkin i K., pp. 15–17, 125–34.

66 Tuller, D. (1996), *Cracks in the Iron Closet: Travels in Gay & Lesbian Russia*. Boston: Faber & Faber, pp. 155–67; Krauze, O. (1994), 'Vashi Pis'ma', *Gay, Slaviane!*, 2, 90.

67 For the delayed sexual revolution, see Borenstein, E. (2008), *Overkill: Sex and Violence in Contemporary Russian Popular Culture*. Ithaca, NY: Cornell University Press; on the queer dimensions, see e.g. Baer, B. J. (2009), *Other Russias: Homosexuality and the Crisis of Post-Soviet Identity*. New York: Palgrave Macmillan. On AIDS in the Soviet press, Healey, D. (18 March 1989), 'Can glasnost cope with aids?', *The Pink Paper* (London), p. 2; Healey, D. (1992), 'Pros & Cons with professor Kon: Russia's pre-eminent sexologist dissects Russia's emerging Lesbian and gay movement', *Xtra!* (Toronto), July, pp. 8–9.

68 14 issues of *Tema* appeared between 1989 and 1993; on its founding editors and the ASM, see Kirsanov (2005), pp. 412–13, 476–9; Dorf, Julie (1990), 'On the theme: Talking with the editor of the Soviet Union's first Lesbian and gay newspaper', *Outlook*, 1, 55–9.

69 Kirsanov (2005), pp. 479–83; Gasparian, A. (24 September 1991), 'Gosudarstvu net mesto v posteliakh svoikh grazhdan', *Moskovskii komsomolets*, 182, 1.

70 Wockner, R. (30 August 1991), 'Heroes of the USSR: Soviet gays and Lesbians fight coup' *Capital Gay*, 509, 3.

71 Kirsanov (2005), p. 483, makes this point.

72 Gessen (1994). Some reformers were queer but hidden; one middle-ranking member of the Yeltsin team who later came out was journalist Andrei Cherkizov (1954–2007); however, his influence on the repeal of the anti-sodomy law was apparently minimal; see Kirsanov, V. (2007), *+31. Russkie Gei, Lesbiianki, Biseksualy i Transseksualy*. Moscow: Kvir, pp. 119–24.

73 On the 1997 criminal code's flaws, see Healey (2001), pp. 249–50; on the 2002 debate over re-criminalization, see Healey (2008).

74 Kirsanov (2005), pp. 455–60; Kirsanov (2007), pp. 106–12. *Adel'fe*, Moscow, Mila Ugol'nikova (ed.), and Tat'iana Ivanova (1996–), 5 issues. Other Moscow lesbian publications include *Ostrov* (1999–2004), 19 issues; *Sofa Safo* (2003), 2 issues; and *Labris* (2004–05), 5 issues (see http://az.gay.ru/books/index_magazines.html, last accessed 15 January 2012).

75   On Triangle see, Legendre, P. (1997), *V Poiskakh Sebia: Polozhenie Geev i Lesbiianok v Sovremennoi Rossii*. Moscow: Charities Aid Foundation, p. 23; conference: Healey, D. (1996), 'Russky "Comrades" Nix commies in election', *Xtra!*, 304 (20 June), 55.

76   Oboin named his archive GenderDok; the newsletter was *Zerkalo*, 'The Mirror' (18 issues, 1995–99); on GenderDok see also Legendre (1997), pp. 23–4.

77   Gusiatinskaia, E. (ed.) (2006), *Antologiia Lesbiiskoi Prozy*. Tver': Kolonna Publications; Kirsanov (2005), pp. 396–400.

78   On the gay men's magazines of the 1990s, see Healey, D. (2010), 'Active, passive, and Russian: The national idea in gay men's Pornography', *Russian Review*, 69(2), 210–30, esp. 215–17.

79   For a resume of Russian homophobia in the 1990s, see Oboin, V. 'Gomofobiia v Sovremennoi Rossii: Vse Ottenki Chernogo', in Viktor Oboin (ed.), *Gomofobiia v Sovremennoi Rossi 1993-2001 g.g. Dokumenty, Fakty*. Moscow: The author.

80   Healey (2010), p. 212.

81   See http://www.gayrussia.eu/gayprides/moscow/ (consulted 16 January 2012).

82   See photo no. 19 from the Bolotnaya Sq. demonstration of 10 December 2011, at http://www.novayagazeta.ru/photos/49997.html (consulted 16 January 2012).

Further reading

Baer, B. J. (2009), *Other Russias: Homosexuality and the Crisis of Post-Soviet Identity*. New York: Palgrave Macmillan.

Essig, L. (1999), *Queer in Russia: A Story of Sex, Self and the Other*. Durham and London: Duke University Press.

"G" [Harlow Robinson] (1980), 'The secret life of Moscow', *Christopher Street*, 15–21 June; reprinted in M. Denneny et al. (eds) (1983), *The Christopher Street Reader*. New York: Coward McCann; Wideview/Perigree, pp. 199–206.

Gessen, M. (1994), *The Rights of Lesbians and Gay Men in the Russian Federation*. San Francisco: International Gay and Lesbian Human Rights Commission.

Healey, D. (2001), *Homosexual Desire in Revolutionary Russia: The Regulation of Sexual and Gender Dissent*. Chicago: University of Chicago Press.

—(2008), '"Untraditional Sex" and the "Simple Russian": Nostalgia for Soviet innocence in the polemics of Dilia Enikeeva', in T. Lahusen and P. H. Solomon, Jr (eds), *What Is Soviet Now? Identities, Legacies, Memories*. Berlin: Lit Verlag, pp. 173–91.

—(2010), 'Active, passive, and Russian: The national idea in gay men's pornography', *Russian Review*, 69(2), 210–30.

Kelly, C. (1999), 'Anna Barkova (1901–1976)', in C. D. Tomei (ed.), *Russian Women Writers*. New York: Garland Publishing, pp. 943–56.

Kharitonov, Y. (1998), *Under House Arrest*. London: Serpent's Tail.

Kon, I. S. (1995), *The Sexual Revolution in Russia*. New York: Free Press.

Moss, K. (ed.) (1996), *Out of the Blue: Russia's Hidden Gay Literature*. San Francisco: Gay Sunshine Press.

Schluter, D. (2002), *Gay Life in the Former USSR: Fraternity without Community*. New York: Routledge.

Stella, F. (2013), 'Queer space, pride, and shame in Moscow', *Slavic Review*, 72(3), 458–80.

Tuller, D. (1996), *Cracks in the Iron Closet: Travels in Gay & Lesbian Russia*. Boston and London: Faber & Faber.

Zhuk, O. (1994), 'The lesbian subculture: The historical roots of lesbianism in the former USSR', in A. Posadskaya (ed.), *Women in Russia: A New Era in Russian Feminism*. London: Verso.

6

Queer Amsterdam 1945–2010

Gert Hekma

Foreplay and context

World War II with the German occupation (1940–45) was a definite break in Dutch history. But this was not so much the case for homosexuals. The general picture is that discrimination was common before, during and after the war and that, in fact, the 1950s had the highest numbers of prosecutions for gay-related sex crimes. But in the post-war years things started to change and there were signs of greater acceptance. In 1946, some courageous men from Amsterdam restarted the homosexual rights movement. They launched a monthly journal in January 1940 just before the occupation but had to stop in its wake on 15 May. They were not the first to start such a movement. In 1912, a chapter of the German WHK (Wissenschaftliches Humanitäres-Komittee or Scientific Humanitarian Committee) was formed; it was called the *Nederlandsch Humanitair Wetenschappelijk Komitee* (Dutch Humanitarian Scientific Committee, NWHK). This was mainly the work of Jacob Anton Schorer (1866–1957) of The Hague though he halted his endeavour in 1940. After the occupation, a younger generation led by Nico Engelschman (1913–88) took over. The new organization was called *Shakespeare Club* and soon changed its name to *Cultuur en Ontspannings Centrum* (Centre for Culture and Recreation, COC). The *NWHK* was originally just a desk and an irregular newsletter with a library in Schorer's house; the COC was a membership organization with an office that organized lectures and social meetings. It published a magazine and founded the *International Committee for Sexual Equality* (ICSE). The Dutch homosexual rights movement has now existed for a century and has had its seat in Amsterdam since 1946. The focus of this chapter, though, is Amsterdam's rise to international fame as a gay and sex capital in the 1960s and 1970s and its slow demise afterwards, while at the same time contesting the idea of the city as a gay utopia. Typically, when homosexuality is discussed in Holland, it nearly always concerns men. And indeed, the specific anti-homosexual article 248bis (1911–71) was concerned 99 per cent of the time with males.[1] In 2007, 96 per cent of anti-gay violence cases reported to the Amsterdam police concerned men.[2] As such the focus of this chapter is more on men than women. We find through the examination of interviews, newspapers, archives and secondary literature that Amsterdam has a reputation as one of the most sexually liberated cities for gay men in particular; in this chapter it is argued that this positive (self) evaluation needs nuancing. Too many problems with straight norms, discrimination and invisibility still haunt this idea of the city being a 'gay and lesbian Mecca'.[3]

Social situation

The discrimination homosexuals faced in the post-war years was manifold. Family, friends and colleagues would often reject homosexuals. This was related to religious beliefs that made homosex a sin unmentionable among Christians. At the same time, it was seen as a medical pathology and criminal offence. The silencing of queer issues may have been advantageous because it meant that the public perception of homosexuality among straight people remained low. The rejection of gay men was stronger than of that of lesbians for three reasons. The first issue was anal sex, the second, effeminacy and the third, the seduction of adolescents. Most insults towards gay people turned on the first two themes with variations of slurs from 'bottom' and 'brown' to 'sissy' and 'nelly'. The third reproach related to relationships between adults and minors of the same sex. In 1911, the Netherlands was the first country to include an article in the criminal law (248bis) that created a different age of consent for homo- and heterosexual relations, 21 and 16 years, respectively. It was based on the idea that since homosexuals did not reproduce they had to recruit youngsters to fill their ranks.[4] This legal discrimination was the reason behind Schorer's decision to start the *NWHK*. Another legal article that affected homosexuals was the one about public indecency. It was not only the ways of having sex that were scrutinized, but also certain ways of being. From the late nineteenth century, the Netherlands witnessed, alongside other Western European countries, a debate about the cause of homosexuality. Around 1900, Amsterdam physicians Arnold Aletrino and Lucien von Römer followed German Karl Ulrichs in describing homosexuality as a natural variation with homosexuals, therefore needing equal rights. Their argument was taken up by medical people who proposed that 'sexual inversion' might be an innate, but pathological condition. So homosexuality was at that time in the Netherlands a sin, crime and disease. It was nothing to be proud of and was often a source of shame and difficulty for the men and women themselves and their families and friends.

The situation worsened after the introduction of new sex laws in 1911,[5] strongly promoted by new Christian parties that participated in the government of the Netherlands from the World War I until 1994. From the 1930s on, medical therapies – including castration for 'sex criminals' – strengthened the social rejection homosexuals faced. This pressure continued to grow until the 1950s. Not only had the number of cases for sex with minors been rising, so too had public indecency. Moreover, municipalities introduced rules that made it illegal to remain for longer than 5 minutes in a public toilet. Amsterdam did so in 1955. But growing sexual repression meant that social resistance mounted.

Gay sex at a breaking point

The homosexual scene had very different forms before the 1960s sexual revolution.[6] In the 1930s, Amsterdam had perhaps a dozen bars catering to gays and lesbians. These did not operate simultaneously. They were of two types: more exclusively homosexual ones and mixed ones in the Red Light District where queers hung out with prostitutes and their clients. Both were often owned or run by lesbians who had made money in the sex industry. The bars were closely watched by the vice squad who visited known venues regularly.[7] Although there was no law forbidding queer bars, the police used its discretionary power. Bar owners protected themselves in different ways against inspections. They had doormen who warned against arrival of 'Russen' (Russians, slang for officers) and 'uilen' (owls, heterosexuals). They also saw to it that clients didn't do anything reproachable (same-sex kissing, intimacy or dancing most obviously). Controlling police officers relied on the notion that gay men were effeminate and lesbians mannish both in clothing and behaviour. So a woman with short hair, drinking gin and smoking cigars was classified as lesbian.

The main part of the gay scene, however, was an extensive public sex circuit in which not only homosexuals but also heterosexuals participated. The delineation of identities was not so embedded in those times. The sexual border traffic was made possible because many young straight men who wanted sex had very few options as women were married and were meant to stay faithful, while the unmarried were meant to keep their virginity. Prostitutes were for many males simply too expensive. Their only means of sexual release was to do it with other, often homosexual men, for money or for free. Some may have paid for the more effeminate men who worked as hustlers. My respondents mentioned an older queen who still worked from his home in the 1950s as a whore in the Red Light District, with rouge, powder and female attire, and attracting a male heterosexual clientele. Gays found it a mystery how they could make money. In other cases, young straight or questioning men derived some economic advantage from having sex with homosexuals – a bed to sleep in, drinks or food, a present or money as in other European cities. Sexual roles were clearly separated in unofficial ideology: real 'straight' men had 'active' (fucker, sucked) and 'unmasculine' gay men 'passive' roles (fucked, sucker). This terminology had less to do with what gay or straight and active or passive meant but more with what was seen as disgusting in terms of transgression of gender roles.

The main place for public sex was in or near one of the city's 50 urinals or dozen parks that witnessed sexual activity. Most cottages were in the city centre and men went from one to the other, making tours to find sex partners. This was the pivotal location of sexual border traffic between straight and gay. It was dangerous both because of police and popular sentiment and also very effective because, as a respondent said, 'there you see first what you elsewhere see last'. Already in the late nineteenth century, public toilets had been designed with little success in such a way as to prevent gay sex: lamps, separated urinals, open space at the top and bottom of cubicle walls so the police could see from the outside what happened within.[8] Swimming pools were less known for homosex and gay saunas developed only in the 1960s. As an urban street culture, queer sex could begin at any place where men met: in 'normal' bars and cinemas, in front of shop windows, at newspaper stalls, in train stations, on markets and fairs. Male hustlers could be found in the centre on Rembrandtplein and Singel until the 1970s, and until 2000 in Central Station. Ganymedes (male prostitutes) and clients could consummate sex not only at the customer's home but also in dark alleys, urinals, parks or 'one hour'-hotels in the Red Light District (where people could rent a room for an hour to have sex). In other words, gay life was until the 1960s part of public life. Notwithstanding social taboos and its public nature, this kind of contact was widespread from at least the late seventeenth century until the late 1970s when it slowly disappeared in supposedly more tolerant times. It moved to semi-public spaces – dark rooms and saunas – and out of the city to highway stops.[9]

The rise of a gay capital

After the war another more respectable scene developed in exclusively gay bars and discos. They rarely catered to lesbian women and straight people. These bars set a new trend of gay men getting into a subculture hidden behind closed doors. The numbers of these bars and discos grew quickly. They were soon left alone by the vice squad and existed for extended periods of time. They also became more fashionable. Bars have always been quite small in Amsterdam because of the architecture of the city but both discos *DOK* and *COC*'s *Schakel* (meaning link) that were founded in 1952 were grandiose by comparison. Soon they attracted great numbers of male homosexuals, not only from Holland but also from England, Germany, France, Belgium and beyond – including US soldiers who were stationed in

Germany. The rise of the gay scene in the 1950s and 1960s paralleled what happened with the Red Light District: growth and internationalization. Along with the bars and discos, hotels started to specialize in gay tourism. The movement from street to bar life was stimulated by the police who liked it better when gays were hidden away in their own subculture instead of hanging around on streets having sex and making trouble with straight men. It was in this period that it became forbidden to stay longer than 5 minutes in a urinal.

The change from street to bar life had another important cause. Gays had been defined as sissies: men not only with same-sex interests but also with an inverted, feminine gender identity. In the 1860s, Ulrichs' had summarized his theory of an innate homosexuality and psychic hermaphroditism for gay men as 'female souls in a male body', with lesbians being 'male souls in a female body'. Effeminate homosexual men and masculine dykes did not look for sex with their equals, but with their opposites: 'real' straight men and women who were not gender-inverted. As in heterosexual relations, the idea reigned that only opposites could be sexually attracted to each other. 'Dykes with dykes' was perceived as incompatible and wouldn't work sexually. In Dutch, queens and trade were *nicht* (sissy, literally niece) and *tule* (tulle, probably referring to the 'beauty' of straight youth). *Butch-femme* had no clear equivalent in Dutch. A *butch* was a *pot* (meaning pot or jar) with some variations, and for *butch-femme*, generally, binaries were applied: brother-sister, boy-girl, trouser-skirt, sling-handbag.[10] Other oppositions like those of class, age or ethnicity could replace or be added to gender differences in sexual relations. What straight people specifically attributed to gay men, effeminacy and an interest in straight men, was theory and practice until the 1950s, for gay and straight men as for psychiatrists. Just before the war a collection of 35 stories of homosexual men and women was published – *De Homosexueelen* – in which homosexuals discussed these 'stereotypes' having purchase in their real lives. Lesbians presented themselves as tomboys with an interest in rough play while male homosexuals expressed a strong dislike for sports like football.[11]

Queens of the 1950s were still effeminate and Paris was for many of them epitome of a culture of elegance. They wore French styles of dress, listened to continental music like French *chansons* and German and Dutch *Schlagers* and danced Viennese style. Dandies were their preferred subcultural icons, not cowboys. But this image and iconography would soon be superseded by a new generation from the late 1950s onwards who saw queens as relics of a repressive past. The new style was decidedly American: blue jeans, lumberjack shirts or white Ts, short hair, pop music and wild dancing, and icons like James Dean. Beer replaced sherry and wine as favourite drinks. And most importantly, there emerged on the scene new 'masculine' gay men who were interested sexually in each other and no longer searched for heteros. They could not understand how their predecessors had desired straight men and cultivated a feminine style.

The change of attitudes from a system of sissies looking for straight guys to gay men deliberately pursuing each other had important consequences for sexual comparisons. The homosexuality of past times was seen as similar to prostitution: situational contacts between unequals with monetary transactions. The new gay men often had more equal relations that resembled marriage. They rose in status from whorish to marriageable and respectable. This change in perception strongly influenced psychiatrists who compared homosexuality in the early 1950s with sex-work and shit (referring to anal sex) and thought sissies seduced boys into homosexual pleasures. A decade later, exactly the same people had changed over to ideas of homophile identities and 'fixed friendships' – with sex, boys and money left out. From sodomy, pederasty and whoring, homosex had finally become acceptable as homophilia (a popular word in post-war Holland), more a special identity than an abject practice. It meant an end to public sexual border traffic and the rise of a privatized gay commercial scene that created safety inside but not beyond its walls.

Interest in trade had been widespread among homosexuals, and also in adolescents. Paedophiles belonged to the gay world as COC iconography demonstrates: many illustrations of its journal *Vriendschap* (Friendship) showcase adolescents under 21 years. Youngsters could easily be found in streets, around urinals and in parks, but entering gay bars was forbidden to them. They had sex with older gay men for money, as a pastime or as a way of experimenting with homosexuality. For various reasons many young men stopped having gay sex in the 1950s and 1960s: because girls were less pressured to remain chaste (some were even able to acquire contraceptives to prevent pregnancy) and also because a greater although negative awareness of homosexuality made it less attractive for adolescents who needed to be seen as hetero and masculine. Youth became less available and more straight. Gay men were forced into each other's arms where they had previously felt uncomfortable. From the 1960s on, relations between adult men became the dominant and desired form of same-sexual pleasure.

Men with paedophile interests still referred to classical times when such relations were highly regarded. Greek and Roman antiquity remained a reference point for the homosexual movement until the 1950s. The renowned Dutch turn-of-the-century author Louis Couperus strongly contributed to this reputation with his classical novels on emperors, Alexander the Great and Elagabalus. This celebration of male eros ended, mainly because sexual equality became the norm and gay men now rather desired each other than the straight or undefined men and youth of the past. Paedophiles were increasingly differentiated from homosexual men, and a clearer separation developed between love for adult men and male youth. The two main paedophile spokesmen became Frits Bernard and Edward Brongersma. They worked for the COC but were sidelined in 1963 although Brongersma continued to lobby as a Labour senator for the repeal of article 248bis, which was finally realized in 1971. Paedophiles saw some success in the 1970s in the slipstream of the gay and lesbian movement. Some psychiatrists, journalists, politicians and police officers supported their cause; since the 1980s, however, paedophilia has been increasingly demonized in Holland.

It wasn't just paedophiles that emerged as a special group in the post-war period. In the early 1950s, the bar of *Hotel Tiemersma* in the Red Light District's Warmoesstraat developed into the first leather venue with the city's first dark room. It meant the beginning of serious masculinization of homosexuals in Amsterdam. In 1965, the *Argos* opened and in 1970 the *LL* bar that soon organized highly appreciated monthly leather parties. Also in 1970, *Motor Sportclub Amsterdam* (*MSA*) became the organization for kinky queers.[12] At the other end of the gender spectrum, *COC* and *DOK* had organized drag parties and fashion designers came to gay bars in spectacular female clothing.[13] In 1961, these shows became a regular feature for mainly straight audiences in the bar *Madame Arthur*.[14]

The sexual revolution

The same people who started the first drag bar also initiated in 1959 the *Fiacre*, modelled after a stylish Paris café of the same name. It would become the great fashionable place of the sixties where many gay artists came to socialize and unwind. The amazing development was the rising number of bars. Even more surprising was the sudden openness of gay men many of whom worked in the art scene and had no longer any intention to hide. Their visibility in ballet, theatre, literature and soon also on TV meant a major breakthrough for public queer live.

This revolution ran parallel to changes in traditional institutions that had been essential in oppressing homosexuality: religion, psychiatry, law, popular opinion. In the 1950s, catholic and protestant psychiatrists met gay clients and started to change their views from rejection to acceptance. The Catholic Church established a social care institution *Open Door* in the heart of Amsterdam where priests, psychiatrists and social workers met 'real life' homosexuals. A protestant psychiatrist studied homosexuals and found seduction played no role in their sexual development.[15] In many ways, the transformation of gay identification from feminine to more masculine roles while relations began to look less like prostitution and more like marriage stimulated a change of view among psychiatrists. Explanations shifted: it was no longer seduction of youth but a deep, unchangeable desire that was the cause of homosexuality. Psychiatrists in turn influenced clergy to adapt their views. Bishops, priests and parsons started to accept the homosexual, although not his sexual practices. These professionals changed course from condemning and castrating to accepting homosexuals.[16] In the late 1960s, public opinion began to shift from negative to positive, paving the way for the abolition of article 248bis in 1971. In 10 years, homosexuality had gone from sin, crime and disease to something close to normal, from an abject practice to a more accepted way of being.

The COC was a major player in these transformations. It changed from an underground organization of men who used pseudonyms to one that participated in public culture and started a dialogue with other groups. In 1965, it founded a journal *Dialoog*, a title that indicated its intention to form a bridge between gay and straight – now in political and no longer in sexual terms.[17] Gay author Gerard Reve became one of its editors. He was already well known but now made headlines because of the 'donkey' court case. In an article in *Dialoog* he expressed his belief that Jesus would return to earth as a donkey that he would fuck out of love and faith. An orthodox protestant MP brought him to court and the case went all the way up to High Court. He was judged not to be guilty of blasphemy: it was, the court said, his private way of believing.[18] Reve was extremely important for homosexual emancipation and beyond because his work also included themes of polyamory and kinky sex. COC's Christian members were critical of Reve's pronouncements but like most other Dutch people they were astounded by the quick and radical changes. In 1965, Reve's work was still unacceptable but in 1968, it became fashionable despite this bestial blasphemy.[19]

In the sexual revolutionary years from 1965 to 1970, Amsterdam's streets witnessed dramatic changes. In 1965, a radical anarchist *Provo* movement squatted houses for the homeless, was against polluting cars and in favour of public transport, and had a 'white bicycle', a 'white women' and a 'white homophile plan'. This meant that bicycles should be freely available and that women and homosexuals should have equal rights.[20] In the first issue of its journal *Provo*, an activist declared himself in favour of 'complete amoral promiscuity'. Though *Provo* suspended its activities in 1967,[21] it set an example for other groups in Amsterdam and elsewhere. Protests started to fill the streets with demonstrations against nuclear weapons, Vietnam War and fascist or colonial regimes. Young artists protested against a fossilized system, radical feminists declared lesbianism to be a political choice against patriarchy, artists created nude shows and published explicit erotic journals. More students than ever started studying and fought for democratization. Squatting became a major housing policy for the alternative scene and several lesbian and queer communal households were set up.

Soon feminists started their own journals, printing and publishing houses, bookshops and bars in which lesbians actively participated. They had leading positions in feminist organizations, struggles for abortion and sex-worker rights, women's studies and cultural endeavours. Many opted for feminist rather than gay activities and often remained invisible as lesbians. The first lesbian movements of the 1970s criticized homophobia of feminists and sexism of gays, but after that decade many participants looked to feminist causes rather than specifically lesbian and gay issues. After a short flowering of lesbian sexual visibility in women's festivals in the famous art house Milky Way (1977–79) and in glossy *Diva* (1982–85), Amsterdam's lesbian life began to stagnate. Some bars and parties started in this period but it remained more difficult to organize lesbians than gay men in terms of this scene. The city had at most two or three lesbian bars in those decades compared with the dozens for gay men.

The gay scene grew from five bars in 1950 with eight new bars and two discos in 1953–57, one to two venues each year in the period 1961–67 and six in 1968 alone to some 30 locations in 1970. Among these new venues of the 1960s were three saunas and one exclusively lesbian bar *Tabu* that opened in 1969. Four mixed pubs were tended by lesbians, two of them already existing in 1950, the famous *Mandje* of Bet van Beeren (1927–83, 2008–present) and the *Monico* of Saar Heshof who herself kept the bar for 60 years (1941–2001). These mixed bars catered to *butches and femmes*, while the *Tabu* attracted an elegant middle-class lesbian public. In this period, only three venues went out of business and four changed owners – indicating that gay bars now had a longer lifecycle.[22] The authorities in the 1960s disliked the many tourists who flocked to Amsterdam for its gay life which was felt to be freer than elsewhere in Europe. The influx continued for many decades, though – and to the city's benefit.

The possibility to be openly gay together with the parallel abolition of religious, criminal and psychiatric discrimination was the great revolution of the 1960s and was an amazing step forward. The ease and eagerness with which many gay men acted upon it remains astonishing. The retreat of official anti-homosexual attitudes into hidden closets and of homosexuals from streets into private and semi-public spheres – also in terms of more acceptable clothing and behaviour in public – was simultaneous. This new 'integration' also made homosexuals increasingly invisible.

The COC may have been exemplary of these developments halfway through the 1960s, but its new and open leadership was soon overrun by a more radical student generation from 1967 on. They demanded social change as a precondition for homosexual integration. Since they were affected as 'minors' by article 248bis, they staged the first gay and lesbian demonstration in February 1969 on the steps of parliament in The Hague against this legal inequality. In 1970, they also organized the first demonstration in Amsterdam and in the late 1960s, they held same-sex 'dance actions' in straight discos. In the early 1970s, these student groups were surpassed by more radical movements that proposed separatism to discover their own culture and what it meant to be gay or lesbian before social integration could be developed. Starting in 1971, *Purple Mina*, *Purple September*, *Lesbian Nation* (the first Dutch lesbian movements), *Faggot Front* and *Red Faggots* mainly operated culturally with parties, bars, books, zines and music. In 1977, lesbians organized the first national demonstration in Amsterdam inspired by the Stonewall examples that developed into the *Pink Saturdays* celebrated to this day in June's final weekend. In less than 15 years, Amsterdam's gay and lesbian world had seen four generations of activists: closeted homophiles, homosexuals desiring personal integration, gays and lesbians looking for social integration and queer separatists. When this last generation stopped its activities with a faggot festival 'Real Men?' in 1980, their message lingered on but Amsterdam witnessed little radical activism thereafter.[23]

Gays and lesbians join social institutions

The new gay and lesbian generation paved the way for the march through the social institutions and for an influx of queer representations in the arts. The late 1970s and early 1980s saw many gay and lesbian caucuses developing in political parties, trade unions, universities, police and army, medical care and churches, and on stages queer plays were performed. Pacifist-socialist member Bob van Schijndel of the Amsterdam city council penned the first 'homo report' in 1982 and demanded more education in schools on homosexuality, protection for cruising queers, a stop to demolition of urinals, lesbian visibility, housing for singles, better care for the elderly, grants for gay and lesbian culture and a HomoMonument to remember the homosexual victims of World War II.

His requests had the following results. Sex education was left to the school's discretion, but the topic is rarely dealt with in a systematic way. It is not included in courses and anti-gay slurs in schools are not countered. The police started to protect cruising gay men but this has continued to be a controversial policy, and its application fleeting. One gay active tearoom that had been removed was reinstalled but had lost its sexual function like most others that remained in place. By 2000, urinal sex had become a relic of past times, while parks like *Vondelpark* and *Nieuwe Meer* (New Lake) continued to function as cruising grounds to this day. Lesbians remain largely invisible in the city. Housing is no longer a specific problem but care for the elderly has remained on the agenda. Cultural activities have been funded on a small scale. In 1987, the HomoMonument was inaugurated in the middle of the city and it has become the heart of queer activities.[24] After 30 years, the policy demands have only been partially realized. All political parties may say they are supportive of gay and lesbian policies, yet concrete results are meagre and financial investments low. The Dutch see sexuality as a private affair and rarely discuss it in terms of intimate citizenship.

When the AIDS epidemic broke out, city officials, health authorities, COC and the gay medical group that had started some years before, met and developed policies of care and prevention. In its first 10 years, the epidemic mainly struck gays, and the cooperation between the different parties has in general been beneficial for all concerned. No dark rooms or saunas were closed although health authorities wanted to do so, and prevention information specifically directed to gay men was distributed.[25] Gay and lesbian groups for example in the police and army contributed their share to changing policies in their institutions. It is only recently that 'company pride' groups started to cater to the interests of gay and lesbian personnel in private corporations.

Gay life after the sexual revolution

Since 1970, the gay scene has continued to develop but not to grow. The number of bars and discos remained relatively stable in the AIDS years although their locations changed. Kerkstraat had developed into a major gay street in the 1960s with bars, the main sauna and some hotels, but it was replaced in the 1980s by Regulierdwarsstraat that became the posh gay place. Amstel and Amstelstraat saw the development of a more popular gay scene where some pubs played Dutch music, while elsewhere Anglo-American pop set the tone. This district traditionally harboured some hustler bars of which only one now remains. The major new development was the rise of the leather scene just before the AIDS-epidemic around the Warmoesstraat and there are still half a dozen bars, a disco, a cinema, specialized hotels and – since the 1990s – two leather shops. In the 1980s, the *LL-bar* and its parties disappeared, but in the 1990s kinky parties and leather weekends became an important feature of Amsterdam. The leather scene diversified and added other fetishes such as rubber, skinhead and sports. Kinky bars organized sex parties for 'horsemen and knights', castigation, BDSM, only or no underwear. The sex club *Church* now caters to the diverse preferences of visitors in Kerkstraat.

Since 1990 two new discos *It* and *Roxy* attracted a mixed public with gay evenings, Love Balls, Pussy Lounges, kinky events, drag kings and a new set of drag queens who preferred to be described as gender transformation artists.[26] In 1999, *Roxy* burned down and in the same year the mayor temporarily closed *It* after the police found hard drugs on the premises. Some people see this as the beginning of the decline of gay Amsterdam because city authorities showed no understanding for the pivotal role of these places of gender extravagance and sexual transgression.

In 1998, Amsterdam held the *Gay Games*, which promised to be the grandest homosexual event in the city ever. Gays and lesbians were very welcome but any sexual explicit display was blocked by the organization: it was to be about friendship. Such events prefigured same-sex marriage, which may similarly be viewed as part of the desexualization of gay life. The following years would see all kinds of minor struggles about sex. A hotel with SM toys on location had to close and a leather shop had problems being licensed. The city shut down a hotel bar because it had no permission for its jack-off parties (which were a remnant of the fight against AIDS). The legal situation of dark rooms was discussed intermittently but they remained untouched by restrictive policies. Gay men's identities were worthy of acceptance, much less their sexual pastimes.

The new millennium: Gays, Muslims and straights

The decline of Amsterdam as a gay capital set in at the moment most people saw as the high point of emancipation: the opening of marriage to same-sex couples in a path-breaking move by the Netherlands government. It was the first country to do so. On 1 April 2001, the first marriages were celebrated in Amsterdam's City Hall. Both homo- and heterosexuals had the idea that this meant the end of the gay movement. The COC still saw a role for itself in emancipating the remaining pockets of orthodox Christians and Muslims (the first mainly outside, the last strongly represented inside the city) and exporting the Dutch message to nations opposed to homosexual rights.

The same year saw two other events that very much defined the next decade of gay politics. On the one hand, an imam wrote that Europeans were less than dogs and pigs because they allowed gay marriage. He said something similar in a TV programme about the rise of anti-gay violence that was mainly attributed to young Muslim men of Moroccan and Turkish descent. His negative remarks, half a year before 9/11, were widely discussed by politicians and in the media. Other imams followed suit saying that the Quran forbade homosexuality. These debates created an opposition of queer and Muslim. This has since been exploited by the radical right, first by Pim Fortuyn whose rise to fame as leader of this movement also took place in 2001. This gay dandy was the first to make homosexuality and the radical right compatible on the contemporary scene. He used his intimate knowledge of Moroccan men to say that he knew they were backward because he slept with them. And he denounced their anti-gay violence.[27] Fortuyn was murdered by an animal rights activist just before the elections of 2002 but his many straight successors on the right followed a similar logic of denouncing Muslims for their anti-gay attitudes: Ayaan Hirsi Ali, Marco Pastors, Rita Verdonk and Geert Wilders. This debate affected gay men deeply, many of whom found themselves going from left to right, while the COC elected a chair who was a close ally of Verdonk. The radical right expressed the idea that there were too many Muslims creating problems. The ethnic composition of the city indeed dramatically changed in the post-war period. From being largely white, it became a more mixed city with 25 per cent of the population being ethnic minorities in 1990 and 40 per cent in 2004. The most important groups of recent immigrants in Holland are of Moroccan, Surinamese, Turkish and Antillean origin, the first two being strongly represented in Amsterdam among 177 other nationalities. Now 60 per cent of those between 5 and 20 years belong to ethnic groups of non-Western origin.[28]

At the same time that the imam spoke out against homosexuals, a gay Arab bar was opened in Amsterdam showing that the purported opposition of homosexuality and Islam is deeply problematic. The ethnic transformation is visible in some gay bars and discos and certainly in the one Arab and one

Surinamese venue but this is less true in other parts of the scene. The gay movement is still by and large white. Since the 1980s, there have been ethnic gay and lesbian groups, first Surinamese and later Arab, Turkish, Muslim and racially mixed. Ethnic minority queers have to face the dichotomy that has been created between gay-friendly Dutch and gay-rejecting Muslims. Many queers from these groups like to go out but rarely to come out. Most local gay activists of colour are atypical recent immigrants. They followed a lover, sought asylum, studied here or came for the city's tolerant reputation. Second-generation New Dutch are rarely to be found among queer activists.[29]

Many Moroccan and Turkish political leaders spoke out in favour of homosexuals, and some like MPs Hirsi Ali and Ahmed Marcouch and Ahmed Aboutaleb (now mayor of Rotterdam) chastized their fellow-Muslims for their restrictive attitudes regarding homosexuals and women. The Labour Party, which had often supported gay and lesbian movements, became hesitant because they did not want to alienate their Muslim constituency by defending sexual freedoms too openly. Leftists stressed that the perpetrators of anti-gay violence were not only ethnic minorities but also white kids, or that Islam played no role in the violence. The number of perpetrators from the city of Amsterdam for 2007 shows that Moroccan young men were indeed overrepresented: 36 per cent of perpetrators of anti-gay violence were Dutch-Moroccan and another 36 per cent white Dutch; their share among young men under 25 years was respectively 16 and 39 per cent.[30]

In recent years, the city's tolerant reputation took some serious blows. Since 2007, Labour leaders want to trim down the *Red Light District* using exaggerated numbers regarding sex worker abuse and trafficking. 'Problems' with drug tourists have caused national authorities to limit the sale of soft drugs to locals and excluding foreign tourists. Populists attribute all national miseries to New Dutch and 'Left Church' multicultural ideals. The present-day demonization of paedophiles stands in stark contrast to greater acceptance in the 1970s. Such sentiments are not peculiar for the Netherlands, but because Dutch were famous for tolerance on such controversial themes, recent changes surprised liberal observers who may have hoped that social progress is inevitable.

Tolerance of homosexuality seemed an exception. The number of Dutch who claim in surveys they accept homosexuality is rising to levels of 95 per cent. This is important and encouraging, but what is its value? Additional questions were posed about what they think of seeing two men or women kissing in public. Some 40 per cent and 35 per cent, respectively, admit to disliking this. Homosexuality may be fine at a distance, but is less tolerated if close by.[31] There are more examples of failing tolerance. Sixteen per cent of young lesbians and 9 per cent of gays under 25 years have tried to commit suicide.[32] Thirty per cent of young queer males would prefer not to be gay.[33] In Amsterdam schools, 53 per cent of the boys and 18 per cent of the girls report anti-gay insults. For 22 per cent of male youth, this is a regular occurrence. Only 11 per cent of boys and girls admit to feelings of same-sex attraction. It seems that many more boys endure anti-gay abuse than have such feelings – a sure sign of straight socialization in a presumably gay-tolerant city.[34] A major problem is lack of support in schools for kids who show non-normative gender and sexual behaviour. This disinterest facilitates anti-queer behaviour of male youngsters who set the tone in schools.

It remains difficult to assess the decline or growth of the gay scene. The number of venues may go up and down but they have remained stable over time. Neighbourhood and company pride groups are a recent addition to gay life. There is a distinct feeling that the number of gay tourists has stagnated but there are no data. Since 2007, the police registered ever more cases of anti-gay violence, but it may be more an effect of the growing attention to the subject and higher levels of people reporting such violence. What seems certainly to have decreased is the number of murders of gay men by male hustlers. In the 1980s, two men per year were killed, but now it is rarer.[35] This decrease is clearly related to the transition from street and bar prostitution to escort services on the internet. This seems to be safer. Remarkable is the growth of the annual *Canal Pride Parade* that takes place on the first weekend of August. It started in 1996, 2 years before the *Gay Games* and attracts growing numbers of visitors. Several hundred thousands are now expected. More organizations join the parade each year: first mainly gay groups and political parties, later big companies, police, fire brigade, municipal and national government and religious organizations. In 2001, an Arab boat was a big hit, while in 2007 another with under sixteens created controversy due to the paedophile scare. Every year there is criticism about there being too little emphasis on politics and too much on commercialization.

Nowadays, the city bears witness to much discussion about solidarity over group boundaries but offers little queer content. Amsterdam has become famous as a gay capital through the hard work of local queers, but support of various other groups is often symbolic rather than systematic. These groups were perhaps eager for economic profits derived from vacant identities but were antagonistic to sexual pleasures. The city has a long way to go to become a place where sexual citizenship in terms of 'doing' rather than 'being' is actively fostered.

Notes

1   Koenders, P. (1996), *Tussen Christelijk Réveil en seksuele revolutie. Bestrijding van zedeloosheid met de nadruk op repressie van homoseksualiteit.* Amsterdam: IISG, p. 864.

2   Buijs, L. J., G. Hekma and J. W. Duyvendak (2009), *Als ze maar van me afblijven. Een onderzoek naar antihomoseksueel geweld in Amsterdam.* Amsterdam: Amsterdam University Press, p. 55.

3   This article is based on the mentioned literature; see for gay and lesbian scene Kooten Niekerk, A. van and S. Wijmer (1985), *Verkeerde vriendschap. Lesbisch*

leven in de jaren 1920-1960. Amsterdam: Sara and Hekma, G. (1992), *De roze rand van donker Amsterdam. De opkomst van een homoseksuele kroegcultuur 1930-1970.* Amsterdam: Van Gennep. On gay and lesbian history Hekma, G. (1987), *Homoseksualiteit, een medische reputatie. De uitdoktering van de homoseksueel in negentiende-eeuws Nederland.* Amsterdam: SUA; (1999) 'Amsterdam', in D. Higgs (ed.), *Queer Sites, Gay Urban Histories since 1600.* London/New York: Routledge, pp. 61–88; (2004), *Homoseksualiteit in Nederland van 1730 tot de moderne tijd.* Amsterdam: Meulenhoff; (2011), 'Queer in the Netherlands: Pro-gay and anti-sex. Sexual politics at a turning point', in L. Downing and R. Gillett (eds), *Queer in Europe: Contemporary Case Studies.* Farnham: Ashgate, pp. 129–42; Oosterhuis, H. (1999), 'The Netherlands: Neither prudish nor hedonistic', in F. X. Eder, L. A. Hall and G. Hekma (eds), *Sexual Cultures in Europe* Vol. 1: *National Histories.* Manchester: Manchester University Press, pp. 71–90; Meer, T. van der (2007), *Jonkheer Mr. Jacob Anton Schorer. Een biografie van homoseksualiteit.* Amsterdam: Schorer; Schuyf, J. (1994), *Een stilzwijgende samenzwering. Lesbische vrouwen in Nederland, 1920-1970.* Amsterdam: IISG. Encyclopedic info in Bartels, T. and Versteegen, J. (eds) (2005), *Homo-Encyclopedie van Nederland.* Amsterdam: Anthos and Hemker, M. and L. Huijsman (2009), *LesboEncyclopedie.* Amsterdam: Ambo.

4   Hekma, G. and T. van der Meer (eds) (2011), *'Bewaar me voor de waanzin van het recht'. Homoseksualiteit en strafrecht in Nederland.* Diemen: AMB.

5   The new stricter laws also regarded sex with dependents, pimping, pornography, contraceptives and abortion.

6   Kooten Niekerk and Wijmer (1985); Hekma (1992).

7   The vice squad soon consisted of 25 officers. They kept a list of known homosexuals that contained before the war 1.7 per cent of the adult men in town. See Koenders (1996), p. 221.

8   Duyves, M. (1992), 'In de ban van de bak. Openbaar ruimtegebruik naar homoseksuele voorkeur in Amsterdam', in J. Burgers (ed.), *De uitstad. Over stedelijk vermaak.* Utrecht: Van Arkel, pp. 73–98.

9   Ibid.

10 Dutch gays and lesbians had their own coded language and also their own terms, see Joustra, A. (1988), *Homo-erotisch woordenboek.* Amsterdam: Rap and Kunst, H. and X. Schutte (1991), *Lesbiaans. Lexicon van de Lesbotaal.* Amsterdam: Prometheus.

11 Stokvis, B. J. (1939), *De homosexueelen. 35 autobiographieën.* Lochem: De Tijdstroom.

12 Claeys, P. (2009), *Leren Leven. Een verkennend onderzoek naar de geschiedenis van de Amsterdamse leerscene.* University of Amsterdam, BA thesis.

13 Heymans, M. (1966), *Knal.* Assen: Born.

14 Rotsteeg, M. (1996), *Cherchez la femme. Travestie als fenomeen.* Amsterdam: Vassallucci.

15 Bos, D. (1994), 'Een typisch menselijk verschijnsel. Homoseksualiteit herzien, 1948–1963', *Psychologie en Maatschappij,* 18, 192–209.

16 Bos, D. (2010), *De aard, de daad en het Woord. Een halve eeuw opinie- en besluitvorming over homoseksualiteit in protestants Nederland, 1959–2009.*

Den Haag: SCP; Oosterhuis, H. (1992), *Homoseksualiteit in katholiek Nederland. Een sociale geschiedenis 1900–1970*. Amsterdam: SUA.

17 Warmerdam, H. and P. Koenders (1987), *Cultuur en ontspanning. Het COC 1946–1966*. Utrecht: Homostudies.

18 Fekkes, J. (1968), *De God van je tante ofwel het Ezel-proces van Gerard Kornelis van het Reve*. Amsterdam: De Arbeiderspers.

19 Maas, N. (2010), *Gerard Reve. Kroniek van een schuldig leven*. Vol. 2: *De 'rampjaren' 1962-1975*. Amsterdam: Van Oorschot.

20 Weerlee, D. van (1966), *Wat de provo's willen*. Amsterdam: De Bezige Bij.

21 Kempton, R. (2007), *Provo. Amsterdam's Anarchist Revolt*. New York: Autonomedia.

22 Hekma (1992).

23 Hekma, G., D. Kraakman, M. van Lieshout and J. Radersma (eds) (1989), *Goed verkeerd. Een geschiedenis van homoseksuele mannen en lesbische vrouwen in Nederland*. Amsterdam: Meulenhoff; Klein, M. van der and S. Wieringa (eds) (2006), *Alles kon anders. Protestrepertoires in Nederland, 1965-2005*. Amsterdam: Aksant.

24 Bartels, T. (2003), *Dancing on the Homomonument*. Amsterdam: Schorer.

25 Mooij, A. (2004), *Geen paniek! Aids in Nederland 1982–2004*. Amsterdam: Bert Bakker.

26 Langer, M. (1993), *Alle geheimen van de It*. Amsterdam: Arena; Rotsteeg (1996).

27 Hekma, G. (2002), 'Imams and homosexuality: A post-gay debate in the Netherlands', *Sexualities*, 5(2), 269–80; (2011), 'Queers and Muslims: The Dutch case', *Malacaster International*, 27, 27–45.

28 Data on www.os.amsterdam.nl.

29 Keuzenkamp, S. (ed.) (2010), *Steeds gewoner, nooit gewoon. Acceptatie van homoseksualiteit in Nederland*. Den Haag: SCP, pp. 320–2, *passim*.

30 Buijs et al. (2009), p. 50.

31 Keuzenkamp, S., D. Bos, J. W. Duyvendak and G. Hekma (eds) (2006), *Gewoon doen. Acceptatie van homoseksualiteit in Nederland*. Den Haag: SCP; Keuzenkamp (2010).

32 Keuzenkamp (2010), pp. 143, 191.

33 Graaf, H. de, H. Kruijer, J. van Acker and S. Meijer (2012), *Seks onder je 25ᵉ. Seksuele gezondheid van jongeren in Nederland anno 2012*. Delft: Eburon.

34 Buijs et al. (2009), pp. 62–3.

35 Gemert, F. van (1999), 'Chicken kills hawk: Gay murders during the eighties in Amsterdam', *Journal of Homosexuality*, 26(4), 149–74.

Further reading

Bartels, T. (2003), *Dancing on the Homomonument*. Amsterdam: Schorer.
Bartels, T. and J. Versteegen (eds) (2005), *Homo-Encyclopedie van Nederland*. Amsterdam: Anthos.

Duyves, M. (1992), 'In de ban van de bak. Openbaar ruimtegebruik naar homoseksuele voorkeur in Amsterdam', in J. Burgers (ed.), *De uitstad. Over stedelijk vermaak*. Utrecht: Van Arkel, pp. 73–98.

Hekma, G. (1992), *De roze rand van donker Amsterdam. De opkomst van een homoseksuele kroegcultuur 1930–1970*. Amsterdam: Van Gennep.

—(1999), 'Amsterdam', in D. Higgs (ed.), *Queer Sites, Gay Urban Histories since 1600*. London/New York: Routledge, pp. 61–88.

—(2004), *Homoseksualiteit in Nederland van 1730 tot de moderne tijd*. Amsterdam: Meulenhoff.

—(2011), 'Queer in the Netherlands: Pro-gay and anti-sex. Sexual politics at a turning point', in L. Downing and R. Gillett (eds), *Queer in Europe: Contemporary Case Studies*. Farnham: Ashgate, pp. 129–42.

Hemker, M. and L. Huijsmans (2009), *LesboEncylopedie*. Amsterdam: Ambo.

Koenders, P. (1996), *Tussen Christelijk Réveil en seksuele revolutie. Bestrijding van zedeloosheid met de nadruk op repressie van homoseksualiteit*. Amsterdam: IISG.

Kooten Niekerk, A. van and S. Wijmer (1985), *Verkeerde vriendschap. Lesbisch leven in de jaren 1920–1960*. Amsterdam: Sara.

Kraakman, D., M. van Lieshout and J. Radersma (eds) (1989), *Goed verkeerd. Een geschiedenis van homoseksuele mannen en lesbische vrouwen in Nederland*. Amsterdam: Meulenhoff.

Oosterhuis, H. (1999), 'The Netherlands: Neither prudish nor hedonistic', in F. X. Eder, L. A. Hall and G. Hekma (eds), *Sexual Cultures in Europe*. Vol. 1: *National Histories*. Manchester: Manchester University Press, pp. 71–90.

Schuyf, J. (1994), *Een stilzwijgende samenzwering. Lesbische vrouwen in Nederland, 1920–1970*. Amsterdam: IISG.

7

Ljubljana: The tales from the queer margins of the city

Roman Kuhar

Ljubljana, which is geographically located at the crossroads of Slavic, Germanic and Latin cultures, has a hate/love relationship with the gay and lesbian community in Slovenia. As a space it offered a social, cultural and political platform for the gay and lesbian movement to emerge in the early eighties. At the time Ljubljana was considered the most liberal capital in Yugoslavia and with its geographical closeness to the West, it was a 'natural' place for alternative social movements to emerge. It remains the only city in Slovenia with an organized and recognizable gay and lesbian scene, partly due to the fact that with approximately 280,000 inhabitants it is the only large city in Slovenia. For this reason, the history of the gay and lesbian movement in Slovenia is in fact the history of how this movement emerged and developed in Ljubljana and how it fought for and kept its own space in the city.

It is a popular belief that the fall of the Berlin wall in 1989 represents a crucial turning point in the development of gay movements in Eastern Europe. While that might be true for some Eastern European cities, for the gay scene in Ljubljana this date did not mark the beginning but rather a continuation of relative openness. The movement had already begun to coalesce in 1984 as part of the new social movements which formed a 'tolerated opposition' to the one-party system. It is hard to say to what extent subcultures in the West influenced the emerging Ljubljana gay scene, but unlike other countries in the 'Soviet bloc', the former Yugoslavia had relatively open borders to the West – especially from the seventies onwards – and this enabled gays and lesbians to have contact with the Western gay scene.

Despite initially being a relatively safe haven, Ljubljana nevertheless often turned its back on the gay and lesbian community in the following years. The community was denied access to public space either as a consequence of political conflicts leading to the dissolution of Yugoslavia in 1991 or as a result of the process of re-traditionalization, which emerged in the power vacuum of the early nineties. The efforts and actions which resulted in the increased visibility of the gay scene in the new millennium induced a reaction: violent attacks on visible gay and lesbian spaces by neo-Nazi and similar groups in Ljubljana were blatant attempts to follow old patterns of denying life in city space to queers. Despite the fact that such attacks are usually followed by public condemnation and extensive media attention, it remains the fact that in Ljubljana, with its heteronormative public space, signs of homosexuality are understood as a disturbance to the system. As reported in several research papers gays and lesbians in Slovenia are constantly aware of these potential threats and tend to use a degree of mimicry in order to blend in.[1]

This chapter describes the emergence of queer spaces in the city before the organized movement of the 1980s; it looks at the development of that movement, its effects on the queer geography of the city, and the 're-privatization of homosexuality' in the nineties with the emergence of the internet and queer virtual spaces. It focuses primarily on the emergence of gay scene in Ljubljana in the sixties and later as there are only few records of how gay men and lesbians lived their 'gay lives' before and immediately after the Second World War. According to Vindex's *Homoseksualnost* (1926), the first book on homosexuality in the Slovenian language, the life of homosexuals was an unhappy and isolated one. Vindex, however, does not offer any ethnographic evidence for his claim. Drawing primarily on the ideas of the sexologist Magnus Hirschfeld from Berlin, he urged homosexuals not to feel unhappy as they are not to be blamed for their own homosexuality.[2] His book brought some of the liberal spirit of early twentieth-century Berlin to Ljubljana, and Berlin remained, as we shall see, an important place of inspiration for the Slovenian gays and lesbians.

The newspapers in the 1920s and 1930s only randomly reported homosexuality. The articles were mostly short, partly gossipy criminal reports – usually about certain men who allegedly wanted to have sex with other men. On 22 October 1927, for example, the daily newspaper *Slovenski narod (Slovenian nation)* reported in one sentence that 'police arrested an older man yesterday due to homosexuality'.[3] *Življenje in svet (Life and the world)*, a weekly magazine, featured an article on homosexuality in 1938 in which physician Fran Göstl claimed that homosexuality had spread among Slovenians 'more than one can imagine'. He goes on to explain that homosexuality is a mental disease and a sexual disorder.[4] This seems to have been the prevailing framework of understanding and thinking about homosexuality at the time. There is no evidence that homosexuals were heavily persecuted before and after World War II, despite the fact that

Article 168 of the Penal Code criminalized 'unnatural acts of unchastity between persons of the male sex'. The criminalization of homosexuality was primarily used for the elimination of political enemies such as, for example, catholic priests, or even the mayor of Ljubljana Anton Pesek. When he was elected in 1921 the Minister of Interior refused to place his candidacy before the King for approval due to the accusations that Pesek was a homosexual. Pesek took the case to the court but failed to produce a ruling in his favour and the election results were eventually overturned.[5]

The sixties and seventies: Hide and seek

'I don't recall ever discussing that with my gay friends. I guess we didn't even know about it. Homosexuality was simply just something shameful', said a 66-year-old retired primary school teacher, when asked how the fact that homosexuality was criminalized until 1977 in Slovenia influenced his social and sexual life. He is one of the few older gay men willing to talk about the 'gay lifestyle' in the sixties and seventies.[6] Although the criminalization of homosexuality might not have dramatically affected ordinary gay men, it nevertheless generated stigma and ensured homosexuals kept their 'shameful acts' hidden.

The seeds of the homosexual subculture in Ljubljana can be traced back to the late sixties and early seventies. This was due to the influences of the transnational sexual revolution and relaxed political situation in Slovenia which accompanied a prospering economy. Although homosexuality was often still confined to private spaces, two types of public places started to emerge: cruising areas and places for socializing. None of these places were officially gay – it was simply 'common knowledge' among homosexuals that 'our kind of men' could be found there.

In 1970, a progressive and liberal students' magazine *Tribuna* published what seems to have been the first gay guide to Ljubljana. In an article entitled 'A small homosexual guide', five meeting places were listed where 'kindred souls' could be found. According to the guide, one should visit a certain public toilet during the day, while *Knafljev prehod* (city passage) was frequented by gay men in the evenings. 'Just sit on a bench and wait for someone to join you and start talking to you. You will surely know whether he is the right one or not'.[7]

The guide also listed a candy shop called *Tivoli* (also known as *Pri Petričku*), located in the city centre. Café Union was not mentioned in this piece; it became noted for its gay crowd in the seventies. Although the café was popular among the general public, the imperceptibility of the gay crowd enabled a relatively peaceful coexistence. 'Our project was called "res-publica", which is "public affair" in Latin', remembered one gay man. 'We talked about public places where we would publicly associate with each other like anyone else'.[8] Although the 'res-publica' project might have been something a smaller group of gay intellectuals discussed at the time, it was never realized. For the majority of gay men, candy shop Tivoli, Café Union and also tavern Opera bar were simply meeting places where one could socialize with other fellow travellers. Café Union coexisted with a lively, but hidden and anonymous sexual scene: gay men would meet in several public toilets in Ljubljana (which they called 'a chapel'), in the cruising areas in the parks or in the sauna on Miklošičeva street in Ljubljana. As there were separate days for men and women in the sauna, a distinct and rather openly gay culture emerged there. The public places in Ljubljana which offered a more or less safe space for homo-socializing were typically only for gay men. Lesbians never met in parks, saunas or any other public space. Tratnik and Segan claim that there was a delay in the formation of the lesbian movement because lesbians did not know each other in the context of a broader social network, and instead usually met privately and often via contact ads in newspapers.[9]

The decriminalization of homosexuality on 11 June 1977 was not directly connected to the emerging gay subculture in Ljubljana. Dr Ljubo Bavcon is the legal expert who initiated decriminalization and his proposal was based on scientific research. It was his firm belief that all moralistic and religious 'leftovers' from previous political regimes, such as 'unnatural acts of unchastity', should be deleted from the Penal Code. In an interview for the gay magazine *Narobe* he also mentioned one of his friends who came out to him. 'His story surely had an influence on me and confirmed that my thinking about this issue is correct'.[10]

There is no clear record of whether the police in the sixties and seventies (before decriminalization) collected information on people's sexual orientation. While the police denied having a 'pink list', some gay men reported otherwise: the police did collect information on one's homosexuality, especially for those who were active in the political structure of the socialist government.[11] The information was part of their dossier and could be used if a certain person needed to be discredited. A study from 1996 reports on one interviewee who claimed that the list of homosexuals was marked with the number 47 and that gay men of the time would sometimes refer to each other as being '47'.[12] Similarly, my informant – who was just an 'ordinary' citizen – believes that such a list could have existed as he was caught by police twice or thrice while having sex with a man in 'a chapel' or in the park. The police would ask for his ID and record the name but he was never prosecuted. According to available statistical data, 18 gay men were recorded in Slovenia infringing article 186 of the Penal Code between 1945 and 1951, 30 between 1952 and 1955 and 90 in 1964 and 1965 indicating a marked increase over those years.[13]

'I didn't like the previous political system [communism], but it was quite open in this regard. It is true they have punished the political dissidents, but they did allow people to live as they wish and to love whom they wanted. They didn't interfere with one's private life', remembers Stanko

Jost, director of *Boys* (Dečki), the first Slovenian gay movie from 1977.[14] The movie is based on a novel with the same name by France Novšak, published in 1938. The story is set in a catholic boarding school and depicts a teenage love story between two boys. Jost prepared the script for the movie in 1971, but at first he was not allowed to make the movie as the Cultural Union forbade the shooting. In 1976, he decided to make and finance the movie on his own. This time the authorities did not protest (although the police did pay a few visits during the filming). Once the movie was publicly shown in 1977, however, its further distribution was prohibited. The movie was shown only twice before its second premier in 2004 at the Gay and Lesbian Film Festival in Ljubljana. This screening gave the community a sense of its own history, both in terms of the topic of the film as well as in terms of the screening itself. This sense was extended in 2009, when the festival screened some other Slovenian movies from the seventies – none of which was marked as a 'gay movie', but had clear gay undertones or even featured explicit gay and lesbian scenes, as in Boštjan Hladnik's *Ubij me nežno* (Kill me softly, 1979) and *Maškarada* (Masquerade, 1971). Due to the explicit homoerotic scenes *Maškarada* was not screened in its original version until 1982.[15]

As the borders in Slovenia of the seventies and later were relatively open to the West, there existed exchange not only with Western culture but also its scientific discourse. The influential Slovenian *Research Report on Social Pathology* borrowed extensively from reports by Alfred Kinsey (1948 and 1953) and John Wolfenden (1957). The report defined homosexuality as a 'less dangerous social phenomenon' and argued against repressive measures as a *solution* for homosexuality. While the authors claimed that homosexuality should remain valued as a 'negative sexual activity', they nevertheless opted for its decriminalization. They concluded that in practice, police in Slovenia had already realized that repression was not an effective tool for dealing with the 'deviant sexual behaviour of two consenting adults'.[16]

The possibility for a change to the Penal Code came in 1974, when Yugoslavia adopted a new Constitution, granting each of the six republics the right to its own Code. Janez Šinkovec, the Supreme Court judge at the time, believed that homosexuality should be decriminalized as Slovenia was already lagging behind contemporary jurisprudence. In an interview in 1974 he said: 'I certainly believe that intimate lives of adults . . . are truly their own personal issue and there is no need for the society to feel obliged to intervene in this field'.[17] His statement was in line with liberal interpretations of the private/public divide and western ideas about the role of the state in such matters. However, it took another 3 years before the Penal Code was changed. This created a platform for the future cultural and political 'coming out' of the lesbian and gay movement in Ljubljana in the eighties. Slovenia, Croatia and Montenegro decriminalized homosexuality in 1977, while other republics repealed the article about 20 years later: Serbia in 1994, Macedonia in 1997 and Bosnia in 1998.

The Eighties: First we take . . . Berlin

There is no doubt that the success of the American gay movement of the late sixties and early seventies had an effect on similar movements in Europe, but the beginnings of the Slovenian movement are not so much inspired by the American story. It can rather be traced to the lively gay and feminist scene in Western Berlin in the eighties. 'I will not stop before I have Berlin in Ljubljana', leading Slovenian feminist Mojca Dobnikar famously declared.[18] Visits to Berlin inspired her to start creating 'women's spaces' in Ljubljana, too. Similarly, Bogdan Lešnik, the initiator of the gay movement, also found one of his inspirations in Berlin; he wanted to bring to Ljubljana the Berlin exhibition 'Queers and Fascism'. 'But the very idea [of starting the movement] did not emerge abroad', says Lešnik. They came up with the idea on the basis of relatively liberal and relaxed attitudes about sexualities in the clubs of Ljubljana at the time. They tried to take advantage of this openness and turn it into a social movement and activity. It was only later, says Lešnik, that they realized that initial efforts to change the legislation and the system were not enough, as they had to deal with the people's homophobic mentality as well: 'At the time we didn't know what opinion people had about homosexuality and we were not even much interested in that. Later these [homophobic] opinions not only came to the surface, but also gained political power. A new situation emerged; one that we thought was already surpassed'.[19]

In April of 1984, the first festival of gay culture was organized in Ljubljana, followed by the establishment of the first gay organization in December of the same year. The festival and the organization were called 'Magnus' after Magnus Hirschfeld. The six-day festival – which for the first time created official, if temporary, 'gay spaces' in different locations in Ljubljana – presented the exhibition of European and American gay print media, featured a variety of lectures, including a lecture by the French theorist Guy Hocquenghem, and screenings of films such as Rainer Werner Fassbinder's *The Bitter Tears of Petra von Kant*, William Friedkin's *The Boys in the Band* and the infamous *Cruising*, Frank Ripploh's *Taxi zum Klo* and John Schlesinger's *Sunday Bloody Sunday*.

While Berlin emerged as an important reference point for the gay and lesbian movement in Ljubljana, resulting in a similar queer lexicon and imagery between the cities, Lešnik nevertheless claims that they did not care too much about the preoccupations of the gay movement in the West. 'We had our own [preoccupations]. Only here and there we would take some key words [from them] and use them in our context'.[20]

The emerging gay community demanded its own organized public space (such as bars and clubs) in Ljubljana, next to already existing gay sexual culture in cruising areas. While the sauna on Miklošičeva Street was closed down in early eighties, the 'chapels' and especially the parks were still frequented by gay men. The outdoor gay sexual culture started to die out only later with the introduction of the internet in the mid-nineties.

In 1984, Magnus organized the first gay club nights at the newly established students' alternative club K4 in the centre of Ljubljana. Gay Saturday nights became an important part of Ljubljana's alternative scene. The club has been frequented by people from all over Yugoslavia, Italy and Austria. Despite some interruptions, gay nights at K4 remain to this day an important (and for a long time the only) spatial reference point for the gay and lesbian community in Ljubljana (and Slovenia). However, the gay *Saturday* nights were replaced by the less attractive gay *Sunday* nights in the first year of its operation. It was soon realized by the owners of the club that giving Saturday to the gay community meant losing the key 'party day'. This sent a clear symbolic message as the community was pushed to the margins of the 'party week'. Nevertheless, for a gay man like myself growing up in a rural area of northern Slovenia, the 'Roza nedelja' (Pink Sunday) became some kind of an all-inclusive reference to homosexuality. It was such a strong marker that it has been used also in (heterosexist) public speech in mockery.

The gay and lesbian movement of the eighties helped to relocate the issue of homosexuality from the psychiatric context of the seventies and earlier (reflected primarily in media reports) to the cultural and political contexts of the eighties and after. For example, in 1986, Magnus issued a public manifesto demanding that the school curriculum should include teaching that homosexuality had the same social status as heterosexuality and called for an amendment to the Constitution so that discrimination on the basis of sexual orientation would be prohibited. Although these requests were never fulfilled, such interventions contributed to an increased attention to the gay and lesbian community from the media and the general public.

The formation of the gay movement in Ljubljana may be understood through two contexts. First, the Slovenian movement was influenced by the experiences of the Western movements, which were by then already practising identity politics and experiencing some success. The second context is related to the political agenda of the new social movements in Slovenia. In this sense, as Lešnik (2005) points out, the goal of Magnus was to transform the social relations in a way to guarantee the freedom of expression, including the expression of sexuality.[21] Rather than the question of identity, the initial urge was to bring the question of agency and action to the forefront of the movement. The aim was to make visible and hearable what used to be silent and set at the social margins. It challenged boundaries and the relationship between 'deviant' and 'normal'. On the one hand, Magnus called for the prohibition of discrimination based on sexual orientation, but on the other, it advocated the creation of space for alternative practices. In other words, its original goal was not immersion in mainstream norms.[22]

Ljubljana more or less peacefully (or unknowingly?) incorporated the emerging gay scene into its social and cultural life. All this changed in 1987 when the fourth Magnus festival was scheduled to start on 25 May, corresponding with the late Yugoslavian president Tito's birthday (Marshal Tito died in 1980). Again Berlin played a significant role in the story.

Bogdan Lešnik attended a film festival in Berlin in February 1987 and gave an interview for the festival bulletin in which he mentioned that the Magnus festival would take place on 25 May. The interview was read by a Serbian journalist who launched this information in the Serbian media and informed readers of the apparently astonishing fact that in Ljubljana 'a homosexual is not blamed for or subjected to ridicule. Homosexuality is assumed to be a personal matter'.[23]

Tito's birthday, 25 May was viewed as a kind of a sacred day on which 'ugly things' should be kept out of view of the festive Yugoslav citizens. In this context, homosexuality was constructed as anti-communist. At that time, Slovenia was already suspected of having aspirations to exit from the Yugoslav federation and the festival came as a handy means for putting pressure on the Slovenian government. The incident should therefore be understood in the broader context of political tensions at the time.

When the scandal erupted, the local Slovenian authorities, pressured by the Yugoslav government, issued a public statement, saying that the organization of such a festival would represent a threat to the healthy population in Ljubljana as it was assumed that participants of the festival will not only discuss the 'topic' of the festival, but also *practise it*. The festival could also have negative economic consequences, primarily in the area of tourism. Such a gathering would apparently prevent 'ordinary' tourists from coming to Yugoslavia.[24]

The scandal was blown up to the extent that the Yugoslav media started to report that Ljubljana would host something known as 'the world congress of homosexuals'. Such a reinterpretation is interesting for at least two reasons: the obvious one is that the false magnification of the event effectively contributed to intolerance towards it. Secondly, the introduction of 'queers from abroad' into the story played on the common belief at the time that AIDS was a gay disease from the West. It is not the local gays who would endanger the innocent inhabitants of Ljubljana, but rather those who would come to Ljubljana from abroad. Fearing that Yugoslavia could become a 'promised land for fags', the Bosnian weekly *As* suggested that every straight Yugoslav citizen should wear a badge reading 'Faggots? No, thanks!'.

The scandal showed both how the underlying homophobia in the society could be triggered by moral panic, and also how homosexuality could be used and abused for political reasons. In Slovenia – where media reports were mostly in favour of the Magnus festival – homosexuality was a sign of liberal and progressive elements in Slovenian culture. These seemed endangered by others' conservative and backwards values. In Serbia, on the other hand, homosexuality was imagined as endangering the nation's true (heterosexual) self. Similarly, Bosnian weekly *As* hinted that Slovenian lesbians were prostitutes for capitalist Austrian lesbians at the border crossing. 'These were the big fears of communism', commented Nataša Sukič who established with Suzana Tratnik the lesbian organization LL in

Ljubljana in 1987.[25] To what extent homosexuality was just a tool in a political battle between opposing political forces in Yugoslavia became clear few years later: homosexuality ceased to be a sign of 'progressive Slovenian culture' as soon as Slovenia gained its independence in 1991 and (political) conservatives re-gained the power.

The nineties: Out of the closet . . . into the margins of the city

The new social movements of the eighties were tolerated by the socialist government as they aimed at loosening the political system from within, making it more democratic, but keeping the basic framework of socialist ideology intact. These movements would eventually play an important role in the change of the political system at the end of the eighties, although they found themselves in a strange – perhaps impossible – coalition with conservative groups.

The key tension among these powers was in their interpretation of democracy. While the activists from the new social movements were leftists, putting the human rights of minorities on the top of their agenda, the emerging new right-wing political parties worked within the context of their conservative and Catholic background. The clash between the two streams was most obvious in their opposing ideas on how to deal with the socialist heritage of state feminism and women's rights. It came as no surprise that the new conservative political powers aimed to abolish the right to abortion. While the liberal political parties managed to keep the right to abortion protected by the new Slovenian Constitution, the conservative powers managed to prevent an amendment to the Constitution which would explicitly prohibit discrimination on the basis of sexual orientation.

Following the change of the political system in 1991 involving the secession of Slovenia from Yugoslavia, the gay and lesbian movement institutionalized and took on board the identity model of politics. The politically pragmatic yet essentialist model of identity and its language can already be clearly seen in the first political declaration of the movement after the change of the system entitled 'The right to be different'. The declaration in no way questioned the homo/heterosexual binary. Rather it referred to democratic principles and two identity groups – homosexuals and heterosexuals – and agitated for the equal rights of both.

In the context of the newly found political democracy, the movement took over the language which had proved to be the most successful in the West: the language of human rights for minorities. Such political grammar was also an effect of the institutionalization of gay and lesbian movements which changed into project-based non-governmental organizations typical of the nineties. As the democratic political system is based on the principle of representation, identity politics seemed to be a logical choice, and one which directed the movement towards mainstream 'normalization'. These were not of course specifically Slovenian developments.

The institutionalization of the movement in the early nineties meant that the gay organization Magnus and the lesbian organization LL (established in 1987) got their own small office space in Ljubljana. Located above the club K4, it became another reference point for the gay community. Around such spatial re-organization of the movement emerged a distinctive gay community, which was composed mostly of those who were either willing to help with projects developed by both organizations (for example, a telephone help-line, magazine publication) or agreeing to be their consumers. The community was rather fluid; people who temporarily came to Ljubljana (usually to study at the University of Ljubljana) would join the community and leave it once they moved away. The fluidity of the community remains to this day: it has a relatively solid core of gay and lesbian activists and a broader circle of (temporary) fellow travellers who come and go. The gay community in Ljubljana is therefore not spatially separated in its own quarter as is the case in some Western capitals. Rather there are gay meeting places where the community comes together for a cultural event, lecture or party, and then disperses until the next event. Furthermore, the majority of these places in Ljubljana were not gay *per se* but were constructed as such temporarily during the particular event. There were also no serious attempts to commercialize the community. Aside from one gay sauna and, recently, the small straight friendly Café Open, there are no private commercial initiatives in Ljubljana (or elsewhere in Slovenia) catering exclusively to the gay and lesbian community.

The turning point in creating a relatively stable all-gay spatial reference point (K4 was, remember, only gay on Sundays) came in 1993 when gay and lesbian activists together with other alternative groups were to squat a former Yugoslav military barracks on Metelkova street. The City of Ljubljana decided to demolish the place and possibly build new shopping malls there. The alternative cultural scene in Ljubljana prevented the demolition of the place with their own bodies.[26] Over 200 people turned the place into clubs and rooms where exhibitions, concerts, parties, readings, lectures and other events took place. At first, the City of Ljubljana reacted by cutting off the electricity and water and by filing a legal suit against these people, but later the suit was dropped and what was to be named as 'Metelkova Mesto' (The City of Metelkova) became an alternative cultural centre of Ljubljana. Metelkova Mesto also soon became the centre of the gay and lesbian movement, where both organizations – Magnus and LL – had their own small offices, and managed to convert two rooms into gay and lesbian clubs which are known today as Monokel and Tiffany. These two clubs were the first gay-owned and run (although at first illegal) places in Ljubljana. Though initially without electricity and heating, there was now a permanent space, where the gay and lesbian community finally found its home. Metelkova Mesto takes the form of a square, fenced in with a high wall. This symbolically represented the wall between the safe space within and the homophobic and heteronormative space outside. Metelkova Mesto remains such a space, but is losing the radical (queer) edge it had in the nineties. On the other hand, for some gays and lesbians the place remains 'too radical', 'too political', a kind of a (queer) ghetto, a dirty place of drug users, and nothing like the imagined fancy gay clubs in the West.

In 1994, the gay movement celebrated its tenth anniversary in what became one of the most resounding gay-related scandals of the nineties. Magnus and LL hired the bar at the Ljubljana Caste, a landmark of the town and a high-profile state-owned site. The party was banned only a few hours before it was scheduled to start. The bone of contention was the space, Ljubljana Castle, which is, according to the city councillors at the time, inappropriate to celebrate such anniversaries. The councillors put pressure on the owner of the restaurant at the Ljubljana Castle, who first agreed to the celebration, but then cancelled it. He claimed that he did not know it was a gay celebration and said he feared that 'queers' might ruin his restaurant's reputation.

As in 1987, the scandal 'earned' the movement further media visibility. It was covered by the mainstream media in Slovenia, and the homophobia of the town authorities once again came under attack. 'This event makes Ljubljana even more of a village than it was before', claimed a journalist from the main daily newspaper *Delo*. 'Our piece of advice to the town dignitaries is to publish an announcement stating "No entry to the castle for Blacks, Faggots, Lesbians and Turks"'.[27]

Nearly the same words were used in 2001 by the gay activist and poet Brane Mozetič when suggesting in an e-mail to the mailing list of the gay and lesbian 'scene' (which was by this time connected virtually via a mailing list) that some bars in Ljubljana should hang out a warning stating 'No entrance for faggots, lesbians and dogs'. He was referring to an incident which occurred the previous night to him and his fellow poet, Canadian Jean-Paul Daoust. The incident turned out to be an important touchstone for gay and lesbian life in Ljubljana in the new century.

The 2000s: Action and re-action

On 8 June 2001, Mozetič and Daoust wanted to enter the pub Café Galerija in the centre of Ljubljana after they had performed at the festival of literature and music *Živa književnost* just a few tiny streets away from the bar. It was known as a gay-friendly place. The bouncer prevented them from entering, however, stating that 'they should get used to the fact that this pub is not for *that kind* of people'. The gay community at first reacted with 'protest drinking' similar to those organized by London GLF in the seventies. Around 40 gays and lesbians gathered in Café Galerija a week after the incident and each ordered only one decilitre of mineral water and drank it over a few hours. This practical and symbolic reclamation of space hit the mainstream media, and sparked a lively public debate about Slovenian (in)tolerance. It also added impetus to the first Slovenian Pride parade in Ljubljana on 6 July 2001, which took place just a week after the first Pride parade in Belgrade in Serbia was brutally thwarted when the few participants were beaten up by hundreds of hooligans. There was a lot of fear about what might happen in Slovenia and whether the violence in Belgrade would be replicated on the streets of Ljubljana. The parade took place without any counter protests, however. According to the Slovenian media, around 300 people took part.

Throughout the 2000s, Metelkova Mesto and gay Sunday nights at K4 remained a central gathering place for the gay community in Ljubljana. The turn of the century also saw some new LGBT non-governmental organizations (such as youth organization Legebitra and Association for the integration of homosexuality DIH) emerging with their own offices. These also became places for gay discussion groups and similar activities. Café Open, ostensibly the most public gay space in Ljubljana, opened in 2008 at the fringe of the old city centre. It emerged as the first private initiative that catered explicitly and specifically for the gay and lesbian community and its followers. Although officially a commercial initiative, it became heavily involved with the LGBT non-governmental organizations and the activists' scene as both owners of the Café are active members of the Ljubljana's gay and lesbian scene. This scene is small and characterized by a 'homely' (and sometimes claustrophobic) atmosphere where everyone knows everybody else. Shortly after it opened, in June 2009, Café Open was attacked by a group of eight men. At the time of the attack, the Café Open was hosting a literary reading which was part of the Pride week events leading up to the ninth Pride parade in the city. The group threw a lit torch and stones into the bar and seriously injured gay activist Mitja Blažič. This homophobic attack once again became the leading story in the Slovenian media, transforming Café Open into a symbol of the position of the LGBT minority in Ljubljana. The attack was seen as an effect of the increasing use of hate speech in the Parliament and elsewhere. The LGBT community had long been pointing at increasing intolerance, and the attack on Café Open, the most brutal attack on the LGBT movement in its 25-year history, proved them right.

The day after the attack several activities took place in Café Open, including a 'Petition against homophobia', which was signed publically by numerous left-wing and even some right-wing politicians, the mayor of Ljubljana and some other celebrities. The attack was condemned by politicians, the general public and the media – who covered the ensuing pride parade extensively. Not only were more people marching in the Parade than usual, it was also the first time that one minister from the government – the Minister of the Interior Katarina Kresal – decided to march as a sign of her indignation at the violent homophobic attack. Three men – aged 18–22 – were arrested soon after, charged with hate crime, and sentenced to between 5- and 8-month imprisonments in 2011.

Despite the public response and court verdict that suggested such violence was intolerable, this did not change the disturbing fact that while the first pride parades in the beginning of the 2000s passed off peacefully, more recently there have been violent attacks on participants, most often at night during the ensuing celebrations around Metelkova Mesto. It seems as if such homophobic violence has become a constitutive element of the parades, which – unlike the commercialized ones in the West – still held the shape (and content) of a political protest. The violent history of the recent parades also points at the double-edged sword of greater visibility: while it brings benefits, it also comes with new challenges. How, for example, can such a visibility be construed as safe for those constructed as 'others'? This is one of the issues the LGBT scene in Ljubljana will have to address in the decades to come.

Conclusion

The Slovenian LGBT movement has its own specificities, especially regarding the emergence of the movement. While current gay politics in Slovenia can be described as identity politics, functioning in the context of minority human rights, the first wave of the movement in Ljubljana and its politics in the eighties were much more ambivalent in terms of sexuality categorization. If the political demands of the movement of the time are taken into consideration, its politics can be related to the identity model (that is, the elimination of discrimination based on sexual orientation). However, the cultural and social specificities of the early movement are in many ways closer to the politics of gay liberation from the seventies and even to the queer politics and activism of today in which social and sexual revolution were entwined.

The gay and lesbian urban experience in Ljubljana differs from other European capitals in some crucial respects. In Ljubljana (and Slovenia), the gay and lesbian movement became established in the period after the decriminalization of homosexuality, while at least in some Western states, the decriminalization of homosexuality was one of the movement's primary, if not the first political objective. In this context, the Slovenian movement and primarily the movements which emerged in Yugoslavia before and after the dissolution of the federation in 1991 experienced a 'condensed history' of similar movements from the West. The movements took on board identity-type politics immediately or soon after their formulation and skipped the assimilationist phase of the Western movements associated with the 1950s and 1960s in the Netherlands, Denmark and England in particular.

Secondly, the movements in Western Europe were usually the result of a critical mass of gays and lesbians, who occupied a certain part of urban space. In Ljubljana, the gay community has formed around certain sites (such as Metelkova Mesto, club K4 or recently Café Open). These are only physical reference points, however. They are lynchpins for a relatively strong sense of community – though that community has not been spatially separated in its own quarter of Ljubljana as we might observe in Chueca in Madrid, the Marais in Paris, or Soho in London. This is partly because of the relative size of Ljubljana in comparison to these other cities.

In the quest for 'spaces for alternative practices', the movement encountered numerous obstacles. While in 1987 during the fourth Magnus festival scandal gays were asked to move from Ljubljana due to their threat to the 'healthy citizens', in 1994, when celebrating the tenth anniversary of the movement, they were not denied the space in total, but were asked to 'go somewhere else' as they would ruin the reputation of a place which held some state importance. In other words, the community could be tolerated, but only on the margins of the city. Similarly in 2001, two gays were requested to 'go somewhere else' as what used to be a gay-friendly place was not so friendly anymore. But when the community 'went somewhere else' and found its own space in the fringe of the city centre in Café Open it was attacked again. This time a homophobic attack on Café Open occurred during the Pride week events leading up to the ninth Pride parade in the city. The community was again clearly informed that they do not belong. However, the gay and lesbian community resisted and continues to resist the condition of being victimized. In its endeavours this community has found many supporters, but many townsmen still do not understand why their follow citizens cannot simply live their homosexuality behind the closed doors of their apartments and houses; about 35 per cent of Slovenian citizens would not want them as neighbours.[28] All this makes Ljubljana 'the most beautiful city in the world' (in the infamous words of Ljubljana's mayor) – the most beautiful city for someone else. Not for LGBTQ people. Not yet.

Notes

1   Švab, A. and R. Kuhar (2005), *The Unbearable Comfort of Privacy: The Everyday Life of Gays and Lesbians*. Ljubljana: Peace Institute. See also: Kuhar, R. and J. Magić (2008), 'Izkušnje in percepcije homofobičnega nasilja in diskriminacije', in J. Magić, R. Kuhar and N. Kogovšek (eds), *Povej naprej (raziskovalno poročilo)*. Ljubljana: Legebitra, pp. 6–24.

2   Vindex (1926), *Homoseksualnost*. Ljubljana: samizdat.

3   Drobiž policijske kronike, Slovenski narod, 22 October 1927, p. 3.

4   Göstl, F. (1938), 'Spolne zlorabe', *Življenje in svet*, 12(9), 132–3, 28 February 1938.

5   Cf. Gašparič, J. (2001), 'Knez Eulenburg na ljubljanskem dvoru: afera nesojenega ljubljanskega župana Antona Peska', *Zgodovina za vse*, 1, 59–69.

6   Kuhar, R. (2011), 'Gejevska poroka na Lovčanu v sedemdesetih', *Narobe*, 17/18(5), 18–20.

7   SeXY (1970), 'Mali homoseksualni vodič', *Tribuna*, 19(9), 11, 28 March 1970, p. 11.

8   Soruz, M. (1994), 'Sedemdeseta leta', *Revolver*, 12(39–41), 40.

9   Tratnik, S. and N. Segan (1995), *L (Zbornik o lezbičnem gibanju na Slovenskem 1984–1995)*. Ljubljana: Škuc.

10   Kuhar, R. (2012), 'O ceni demokracije: pogovor z dr. Ljubom Bavconom', *Narobe*, 21(6), 9–11, p. 11.

11   Soruz (1994).

12   Zornik, A. and K. Mirović (1996), *Način življenja gejev v Ljubljani med letoma 1984 and 1993. Diplomska naloga*. Ljubljana: Filozofska fakulteta.

13   Bavcon, L., M. Kobal, L. Milčinski, K. Vodopivec and B. Uderman (1968), *Socialna patologija*. Ljubljana: Mladinska knjiga.

14   Sedlar, A. M. (1994), 'O dečku, ki je igral na kamero', *Novi tednik*, 15 December 2004.

15   Cf. Mozetič, B. (2009), *Homoseksualnost in slovenski film. 25. festival gejevskega in lezbičnega filma (katalog)*. Škuc: Ljubljana. http://www.ljudmila. org/siqrd/fglf/25/homoseksualnost.php (last accessed 25 January 2012).

16   Bavcon, L., M. Kobal, L. Milčinski, K. Vodopivec and B. Uderman (1968), *Socialna patologija*. Ljubljana: Mladinska knjiga, pp. 124–35.

17   Lorenci, J. (12 February 1974), 'Med moralo in svobodo: Sodnik vrhovnega sodišča SRS Janez Šinkovec o homoseksualnosti'. *ITD*.

18   Cf. Vesel, B. and N. S. Vegan (1992), 'Mojca Dobnikar: Ne bom dala miru, dokler ne bom imela Berlina v Ljubljani', *Revolver*, 6, 12–15.

19   Kuhar, R. (2009), 'Trpeči aktivizem mi je bil vedno malo tuj. Intervju z dr. Bogdanom Lešnikom', *Narobe*, 10(3), 8–11, p. 10.

20   Ibid.

21   Lešnik, B. (2005), 'Melting the iron curtain: The beginning of the LGBT movement in Slovenia', in M. Chateauvert (ed.), *New Social Movements and Sexuality*. Sophia: Bilitis Resource Center, pp. 86–96.

22   Ibid.

23   Cited in Kuhar, R. (2003), *Media Representations of Homosexuality: An Analysis of the Print Media in Slovenia, 1970-2000*. Ljubljana: Peace Institute, p. 28.

24   Cf. Ibid.

25   Cf. Kuhar, R. (2007), 'Prečuta noč za lezbični manifest: dvajset let lezbične skupine Škuc LL: intervju z Natašo Sukič in Suzano Tratnik', *Narobe*, 4(1), 9–12.

26   Cf. Bibič, B. (2003), *Hrup z Metelkove: Tranzicije prostorov in kulture v Ljubljani*. Ljubljana: Mirovni inštitut.

27   Gaćeša, Jelena (30 May 1994), 'Umazano roza', *Delo*.

28   European Value Survey (2008), http://www.europeanvaluesstudy.eu/ (last accessed 25 January 2012).

Further reading

Greif, T. (2005), 'The social status of lesbian women in Slovenia in the 1990s', in A. Štulhofer and T. Sandfort (eds), *Sexuality and Gender in Postcommunist Eastern Europe and Russia*. New York: Haworth Press, pp. 149–69.

Kogovšek Šalamon, N. (2012), 'Traits of homophobia in Slovenian law: From ignorance towards recognition', in L. Trappolin, A. Gasparini and R. Wintemute (eds), *Confronting Homophobia in Europe: Social and Legal Perspectives*. Oxford, Portland: Hart, pp. 171–201.

Kuhar, R. (2010), 'Slovenia', in C. Stewart (ed.), *The Greenwood Encyclopedia of LGBT Issues Worldwide. Vol. 2*. Santa Barbara, Denver, Oxford: ABC Clio, pp. 373–91.

—(2011), 'Heteronormative panopticon and the transparent closet of the public space in Slovenia', in R. Kulpa and J. Mizielinska (eds), *De-centring Western Sexualities: Central and Eastern European Perspectives*. Farnham, Burlington: Ashgate, pp. 149–65.

Kuhar, R., Ž. Humer and S. Maljevac (2012), 'Integrated, but not too much: Homophobia and homosexuality in Slovenia', in L. Trappolin, A. Gasparini and R. Wintemute (eds), *Confronting Homophobia in Europe: Social and Legal Perspectives*. Oxford, Portland: Hart, pp. 51–77.

Kuhar, R. and J. Takács (eds) (2007), *Beyond the Pink Curtain: Everyday Life of LGBT People in Eastern Europe*. Ljubljana: Peace Institute.

Kuhar, R. and A. Švab (2013), 'The interplay between hatred and political correctness: The privatization of homosexuality in Slovenia', *Southeastern Europe*, 37(1), 17–35.

Lešnik, B. (2005), 'Melting the iron curtain: The beginning of the LGBT movement in Slovenia', in M. Chateauvert (ed.), *New Social Movements and Sexuality*. Sophia: Bilitis Resource Center, pp. 86–96.

Sobočan, A. M. (2011), 'Female same-sex families in the dialectics of marginality and conformity', *Journal of Lesbian Studies*, 15(3), 384–405.

Švab, A. and R. Kuhar (2005), *The Unbearable Comfort of Privacy: The Everyday Life of Gays and Lesbians*. Ljubljana: Peace Institute.

Slovenian LGBT fiction in English

Mozetič, B. (2004), *Butterflies*. New York: Meeting Eyes Bindery.

—(2005), *Passion*. Jersey City: Talisman House.

—(2008), *Banalities*. New York: A Midsummer Night's Press.

—(2011), *Lost Story*. Jersey City: Talisman House.

Tratnik, S. (1999), 'Under the ironwood trees', in N. Holoch and J. Nestle (eds), *The Vintage Book of International Lesbian Fiction*. New York: Vintage.

—(2003), 'My Name is Damian', *Tessera*, http://pi.library.yorku.ca/ojs/index.php/tessera/article/viewFile/25514/23691.

—(2008), 'Geographical positions', in M. Čandar and T. Priestly (eds), *Angels beneath the Surface: A Selection of Contemporary Slovene Fiction*. Berkeley: North Atlantic Books.

—(2012), 'Reckless Boy', in J. G. Coon, A. Fincham and J. Beckett (eds), *Ljubljana Tales*. London: New Europe Writers.

8

Mapping/Unmapping: The making of queer Athens[1]

Dimitris Papanikolaou

In today's Athens queer geography looks fixed. Or, at least, this is what the yearly publication 'Athens Gay Map' published by gayguide.gr wants to suggest. Made financially possible by advertising from various commercial establishments, this free map of Athens, with additional small sections on Mykonos and Thessaloniki, lists the main bars and saunas, the restaurants and cafés that a homosexual clientele might be interested in visiting; these are also the same places that stock and offer the free publication, thus helping tourist and resident alike to continue their queer walk of the city, with 'knowledgeable' steps. The map's main focus is the newly gentrified area of Gazi, in the northern shadow of the Acropolis. It is in Gazi and its environs, the areas of Kerameikos, Metaxourgeio and Psyrri, that since the beginning of the twenty-first century, gay and lesbian bars and restaurants, saunas, cafés and even 'community centres' have been springing up, making this the new 'gay area' of the Greek capital.[2]

The area of Gazi is only the latest in a series of neighbourhoods that have experienced a concentration of 'gay spots'. Asking about the 'gay history of Athens', one often comes up against the story of older bars and cafés with 'a special clientele', rising and falling in popularity, changing places, areas, names and outlooks. For this reason, the official history of 'gay Athens' is often thought to have started in the early 1970s, when bars frequented by a visibly homosexual clientele began to spring up one after the other in Plaka; they had to close down en masse in the 1980s as a result of a government decision not to renew licenses, in a policy apparently aimed at turning the district into the sanitized tourist hub it is today. Kolonaki and Thisseion then took the place of Plaka in the 1980s and 1990s; rising property prices in the city centre triggered a subsequent move to the newly gentrified areas of Gazi, Psyri and Metaxourgeio in the new century.

Even though less visible than that of gay men, 'lesbian life in Athens' seems to have followed a parallel path – perhaps with an additional preference for less central areas. In a recent article in the magazine *E Ntalika* [The Truck], published by the Lesbian Group of Athens (LOA), contributor Maria Papado (a pseudonym) offers a piece on 'My nights in the bars of Athens: Mapping the Lesbians'.[3] The article narrates the author's experience in the lesbian bars of Athens since the late 1970s and in the chronological order these bars were established. From the bar *Dolly's* in Kypseli (frequented by 'women from another era, who loved with passion, with power, with shame and with violence') and the restaurant-bar *different* in Koukaki, to *Ornela's* in the centre ('women from all social classes could meet there'), *Syre ki ela* and *Tesseris toichoi* [Four Walls] in Kypseli of the 1980s, a series of lesbian bars in the Thisseion area and Ermou street in the 1990s (*Taxidi* [Journey], *Lizard*, *Circe*, *Allothi* [Alibi], *Odysseia*), to the contemporary *Porta* [Door], *Aroma gynaikas* [The Scent of a Woman], *Almaz* in Gazi, *Myrovolos* in Metaxourgeio, *fairy tale* in Exarchia and *Troll* in Kolonos. Not only the locations, but even the titles of these establishments tell a story of identity in constant negotiation between making a statement and keeping it discreet.

In an exercise in editorial playfulness, the article sports two illustrations: what looks like a medieval map converted into a 'Lesbiographia Atheniensis', and the reproduction of a famous photograph from the lesbian bar *Monocle* in Paris, photographed by Brassaï in the early 1930s. Talking about the bars of the past, the implication goes, is not only 'an old story'; it is also old-style history.[4]

As with many other accounts of 'Athenian gay life in the past' that have been published recently in community press,[5] the article in *Ntalika* charts the history of the queer city through the story of specific gay (or gay-friendly) bars. The period before the bars is thought of as 'a bygone era'. And since these bars were established in different areas of the Greek capital at different moments of the last four decades, their listing tends to read like a progression, from neighbourhood to neighbourhood and from one decade to the other, reaching its conclusion in today's Athens.

A linear history of gay Athens after World War II, such as this, often also mentions the main parks of Pedion Areos and Zappeion in central Athens and the area around the municipal clock in Piraeus, as known male homosexual pickup places over the decades. The list of pickup places expands with the legendary cinemas of the centre, such as *Rosiclair*, *Mondial*, *Cineak*, *Ellas*, *Athenaikon*.[6] The area of Syngrou avenue, running from the centre to the south of the city, is also often mentioned for its notoriety in the 1970s and 1980s as a pickup place for transgender sex workers (what Greeks at the time called the *travesti*), as well as a symbolic site, around which a homophobic representation of sexual subcultures was popularized in the Greek public sphere in the 1980s. That said, Syngrou is today also often discussed as a *lieu de mémoire* in the city's queer history/geography.[7]

I start this chapter by listing a number of nightlife spots or pickup places, in order to show both their importance for putting together a 'gay history' of a city like Athens, and the limitations such an approach is bound to have. The importance is obvious from the articles in the community press I have just quoted: often, these recollections about bars and cruising spots are written as an elaborate exercise in community history. In this way, the map of a nightlife becomes an urban history of gay life; and the recollection of the experience of visiting these places becomes an act of discursive identity formation.

But then, again, as this chapter will keep reminding, the queer experience of a city cannot be, and is never in practice, exhausted by visiting or researching its commercial and nightlife establishments. This is a surface map, and a very incomplete surface map at that. At best, it offers a partial experience of gay life, but even at that level it also distorts the narratives of queerness that lurk in the city's corners.

For instance, a number of my informants, homosexual men and women aged between 40 and 90 who offered their recollections during my research for this chapter, insisted on mentioning a series of 'other' locations with which they would identify their queer experience of the city. The men tended to remind me of the importance of central cinemas, public baths and lavatories, but also of places of transit, such as the big train and metro stations or the legendary coffee shop *Neon* in Omonoia, frequented by soldiers and sailors, as well as the seaside areas and the beaches near Athens. Women insisted on other types of place in which lesbians would socialize more openly and where they could meet other 'women interested in women' in the 1960s, 1970s and 1980s; they mentioned private salons, restaurant-bars owned by lesbian singers, or sports clubs, community card-playing clubs and gambling dens (*hartopaiktikes lesches*).[8]

Therefore, in my attempt to further explore narratives about gay and lesbian experiences of the city of Athens after World War II – and taking my informants' experiences/testimonies into consideration – I realized that I had to distinguish between two versions of the city: the easily mapped city of gay bars and cafés on the one hand, and the city of oral narratives, memories and intense negotiations of queer identity on the other. A city like Athens still lacks a settled narrative of its homosexual history and, as Athens Pride has made clear in recent years, even the idea of a gay history remains a hotly debated issue.[9] For this reason, the distinction between the gay city and the queer city, the mappable urban place of non-normative sexual identities and the unmapped space of non-normative desire, tends to become more pronounced, historically meaningful and representationally significant.[10]

In what follows, I will focus on a period starting with the Greek dictatorship (1967–74) and discuss the emergence of non-normative identities in the mappable space of the Greek capital. I will analyse the importance of this first concrete mapping of gay Athens in a specific historical context and the radical politics it was eventually associated with. But, in the meantime, I will argue that a sense of Athens as a place for the expression of non-normative desire predated 1967, continues to this date and can be felt in the gestures made by people to evade maps, to hide from surveillance and to co-ordinate a fluid experience of queer space in the city. This, as I will explain, can be conceptualized as an exercise in unmapping. My argument is that it is only through this constant dialogue of mapping and unmapping that one could today narrate a history of queer Athens.

'Every night queers wander around central Athens': Mapping the homosexual subculture of the capital, ca. 1970

Many politicians in public office, often those wanting to show off as strong men, announced that they had cleansed Athens of the queers. This is nowhere the case. On the contrary, today, almost all of the 300 semi-legal bordellos of the capital have a queer man as an assistant. Moreover, every day, after midnight, queers dressed in women's clothes wander around the Hilton hotel of central Athens, as well as in the Metaxourgeio area, in Kolonos, and elsewhere. The queers are a unified group. Part of this group are the effeminate men, who at night wander around the dark depths of the parks or socialize with macho guys in the lowly tavernas. All these people know each other very well. It is this group of people who speak the language of Kaliarnta.[11]

This is how Elias Petropoulos, a Greek ethnographer known for his work on subcultures, opens his book *Kaliarnta: The Dictionary of Greek Queers*, in 1972. *Kaliarnta* was the first attempt to collect words of a slang spoken in a queer subculture, the equivalent of the English Polari. It was first published during the Greek military dictatorship of 1967–74. Under its ethnographical guise, it presented the first open acknowledgement of a vibrant queer subculture in Greece, and to an extent, the first attempt to map its spaces and its sexual logistics. The book has its own history of suppression and persecution, as it faced the hostile response of the dictatorial regime during the first years of its circulation; it eventually became a bestseller, especially after the restitution of democracy in 1974.

It is interesting, at any rate, to observe that this 'glossary of a subculture's sociolect', starts not with a description of linguistic structures or vocabularies, but, as the paragraph above shows, with a short foray into sexual geography. Petropoulos begins by assuring his readers that, even though officials have declared the city of Athens 'cleansed from vice', 'the queers' are still everywhere. At night they come out, as 'a unified group', and populate the streets, the bordellos, the neighbourhoods, the specific bars and tavernas 'where everyone knows everyone else'.

The narrative is typical of Petropoulos's inimitable style of research and writing, a mixture of autobiography, crime fiction and participatory observation of subcultural life, which made him one of the best-selling non-fiction authors in post-war Greece. In later editions of his *Kaliarnta* book he went even further in his attempt at sexual geography, explaining the ruses he employed in order to break into 'the completely enclosed caste of the queers'.[12] For a year in 1968, he says, he would go around 'those places which the queers frequent': tavernas in Piraeus, 'the notorious bar *Sou-Mou*' on Iera Odos to the West of the centre, or places near the slaughterhouses of Kifissia, the northern suburb; but also in the very centre of the city, in the public lavatories of Omonoia and Syntagma Squares, in the park of Pedion Areos, and, 'after midnight', in the area behind the Hilton hotel, on Vassileos Konstantinou Avenue.[13] In order to develop this ethnography, Petropoulos adds, he even had to produce a detailed map (reproduced in later reprints of the book), and ask for the help of members of the vice squad to expand it. This self-sketched small map shows the various 'hangouts of homosexuals' (the public baths, the tavernas, the streets) marked with small boxes, and the itineraries possibly connecting them marked with arrows. The name of the policeman used as an additional informant still remains in the lower right hand side of the map, along with his telephone number. This small piece of paper, sketched by an ethnographer and finalized with the help of a policeman, remains to this day, and to the best of my knowledge and research, the earliest cartographic account of a homosexual subculture of Athens, the first graphic map of Athens as a city containing a queer geography.

As I will explain in the second part of this chapter, the timing of this early map of gay Athens, first produced as an ethnographic note in 1968, implicitly referred to in the first edition of *Kalianta* (1972) and eventually reproduced in a later edition of this book (1980), was far from coincidental. This map relates to a specific *arrangement of the queer city* that evolved in the Greek 1970s and has left its mark on queer negotiations of Athens since. As I will show, the experience of life under the Colonels' dictatorship (1967–74) and the transition to democracy changed the conditions for queer socialization and offered new opportunities for the public expression of non-normative sexuality after the Junta. Yet this connection was by no means straightforward. Homosexual lifestyles would become more visible from the late 1960s onwards, especially in areas of Athens like Plaka; thus the secrecy and the feeling of the underground described by Petropoulos in his *Kaliarnta* was becoming obsolete, at the very moment when his book was becoming a bestseller. But more of that later. For the moment, the reason I am interested in Petropoulos's narrative is because of its end product: the *possibility* of a map of a queer under-city; the *mapping* of queerness itself.

Why would one want to map the queer city? When does this happen? What energies does such a gesture produce in return? How much does it collude with systems of control? Petropoulos produced an account of 'the space where [Athenian] queers fraternized and socialized'. In so doing, he also made their presence concrete, their language collectable, their 'enclosed caste' visible, their lifestyle iterable. For years after its first publication, the 'homosexual dictionary' published in *Kaliarnta* was used by Greek homosexual men and women, passed from hand to hand as an alphabet of identity. I remember borrowing it from a lesbian friend in 1993, after a night out in one of the then multiplying Athenian gay clubs. And I recall vividly how I was compelled not by the obscure 'queer language' printed in the Lexicon, the book's main part, but by the topographical details in those first pages: a map of a hidden, subcultural queer Athens coming from a past not long gone, yet at the same time feeling so remote. The hidden tavernas and the subterranean lifestyles that were described in that book were certainly different from what I was experiencing in the very same city 20 years later. For a reader like me in the 1990s, Petropoulos' map was not offering a history anymore, but a queer *prehistory* of Athens. It still does, at least for some.[14]

Having said this, Petropoulos' version remains a very problematic account: it creates a romanticized view of Greek queer lifestyle in the 1960s as subcultural and hidden, but overdoes the description of how completely marginal, sealed off and clandestine it was. Equally problematic is the fact that this account was produced with the collusion/help of state control, while also aiming to titillate a wider middle class audience *and* present itself as a call for sexual liberation in the climate of the 1960s. When readers, like me, read this linguistic and topographical account as a fixed genealogy for their identity in subsequent decades, they had to ignore or downplay these problematic aspects.

But isn't this always the issue with maps? They tend to produce in one's mind a vision of space settled in historical time, an objectified topography. Once you see a map, you tend to forget the activity of mapping that produced it in the first place, its historicity; you concentrate on the information at hand and forget its texture, or its gaps. Yet the difficult questions are exactly these: by whom and for whom was the mapping carried out in the first place? Which side was it on, control or its subversion? And how about un-mapping? How about the urge to react to the map, to undermine, dislocate, denounce the authority of a certain mapping? Who looks for a map? Who is being mapped? Who wants to avoid it?[15]

While I was collecting material for this chapter, and especially in a series of interviews with older gay men and women who talked to me about their past experience of 'queer Athens', I realized that my willingness to ask about a 'queer city' was often met with suspicion. It was as if my own frame of questioning was the problem: trying to collect material on 'queer Athens' was seen as already using a frame of theory and a shape of inquiry that was more tuned to a different historical experience of sexual identity – both in generational and spatial terms. It was as if I was coming with a prefabricated conceptual map, and was asking my informants to conform to a role already assigned to them, a role that would fit this pre-existing frame.

In one particular instance, as I was inquiring about the specific places queers used to meet in the 1960s and 1970s, and about how they would find out about them, one of my interlocutors exclaimed: 'You remind me of those gay French friends who came to visit me in the early 1970s. To my surprise, I realized they already knew everything about where to go, the parks, the cinemas, the bars . . . they had a map in their heads already, perhaps had seen it in a foreign book; I, on the other hand, had different priorities at the time, and was not very sure how well I knew all these things then . . .'. For him and his circle of queer friends living in the city, he explained, things were much more complicated, much less clear-cut, not only in relation to space and place, but also regarding their own sexuality and sexual identity. It is not as if his tourist friends had wanted to experience a city he had no idea about – he repeatedly assured me that he knew of all the places they had wanted to go; what was awkward was that they were following a different script about identity and the city than he was accustomed to.

What I am reporting here obviously holds a more general value. After all, recent accounts of 'queer geography' as well as 'non-metropolitan sexualities' have been eager to promote a rethinking of the relationship between body, space, place and its more fluid sexual dynamics, urging us to 'expand [our] empirical terrain to include more of these messy realities [of human experience], including fluidity, hybridity, incompleteness, moralities, desire and embodiment'.[16] But I would further argue that, in places like Athens, where public accounts and representations of homosexual life in the modern history of the city have been scarce, where there is no settled and popular account of the 'history of the homosexual city', of a specific subculture and its iconic moments of representation within the twentieth century, mapping becomes much more slippery territory: always incomplete, but also always there. On the one hand, mapping pursued and presented as a desire to organize and communicate versions of the past and the present, a desire *for* history. On the other hand, mapping widely felt as a contentious issue, a gesture belying containment and undesirable fixity, which is thus resisted with strategies of *unmapping*. With the term *unmapping* I want to describe both the effort to evade surveillance, as well as the urge to underline, sometimes nostalgically, the fluidity of sexuality in the city 'before [or beyond] gay maps'. Mapping/unmapping can thus often be seen as a system made up of two currents working in parallel, its cultural circulation and politics becoming a good vector through which to assess complex dynamics of control, power and the negotiations of identity in specific historical moments.

In the next two sections, I will explore this convergence of queer mappings/ unmappings of Athens in the 1960s and 1970s. I will also point at a period in the second half of the 1970s, when an organized homosexual movement made possible the articulation of a coherent narrative about homosexual culture and its place in the city (and, metonymically, in Greek society). Yet, as I will also argue, this gesture did not exhaust the possibilities, or the different turns, that the queer city can take.

'A gay bar in Athens!'

'When I first heard about a gay bar in Athens, it was in the 1970s. I was amazed; a gay bar in Athens! To my further amazement, someone said that there were, already, not one but six or seven of them'. Jeffrey,[17] a British writer who has lived most of his adult life in Athens ('but, you see, I was always in liaisons, I was not going around much') is reminiscing about the time he returned to the city he loved after the military Junta that ended in 1974. In the years he had been away, many things had changed. But did these first gay bars mean that, for the first time, gay life in the 1970s was becoming concrete, and, ultimately, easier, I ask. 'Oh no, no.' Jeffrey replies. 'Because, you see, in the Athens of the 1950s and '60s I had been living before, anybody who wanted to find homo-sex could go out and find it within twenty minutes'. The only difference in the 1970s, he continues, was that now 'specific places catered to a more homosexually orientated clientele'. And gay life in that period, under the influence of the lifestyles of a younger generation, of tourism and of 'images coming from abroad', was becoming, even in Greece, 'more specific, more narrow even'. Already in the 1970s, Jeffrey concludes, one could be nostalgic for what had gone before.

Loukas Theodorakopoulos,[18] a well-known gay activist, whose story will become crucial in the argument of the last part of this chapter, similarly explains that when he first arrived in Athens in the late 1940s, the streets were glowing with eroticism. 'There were the parks, some central cinemas around Panepistimiou street, where men picked up men in the back rows while families enjoyed the film in front rows. There were the public baths. But, mostly, there was a sexual availability on the street, in the bus, in the square, in the public area. To such an extent, that I used to call [the very central] Patission Avenue the Twink-Street [teknostrít]. One could easily pick men up there'.

Both Jeffreys' and Theodorakopoulos' accounts of Athens in the 1950s and 1960s could be analysed in the terms Matt Cook's analysis has favoured for a similar discussion of London in the earlier twentieth century. Instead of seeing the city as a catalyst for modern gay life and the necessary prerequisite for a gay identity to emerge, Cook has insisted that we need to demonstrate 'the impossibility of conjuring a unitary gay metropolis or a singular gay urban type, and [the need to] indicate instead the controlled plurality which characterized the relationship between [the city] and homosexuality'.[19] According to this view, the modern city did not (help) give rise to a singular 'homosexual' identity, but became the theatre of multiple engagements with sexuality and diverse expressions of identity and attachment.

There are two minor problems with this analysis, however. The first is that, as it underlines the fluidity of attachments and negotiations offered in the modern city, it often underestimates the presence of specific identity narratives and specific spatial arrangements for homosexual identity, at least *for some*. Of the two informants I have just quoted, one, Jeffrey, is a middle class, cosmopolitan, educated man, who enjoyed a life of relative freedom of movement between countries and a steady income as a journalist and writer, as well as *de facto* membership to the group of expats living in Athens in the 1950s and 1960s. A number of these expats, such as James Merrill or Chester Kallman (to name two of the most famous), identified as homosexual, enjoyed relationships with local Greeks ('a particular hit were the Greek policemen; who were often passed on from one expat to the other'), enjoyed diplomatic protection and certainly a protection offered by their class, passport and financial means. They socialized in specific places and organized parties. They may have experienced in Athens a city where some attitudes were more relaxed, a city still locked in their eyes in a time warp 'before homosexuality'. But this view was shaped by their own experience of identity, and identity *in place*, which was very much informed by their own metropolitan attitudes to sexuality. They could feel at ease in a peripheral yet European city like Athens, with a penal code that did not criminalize homosexuality and a helpful attitude towards western foreigners in a period of austerity and reconstruction. But their 'fluid experience' of Athens was possible especially because they had had the experience of homosexual life in London, New York or Paris – cities where they could always, after all, return if they wanted to. For some of them, moreover, Athens was appealing in that it could fuse a classicizing with an orientalist topography, and this, in the case of a western gay expat cruising for sex, could also mean the fusion of fantasy with availability. Crucially, the erotic/identitarian negotiations these people were able to engage in may not have been available to other people, in the same city, at that same moment in time.

The story of Theodorakopoulos, on the other hand, is different. A working class man from rural Greece, who fought in the Civil War (1946–49) and was persecuted by the right-wing paramilitaries after he returned to his village, found himself seeking exile in Athens, where he also had his first experience of gay sex. He initially believed, he tells me, that he could continue engaging in same-sex relationships as an unmarried man, as long as he kept the active role in sexual intercourse. Today he recalls this as a first phase of his homosexual life ('I was operating under a false consciousness then, you could say') and can narrate in detail how ('through the reading of foreign books, mainly') he came round to developing a different view about sexuality, eventually assuming an activist homosexual identity. In the 1970s, by then a well-known poet and translator, he became one of the first intellectuals to 'come out' in Greece, translated seminal books (such as

Altman's *Homosexual Oppression and Liberation*) and wrote extensively
about sexual oppression in Greece.

Theodorakopoulos' experience of the same-sex paths of the city in the
1950s and 1960s is still recalled as part of a larger culture of homosociality
and uncontainable homoerotic desire that was not, as a whole, related to
a specific identity narrative. His experience, nevertheless, was unfolding at
the same time as the similar experiences of the expat groups, who clearly
had a sexual identity script in their minds and seem to have established an
understanding of this identity as 'freer when far from home'. The result is the
formation of opposite itineraries. If for Theodorakopoulos the city of Athens
was the place where he opened up to an erotics of identity that eventually
became the bedrock of a militant homosexual identification, for Jeffrey it
was the place where certain constraints of a metropolitan gay identity could
be lifted, released. Different maps; different mappings. Working in tandem,
often with different aims, even though sometimes intersecting.

But there is also a second problem with the narrative of the 'multiple,
fluid and uncontained queerness' of an Athens 'before homosexuality' in
the 1950s and 1960s. Recent research has unearthed traces of a vibrant
homosexual subculture existing in Athens long before the 1950s and the
1960s, a topography of homosexual lifestyles that peaks in the 1920s and
1930s, and has even left a small mark in the public domain. In *E eromene tes*
[Her Woman Lover], for instance, a pseudonymous autobiographical diary
novel first published in 1929 and then largely forgotten until it was unearthed
and republished to great acclaim in 2005, the female narrator describes her
love affair with another woman in the Athens of the 1920s. What comes
out of the novel is an Athens that much (perhaps too much) resembles the
Paris of the *Années folles*. The two girls and their friends go around in cars,
they receive invitations to special balls (their experiences there read like
the Parisian balls of the *Magic City* and the bar *Monocle*), they use special
places to hang out and, of course, they read the latest homoerotic literature
to come out of France.[20]

In a similar fashion, the 'biographical novel' *Kourasmenos apo erota*
[Tired of Love],[21] a roman à clef providing a very popular version of the life
of the dandy poet Napoleon Lapathiotis in 1927, spends page after page
recounting the negotiations of men for sex in the Zappeion park in central
Athens, as well as the tavernas and the cafés these men go to. Newspaper
reports during those same years of the 1920s and early 1930s, emphasized
the presence of a 'hidden Athens', often in specially commissioned articles
also describing (and reproducing photographs and graphic accounts of) the
'debauched life of the big European Cities'.[22] The point here is much less
that Athens, especially in the 1920s and 1930s, seems to have had a vibrant
queer subculture that resembled that of the big European metropolis. The
more crucial point is that there was a popularized narrative of the 'queer
city' circulating widely throughout the earlier part of the twentieth century,
shaping the centre as it did the periphery. This narrative was easily available
for controlling gestures of mapping: most newspaper pieces in the 1930s,

called for the authorities not to let Athens become 'debauched Paris', while at the same time rejoicing in the act of fully describing queer scandals, or the nocturnal activity in the central parks. But the narrative was also available to enhance stories such as the published versions of 'memoirs' *Her Woman Lover* and *Tired of Love*, and inform the experience of queer subcultures in the periphery. Maryse Choisy, a famous French feminist journalist who visited the Greek capital in 1929, reported that she had visited lesbian salons and had met 'the most famous lesbians of Athens', in the same way that she had done so 'in Paris, in London and in New York'.[23] We may never find out the exact places and bars Choisy saw during her stay in Athens, or even whether she was exaggerating when she wrote this phrase for a Parisian audience. What is certain, though, is that there was a commonplace view of the 'Lesbian salons of New York and Paris' circulating globally in the late 1920s and 1930s, and somehow the experience of homosexual life in other parts and urban centres of the world was modelled upon them – either as an experience, or as an expectation and frame of reference.

Such references to a queer subculture in Athens subside in the 1940s, 1950s and the early 1960s before they pick up again in the 1970s. It has been argued that this was the result of post-1930s austerity and control – in a manner very similar to the situation that George Chauncey has described in *Gay New York*.[24] However, what should also be noted is that in the 1940s and 1950s the idea of the 'sexual city' seems to become less pronounced in Greek media and cultural texts – moral panics exist, for sure, yet they are less concerned with the image of the queer European metropolis and its impact on Greek urban life. Rather than Athenian queer life itself, it is its narrative mapping as something concrete that seems to have subsided; this is exactly what would come back, with new force, in the late 1960s.

'Sexual Inflation'

While waiting in front of the [Panathenaikon] Stadium I gave a backward glance to two green-berets – one of them had a rare beauty. And suddenly, a strange buzz started around me. One of the two guys turns and whispers something to his colleague. Then the two of them turn and whisper something to two others and they, in their turn, start gazing at me! It seems that in Greece there have been changes I have not yet fully comprehended: offer seems to be four times the demand! In the future, it would be more prudent if one takes this type of inflationary expectation into account! Later on, as they mounted the army truck to go, all four of them would wave goodbye and gesture that they would be there tomorrow too.

This is what Triantafyllos Pittas, a homosexual writer out only to a small circle of friends, wrote in his private diary on 29 July 1970. For more than a decade, Pittas had been filling his notebooks with chance encounters in the city, just like the one I have just copied: encounters in the two main parks, Zappeion and Pedion Areos, but also in other small parks of Athenian neighbourhoods; on the bus but also on the street; in front of shop windows and in cafes; with fear that a passionate youth may be a police set up, but also with a marked boldness in approaching willing strangers. And now, in 1970, Pittas seems to have been at ease and could even joke about cavorting with members of the Greek army, in the middle of a dictatorship, in the centre of Athens and in broad daylight.

It is exactly the same period during which the ethnographer Petropoulos produced his *Kaliarnta: Dictionary of Greek Queers*, the book I discussed at the beginning of this chapter. In Petropoulos's account '[Athenian] queers are a very closed caste which [he] had to try hard to penetrate', their language incomprehensible, their places hidden, their itineraries and encounters a city beneath the city. On the opposite side, Pittas' private diary entries talk about open gestures, a continuum between homosociality and homosexuality, a diffusion of queerness in the centre (and even, the most iconic places) of the city.

All this happens during a regime that boasted about its moralistic credentials and put the motto 'Fatherland, Religion, Family' at the heart of its public credo. In an anecdote that made international headlines, the regime's Minister of Public Order, Colonel Ladas, would even go as far as to beat up, in his office, two journalists who had dared to publish a piece with reference to homosexuality in Ancient Greece.[25] The same colonel was eager to organize police clampdowns in places with homosexual activity (especially in the cinemas of central Athens), even though this was neither consistent nor always very effective.[26]

Since 1969, exactly during the same period, bars and cafes with names such as *Mykonos, Zodiac, Giannis' Bar, Vangelis' Bar, Mouses*, started opening in rapid succession and close proximity to one another, in a small area mostly around the narrow streets Tholou and Thrasyvoulou of Plaka, making this the *de facto* 'gay area of Athens'. In this case, the regime, eager to promote Greece to foreign tourists, seems to have turned a blind eye.

The Junta, therefore, stands as both a period of repression for homosexuals (with politicians announcing that 'they had cleansed the capital of the vice'), and a moment of new opportunities for the public display of homosexual identity. Rather than a contradiction, these inconsistencies could be seen as signs of a sexual economy at a time of change. Some people, like Petropoulos, opted not to see these changes happening; others, like Pittas, were content with the unresolved tensions that lay behind them. Yet others, such as Loukas Theodorakopoulos, finding themselves on the wrong side of control, decided to challenge the regime directly.

Theodorakopoulos and some of his friends were prosecuted in October 1968 in an orchestrated clampdown. Having subsequently defended himself vocally in court, Theodorakopoulos went on to write a memoir about the experience. His book would become a reference point for the emerging sexual identity movement of the 1970s in Greece and one of the reasons for this, I would argue, is the way it interwove a politics of sexual identification with a spatial poetics, an effort to perform homosexuality in a new map of the sexual city.

The police, the party and the memoir

The manuscript for Loukas Theodorakopoulos' memoir *Kaiadas* was ready by 1972, but no editor risked publishing it until the Junta was over. It was finally printed in 1976, 2 years after the fall of the regime, by one of the most progressive publishing houses of Athens of the time, Exantas Publications. On the surface this is a personal account of persecution: it tells the story of a clampdown against a party organized by a homosexual man in his house in the district of Koukouvaounes of Athens in October 1968. The clampdown and subsequent media event around it were overseen by Colonel Ladas. Details of the event, along with the names and photographs of those detained, were widely reported in the heavily censored newspapers of the time – even though there was no clear charge according to the Greek penal code, and eventually everyone was acquitted.

Theodorakopoulos' narrative offers an account of the everyday life of a homosexual man in late 1960s Athens. It starts with his decision to go to a 'gay party'; it goes into a digression about how each one of his group of friends negotiated the role of sexual identity in their own lives; then it describes in detail the type of people gathered in the party and, eventually, their reaction when they realized they had been set up by the police. The narrative follows these people afterwards, in custody, as they are awaiting questioning. From the very first page the narrator is unapologetic about his own identity and extremely critical of the whole police operation. *Kaiadas*, therefore, is framed by a strong political agenda, made apparent from the first pages: the book's aim is to turn an event of persecution into an eloquent identity narrative; a public humiliation ritual into an active coming out gesture; a story of shaming into a paean to (homo)sexual liberation, the first such text to be published in Greek.

If its political agenda is more than clear, *Kaiadas* eventually gravitates towards two dimensions whose critical role is not immediately obvious: identification and space. The narrator is obsessed with the diverse forms and politics of identification. As the guests are coming into the trapped house, long descriptions focus on how each one looks, how effeminate or not they are, how they themselves negotiate their different sexual preferences with their identities, whether they are also married, and which of these characteristics are then used by the police to identify their suspects and decide who they would press more during questioning.

The second centre of gravity in the narrative is space: a long description of the guests' efforts to find the location of the party, with detailed and very self-conscious references to roads, wrong turns and dead ends, is followed by painstaking descriptions of the police headquarters, the rooms the men are kept in, the exact places they decide to sit and wait for questioning and finally the courtroom. Space is seen, alternatingly, as identity marker, trap, site of surveillance and place of expression. At the beginning of the memoir, the narrator outlines how he 'once had had a difficulty with homosexual-only get-togethers'; eventually, he adds, he had come round to realize people's need to 'live, for a couple of hours, in an atmosphere of freedom, impossible to have in a public space'.[27] The whole book could be seen as an effort to open up space, to turn private spatial arrangements into public statements.

Even the title of the book is the name of a place: 'You should have all been thrown off the Kaiadas early on' Colonel Ladas exclaims at one point, as he is overseeing questioning. He refers to the gorge where, according to popular belief, ancient Spartans used to throw off unhealthy babies. What *Kaiadas* the memoir, therefore, performs, is an attempt to reframe the abusive spacing of persecution and abjection, in the same way that it turns the biopolitical mandate to identify and control homosexuals into a celebration of their existence no longer in the hidden corners of the big city, but (given the national circulation of the memoir) in the space of national life and culture.

Kaiadas starts by recalling private arrangements of an earlier homosexual lifestyle in the city, explaining how people tried to manage everyday life between islets of freedom and frames of control. Yet it ends with a different and concrete economy of belonging and a call for public identity. In this context, it is telling that from its first edition *Kaiadas* included, as an appendix, a translation of Guy Hocquenghem's famous coming out 1972 interview from the *Nouvel Observateur* under the title 'The French May 1968 and the homosexual revolution'.

The timing of this memoir's publication could not have been more fortuitous. In 1976, the now democratically elected government suddenly attempted to pass a law 'on sexual diseases'. Against expectations raised by the transition to democracy, the legal framework concerning (homo)sexual conduct and public presence in the city was now being tightened. The initial draft of the law stipulated that illegal sexual activity, prostitution and homosexuality, should be further controlled; that all prostitutes, transgender people and homosexuals should be screened for venereal diseases, and that, in some cases, they should be deported to remote islands.[28]

Reaction was immediate and helped organize a grassroots homosexual movement, the Greek Homosexual Liberation Front (AKOE). Significantly, the movement adopted *Kaiadas* as one of its foundational texts. Theodorakopoulos became the editor of the Front's main journal, *Amphi*, and started organizing weekly meetings in the small basement office space of the magazine on Zaloggou Street in central Athens. A number of my informants remember this as a crucial point in the history of queer Athens.

For the first time there was a place, a well-known address, clearly associated with *the politics* of non-normative sexual identity. AKOE further introduced a new activist politics of space. Many informants, for instance, remember that in the open activist gatherings in cinemas, core members of AKOE would sit among the audience, and then suddenly stand up delivering parts of the movement's political lines. By doing this they were turning the row of cinema seats – one of the celebrated 'queer sites' of a previous era – into a political arena for the political expression of identity.

Kaiadas and AKOE proposed their own spatial and cultural politics of non-normative sexuality in Greece and Athens of the 1970s, at a time when existing strategies of mapping and unmapping had become tenuous. Theirs was a desire to construct an identity *in place* (including the topography of the city and the nation), while at the same time unhinging this emerging identity from the spaces of seclusion and exclusion where it had been relegated by control.

The homosexual topography and political agenda proposed by *Kaiadas* and AKOE did not supersede previous arrangements. Experiencing the corners but also the impulses, the excitement but also the oxymoronic dead-ends of queer Athens still remained the territory of mapping/unmapping. The difference now was that, after *Kaiadas* and AKOE, it was impossible to consider this experience as being 'in a time warp' and outside history. In other words, homosexual politics did not create an all-encompassing homosexual topography; what it did was to provide a frame, to make the historicization of the queer city an imperative and politically meaningful gesture.

Coda: Homosexual topography and the queer city

In the same issue of the magazine *The Truck* where the account of the history of Athenian lesbian bars was published, one can find an article under the title 'How to be a lesbian in Athens'. It talks about . . . cycling. Lesbians are like cyclists in this city, argues contributor Lillybillies.[29] Like cyclists, they are still invisible; they know another one when they see one; they demand recognition of their rights; they collectively stage their own rituals of claiming space in the centre of Athens [since 2010 cyclists have been organizing big gatherings to demand the introduction of bicycle lanes in the capital]. But they also know that they can always craft their own, very personal, itineraries in the city, 'even if the official structures are not there to support them'.

The analogy is useful in reminding us of the dialectic between visibility/invisibility that frames any strategy related to public space. Even gestures aiming to reclaim public space and demand visibility for a minority are bound to create their own exclusions. Thus lesbian Athenians have felt excluded by practices of control and effacement, but they also often find themselves excluded from the visibility gained by gay men (a situation that my own chapter here could not help but replicate to an extent); as gestures of claiming space in both the urban centre but also in the public sphere are multiple and polymorphous today, other sexual minorities – including trans, transqueer or intersex people – are bound to keep finding themselves in the position of the cyclist: at turns supported, forgotten or pushed aside.

But this is exactly the reason why I have tried to talk in this chapter about diverse strategies of mapping/unmapping and the ways they coincide and work together in time, some of them on the side of control, others on the side of subcultural experience. My aim was to show and historicize a larger dynamic with a more general application. In this context, my last section on the 1970s can also be treated as a paradigmatic story. As 'queer space' became debated in Athens in the context and within the agenda of the emerging homosexual liberation movement, the already existing multiplicity of mappings/unmappings stopped being a balanced ecosystem of different coinciding strategies, and became instead a source of tension.

My argument is, therefore, twofold: I have shown why the tension between mapping and unmapping that unfolded in the 1970s produced a certain Athenian *homosexual topography* that many today recognize as the first step in the 'proper' gay history of the city. But I have also argued that the *queer city* pre-existed and superseded this resolution; it remained as an opportunity and made itself felt through a palimpsest of mapping/unmapping that I have traced in existing archival material and through interviews with informants. What I have ultimately tried to chart is a certain making not of a homosexual, but of a queer Athens; a queer Athens understood not as a stable topography or as a finished historiographical project, but as an epistemological and identitarian question unfolding in historical time.

The cycling metaphor can be seen, for this reason, as a wider symbol for the palimpsestic experience of queer Athens I have charted here: both the experience of specific people I have reported throughout, and the possible experiences of others not represented in these accounts. I like to think of cycling as the best visualization for this process of mapping/unmapping. Always trying to put oneself on the map; negotiating one's position around it; and always able to find those alternative routes that, for a moment at least, look like an escape.

Notes

1   Apart from archival and published sources, material for this chapter was also drawn from interviews with 15 Athenian men and women of different ages. For their help with the collection of material, I would like to thank Dimitris Antoniou and Dimos Kouvidis and for their comments on the final manuscript, Soo-Young Kim, William McEvoy, Dimitris Plantzos and the editors of this volume.

2   The 2004 Athens Olympics are generally considered responsible for
nominating Gazi as the Athenian 'gay village', especially in foreign
publications. See the recent discussion on Gazi in gay magazine *Antivirus*
(2009), 30, 38–9. On identity and the experience of living in Gazi, see
Giannakopoulos, K. (2010), 'Ena keno mesa sten pole: Choros, diafora
kai outopia ston Kerameiko kai sto Gkazi' [A void in the city: Space,
difference and utopia in Kerameikos and Gazi], in K. Giannakopoulos and
G. Giannitsiotes (eds), *Amfisvetoumenoi choroi sten pole*. Athens: Alexandreia,
pp. 117–38; Giannakopoulos, K. (2012), 'Politismikes ennoiologeseis
tes monaxias: Syggeneia, koinoteta kai politikes tou LOAT kinematos'
[Cultural significations of loneliness: Kinship, community and politics of
the LGBT movement], in A. Apostolele and A. Chalkia (eds), *Soma, fylo,
sexoualikoteta: LOATK politikes sten Ellada* [Body, gender, sexuality: LGBTI
politics in Greece]. Athens: Plethron, pp. 173–96. Cf. Marnellakis, G. (2007),
'E arhitektonike tes sexoualikotetas' [The architecture of sexuality, intw. to
Dimitris Angelidis], *10%*, 19 (June–September) http://www.10percent.gr/old/
issues/200706/03.html.

3   Papado, M. (2012), 'Oi nychtes mou sta bar tes Athenas' [My nights in the
bars of Athens], *Ntalika*, 6, 14–17.

4   Even though this chapter largely focuses on Athenian experiences of gay men,
women's perspectives have been taken into account and, as much as possible,
represented. If they read as supplementary or less pronounced, this, I fear,
reflects less the drawbacks of my research design, and perhaps more the actual
negotiations on the ground, and a different (even though currently changing)
economy of public visibility enjoyed by the two groups. For an ethnography
of lesbian visibility in Athens see Kantsa, V. (2010b), *Dynamei files dynamei
eromenes*. Athens: Polychromos Planetes; Kantsa, V. (2010a), 'Perpatontas
agkaliasmenes stous dromous tes Athenas: Omofyles sejoualikotetes kai astikos
choros' [Walking together on the streets of Athens: Homosexualities and urban
space], in K. Giannakopoulos and G. Giannitsiotes (eds), *Amfisvetoumenoi
choroi sten pole*. Athens: Alexandreia, pp. 195–225; Kantsa, V. (2012), 'Aorates/
Orates' [Visible/Invisible], in A. Apostolele and A. Chalkia (eds), *Soma, fylo,
sexoualikoteta: LOATK politikes sten Ellada* [Body, gender, sexuality: LGBTI
politics in Greece]. Athens: Plethron, pp. 29–52.

5   Cf. Aggelides, D. (2009), 'Gay chronocapsoula' [interview about gay life
in 1970s Athens]. *10%*, 26. http://www.10percent.gr/periodiko/teyxos26/1203-
2009-06-19-09-14-03.html; Tsitirides, G. (2011), 'Gyrizei to Granazi'
[interview about gay life in 1970s Athens]. *Fagazine*, 3, 38–41.

6   Cf. Aggelakes, A. (1989), *Alesmoneta cinema* [Unforgettable Cinemas].
Exantas: Athens, pp. 26–7.

7   Cf. the roundtable discussion on 'Sygrou in 1980' held in December 2011,
available online at http://www.youtube.com/watch?v=A7JSEFjzlIc.

8   A series of sensationalist books that appeared in the 1980s, with titles
such as *The Pavement* and *Lesbians* (Sioumpouras, F. (1980), *Pezodromio:
Omofylofiloi, travesti, egheirismenes, lesvies, diafthoreia – pornes, prostates*
[Pavement: Homosexuals, transvestites, transsexuals, lesbians, houses of
debauchery, prostitutes, pimps]. Athens: Kaktos; Niarchos, Th. (1986), *Lesvies:
Synenteuxeis kai prosopikes martyries* [Lesbians: Intreviews and testimonies].

Athens: Niarchos). They provide homophobic, yet still useful, descriptions of all those spaces in the city. Cf. the different presentation of Omonoia as a homoerotic site, by respected writer Ioannou, G. (1980), *Omonoia 1980*. Athens: Odysseas.

9   Since its beginning in 2005, Athens Gay Pride has become a very politicized venture, with a marked priority to 'help assess the history of the Greek homosexual community . . . and its organized movement', since 'historical consciousness is the prerequisite for the building of an identity and a community' (*Athens Pride* (2008), p. 3).

10 For the sake of concision, the experience of travestí and transsexuals was not addressed in this chapter. For some early accounts, see Vakalidou, E. (2007), *Mpetty* [autobiography of transgender activist Betty]. Athens: Typotheto; Paola (2008), *To Kraximo* [re-print of the 80s magazine Kraximo, published by transgender activist Paola]. Thessaloniki: Gorgo; as well as the recent visual ethnography conducted by Panapakidis, K. (2012), *Drag Narratives: Staged Gender, Embodiment, and Competition*. Doctoral thesis, Goldsmiths, University of London.

11 Petropoulos, E. (1980 [1972]), *Kaliarnta*. Athens: Nefele, p. 9.

12 Ibid., p. 207.

13 Ibid., pp. 91, 206.

14 There has been, however, some criticism, most notably from the queer anarchist collective Terminal 119 (2012), 'Ta kaliarnta tou Elia Petropoulou: E oratoteta kai to perithorio tes omofylofilcs empeirias' [Petropoulos's Kaliarnta: Visibility and the margins of homosexual experience], in A. Apostolele and A. Chalkia, *Soma, fylo, sexoualikoteta: LOATK politikes sten Ellada* [Body, gender, sexuality: LGBTI politics in Greece]. Athens: Plethron, pp. 79–92. See also Papanikolaou, D. (2011), 'O Elias Petropoulos, e dekaetia tou 60 kai to antisystemiko mas apothemeno' [Elias Petropoulos and the study of Greek subcultures]. *The Books' Journal*, 7, 62–9.

15 My discussion here and in the relevant bibliography, owes a lot to Michel DeCerteau's work, especially the essay 'Walking in the City' (2011) in *The Practice of Everyday Life*. University of California Press, pp. 91–110. An interesting parallel discussion is the one conducted by geographers and social scientists on 'cognitive mapping', cf. Downs, R. and Stea D. (eds) (1973), *Image and Environment: Cognitive Mapping and Spatical Behaviour*. Chicago: Aldine; Pile, S. (1996), *The Body and the City: Psychoanalysis, Space and Subjectivity*. London: Routledge.

16 Knopp, L. (2007), 'From lesbian and gay to queer geographies: Pasts, prospects and possibilities', in K. Browne, L. Jason and G. Brown (eds) (2007), *Geographies of Sexualities: Theory, Practices and Politics*. Aldershot: Ashgate, pp. 21–8, p. 27; see also Bell, V. and G. Valentine (eds) (1995), *Mapping Desire: Geographies of Sexualities*. London: Routledge; Valentine, G. (ed.) (2000), *From Nowhere to Everywhere: Lesbian Geographies*. Cambridge: Polity Press; Betsky, A. (1997), *Queer Space: Architecture and Same Sex Desire*. New York: William Morrow & Co; Browne, K., L. Jason and G. Brown (eds) (2007), *Geographies of Sexualities: Theory, Practices and Politics*. Aldershot: Ashgate.

17 Jeffrey is a pseudonym of a British writer and journalist in his 80s, who lives in central Athens.

18 Loukas Theodorakopoulos, born in 1925 in Amfissa, was a legendary figure of the Greek gay movement. He was interviewed for this research on 7 May 2012 and wanted to be quoted with his real name. He passed away on 26 April 2013, as this piece was being edited for publication.

19 Cook, M. (2003), *London and the Culture of Homosexuality, 1885–1914*. Cambridge: Cambridge University Press, p. 5.

20 What I am describing here is, obviously, not specific only to Athens. In her research on Berlin, Marti Lybeck (2009) has shown a similar pattern at work, insisting on the importance of writing and reading to the constitution of lesbian lifeworlds. See: Lybeck, M. (2009), 'Gender, sexuality, and belonging: Female homosexuality in Germany, 1890–1933', *Bulletin of the German Historical Institute*, 43, pp. 29–42.

21 Tsoukalas, G. (1927), *Kourasmenos apo erota*. Athens.

22 On 2 February 1929, for instance, an article in the popular newspaper *Akropolis* describes the performance of naked dancers in Athenian bars, noting that 'Athens is having fun; everything looks like an imitation of Europe'. See also an indicative sequence of titles from the same newspaper in 1932: 'Women having orgies in the literary salons of Paris' (*Akropolis*, 25 September 1932); 'How debauchery swamps the female world of Athens' (24 October 1932); 'The nocturnal Paris of debauchery and vice: A night in a bar with young transvestites' (20 November 1932); 'Transvestite youths in Athens' (24 November 1932); 'A wave of effeminate youths swamps Athenian society: Satanic ambushes in cinemas and schools' (25 November 1932).

23 Choisy, M. (1930), *L' Amour dans les prisons*. Paris: Montaigne, p. 144; Choisy, M. (1929), *Un Mois chez les hommes*. Paris: Editions de France.

24 Varelas, L. (2008), 'Evremata kai nees protaseis gia to romantzo *E Eromenes tes* tes Ntoras Rozette' [New findings on Rozette's *My Woman Lover*]. *Nea Estia*, 1808, 261–300; cf. Chauncey, G. (1995), *Gay New York: The Making of the Gay Male World*. London: Flamingo.

25 Clogg, R. (1972), 'The ideology of the "revolution" of 21 April 1967', in R. Clogg and G. Yannopoulos (eds), *Greece Under Military Rule*. London: Secker & Warburg, pp. 36–58, p. 41.

26 Aggelakes, A. (1989), *Alesmoneta cinema*. Athens: Exantas.

27 Theodorakopoulos, L. (1976), *Okaiddas*. Athens: Exantas, p. 27.

28 Theodorakopoulos, L. (2005), *Amfi kai apeleutherose*. Athens: Polychromos Planetes.

29 Lillybillies (2012), 'Pos na eisai lesbia sten Athena' [How to be a lesbian in Athens]. *Ntalika* 6, 18–19.

Further reading

Aggelakes, A. (1989), *Alesmoneta cinema* [Unforgettable Cinemas]. Exantas: Athens.

Apostolele A. and A. Chalkia, *Soma, fylo, sexoualikoteta: LOATK politikes sten Ellada* [Body, gender, sexuality: LGBTI politics in Greece]. Athens: Plethron, pp. 29–52.

Athens Pride (2008), *E Istoria tou lesviakou-gei-amfi & trans kinematos sten Ellada: Mia prote apotimese* [The history of the lesbian-gay-bi & trans movement in Greece: A first survey]. Athens: futura.

Giannakopoulos, K. (2010), 'Ena keno mesa sten pole: Choros, diafora kai outopia ston Kerameiko kai sto Gkazi' [A void in the city: Space, difference and utopia in Kerameikos and Gazi], in K. Giannakopoulos and G. Giannitsiotes (eds), *Amfisvetoumenoi choroi sten pole*. Athens: Alexandreia, pp. 117–38.

Ioannou, G. (1980), *Omonoia 1980*. Athens: Odysseas.

Kantsa, V. (2010a), 'Perpatontas agkaliasmenes stous dromous tes Athenas: Omofyles sejoualikotetes kai astikos choros' [Walking together on the streets of Athens: Homosexualities and urban space], in K. Giannakopoulos and G. Giannitsiotes (eds), *Amfisvetoumenoi choroi sten pole*. Athens: Alexandreia, pp. 195–225.

Marnellakis, G. (2007), 'E arhitektonike tes sexoualikotetas' [The architecture of sexuality, intw. to Dimitris Angelidis), *10%*, 19 (June–September), http://www.10percent.gr/old/issues/200706/03.html

Petropoulos, E. (1980 [1972]), *Kaliarnta*. Athens: Nefele.

Theodorakopoulos, L. (1976), *O Kaiadas*. Athens: Exantas.

9

Istanbul: Queer desires between Muslim tradition and global pop

Ralph J. Poole

12 points

May 2005. It is hot, crowded and noisy. Everybody is singing, cheering and dancing to the music from the huge screen. There is an overbearing sense of community with everybody drinking, sweating and partying together. The atmosphere is charged with erotic energy. This is just a first impression, though. There is something strange about this picture.

I am in a bar in Istanbul (called not so subtly The Other Side) surrounded mostly by men, mostly Turks, most in their early twenties. They are cheering for a song sung by a Greek performer: Helena Paparizou's 'My Number One' – the 2005 winner of the Eurovision Song Contest. Paparizou garnered a score of 12 points – the highest possible, and awarded by their Turkish neighbour. Why would a group of presumably exclusively gay men in a Turkish bar cheer for a Greek band, given the long-standing political animosity between the two nations and the fresh tension sparked by new controversies over Cyprus' role in Europe? There is an easy answer: it is fun to be together, enjoy dance music and to flirt. But there is also a more intricate answer that needs additional explanation.

Growing up in Europe in the 1970s, it was a must for everyone to watch the Grand Prix Eurovision de la Chanson, as the annual Eurovision Song Contest (ESC) was still called then, before its name was anglicized. Since its inception in 1956, the event has become a European institution, delineating one understanding of the European community. Originally with only seven participating countries, the contest has steadily grown – as has Europe. In 2012, 43 countries participated, making it necessary to divide the formerly one-night event into two semi-finals and a final. In the course of time, the field has included most Eastern European countries and countries not considered European in other contexts: Israel and Turkey (since 1973 and 1975 respectively) among the first, and Armenia, Azerbaijan and Georgia among the latest additions. This can be seen as a means 'of indicating a pro-European stance or a European affiliation' for these countries, often foreshadowing future membership in the EU.[1] 'Therefore', cultural historian Heiko Motschenbacher explains, 'one can see the ESC as a musical test for what may lie ahead in politics. If certain countries can compete in a pop music competition, they may eventually try to cooperate on a political level'.[2] For a long time, Turkey was without luck in the contest.

But a definite turning point for Turkey was the spectacular victory in May 2003, with many countries awarding it a full 12 points. After a quarter of a century of trying and with much embarrassment this was, as musicologist Thomas Solomon suggests, a 'historical moment'. The failure to score points in the contest up to then has been perceived in Turkey 'as an allegory of its aspirations to join the European Union and its frustratingly slow movement towards that goal, and proof of the perception, warranted or not, that Europeans do not accept Turkey as a European nation'.[3] The success of 2003 sparked new hope. Solomon makes a strong – not aesthetic, but political – claim that part of the sudden victory was due to Turkey's surprising opposition to the United States' wish to set up a military base in southern Turkey to provide a northern invasion route into Iraq. This resistance brought Turkey many sympathizers at a time of growing anti-war sentiment in continental Europe. But it was also Sertab Erener's song 'Everyway that I can' with its hybrid musical aesthetics including English lyrics, Middle Eastern rhythms and a mix of belly-dancing and hip-hop moves, that 'projected a Euro-friendly version of Turkey just at the time much of Europe was predisposed to be friendly with Turkey'.[4]

So why did the gay crowd cheer for Helena Paparizou in that gay bar that evening? Certainly, there was an aesthetic point of comparison: 'It seemed that Greece found the right combination of a solid pop song, English lyrics, and "ethnic" stylings in its music and performance, comparable in many ways to Sertab's 2003 performance'.[5] But this only very partially explains the hurrahs of my gay Turkish friends. More obviously there was Helena's 'highly polished' stage performance that contrasted to Sertab's faux-harem machinations.[6] Helena was surrounded by four gorgeous, bare-chested male dancers. These boys not only looked very gay, but judging from the enthusiasm of the bar's crowd the whole song-and-dance number exuded a distinct gay sensibility, much more so than Sertab's performance.

Both songs not only became immensely popular in Turkey in general and in the gay scene in particular; they highlighted the lasting appeal of the ESC for a gay male audience.[7] All over Europe, the event is followed by its gay fans who often gather for celebratory parties hosted in gay bars. The contest has been called 'Gay Christmas', a sort of holiday not unlike

Gay Pride celebrations.[8] But the ESC does not transcend nationality; 'rather, Eurovision provides a rare occasion for simultaneously celebrating both queerness and national identity'.[9] Istanbul is no exception here, and yet it is only recently that such parties are organized as part of a growing community and increasingly visible gay urban scene. Istanbul, although not the country's political capital, clearly can be considered its gay capital. And yet, as much as queer moments just described link Istanbul to social practices of other European queer metropoles, the largest Turkish city at the same time remains very much entangled in the nation's overall struggle to find a distinct cultural identity between its currently resurfacing Ottoman past with the political backlash that entails and the ongoing precarious move towards a future membership in the EU. The following chapter proceeds from this example of a local gay cultural practice in Istanbul's gay bar scene to look at the way an understanding and treatment of homosexuality has evolved in the nation in general and in the city in particular. A look at two major radical transitional periods in Turkey's history, namely the founding of the Turkish Republic in 1923 and the 1980 military coup d'état, will serve as backdrop to an ensuing discussion of particular sites of contemporary gay practice in Istanbul such as bars and baths.

Turkey's transitional periods: Kemalist modernization and military coups

Speaking about homosexuality in Turkey proves to be an endeavour charged with ambiguities and paradoxes. A secular nation modelled on Western legal standards, Turkey also remains a predominantly Islamic society. Turkish homosexuality is located at the crossroads of both East and West with strict religious tradition competing against the claims of a secular nation state, and nowhere is this more obvious than in Istanbul, a city that not only in geographical terms is precariously located right on the East-West-schism. For an understanding of the current situation of homosexuals in Turkey, it is necessary to acknowledge the profound change that Kemalism, that is, the project of modernization launched by the republic's founding father Mustafa Kemal Atatürk, and the ensuing concept of Turkish citizenship brought along. Since this project was conceived to oppose everything that the traditions of the Ottoman Empire entailed, its nationalist agenda can also be understood in sexual terms, since 'sexuality, family relations, and gender identities came to occupy a central place in discourses about modernity'.[10]

With women having to discard their veils and moving out into the public, both radical renunciations of the Ottoman separation of genders, the forcefully modernized man also had to adapt to a changed sexual discourse. On the upside, this meant for a woman hitherto unknown access to sites of education and work, on the downside an increased monitoring of her virtue and honour. And as for the changing concepts of masculinity, the dissolution of gendered spheres did not come along with a loosening of strictly divided sexual identities. On the contrary, 'masculinity is generally regarded as superior to femininity. Those who seek to live up to the former are expected to be sexually active, initiate sex and penetrate female or feminine bodies'.[11]

Whereas formerly and by way of the division of spheres, the stronghold of homosociality may at times have included clandestinely tolerated homosexual practices, now both men and women were called upon to share all spheres making same-sex interactions more difficult and indeed unwanted. Modelled after Western conceptions of heteronormativity, the Kemalist project literally left no queer spaces. Pointing to the Turkish Constitution's Article 66 of 1982 ('Everyone bound to the Turkish state through the bond of citizenship is a Turk'), communication theorist Lukasz Szulc pointedly claims: 'Every citizen of Turkey is a (straight) Turk', and human rights defender Hakan Ataman adds that the 'Kemalist perception of citizenship therefore excludes LGBT people in Turkey'.[12]

The military has seen it as one of its prime goals to uphold the Kemalist ideology, even though acting mostly in the background. But the three coups of 1960, 1971 and 1980 prove the willingness of the military to intervene in governmental states of affairs, if the generals decide that the Kemalist ideals are in danger of being forsaken. Of the three coups, the 1980 takeover, which resulted in 3 years of strict military rule, had the strongest effects on the LGBT community in urban centres such as Istanbul and Ankara. There were severe restrictions for anyone not adhering to the Kemalist ideal of Turkish citizenship and especially for those deemed morally deviant. After a crowing liberation and visibility of gays and lesbians during the 1960s and 1970s, nightclubs in these cities were now shut down, burgeoning gay organizations were banned and transsexuals were imprisoned.[13]

Due to these extreme measures, however, new social movements gradually started to emerge as soon as the elected government had taken over again in 1983, among which was the founding of professionals LGBT organizations. In 1993, the first Gay Pride Week was first permitted and then banned at the very last minute, resulting in the arrest of 28 foreign delegates; the massive protest of activists that followed led to the launching of the first two Turkish LGBT organizations: Lambda Istanbul in the same year and Kaos GL in Ankara a year later.[14] The first Gay Pride Week then was celebrated in 2003, and in 2004 the First Gay and Lesbian Film Festival took place in Istanbul, which was so heavily controlled by the police that being present at that event I had to wonder whether the police was meant to protect us from (non-existent) protesting crowds or whether we were being monitored and threatened by the police instead. Unfortunately, the event was not repeated and cinéastes interested in the newest queer films again had to resort to the prestigious International Istanbul Film Festivals, which for some time has included a fair share of such national and international productions. The still ongoing effort to 'cleanse' the morals of citizens led (among other things) to the effort of closing Lambda Istanbul in 2008. The court decided that the existence of such an institution (besides not carrying a proper Turkish name) would infringe the 'public morale' and the protection of family values. The Supreme Court of Appeals, however, overturned this order and Lambda was allowed to continue operating, if under close scrutiny.

Turkish sex

(Homo)sexual practices, gender norms and queer life in Istanbul cannot be viewed without taking into account the sexual customs at large which are still heavily influenced by their Muslim heritage. Since Islam is a religion based on a legal framework, there is no morality and sin in a western, Christian sense, but rather the abidance or violation of laws. Accordingly, to act ethically for Muslims means compliance with the Sharia. With respect to sexuality, this implies that the sexual act can only be performed between legitimate persons. From a legal-Islamic perspective, homosexuality is fornication, *zina*, because it is defined as illegitimate and thus illegal penetration.[15] And yet, according to many records 'pederasty' – the term given to male-male sexuality – in Muslim regions was practised at least since the eighth century and almost always tolerated as a social practice. How can we account for this paradox? In Arabic countries as well as in Turkey, active and passive sexual roles are the constituting paradigm of masculinity and femininity. Homo- and heterosexuality are thus defined not so much by a concrete choice of object, but rather by sexual practices. Arno Schmitt describes this gendered logic in one of the few studies on the topic, *Sexuality and Eroticism Among Males in Moslem Societies*, which came out in 1992: 'Men consider themselves to be stronger physically, intellectually, and morally, and be able to control instinct and emotion – unlike women, children . . . and transvestites'.[16]

A derogatory view on male homosexuality therefore relates predominantly to men who engage in receptive anal intercourse.[17] 'Gay' generally defines the one who takes this role. His social depreciation relates above all to his betrayal of the masculine ideal. The active male may even gain admiration because he has proven his masculinity without a proper external 'object of desire'.[18] Mehmet Ümit Necef confirms that the notion of 'homosexuality' basically is a Western import, whereas traditionally there is a distinction according to sexual roles between *kulanpara* (from Persian meaning 'fucker of boys') and *ibne*. The practice of hate speech, for example, shows that *ibne* does not invariably signal homosexual behaviour but is an appearance that lacks male sovereignty, similar to 'fag', 'pansy' or 'pussy' in English. *Ibne* means 'being fucked' in a rhetorical-symbolic way, in the sense of being unmanly and impotent, but also more generally of not being able to offer resistance.[19] On the contrary, this means that a colloquial threat like 'I fuck you' ('Ich ficke dich' in German – where it is frequently used among young Turks), implies the willingness to fight coupled with a confidence of victory as in Hermann Tertilt's ethnographic study on youth gangs, *Turkish Power Boys*.[20] In general, of the 80 entries in the contemporary Turkish vocabulary that allude to same-sex sexuality, only ten refer to female homosexuality and only five to men as active partners in sexual intercourse, whereas more than 50 terms refer to men letting themselves be 'penetrated' by other men thus indicating again a cultural preoccupation with the putatively emasculated male.[21]

The common social practice in Muslim countries calls for heterosexual marriage as the favoured way to bypass impeding marginalization. In moderate, Europeanized families, many of which live in Istanbul, it is now more common for young unwed men to live alone outside of the parental home, though a son's announcement of being gay still often leads to an appointment with a therapist. This routine is common across the country, but especially prevailing in a metropolis like Istanbul, and supported by the Turkish psychiatry that is known to be overly conservative.[22] Homosexuality thus continues to be considered a passing phase or sickness that may be overcome with professional help.[23] The situation for lesbian women is even less encouraging. Some efforts by lesbian activists notwithstanding, who in the 1990s founded organizations such as Sappho'nun Kızları (Saphho's Girls) and Venus'un Kızkardeşleri (The Sisters of Venus), lesbianism remains almost completely invisible in public life; there are currently, for example, no bars in Istanbul addressing a specific lesbian clientele.[24] Transvestism and transsexuality, on the other hand, are spread widely and play a much larger role in Turkey compared to Western Europe and the United States, precisely due to a strict practice of gender dichotomy.

Emrecan Özen describes such sexual codes in a campy way. In an internet tourist guide catering to gay patrons, he 'warns' Western tourists visiting Istanbul thus: 'For some hetero men, a gay arse is the next best thing if they cannot find a woman that night! With these types, you've got nothing to do if you're looking for a long and versatile session – your only chance is to spread the legs and try and enjoy yourself till he cums'.[25] It is not easy to tell whether trendy youngsters in bars like 360°, Barbahçe, Beşinci Kat or most recently XLarge Club, all of which are located in the most Westernized part of Istanbul's centre, Beyoğlu, are just playing it cool – and queer – showing off their muscled-up bodies, or whether straight-looking bears drinking beer in Tekyön are later up for the transvestites of Sahra Bar, where it is just as likely to be ripped off by some sleazy pimp as it is to be offered money by an eager patron. Trusting appearances may likely lead to comic misunderstandings, harsh disappointments or more serious trouble.

Istanbul hamam: Architecture of seduction

When the film *Hamam*, a 1997 Italian-Turkish co-production by exile Turkish director Ferhan Özpetek, was screened in Turkey, there was a great outcry claiming that this was a totally distorting, Orientalizing, and wholly untrue account of what goes on in a traditional Turkish bath. The film narrates the homoerotic confusion of the Italian protagonist Francesco who through an enforced sojourn in Turkey discovers his love for the local bath culture and in consequence for men. The public disclosure of a strictly taboo homosocial and indeed homosexual practice was felt to be a true scandal. This was especially the case as it was narrated and viewed from a tourist's perspective that purportedly calls up stereotypical notions of (homo)sexual tourism that has for centuries been part of male Western travelogues recounting their Istanbul visit. A Turkish bathhouse-guide, available at every major tourist site in Istanbul, claims that such Western perceptions of Turkish bathhouses are filtered through the lens of Orientalism and thus warns the tourist not to give in to 'the general western impression of the Turkish bath as representing the "mystique of the harem"'. Instead, sexual activity is 'far from the rule'.[26] In travel guides more specifically aimed at a gay audience, you will read a very different interpretation of the hamam experience. Often they serve as a glib warning to be careful not to be ripped off by rent boys offering overprized and unprofessional 'erotic massages' in places like the 'sleazy' Aquarius Sauna, and not to take the 'action' on offer in Cihangir Sauna for granted. What these guides thus imply – the warnings for caution notwithstanding – is the fact of quite unrestrained, if often purchasable sexual activity in hamams contrary to official claims.[27]

This flies in the face of traditional narratives surrounding bathhouse rituals and practices. Traditionally, for the devout Muslim, the hamam unifies the sacred and the sexual. The hamam figures as concrete *and* symbolic space since it serves as transition between the quotidian organization of sexual activity and the experience of religious prayer. According to Muslim belief, purity is an essential element. After any kind of physical activity – especially including the sexual act – and before each prayer, a Muslim should wash himself. That is the reason why traditional hamams are always in close vicinity to a mosque. According to Abdelwahab Bouhdiba, the act of washing is not only to be understood as cleansing of a body soiled by sex, but in its restored purity also as the preparation for the sexual act: 'The hamam is the epilogue of the flesh and the prologue of prayer. The practices of the hamam are pre- and post-sexual practices'.[28] Bouhdiba speaks of a 'hamam complex' through which the sexual life is organized around the visit to a bathhouse, which especially for the adolescent male serves as rite of passage, since attending the male hamam signifies his 'derealization of the female world' and the entry into an 'all-male community'.[29] The exceptional space that the hamam occupies in the life of a traditional Muslim may be seen by the fact that this it is one place where the Quran may not be read, where instead the body should relax, preparing the mind for the spiritual experience to come. As such, the bath visit could serve as a survival strategy for Muslims since it has given the society leeway to release sexual tension.

In the course of Turkey's modernization and Westernization epitomized in refashioning Ottoman Istanbul into a global hub, such habitualized homosocial and homoerotic practices were classified, pathologized, repressed and criminalized. This was part of the larger historical context already underway during the nineteenth century in which the young Turkish republic restructured its society through urbanization based on European, and especially French models. New public spaces were created changing the metropolitan cartography to include boulevards, theatres, parks and cinemas. Beyoğlu's grand pedestrian avenue İstiklal Caddesi, now a major pedestrian, shopping and clubbing site, is a prime example. These places were supposed to have a de-Orientalising effect, and *de facto* they did succeed in blurring otherwise rigid gender boundaries. Even though this was mainly a phenomenon of the societal elite, this process in turn led to the privatization and thus demise of bathing culture. Going to baths was considered to be old fashioned and leading to backwardness. Public bathhouses symbolized Islamic traditionalism and were contrary to the wished-for ideals of a modernized elite. Atatürk's reforms in the early twentieth century called for a reformist, republican nation, and bathhouses as quasi-religious institutions stood against these secular and nationalist ideas.[30] Visiting the hamam not only became something like a religious confession, it also turned into a class issue.

This changed only with the emergence of a recent trend in tourism during the latter half of the twentieth century, when tourists – and among them gay tourists – started to look for erotic exoticism linked to an Ottoman history instead of a modernized Turkey. The Turkish bath was rediscovered as a source of income and therefore many of the almost defunct and shabby bathhouses such as Istanbul's Cağaloğlu Hamamı and Çemberlitaş Hamamı were restored to former Ottoman splendour. This wave of restoration was part of a public change of heart towards the 'lost' Ottoman cultural heritage. And it was this double effect that Özpetek's film *Hamam* captured, where the hero Francesco inherits a decrepit and defunct bathhouse and instead of selling it off decides to restore and reopen it. In the course of this endeavour, he falls in love and has sex with the pretty Turkish boy Mehmet.

Even though this revival is rooted in an effort to attract foreign tourists, it has a secondary effect on the native modern, young, urban middle-class – with Mehmet as a representative – who is increasingly willing to participate in the renaissance of a long-lost culture. Nina Cichocki calls this 'internal tourism', when 'the otherized Ottoman past becomes a foreign country – within (the) home country – where Turks like to travel as tourists, follow tips given by guide books and visit such sites as the *hamam*'.[31] Cichocki explicitly exempts Özpetek's film as well as the resurgence of a queer *hamams'* desire via the hamam-revival in general from this phenomenon, and yet my claim is that Özpetek, himself an openly gay director, deliberately reminds us of this cultural practice of remembering in his films, especially *Harem suaré*, a historical film about the harem of the last Ottoman sultan. It is through the economy of gazing that Özepetek enters the cultural practice of cruising.[32] The recoding of a formerly sexual practice of Muslim cultures, which was based on a traditionalized segregated gender order and which never understood sex between men as homosexuality, makes possible an encounter like that of Francesco and Mehmet that is based on a non-traditional, mutual and genuinely homoerotic desire. Mehmet, belonging to a new generation of Istanbulites that is willing to embrace such notions of 'gayness', meets Francesco in this architectural space represented by renewed possibilities for seduction. The film, thus, at the same time extracts forgotten layers of Ottoman homosocial agency in the hamam experience, and resets them to contemporary sexual practices in an increasingly queer and Europeanized Istanbul.

Istanbul at night: Queer music and bars

At night in Istanbul's party district, Beyoğlu, you can see transvestites walking on Tarlabaşı Street, as well as in Cihangir, around Taksim Square, and along the side streets of İstiklal Avenue, all of which comprise the traditional Western-Christian bohemian neighbourhoods of Beyoğlu. In this area, there are also most gay bars and clubs, some with back rooms. It is also the area of prostitution, especially for men seeking transsexual partners.[33] Therefore, this group has specifically been the target of policing. Since it is very difficult for transgender people to find regular employment and even licensed bordellos are closed to them, most earn money as street workers and are thus easy prey for police harassment, blackmailing, arrests and abuse.[34] By contrast, Russell Ivy, studying gay travel patterns, finds Istanbul a particularly interesting example of a place 'with a modest build-up of gay infrastructure' that serves as an 'island' 'surrounded by a region with little to no gay infrastructure.'[35] Istanbul has been called 'the first (most important) gay city in Turkey and the second (most important) in Eastern Europe (after Mikonos, Greece)' (www.istanbulguide.net) and therefore, Istanbul could be perceived as the most important gay city in the Islamic world.

A pop cultural case in point reflecting such vagaries of queer Istanbul is Mehmet Murat Somer's 'Hop-Çiki-Yaya' thriller series.[36] This crime series set in contemporary Istanbul features an unnamed transvestite amateur sleuth, who, made-up as a flamboyant drag queen 'with an Audrey Hepburn alter-ego', runs an underground transvestite bar at night while by day – and clad in all-male attire – he runs a lucrative hacker business.[37] Turkish author Somer explains the title in an interview: 'Hop-Çiki-Yaya was a cheerleading chant from Turkish colleges in the early 1960s, and it came to be used in comedy shows to mean gays. If somebody was queenish, then they'd say "Oh, he's Hop-Çiki-Yaya"'. By the 1970s, it wasn't being used anymore – so I brought it back'.[38] What is most interesting is that this character, although ostensibly a transvestite and homosexual in the sense that he/she desires men and defies given gender norms, highlights their flexibility through temporal and spatial anchors. Whether on the hunt in Westernized liberal Beyoğlu, the queer hub of the city, or investigating in the visibly more Muslim Eminönü, the former centre of Constantinople, he/she moves about the city effortlessly crossing the gendered East-West-schism.[39]

As could be seen in Turkey's victory at the ESC that installed Sertab Erener as a national heroine who 'conquered Europe' music has played a crucial role in the self-definition of the Turkish nation state as well as in the self-fashioning of various groups including queer audiences.[40] 'Arabesk' in particular is a musical style that is closely connected to Turkey's recent national and cultural history. Besides its immense and at times subversive power, which is mostly at odds with the state-regulated efforts to forge a common national identity, Arabesk also pays tribute to a questioning of how to situate an overwhelmingly popular and socially pervasive music genre within the discourse of globalized pop music. Sertab Erener's performance at the Eurovision Song Contest, for example, used elements of Arabesk and it proved to be the formula for international success; Tarkan is an even more famous example about which more is discussed later. Indeed, perhaps Arabesk poses the greatest potential for thinking about how queerness functions in contemporary Istanbul, blending together gay, straight and queer elements and providing an opportunity for subversion through tradition instead of against it.

As a cultural practice, Arabesk was always quintessentially queer, blurring high and low, modern and traditional elements, and emerging on the scene from the fringes of the city during the 1950s and 1960s, where the traditional habits of immigrants from predominantly impoverished southeast Anatolian (mostly Kurdish) rural areas blended with contemporary urban lifestyles.[41] From the very start and given Turkey's Kemalist ideology, Arabesk's foreignness and alienness – its 'Arabic' style[42] – could not easily be assimilated and it posed a threat to the politics of the Turkish nation state in general and to Istanbul in particular. In suggestive sexual metaphors, Alev Çınar remarks that the notion of the 'provincial other' as 'the alien infesting the city' has created personifying depictions of Istanbul as a beleaguered place suffering from corruption, alienation and degeneration; it is 'open to penetration and destruction, a place that is defenceless in the face of the modernizing and Westernizing influences of the secular state'.[43]

On the whole, Arabesk has remained in the stronghold of a masculine culture that 'is strongly associated with mustaches, masculine friendship, and *rakı*-drinking, cigarette-smoking rituals'.[44] Nevertheless, the longstanding 'Othering' of Arabesk singers as well as the melodramatic lyrics of their songs have put these male performers in a somewhat ambiguous category of masculinity. The considerable popularity of transsexual performers in this genre further adds to the complexity of body politics that distinguishes Arabesk in general. Despite the queerness of the practice, it could still be quite a precarious existence for performers. Following the 1980 military coup, the restrictive politics included a policing of Arabesk music and films that in turn resulted in the exile of stars like transsexual Bülent Ersoy, to pick an especially notorious and famous example.

Ersoy was one of the first widely known Turkish transsexuals, quickly gaining cult status within the Arabesk community. After her sex reassignment surgery in 1981, she not only faced transphobic reactions from the government leading to her ban on public performances, her petition to be legally recognized as a woman was rejected as well. Her operation was performed in London because local sex reassignment surgery was illegal in Turkey at the time. Her highly visible stardom might even have accelerated the restrictive measures of the military government on Arabesk. Despite being forced to leave the country due to persecution, she successfully continued to perform in West Germany until her return in 1988, after which she filed a court case, fighting for her legal recognition as a woman. Due to the changed Turkish Civil Code in 1988,[45] which added the amendment that male-to-female post-operative transgender people could now obtain the 'pink card' to certify their new female gender, Ersoy continued her career as a female performer in Turkey, although retaining her rather male first name Bülent.

Although the change in legislation was brought on by Ersoy's court case, resulting in a rather progressive legal regulation,[46] the ensuing situation for transgender people has not been without conflicts. On the contrary, as Deniz Kandiyoti points out, the pressures to eliminate any ambiguity in matters of gender have caused serious problems for transgender people such as 'potential medical malpractice'.[47] The established hegemonic structure, though somewhat loosened in recent years, still today maintains a strictly dichotomous gender system, denying the existence of homosexual and transgender identifications. Therefore, a male-to-female transsexual like Ersoy is more likely to be considered an aberrant woman and thus her former biological male sex will simply be ignored. As many cases from Istanbul's transgender scene prove, one of the ways to 'come out' of the prescribed invisibility of closeted sexual behaviour still remains the choice of a 'corrective' surgical procedure.

This claim of a specifically Turkish mode of living transsexuality accounts not only for the ambiguous fascination that transsexuals evoke in the broad public, but also for the perception of transsexuality as a signifying cultural practice of paradoxical and disparate public performance, especially with regard to highly visible actors like Arabesk singers. Thus, an example like Bülent Ersoy's speaks for Arabesk as 'all encompassing metaphor' expressing the pervasive identity problem of a Turkish society that is 'strangely composite' and as such unwillingly 'appropriating and incorporating into its closed circle what does not fit into the existing scheme of things'.[48]

A different example of how Arabesk has been queered in the last years is Tarkan. Turkish singer Tarkan for years has been one of Turkey's most prominent pop exponents and exports. His music style and performance mixes belly-dance, rap, break-dance, Turkish classical music and western pop. In 2006, he released his first all-English album *Come Closer*, produced in the United States, thus aiming, with his music style and star image, to join the global market forces. Like Sertab Erener in her ESC performance, Tarkan 'attempts to steer a middle course between the Scylla of Western pop music and the Charybdis of "traditional" Turkish music'.[49]

And yet, refocusing the perspective from a global scope back to Turkey, Tarkan is but one example of a booming pop-culture within his homeland Turkey, centred in Istanbul's clubbing scene, but present – via radio, television, internet, cell phones and iPods – in virtually every household throughout the country. Tarkan, who as a child of Turkish *Gastarbeiter* in Germany moved with his family to Turkey in his early teens and now lives in Istanbul and New York, is a 'product' of migrant politics due to transnational economics. When viewed solely from a western perspective, he figures as thoroughly westernized and highly sexualized orient-export. Yet his music is actually rooted in the Turkish tradition of Arabesk culture that is historically and geographically locatable as non-western.

As can be seen in his videos,[50] Tarkan's allusion to Oriental belly-dancing re-creates and moulds himself into a representation of an Oriental Other which in turn brings him precariously close to feminized, exoticized and colonial notions of the Orient, mostly associated with sexually attractive and available women, but including men as well. More than other Arabesk singers, Tarkan situates himself within a cultural context of the Middle East, where belly dancing, for example, has long been both a social – or folk – practice as well as a profession performed by women *and* men alike. Thus, even though a male dancer's sex would be discernible, his male gender was disputable from the viewpoint of cultural outsiders. For the latter, the scandal of the male dancer was his dubious sexual allure as seemingly being available, yet remaining frivolously aloof.[51]

On the other hand, Tarkan's body – his style and movements – adheres to the western discourse of double entendre. In so doing, he covertly uses a second language that is queerly coded. It is an 'open secret' within the gay community, both in Istanbul's clubbing scene as well as abroad, that Tarkan himself is gay. This is not to say that we can automatically conflate his private predilections with his public star persona. But I suggest that Tarkan delib- erately mixes musical genres of different cultures as well as creates hybrid body images that cover *and* reveal various things simultaneously. In this way, his body represents a terrain upon which the gender and sexual conflicts in modern Turkey play themselves out, in a highly spatialized fashion.

To quote Stephen Amico's findings, analysing the connection of house music and homosexuality, Tarkan here takes part in a cultural dilemma where 'gay men are forced to resort to re-appropriation, *bricolage*' when attempting to imitate 'straight' society.[52] Tarkan's local success and global appeal are markers not least of a transnational queer community in which a shared bond of common knowledge is characteristic of the versatility of queer culture that is also manifest in the transnationality of the Eurovision Song Contest. The worldwide fandom of the ESC forges an 'imagined queer community', which also manifests itself through the very concrete and physical experience of partying together at the ESC celebration in the gay bar in Istanbul that I took part in.[53] 'Queer culture', Michael Warner claims, 'has found it necessary to develop this knowledge in mobile sites of drag, youth culture, music, dance, parades, flaunting, and cruising'.[54] These sites are mobile, not easy to recognize, and yet full of potential, and in Istanbul in particular, are as 'fragile and ephemeral' as ever.[55]

This notwithstanding, with Istanbul's growing touristic appeal and global importance the gay scene is still on the rise in this megacity where, according to our insider tourist guide Emrecan Özen, gay life 'is probably the best way to experience Istanbul's highly cosmopolitan atmosphere and diverse cultural fabric that is stretched from East to West'.[56] In 'The Gay Map of the Islamic World' published by *The Advocate*, Turkey ranks highest of all Islamic countries most likely to be visited by members of the LGBT community.[57] While the article claims that '[d]reams of European Union membership are a liberalizing force', igniting 'burgeoning gay tourism infrastructure in Istanbul', the fact remains that after a peak in queer visibility and freedom in the mid-2000s, an increasingly palpable conservatism of Turkey's Prime Minister Erdoğan and his Justice and Development Party (AKP) has caused an Islamic backlash for the queer Turkish community. Therefore, it remains to be seen whether Istanbul can uphold the claim to being the queer metropolis of the Islamic World. What has been shown in this chapter, however, is the fact that ever since Turkey's inception as a modernized, secular nation, political efforts to forge a national identity were at odds with social practices that successfully subverted such efforts. Istanbul's LGBT community managed the paradoxical feat of embracing transnational notions of queerness while staking out sites of resistance, here exemplified in the vagaries of the histories of Istanbulite bars and baths. This blending and interlacing of subversion alongside tradition instead of against it has led to a highly flourishing, if greatly contradictory queer capital where the modern and traditional, the rural and the urban, the margin and the centre, and above all gay and straight merges into a hotbed of contemporary queerness at the crossroads of East and West.

Notes

1   Motschenbacher, H. (2010), 'The discursive interface of national, European and sexual identities: Preliminary evidence from the eurovision song contest', in B. Lewandowska-Tomasczcyk and H. Pulaczewska (eds), *Intercultural Europe: Arenas of Difference, Communication and Mediation*. Stuttgart: ibidem, p. 85.

2   Ibid., p. 86.

3   Solomon, T. (2007), 'Articulating the historical moment: Turkey, Europe, and eurovision 2003', in I. Raykoff and R. Deam Tobin (eds), *A Song for Europe: Popular Music and Politics in the Eurovision Song Contest*. Aldershot: Ashgate, p. 136.

4   Ibid., p. 145. As Matthew Gumpert states, 'the ESC has *always* been a transparently political event, not only in the sense that singers are encouraged (according to the ESC rulebook) to reflect the national identity of the culture they represent, or in the way host nations use the opportunity (as they do at the Olympic Games) to export their own cultural capital, but in the voting process itself'. See: Gumpert, M. (2007), '"Everyway that I can": Auto-Orientalism at Eurovision 2003', in I. Raykoff and R. Deam Tobin (eds), *A Song for Europe: Popular Music and Politics in the Eurovision Song Contest*. Aldershot: Ashgate, pp. 147–57, p. 148.

5   Solomon (2007), p. 143.

6   O'Connor, J. K. (2007), *The Eurovision Song Contest: The Official History*. London: Carlton, p. 182.

7   Feddersen, J. (2010), *Wunder gibt es immer wieder: Das große Buch zum Eurovision Song Contest*. Berlin: Aufbau, pp. 60–5.

8   Wolter, I. (2006), *Kampf der Kulturen. Der Eurovision Song Contest als Mittel national-kultureller Repräsentation*. Würzburg: Könighausen & Neumann, p. 139.

9   Rehberg, P. (2007), 'Winning failure: Queer nationality at the eurovision song contest', *SQS: Journal of Queer Studies in Finland*, 2(2), 60.

10 Kandiyoti, D. (1997), 'Gendering the modern: On missing dimensions in the study of Turkish modernity', in S. Bozdoğan and R. Kasaba (eds), *Rethinking Modernity and National Identity in Turkey*. Seattle and London: University of Washington Press, p. 114.

11 Szulc, L. (2011), 'Contemporary discourses on non-heterosexual and gender non-conforming citizens of Turkey', *International Review of Turkish Studies*, 1(2), 17.

12 Ibid., pp. 11 and 131.

13 Still today, the military considers it an obligation to safeguard the nation's morals (Klaudia, G. (2008), *Die Vertreibung aus dem Serail: Europa und die Heteronormalisierung der islamischen Welt*. Hamburg: Männerschwarm, pp. 109–10, Thumann, M. (2011), *Der Islam-Irrtum: Europas Angst vor der muslimischen Welt*. Frankfurt/M.: Eichborn, pp. 216–17; Sinclair-Webb, E. (2006), 'Military service and manhood in Turkey', in M. Ghoussoub and E. Sinclair-Webb (eds), *Imagined Masculinities: Male Identity and Culture in the Modern Middle East*. London: Saqi, pp. 65–92, p. 69; Altinay 78–9). In its rules homosexuality, transsexuality and transvestism (*eşcinsellik, transseksüellik ve travestilik*) are considered 'profound psychic disturbances' that are not compatible with military service involving armed combat. As proof of these the military requires medical and psychiatric reports as well as photographs of the individual performing passive anal intercourse. These photos often 'miraculously' show up on the internet, causing an involuntary outing for many.

14 Gecim, H., 'A brief history of the LGBT movement in Turkey', http://ilga.org/ilga/en/article/420 (consulted 8 February 2013).

15 Ghadban, R. (2004), 'Gescheiterte Integration? Antihomosexuelle Einstellungen türkei- und arabischstämmiger MigrantInnen in Deutschland', in LSVD Berlin-Brandenburg e.V. (ed.), *Muslime unter dem Regenbogen: Homosexualität, Migration und Islam.* Berlin: Querverlag, pp. 44–5, 52, 55.

16 Schmitt, A. and J. Sofer (eds) (1992), *Sexuality and Eroticism Among Males in Moslem Societies.* New York: Harrington Park, p. 2.

17 Bochow, M. (2004), 'Junge schwule Türken in Deutschland: Biographische Brüche und Bewältigungsstrategien', in LSVD Berlin-Brandenburg e.V. (ed.), *Muslime unter dem Regenbogen. Homosexualität, Migration und Islam.* Berlin: Querverlag, p. 172.

18 Ghadban (2004), p. 223.

19 Bochow (2004), p. 175.

20 Tertilt, H. (1996), *Turkish Power Boys: Ethnographie einer Jugendbande.* Frankfurt a.M.: Suhrkamp.

21 Günay, K. A. (2003), 'Homosexualität in der Türkei und unter Türkeistämmigen in Deutschland: Gemeinsamkeiten und Unterschiede', in M. Bochow and R. Marbach (eds), *Homosexualität und Islam. Koran, Islamische Länder, Situation in Deutschland.* Hamburg: MännerschwarmSkript, p. 126.

22 Thurmann (2011), p. 213; Oksal, A. (2008), 'Turkish family members' attitudes toward lesbians and gay men', *Sex Roles*, 58, p. 514; 'We need a law for liberation: Gender, sexuality, and human rights in a changing Turkey' (21 May 2008), *Human Rights Watch.* http://www.hrw.org/reports/2008/05/21/we-need-law-liberation (consulted 8 December 2011), pp. 89–91.

23 Günay (2003), p. 124. See also Kilic, D. and G. Uncu (1996), 'Turkey', in R. Rosenbloom (ed.), *Unspoken Rules: Sexual Orientation and Women's Human Rights.* London: Cassell, pp. 205–06. A recent murder case, called 'the first gay honor killing in Turkey' (see: Bilefsky, D. (26 November 2009), 'Soul-searching in Turkey after a gay man is killed', *New York Times.* http://www.nytimes.com (consulted 3 October 2012)), therefore is a case in point. In Istanbul in 2009, Ahmet Yildiz, who lived openly as a gay man and was the first 'Mr. Bear' to represent Turkey at the International Bear Rendezvous in San Francisco in 2007, was shot by his father, who had warned him to return to their village to see a doctor and imam for a 'cure'. While this may or may not be a single case depending on the number of unreported cases, there were as much as 11 killings of transgender people registered in 2008–09 alone, mostly in Istanbul and Ankara and they must be regarded as hate crimes even though police officials claim: 'A person is not killed because they are homosexual, it is because of other things'. (Qtd. in 'Turkey: Pride and Violence' (22 June 2009), *Human Rights Watch.* http://www.hrw.org/news/2009/06/22/turkey-pride-and-violence (consulted 8 December 2011)). Furthermore, while at least some of these murderers were caught, they are usually facing a lower sentence due to the claim of being 'provoked' under Article 29 of the Turkish Criminal Code (ibid.).

24 See also the collegiate student association Legato, an acronym for Gey ve Lezbiyen Topluluğu (Lesbian and Gay Association) that first was launched

in Ankara in the 1990s and then reached out across the country now being Turkey's largest LGBT organization and explicitly including lesbian images and stories on their webpage and print fanzine, published in Istanbul (Gorkemli, Serkan (4 November 2011), 'Gender Benders, Gay Icons and Media: Lesbian and Gay Visual Rhetoric in Turkey', *berfroirs*. http://www. berfrois.com/2011//11/turkish-queer-icons/ (consulted 3 October 2012)).

25 Özen, E., 'Tourist guide to Istanbul gay nightlife'. http://www.nighttours.com/ istanbul/gayguide/ (accessed 9 February 2012).

26 Yılmazkaya, O. (2003), *Turkish Baths. A Guide to the Historic Turkish Baths of Istanbul*, trans. N. F. Öztürk. Istanbul: Çitlembik, pp. 56–7.

27 The historical Çukurcuma bath, for example, was a highly popular hamam where especially tourists could intimately meet Turkish men of all ages. It was closed late 2006 supposedly for renovation, but I cannot but wonder, having seen the rampant (and mostly unsafe) sexual activity there, whether it is more likely that policing actions caused the shutdown.

28 Bouhdiba, A. (2004), *Sexuality in Islam*, trans. A. Sheridan. London: Saqi, p. 165.

29 Bouhdiba (2004), p. 169.

30 Cichocki, N. (2005), 'Continuity and change in Turkish bathing culture in Istanbul: The life story of the Çemberlitaş Hamam', *Turkish Studies*, 6(1), 100–2.

31 Cichocki (2005), p. 108.

32 Mooshammer, H. (2005), *Cruising: Architektur, Psychoanalyse und Queer Cultures*. Wien: Böhlau, pp. 7–8.

33 For a recent butching up of gay street prostitution with rent boys showing off an exaggerated masculinity, see Özbay, C. (2010), 'Nocturnal queers: Rent boys' masculinity in Istanbul', *Sexualities*, 13(5), 645–63.

34 This state-sanctioned homophobia means gay bashers act with impunity as is documented in the *Human Rights Watch* report on Turkey 'We need a law for liberation' and its follow-up 'Turkey: pride and violence'.

35 Ivy, R. L. (2001), 'Geographical variation in alternative tourism and recreation establishments', *Tourism Geographies: An International Journal of Tourism Space, Place and Environment*, 3(3), p. 353.

36 There are three novels published and translated so far: *The Prophet Murders* (2008), *The Kiss Murder* (2009), and *The Gigolo Murder* (2009).

37 'Mehmet Murat Somer – the Euro Crime Interview'. *Euro Crime* (8 May 2008). http://eurocrime.blogspot.com/2008/05/mehmet-murat-somer-euro-crime-interview.html (consulted 4 January 2012).

38 Wiegand, C. (14 May 2008), 'Different Beats', *The Guardian* (London), http://www.guardian.co.uk/books/2008/may/14/crimebooks.chriswiegand (consulted 4 January 2012).

39 Somer is well aware that his books may not find an audience with every Turkish reader. His initial struggle to find a publisher and then being represented by the prestigious Iletisim company, which also publishes Nobel laureate Orhan Pamuk, for Somer are signs that he needs 'Iletisim's stamp of approval' to protect his books 'from a hostile reception' (Wiegand [2008]).

40 Gumpert (2007), p. 147.

41 Stokes, M. (1992), 'Islam, the Turkish state and Arabesk', *Popular Music. A Changing Europe*, 11(2), *A Changing Europe*, 213–27.

42 Etymologically, the adjective 'arabesk' or 'arabesque' derives from the 'French, from Italian *arabesco* Arabian in fashion, from *arabo* Arab, from Latin *Arabus*' (see http://www.merriam-webster.com/dictionary/arabesque, consulted 31 January 2009).

43 Çınar, A. (2001), 'National history as a contested site: The conquest of Istanbul and Islamist negotiations of the nation', *Comparative Studies in Society and History*, 43(2), 386.

44 Özbek, M. (1997), 'Arabesk culture: A case of modernization and popular identity', in S. Bozdoğan and R. Kasaba (eds), *Rethinking Modernity and National Identity in Turkey*. Seattle and London: University of Washington Press, p. 223.

45 For a renewed effort in changing and thus liberalizing the Civil and Penal Code see the publication by Women for Women's Human Rights. New Ways (2005), *Turkish Civil and Penal Code Reforms from a Gender Perspective. The Success of Two Nationwide Campaigns*, Istanbul, as well as Şahika, Y. et al. (2000), 'Group psychotherapy with female-to-male transsexuals in Turkey', *Archives of Sexual Behavior*, 29(3), 279–90.

46 The Amendment to the 29th clause of law no. 743, Turkish Civil Code, 12 May 1988, 19812, states: 'In cases where there has been a change of sex after birth documented by a report from a committee of medical experts, the necessary amendments are made to the birth certificate'. According to Kandiyoti, this ruling '*may* appear as more advanced than that of many European countries, where the original record of one's sex of birth is not thus obliterated' (Kandiyoti, D. (2002), 'Pink card blues: Trouble and strife at the crossroads of gender', in D. Kandioyti and A. Saktanber (eds), *Fragments of Culture: The Everyday of Modern Turkey*. London: I. B. Tauris, p. 291, emphasis added).

47 Kandiyoti (2002), p. 279.

48 Öncü, A. (2002), 'Global consumerism, sexuality as public spectacle, and the cultural remapping of Istanbul in the 1990s', in D. Kandioyti and A. Saktanber (eds), *Fragments of Culture: The Everyday of Modern Turkey*. London: I. B. Tauris, pp. 171–90, p. 186; also Öncü, A. (1999), 'Istanbulites and others: The cultural cosmology of being middle class in the era of globalism', in Ç. Keyder (ed.), *Istanbul: Between the Global and the Local*. Lanham, MA: Rowman & Littlefield, pp. 95–119, p. 115.

49 Gumpert (2007), p. 151.

50 For a closer analysis see my essay: Poole, R. J. (2009), 'Arabesk. Nomadic tales, oriental beats, and hybrid looks', in Beate Neumeier (ed.), *Dichotonies: Gender and Music*. Heidelberg: Winter, pp. 245–65.

51 Shay, A. (2005), 'The male dancer in the middle east and central Asia', in A. Shay and B. Sellers-Young (eds), *Belly Dance: Orientalism, Transnationalism, and Harem Fantasy*. Costa Mesa: Mazda, pp. 70, 82.

52 Amico, S. (2001), '"I want muscles:" House music, homosexuality and masculine signification', *Popular Music*, 20(3), 369.

53   Rehberg (2007), p. 60.
54   Warner, M. (2005), *Publics and Counterpublics*. New York: Zone Books.
55   Ibid., p. 198.
56   Özen, E., 'Tourist guide to Istanbul gay nightlife'. http://www.nighttours.com/
     istanbul/gayguide/ (accessed 9 February 2012).
57   'The gay map of the Islamic world' (14 August 2007), *The Advocate 990*.
     http://www.questia.com (consulted 17 November 2011).

Further reading

'Mehmet Murat Somer – the Euro Crime Interview', *Euro Crime* (8 May 2008).
    http://eurocrime.blogspot.com/2008/05/mehmet-murat-somer-euro-crime-
    interview.html (accessed 4 January 2012).
'The gay map of the Islamic world', *The Advocate 990* (14 August 2007). http://
    www.questia.com (accessed 17 November 2011).
'Turkey: Pride and violence', *Human Rights Watch* (22 June 2009). http://www.hrw.
    org/news/2009/06/22/turkey-pride-and-violence (accessed 8 December 2011).
'We need a law for liberation: Gender, sexuality, and human rights in a changing
    Turkey', *Human Rights Watch* (21 May 2008). http://www.hrw.org/
    reports/2008/05/21/we-need-law-liberation (accessed 8 December 2011).
Amico, S. (2001), '"I want muscles": House music, homosexuality and masculine
    signification', *Popular Music*, 20(3), 359–78.
Ataman, H. (2011), 'Less than citizens: The lesbian, gay, bisexual, and transgender
    question in Turkey', in R. Özgür Dönmez and P. Enneli (eds), *Societal Peace and
    Ideal Citizenship for Turkey*. Lanham: Lexington, pp. 125–57.
Bilefsky, D. (2009), '"Soul-searching in Turkey after a gay man is killed', *New York
    Times* (26 November). http://www.nytimes.com (accessed 3 October 2012).
Bochow, M. (2004), 'Junge schwule Türken in Deutschland: Biographische Brüche
    und Bewältigungsstrategien'. *Muslime unter dem Regenbogen. Homosexualität,
    Migration und Islam*. Ed. LSVD Berlin-Brandenburg e.V. Berlin: Querverlag,
    pp. 168–88.
Bouhdiba, A. (2004), *Sexuality in Islam*, trans. A. Sheridan. London: Saqi.
Cichocki, N. (2005), 'Continuity and change in Turkish bathing culture in Istanbul:
    The life story of the Çemberlitaş Hamam', *Turkish Studies*, 6(1), 93–112.
Çınar, A. (2001), 'National history as a contested site: The conquest of Istanbul and
    Islamist negotiations of the nation', *Comparative Studies in Society and History*,
    43(2), 364–91.
Feddersen, J. (2010), *Wunder gibt es immer wieder: Das große Buch zum
    Eurovision Song Contest*. Berlin: Aufbau.
Gecim, H. (2004), 'A brief history of the LGBT movement in Turkey'. http://ilga.
    org/ilga/en/article/420 (accessed 8 February 2013).
Ghadban, R. (2004), 'Gescheiterte Integration? Antihomosexuelle Einstellungen
    türkei- und arabischstämmiger MigrantInnen in Deutschland', in LSVD (ed.)
    Muslime unter dem Regenbogen: Homosexualität, Migration und Islam. Berlin-
    Brandenburg e.V. Berlin: Querverlag, pp. 217–25.
—(2004), 'Historie, Gegenwart und Zukunft der Einstellung zur Homosexualität
    und Pädophilie in islamischen Ländern', in LSVD (ed.), *Muslime unter dem*

Regenbogen: Homosexualität, Migration und Islam, Berlin-Brandenburg e.V. Berlin: Querverlag, pp. 39–63.

Gorkemli, S. (2011), 'Gender benders, gay icons and media: Lesbian and gay visual rhetoric in Turkey', *berfroirs* (4 November). http://www.berfrois.com/2011//11/ turkish-queer-icons/ (accessed 3 October 2012).

—(2012), '"Coming out of the internet:" Lesbian and gay activism and the internet as a "Digital Closet" in Turkey', *Journal of Middle East Women's Studies*, 8(3), 63–88.

Gumpert, M. (2007), '"Everyway that I can": Auto-orientalism at eurovision 2003', in I. Raykoff and R. D. Tobin (eds), *A Song for Europe: Popular Music and Politics in the Eurovision Song Contest*. Aldershot: Ashgate, pp. 147–57.

Günay, K. A. (2003), 'Homosexualität in der Türkei und unter Türkeistämmigen in Deutschland: Gemeinsamkeiten und Unterschiede', in M. Bochow and R. Marbach (eds), *Homosexualität und Islam. Koran, Islamische Länder, Situation in Deutschland*. Hamburg: MännerschwarmSkript, pp. 116–39.

Hamam – Il bagno turco. Dir. Ferhan Özpetek. Italy/Turkey/Spain, 1997.

Kandiyoti, D. (1997), 'Gendering the modern: On missing dimensions in the study of Turkish modernity', in S. Bozdoğan and R. Kasaba (eds), *Rethinking Modernity and National Identity in Turkey*. Seattle and London: University of Washington Press, pp. 113–32.

—(2002), 'Pink card blues: Trouble and strife at the crossroads of gender', in D. Kandiyoti and A. Saktanber (eds), *Fragments of Culture: The Everyday of Modern Turkey*. London: I. B. Tauris, pp. 277–93.

Kiliç, D. and G. Uncu (1996), 'Turkey', in R. Rosenbloom (ed.), *Unspoken Rules: Sexual Orientation and Women's Human Rights*. London: Cassell, pp. 203–7.

Klaudia, G. (2008), *Die Vertreibung aus dem Serail: Europa und die Heteronormalisierung der islamischen Welt*. Hamburg: Männerschwarm, pp. 109–10.

Mooshammer, H. (2005), *Cruising: Architektur, Psychoanalyse und Queer Cultures*. Wien: Böhlau.

Motschenbacher, H. (2010), 'The discursive interface of national, European and sexual identities: Preliminary evidence from the eurovision song contest', in B. Lewandowska-Tomaszczyk and H. Pulaczewska (eds), *Intercultural Europe: Arenas of Difference, Communication and Mediation*. Stuttgart: ibidem, pp. 85–103.

Necef, M. Ü. (1992), 'Turkey on the brink of modernity: A guide for Scandinavian gays', in A. Schmitt and J. Sofer (eds), *Sexuality and Eroticism Among Males in Moslem Societies*. New York: Harrington Park, pp. 71–5.

O'Connor, J. K. (2007), *The Eurovision Song Contest: The Official History*. London: Carlton.

Oksal, A. (2008), 'Turkish family members' attitudes toward lesbians and gay men', *Sex Roles*, 58, 514–25.

Öncü, A. (1999), 'Istanbulites and others: The cultural cosmology of being middle class in the era of globalism', in Ç. Keyder (ed.), *Istanbul: Between the Global and the Local*. Lanham, MA: Rowman & Littlefield, pp. 95–119.

—(2002), 'Global consumerism, sexuality as public spectacle, and the cultural remapping of Istanbul in the 1990s', in D. Kandioyti and A. Saktanber (eds), *Fragments of Culture: The Everyday of Modern Turkey*. London: I. B. Tauris, pp. 171–90.

Özbay, C. (2010), 'Nocturnal queers: Rent boys' masculinity in Istanbul',
    Sexualities, 13(5), 645–63.
Özbek, M. (1997), 'Arabesk culture: A case of modernization and popular identity',
    in S. Bozdoğan and R. Kasab (eds), *Rethinking Modernity and National Identity
    in Turkey*. Seattle and London: University of Washington Press, pp. 211–32.
Özen, E. 'Tourist Guide to Istanbul Gay Nightlife'. http://www.nighttours.com/
    istanbul/gayguide/ (accessed 9 February 2012).
Poole, R. J. (2009), 'Arabesk. nomadic tales, oriental beats, and hybrid looks',
    in B. Neumeier (ed.), *Dichotonies: Gender and Music*. Heidelberg: Winter,
    pp. 245–65.
Rehberg, P. (2007), 'Winning failure: Queer nationality at the eurovision song
    contest', *SQS: Journal of Queer Studies in Finland*, 2(2), 60–5. http://www.
    helsinki.fi/jarj/sqs/sqs2_07/sqs22007rehberg.pdf (accessed 4 December 2011).
Schmitt, A. (1992), 'Different approaches to male-male sexuality/eroticism
    from Morocco to Usbekistān', in A. Schmitt and J. Sofer (eds), *Sexuality and
    Eroticism Among Males in Moslem Societies*. New York: Harrington Park,
    pp. 1–24.
Shay, A. (2005), 'The male dancer in the middle East and Central Asia', in A. Shay
    and B. Sellers-Young (eds), *Belly Dance: Orientalism, Transnationalism, and
    Harem Fantasy*. Costa Mesa: Mazda, pp. 51–84.
Sinclair-Webb, E. (2006), 'Military service and manhood in Turkey', in
    M. Goussoub and E. Sinclair-Webb (eds), *Imagined Masculinities: Male Identity
    and Culture in the Modern Middle East*. London: Saqi, pp. 65–92.
Solomon, T. (2007), 'Articulating the historical moment: Turkey, Europe, and
    Eurovision 2003', in I. Raykoff and R. Deam Tobin (eds), *A Song for Europe:
    Popular Music and Politics in the Eurovision Song Contest*. Aldershot: Ashgate,
    pp. 135–45.
Stokes, M. (1992), 'Islam, the Turkish state and Arabesk', *Popular Music.
    A Changing Europe*, 11(2), 213–27.
Szulc, L. (2011), 'Contemporary discourses on non-heterosexual and gender non-
    conforming citizens of Turkey', *International Review of Turkish Studies*, 1(2),
    10–31.
Tertilt, H. (1996), *Turkish Power Boys: Ethnographie einer Jugendbande*. Frankfurt
    a.M.: Suhrkamp.
Thumann, M. (2011), *Der Islam-Irrtum: Europas Angst vor der muslimischen
    Welt*. Frankfurt/M.: Eichborn.
Warner, M. (2005), *Publics and Counterpublics*. New York: Zone Books.
Wiegand, C. (2008), 'Different beats', *The Guardian* (London), 14 May. http://
    www.guardian.co.uk/books/2008/may/14/crimebooks.chriswiegand (accessed
    4 January 2012).
Wolther, I. (2006), *Kampf der Kulturen. Der Eurovision Song Contest als Mittel
    national-kultureller Repräsentation*. Würzburg: Könighausen & Neumann.
Women for Women's Human Rights/New Ways (2005), *Turkish Civil and Penal
    Code Reforms from a Gender Perspective. The Success of Two Nationwide
    Campaigns*. Istanbul.
Yılmazkaya, O. (2003), *Turkish Baths. A Guide to the Historic Turkish Baths of
    Istanbul*, trans. N. F. Öztürk. Istanbul: Çitlembik.
Yüksel, Ş. et al. (2000), 'Group psychotherapy with female-to-male transsexuals in
    Turkey', *Archives of Sexual Behavior*, 29(3), 279–90.

10

Queering Budapest[1]

Judit Takács

For a few decades now we can be sure that *what queers want is not just sex*[2] – but a lot more, including a critical reorganization of the use of space. Queering, at least in this chapter, refers to examining whether and to what extent the socially constructed non-heteronormative intimacies and desires became constitutive elements in the (social) life of Budapest. It will examine where, when, how and by whom these desires have been recognized, articulated, incited and satisfied, as well explore the regulating attempts deployed mainly to inhibit and not liberate them.

Sexuality, the expression of socially constructed intimacies and desires, is interpreted here as being constructed as one of the 'significant axes of difference',[3] together with gender, age, class and ethnicity, around which struggles have been and are organized in urbanization processes, too. Similar to other social relations through which power is mobilized, social relations organized around sexual difference are made socially perceivable by objects and symbols, including specific uses and codes of space. In the following sections, as far as the – at times sporadic – historical evidence allows, a mosaic will be presented on how non-heteronormative forms of sexuality have positioned gay and lesbian people in Budapest during the last few decades.

Before state socialism

The area that is referred to as Budapest today has been known for its thermal springs rich in sulphur since at least the Roman times. Within the bathhouse culture that flourished for centuries in Budapest, a distinct bathhouse oriented gay culture emerged. During the twentieth century, bathhouses were reserved for men only during certain days of the week and became important social spaces especially for gay men, providing a hassle-free environment in which they could meet and physically interact with one another without raising suspicion.

During the late nineteenth century it was also a bathhouse, the Rudas Thermal Bath that provided a home for Károly Kertbeny, who lived there for the last 7 years of his life. Kertbeny Károly Mária, born as Karl Maria Benkert in Vienna in 1824 'as a son of Hungarian parents' coined the terms *heterosexual* and *homosexual* and is regarded as one of the founders of the gay rights movement.[4] While his mother tongue was German, he declared himself Hungarian: 'I was born in Vienna, yet I am not a Viennese, but rightfully Hungarian'.[5] In 1847, he officially changed his name to Kertbeny.[6] In Hungarian literary history, he is recorded as a not very significant translator and writer but in LGBT history he is remembered for his inventiveness in sexual terminology and for the theoretical case he made for homosexual emancipation. In 1868, in a private letter written to Karl Heinrich Ulrichs he presents a surprisingly modern argument for human rights:

> To prove innateness . . . is a dangerous double-edged weapon. Let this riddle of nature be very interesting from the anthropological point of view. Legislation is not concerned whether this inclination is innate or not, legislation is only interested in the personal and social dangers associated with it. . . . Therefore we would not win anything by proving innateness beyond a shadow of doubt. Instead we should convince our opponents—with precisely the same legal notions used by them—that they do not have anything at all to do with this inclination, be it innate or intentional, since the state does not have the right to intervene in anything that occurs between two consenting persons older than fourteen, which does not affect the public sphere, nor the rights of a third party.[7]

At the beginning of the twentieth century, in line with the efforts to develop tourism as a potential new source of income, a special programme was introduced by the municipality to reinvent Budapest as a 'City of Spas'. For this venture, natural resources like the hot springs that had been the source of enjoyment and recreation for the population for centuries, and the cultural value of baths that had developed especially after the Turks occupied Buda in the sixteenth–seventeenth centuries and built Turkish bathhouses, were cited. However, until the 1910s, bathhouses were located only on the Buda side of the city. The first thermal bath built on the Pest side of the city in 1913, the Széchenyi Thermal Bath, with its open air pools and neo-baroque buildings became one of the favourite spa swimming baths of Budapest and a popular venue also for mainly men sharing same-sex desires.

The role of bathhouses was also emphasized in one of the first Hungarian books that was fully devoted to the modern aspects of the 'homosexual problem'. The book suggested that this problem – recurred suddenly after World War I as a mass phenomenon, and as a 'burning issue of the modern era'[8] – was one that could not be ignored. According to the author's own estimate in the 1920s, the number of *urnings*[9] was over 10,000 in Budapest, where they had several venues to meet and interact, including bathhouses and vapour baths, but also inner city locations, such as the Erzsébet square, the Kálvin square, the Emke corner or the Buda side of the Margit bridge, most of which have remained popular cruising areas for several decades. The author explains that in comparison to villages, Budapest, like other cities, could provide a better environment for homosexuals to 'exit an introverted passive sexuality'[10] and start to become sexually active. In the author's view, the main urban advantage is the 'immense ease of disappearance'[11] that can protect homosexuals from the dangers of blackmail.

In 1929, as a joint effort of journalists and police officers a two-volume work was published on *Modern Criminality* where under the heading 'Crime promoting circumstances' a whole chapter was devoted to homosexuality, or more precisely, its punishment and cure. According to the authors, the proportion of homosexuals used to be half a per cent of the population, but due to the war, and the long terms of internment for prisoners of war which went with it, this rate has recently reached 1 per cent. In modern big cities this rate might be even higher: in Budapest, for example, the male population was 438,456 in 1925, while the number of homosexual men can be estimated at more than 5000,[12] which is more than 1 per cent.

In 1934, a Hungarian neurologist, Zoltán Nemes Nagy devoted a whole chapter of his sexual pathological studies to 'Homosexuals in Budapest'.[13] This chapter starts with the statement that 'Budapest is the first metropolitan city in the whole world where semi-official records are compiled on homosexuals' for about 15 years.[14] The author estimates that 'the real number' of homosexual men in Budapest is about 15,000, most of whom will never be detected as they belong to 'upscale circles, carefully trying to avoid publicity'.[15] There were also well-known homosexual meeting places listed,[16] including bathhouses, public beaches with separate cabins, surroundings of public toilets and steam chambers with limited lighting.

On the basis of historical evidence on elements of homosexual life before World War II, Budapest can be described as a spatially ordered modern city, characterized by specialized public-space use, serving mainly the interest of the higher middle classes.[17] As a uniquely modern kind of social psychological space, the city provided a new dynamic: this was where one could submerge in the world of strangers, and where one could not only be, but might also act as a homosexual. Budapest, before World War II, with its established meeting places and patterns of decodable behaviour seemed to be able to provide this new dynamic for homosexual life; and as it could be seen, it is not too difficult to find empirical evidence for the existence of this semi-secretive homosexual infrastructure, for example, in the form of the surveillance system that was introduced to control it.[18]

Queering Budapest means starting from the first historical recollections of same-sex desire, focusing on the way it guided the use of space. At the same time, it is important to point out that these same recollections were often sporadic and piecemeal, reflecting the desires of men over women, whose same-sex identifications and practices left fewer detectable marks in the public realm. Given that since at least the early 1920s lists of male homosexuals had been compiled in Budapest points to the fact that same-sex desires have been both recognized and misrecognized during the first half of the twentieth century. These gendered processes of visibility and invisibility remained a feature of queer Budapest for the better part of the century.

During state socialism

As with other *iron-curtained* countries, non-heteronormative representations of same-sex desires during state socialism were not at all widespread in Hungary. In fact, heteronormative representations of same-sex desires were not at all widespread either – however, at least some of these were quite well documented, for example, in secret police and state security files.

The practice of specialized state surveillance on homosexuality continued after World War II, especially during the rise of the Hungarian state socialist political system. Compiling 'homosexual inventories' providing potential blackmail victims to be coerced into becoming police informers was part of regular police work in urban areas and especially in Budapest. These practices are reflected in archival documents, including the instructions of the National Police Headquarters of 1958 on how to keep criminal records.[19] According to these instructions, there were 13 types of criminal records, and data on homosexuals had to be kept in at least three of them, including the 'Preliminary records of persons suspected of crime'; the 'Record of regular criminals' and a photo register of convicted homosexuals. Preliminary records of homosexual persons suspected of crime were kept only in the capital city: this was not required in the countryside or in smaller cities and towns. The goal of keeping a register of 'regular criminals' was to collect data on people who were criminally active and socially very harmful, people with a criminal record, including homosexuals and prostitutes. During the 1950s, therefore, the Police Chief of Budapest had access to a special data set of people with 'proved homosexual inclinations', including information on friends who also participated in perversion against nature, their photos, their nicknames and also their female nicknames, if they had any, as well as the 'method' of committing perversion against nature.

Even though homosexual activity between consenting adults, or more precisely between men, was decriminalized in 1961, with reference to medical arguments emphasizing that homosexuality was a biological phenomenon and should not be treated as a crime, there were different ages of consent set for heterosexual and homosexual relationships. Many of these differences remained in operation until 2002.[20] Additionally, the circle of potential perpetrators and victims also changed: gender equality was introduced as the definition of perversion expanded to include men and women's activities; bestiality, however, fell from the penal code. Additionally, there was a special clause introduced on 'perversion against nature conducted in a scandalous manner', for which one could get up to 3 years of imprisonment. Especially the clauses on the different ages of consent and potentially causing public scandal provided good opportunities for state authorities such as the police – as well as blackmails at a local, interpersonal level – to keep (alleged) homosexual women and men under close control.

When the private life of citizens became an object of regular supervision and surveillance, the 'totalitarian androgyny'[21] of the 1950s was replaced by a milder form of authoritarian control in many Soviet bloc countries, including Hungary, by the 1960s, that left some – at least not directly controlled – space for private life. Nevertheless, state socialist morality celebrated a specifically asexual 'socialist reproduction' – that is to say the party-state building/constructing capacities of labour force reproduction – and not pleasure. Sexuality was surrounded by hypocritical silence not only in everyday life but also in academic circles, reflecting a general impassivity in relation to this field.

The first empirical sexual-sociological survey of this period was conducted in Budapest in 1971 focusing on the sexuality related attitudes of young Hungarian workers and university students.[22] When respondents had to form a hierarchy of 11 values, including *physical health, happy marriage, children, living without financial problems, interesting work, professional success, a lot of spare-time, good friends, belief in something, eating-drinking*, having an 'orderly sexual life' (whatever that meant exactly for the respondents) was not among the main priorities. The findings of this pioneering research also illustrated that in comparison to university students young workers started sexual life earlier but had less sexual knowledge: their sexual scripts included less foreplay, and less frequent use of contraception. They put more emphasis on virginity and expressed less tolerance towards homosexuality.

It was under state socialism that the first Hungarian sexual-psychological overview of the 'modern theory of sexuality' was published, in the early 1970s. In the chapter on the 'problem of the sexual instinct' a paragraph was devoted to homosexuality. Here it was simply defined as 'sexual contact with a same-sex partner'[23] in the context of sexual perversions. This report, while still pathologizing gays, represented a step in the direction of creating more public knowledge on homosexuality.

Intimacy issues were practically silenced in state socialist Budapest, giving it some of its defining features. Budapest was thought to possess 'a sense of outright uniformity and boredom'.[24] In this way, it was not unlike other state-socialized cities, which scholars have characterized as 'under-urbanised' in various ways, with less urban diversity and less urban marginality, as well as different uses of space.[25] Less urban diversity was derived from the limited capacity of urban services: for example, there were only a few places to go out and socialize, and existing cafés, terraces or restaurants were shut early at night. There were also fewer overt signs of urban marginality such as crime, poverty and homelessness resulting partly from the successful anti-marginalization strategies of the party-state together with strict police control. Unlike the Budapest at the turn of the century, the urban environment of state socialist cities did not encourage people to submerge in the world of strangers by meeting and interacting with each other. Thus, the unique social-psychological space of the public realm was a missing feature.

In a recently published collection of lesbian life histories, Hungarian lesbian women reported on their personal experiences of the 'secret years'[26] during state socialism when the social visibility of lesbian lives was very limited. A 71-year-old woman pointed to isolation as one of the main problems of lesbians in that period: 'those who had a partner were not so awfully miserable. The misery was to find a partner'.[27] A 62-year-old woman described her sexual life as a 'hopeless desert' before the early 1990s: 'I didn't have the slightest idea where I should try to look for them. The women,' she explained.[28]

Given a social environment that deprived women of having individual encounters with like-minded lesbians as well as the social and cultural representations of same-sex desire, the 1982 presentation of *Egymásra nézve* (Another Way),[29] the first mainstream film from Eastern Europe to portray a lesbian relationship, was a great breakthrough. In the words of a now 82-year-old woman: 'I know that a lot of people saw it, and it became a topic of social discussion. It was a very good film, being brave not only concerning this specific topic [of lesbian love], but it was also brave politically . . . and about Galgóczi, the writer, it was quite well known that she was a lesbian'.[30] A 48-year-old woman also reflected on the formative experiences related to this motion picture, which soon became a Hungarian lesbian cult film 'that was seen by everyone [every lesbian] for about 30 times. Then I heard that women gave classified ads with this code word *"egymásra nézve [another way]"* so that it could be recognised [by other lesbians]'.[31]

The screenplay of the film by Erzsébet Galgóczi was based on Galgóczi's 1980 novel, *Törvényen belül* (Another Love). Kevin Moss, an American expert of Russian and Eastern European gender studies, interpreted the role of the filmmakers in the context of privilege:

> Galgóczi was herself a closeted lesbian, so in this case there was at least one lesbian involved in the production. She was at the time the head of the Hungarian Writers' Union. Makk was an established and well-known director at the time, and the film went on to win the FIPRESCI critics award at Cannes. It may have been Galgóczi and Makk's privileged positions that permitted them to tackle two topics – political and sexual dissidence – that were taboo for other writers and filmmakers in Hungary and elsewhere in Eastern Europe at the time.[32]

The film became a topic of extensive discussion especially among Hungarian film reviewers; trying to frame a 'passion that can defy social conventions'.[33] Additionally, the novel, on which the screenplay was based, received a lot of attention in Hungarian media, especially in view of the fact that the 50,000 copies of the first edition disappeared from bookstores in Budapest within weeks.[34]

Just as Another Way carved a place in public discourse for same-sex desire among women, so too did the 1984 book *Furcsa párok* (Strange couples). This book, based on 'hundreds of interviews' conducted with mainly homosexual men, conveying a very pronounced, 'pro-gay' message that 'homosexuality is not an illness but a [form of] behaviour',[35] also received a lot of media attention. In 1987, a Hungarian writer published a collection of 'homosexuals' confessions'. The book starts with the author's observation regarding the significant increase in the proportion of Hungarian lesbian women and homosexual men since the 1960s–1970s 'due to the dissolution of the traditional family concept'.[36] This observation, which cannot be supported by empirical evidence, most probably reflects the increasing number of public discourses focusing on the manifestations and social consequences of same-sex attractions.

During the 1980s, cultural and media visibility of same-sex attraction started to increase especially as the AIDS epidemic reached Hungary: in this context, the need to control gay sex was paramount. There is evidence that an official report was presented to the Central Committee of the Hungarian Socialist Workers' Party on AIDS-related international situation and the Hungarian measures as early as 1985.[37] In fact, Homeros-Lambda, the first Hungarian homosexual organization was established in 1988 primarily, or at least pronouncedly, for AIDS prevention-related reasons. According to an excerpt from the articles of the foundation of Homeros-Lambda enhancing 'supervisability' of homosexual activities seemed to be one of the main goals of the association: 'All the epidemiological, social and political evidence shows that this minority, obliged to conceal its identity, is growing more and more remote and less and less supervisable as a result of increasing prejudice and intolerance'.[38]

Later Lajos Romsauer, an acknowledged psychiatrist, founding member and leading representative of Homeros-Lambda, recalled that founding Homeros-Lambda was such an event that even the Council of Ministers – that is, the cabinet of the party-state during state socialism – was summoned. He added that

> the police came to collect me several times. They were primarily interested in our political views and our connections. They resented it when I told them that we support the party as there are homosexuals not only among the party members, but also among the party leaders. . . . They also tried to get me involved in investigations of crimes against homosexual victims, and encouraged me to open my ears so perhaps I might hear some information they could use.[39]

In a retrospective interview, conducted after the dissolution of the organization, Romsauer stated two main reasons for organizing Homeros-Lambda. Because of the spread of AIDS 'we wanted to make our membership aware of the methods of protection, and call the country's attention to the presence of homosexuals [in society]'.[40] However, there was another important reason why people with same-sex attraction joined Homeros-Lambda: they simply wanted to meet each other. Romsauer added that the organization had its peak in 1989 when they opened the Lokál in the Kertész street, being 'the first fully gay bar'[41] of Budapest: 'On the first day 46 members joined, and the number of members increased to 400 within a few months. The association functioned really well while we had this central meeting place. When the Lokál closed down, and there was no place to look for a partner there wasn't any real interest in joining [Homeros-Lambda] any longer either'.[42]

In state socialist Budapest, gay men had been inventing and applying various partner-seeking strategies, involving bathhouses, public toilets, cinemas, and personal tricks, to name but a few.[43] A 75-year-old gay man, for example, explained that practically all public toilets were potential meeting places for gay men. However, there were also certain risks involved: 'I had a case once,' he said,

I was caught . . . well, I wasn't caught effectively in the middle of the act but he [a plain-clothes policeman] noticed that I stayed around the toilet, going up and down, and then he came up to me and asked for my ID, where he saw what my job was and where I worked, and then he asked how a person with such qualities can be involved in a thing like this . . . well, tell me a better place in Budapest where I can meet gays, I am telling him, tell me, and then I will start going there. . . . I can meet gays only at toilets and bathhouses.

Another 75-year-old man referred to the old Híradó cinema as an accidental gay meeting venue, functioning a bit like a tame dark room. It was an irregular cinema, with continuous screening of only newsreel programmes: 'People were standing by the rows of seats at the two sides, waiting for a seat to be released . . . and suddenly I noticed that someone approached me and started to paw me in the dark', he said, remembering the first experience he had there.

As was demonstrated by the case of Homeros-Lambda, the first Hungarian homosexual organization, and especially their Lokál bar, after many decades of spatially deprived public existence, there was a tremendous need to have places where – slightly rephrasing Henning Bech's book title – 'men can meet'[44] and women can meet . . . Perhaps Budapest could be referred to as 'the California of Eastern European homosexuals' in a context of 'pink love under the red star',[45] especially if the Hungarian situation was compared with those of the Soviet Union or Romania, where homosexual acts remained illegal until the 1990s. However, people with same-sex desires might have preferred to have other reference points for Budapest.

After state socialism

The transition from an authoritarian state socialist regime to a democratic political system combined with consumer capitalism after 1989 increased the potential for personal freedom, contributing to the relaxation of prudishness that formerly characterized sexual values in Hungary. As Long noted 10 years later, a 'capitalist economy's individualist dislocation of old roles (and consumerism's eroticization of absolutely everything) has granted apparent new freedoms to personality and desire'.[46] However, empirical evidence from the early 1990s suggests that in the former state socialist region, including Hungary, democracy was interpreted mainly in political-institutional dimensions, stressing the importance of political freedom, equality of rights and the freshly re-introduced multiparty system much more than that of moral and sexual freedoms.[47]

While in 1988 the establishment of the first Hungarian homosexual organization, the Homeros Lambda, was officially supported by state socialist authorities in the name of struggle against AIDS and as an – indirect – means of defending society at large, in the 1990s it had been more complex to establish formal non-governmental organizations for representing the interest of 'gay people'. In 1994, the Rainbow Association for Gay People (*Szivárvány Társulás a Melegekért*) was refused formal registration as an association partly because the allegedly non-standard Hungarian term '*meleg*' (gay) was used in its name, as a form of self-description and opposing the perceptions related to the standard use of the 'homoszexuális' (homosexual) term in sexually charged as well as medically and otherwise oppressive ways. A more substantial argument for refusing the registration by the Metropolitan Court of Budapest was however that persons under 18 should not be allowed to become members of an organization advocating the rights of homosexuals – stress on homosexuals – because, in their view, creating 'an infrastructure necessary for institutionalized homosexual life bore the risk of causing the crime of "unnatural sexual conduct" (same-sex sexual activity with a person under 18) to be committed'.[48] The Szivárvány Association has never been registered but a smaller part of its membership formed the Háttér Support Society for LGBT People at Budapest in 1995.[49] Since then Háttér, the most active, continuously existing organization in this field, has maintained a help line, a legal aid service, and several AIDS prevention and other outreach programmes.

During the 1990s, there were altogether three officially recognized NGOs for lesbians and gays registered in Budapest, including Háttér. The Lambda Budapest Association, publishing the Mások gay magazine between 1989 and 2009, was officially formed in 1991, while Labrisz, the only exclusively lesbian Hungarian association was officially established in 1999, but the core of the organization existed from 1996. It was the pioneering work of the Labrisz Lesbian Association that brought LGBT topics into Hungarian schools by introducing the Getting to Know Gays and Lesbians (*Melegség és megismerés*) educational programme for secondary school students and teachers in 2000.[50]

At the beginning there were no other gay and/or lesbian associations registered even in the larger cities of the Hungarian countryside. Budapest seemed to be the only place that could provide relatively tolerant, less directly controlled urban environments, where the sociocultural infrastructure for LGBT people in Hungary could start to develop, including formal and informal meeting places, organizations, and entertainment options. Additionally, the historically developed hydrocephalus character,[51] remaining a main feature of late twentieth-century Budapest, could also have been reflected in this centralized development.

Even though gay gentrification hadn't really been happening in Budapest, during the 1990s there was an increase in commercial and entertainment space especially used by gay men: to a lesser extent but following a similar pattern of white middle-class male market-oriented development,[52] characterizing North American and West European urban gay scenes since the last decades of the twentieth century. Between 1989 and 2011, altogether about 30 gay bars opened in Budapest: most of them serving the needs of gay men and surviving only short periods of time, while a few of them, like the legendary Angel Bar, existed for almost 15 years, though in several consecutive locations. The history of gay bars in Budapest, starting with the Lokál Bar in 1989, illustrates not only how sexuality has been increasingly commodified within the gay bar-oriented subculture, but also how consumer citizenship can create and sustain inequalities[53]: holding economic rights with which one can buy access to certain restricted places, could perhaps guarantee partial tolerance towards the still largely 'immoral' gay citizens – but only a fraction of gay men have enjoyed such economic rights in Hungary, not to mention lesbian women, most of whom have never really been enchanted by the cramped space provided for them in gay bars. According to a leading Hungarian gay activist, submerging oneself in the bar-centred subculture can contribute to the maintenance of 'politically opportunistic' lifestyles:

> Gays are no longer locked into the world of cruising areas, bath houses and public toilets. Nowadays they are ALLOWED [emphasis of the interviewee] to visit the gay bars, [typically] situated in the basements of side-streets. A lot of people have peace with this situation: "*At night I can run around the five gay bars, there are gay discos, I can go to a private party organised in the countryside*". But it is still that level very close to practical sexuality, an instinctual level ... it is like masturbating ... "*but*

*to live together with another man, to integrate this into my everyday life? That is too much yet.".... * This is opportunism, from a radical queer perspective it is sly opportunism. . . . It is still [about] hiding: it is not a real life, not a full one.[54]

However, the achievement of full equality of rights especially regarding the institutionalization of same-sex partnerships, including same-sex marriage or registered partnership, was seen by the majority of Hungarians, including gays and lesbians, as a rather unthinkable arrangement or as a utopian activist project for a long time. Large-scale opinion poll results indicated that rejecting the idea of same-sex marriage remained the dominant opinion of Hungarian respondents between 1988 and 2003.[55]

Nevertheless, it should be noted that the topic of same-sex marriage was put on the Hungarian political agenda as early as 1993 when Homeros-Lambda submitted a petition to the Constitutional Court claiming that the lack of same-sex marriage was unconstitutional. By 1995, the Constitutional Court had reached a decision to open up cohabitation for same-sex couples, being a factual legal relationship, coming into existence without official registration. There have been several manifestations of the existence of 'structural stigma'[56] affecting gay and lesbian citizens in Hungary, including the different ages of consent for same-sex and different-sex partners before 2002, and the present lack of legal institutions such as same-sex marriage, and joint adoption by same-sex couples. It was not until 2007 that the legal option of registered partnership for same-sex couples was adopted by the Hungarian Parliament, and same-sex registered partnership legislation has been in operation only since 1 July 2009. Until the end of 2011, there had been altogether 192 same-sex partnerships registered – 134 by male couples and 58 by female couples[57] – in 40 per cent of all cases in Budapest.[58] The introduction of same-sex registered partnership or marriage has special importance because if such legal institutions exist, people are more likely to directly encounter manifestations of gay and lesbian 'modes of existence'[59] as ordinary facts of everyday life, the social contexts of which are usually not secret meeting places but public space. European empirical findings suggest that these personal encounters can contribute to the formation of more realistic and less prejudiced views on the lived realities of same-sex relationships.[60]

However, during 1998–2000, just a few years after cohabitation of same-sex couples was legally recognized in Hungary, empirical research findings on the value orientation of gay men living in Budapest demonstrated that family formation-related issues, seen by many as unrealistic options, were still largely missing from the mental maps of gay respondents. In comparison to other male respondents of Budapest, *family security* and *national security* were much less preferred values by gay respondents, while *inner harmony, true friendship, true love* and *beauty (in nature and art)* were much more preferred ones.[61] The lower prevalence of *family security* by gay respondents could reflect that they were aware of the legal and practical difficulties in establishing their own family, especially in a social context dominated by heteronormative definition of family, being formed within heterosexual marriage. This awareness could prevent gay respondents from realistically considering *family security* as a value to be achieved: in this context higher levels of preference of *true friendship* and *true love* can also be seen as substitutes for the often problematic and institutionally denied *family security*.

Narratives of Hungarian gay men reporting on their partnership experiences starting from the early 1990s, when more publicly accessible space became available for homoerotic practices, also reflected a certain temporally and technologically determined evolution of ways to find and meet other gay men. For at least one generation of gay men who became young adults after the political system change of 1989, printed ads were the most effective channel to find gay partners: *At the beginning, there was the [Mások] magazine and the ads, and cruising on the streets. The eye-contact game, you know. . . . Then, there were the bath-houses, of course. And as technology developed, people completely moved to the internet for finding new contacts* (38-year-old gay respondent); while the next generations could start to search for other gays already on the internet: *I started my gay life at the age of 17. I know my friends from internet chat-rooms or via other friends from a gay bar or a party* (27-year-old gay respondent).[62] Like in other countries where LGBT communities became increasingly 'cyberised', in Hungary it was cyberspace that to a large extent provided a 'safe environment to encounter and experiment with queer identities'.[63]

In addition, a conspicuously new tendency characterizing the Hungarian LGBT movement since the last decade of the twentieth century was the gradual extension of public space use by organizing LGBT public events. The first attempts began in 1992 with the organization of the first Pink Picnic, held in a hidden glade of the Buda hills, being a somewhat shy precursor of the Budapest Pride marches that started in 1997, and being organized every year since as a main event of the annual LGBT Festival. Between 1997 and 2007 the Budapest Pride marches passed off peacefully without any violent incidents. 2007 was the first year in the history of LGBT festivals in Budapest when counter demonstrators attacked the Pride march with extreme violence.

The violent attacks during and after the 2007 Budapest Pride, followed by the violent attacks of the 2008 Budapest Pride march, reflected the functioning of systemic violence.[64] These acts were impulsive manifestations of hate for the sole purpose of degrading and humiliating the victims, leaving behind the shared knowledge that anyone can be liable to violation solely on account of their assumed non-heteronormative identities. After these events, many LGBT people felt restricted in their use of public spaces, being aware of potential attacks, abuse and other acts of hostility; in direct response to the 2008 incidents, an amendment containing specific provisions, being in operation since 2009, to punish violent behaviour aimed at hindering other persons' participation in a public demonstration was adopted in the Criminal Code.

In 2009, a Hungarian opinion poll[65] found that only 20 per cent of the population approved of 'the right of gay people to publicly show their difference', while 68 per cent disapproved because 'it is a private matter that does not belong to the street'. Additionally, 31 per cent of respondents expressed the opinion that the event would be more acceptable if participants would 'respect public taste'. The *public taste* discourse was also echoed in a 2009 police press release, in which participants of the Pride march were warned to abstain from behaviour disrespecting 'public taste', thereby contributing to the perception of the event as being an over-sexualized exposure of sexual activities that should not be brought to the public. In 2010, the police issued a very similar press release; only this time it was 'public morality' that should have been respected. In order to come to a halt in the development of a close association of the annual Pride marches with the disruptions of public morality and public order by the police, in 2012, an LGBT organization requested from the Metropolitan Police an official list of cases related to disrespecting public morality occurring at any LGBT public event in the last 15 years. In their response, the police admitted that there had not been any cause to investigate any such cases during the last 15 years in Budapest.[66] Another recurring topic the Metropolitan Police of Budapest tends to worry about is the disproportionate hindrance to traffic that the annual Pride marches can cause in the capital: each year since 2008 the police tried to ban the marches on this basis but always reversed its decision at the end. The repeated banning attempts and press releases with offensive contents can be seen as quasi-ritualistic elements in a constrained relationship, where at least one of the parties wishes the other would somehow disappear by applying the appropriate magic charms . . .

A series of somewhat less scandalized public events that have become an established part of the annual LGBT festivals, started in 2002, when a new tombstone was erected for Károly Kertbeny, the creator of the words *homosexual* and *heterosexual*, in the Fiumei Street National Cemetery of Budapest, where he was originally buried in 1882. In the same year, near Kertbeny's tombstone a neglected joint grave of a police constable and a teacher, buried in 1940 and in 1945, respectively, was also discovered by accident. Since then the Lambda Budapest Association has had the couple's grave renovated and each year a memorial ceremony is organized at both Kertbeny's and the same-sex couple's gravesites.

These memorial ceremonies can be interpreted as being part of an LGBT collective memory-making project, within which Hungarian LGBT activists attempt to discover and regain their past at the same time. The establishment of the Kertbeny memorial and its ritualized commemoration can be seen as the creation of gay history through the recuperation of not just a gay ancestor of any kind but an 'ancestor of politicized gays who are engaged in political struggle',[67] being a well-known tactic of sexual-political movements:

> By creating a memorial ritual which constructs Kertbeny and the two other men . . . as "heroic" ancestral figures for present-day gay Hungarian men, gay activists have developed a technique which grounds them, personally and politically, in national presence and significance. In doing so, these activists are proposing a vision of history that suggests . . . that they are equal and legitimate members of the Nation's past, and that they therefore belong in its present as well. Thus, through the Kertbeny ritual, Hungary's gay activists are making a powerful – and revolutionary – argument for inclusion into Hungarian society.[68]

Renkin also adds that the introduction of the Kertbeny ritual is 'much more an act of creation, of the establishment of a memory and history that previously did not exist, than a "recovery"'.[69] The Fiumei Street National Cemetery indeed functions as a National Pantheon, a special *site of memory*,[70] particularly important for Hungarians. Thus the act of finding the place of or creating space for Kertbeny there has equally great importance for present day activism: it is a symbolic act of claiming social acceptance through cultural integration by demonstrating that gay memories are fully and inseparably incorporated into 'real' Hungarian memories.[71]

Conclusion

This chapter has focused on uses of space by homosexuals, urnings, gays and lesbians, LGBT people and queers, in a socially and historically ordered sequence, starting in the City of Spas and continuing in the 'city of spies'. I have shown how the emergence of the public realm in the spatially ordered modern city offered extra opportunities for queers to submerge into the world of strangers, where one could not only be, but also act as a homosexual – with established meeting places and patterns of decodable behaviour. Same-sex desires have been socially recognized and, at the same time, misrecognized in Hungary since at least the first half of the twentieth century, and these processes continued during the state socialist period, too.

The totalitarian androgyny of the first decade after World War II brought the renaissance of compiling 'homosexual inventories' to recruit police informers, as a regular part of police work. Also as a new achievement of state socialist gender equality policies, men and women could equally be prosecuted on perversion against nature charges for a while. During state socialism, public expressions of sexuality were heavily mediated. After the change in the political system and after many decades of spatially deprived public existence of non-heteronormative desires, Budapest was the place, where the sociocultural infrastructure for LGBT people in Hungary could start to develop again.

Today Budapest – while its historically determined hydrocephalus feature has definitively started to fade mainly because of the accelerated expansion of queer cyberization – has a fairly well-developed organizational and entertainment landscape that can be readily navigated by LGBTQ groups and individuals. On the other hand, city life in Budapest is far from instantiating 'social relations of difference without exclusion'.[72] It can only be hoped, especially in the present circumstances, that the largely unrealized social ideal of a city life characterized by 'openness to unassimilated otherness'[73] can soon become an ongoing everyday project in Budapest and elsewhere.

Notes

1 This research was supported by Grant 105414 from the Hungarian Scientific Research Fund. The author is grateful to Boldizsár Vörös for his advice on historical sources.

2 Warner, M. (1993), *Fear of a Queer Planet: Queer Politics and Social Theory.* Minneapolis: University of Minnesota Press, p. vii.

3 Knopp, L. (2003), 'Sexuality and urban space: A framework for analysis', in Alexander R. Cuthbert (ed.), *Designing Cities: Critical Readings in Urban Design.* Oxford: Blackwell, pp. 193–203, p. 199.

4 Kertbeny, K. (ca. 1856), *Öneletrajz (töredék) – Autobiographiai jegyzetek [Biographical notes].* Budapest: National Szechenyi Library, OSZK Kézirattár [Manuscript Archive] OctGerm 302/120-125, p. 120.

5 Kertbeny, K. (1880), *Kertbeny ismeretlenhez [Kertbeny's letter to an unknown addressee].* Budapest: National Szechenyi Library. OSZK Levelestár [Letter Archive].

6 According to Kertbeny's autobiographical notes '[F]rom this time on Kertbeny decided to devote himself to the representation of Hungarian literature as a life aim. But until now his name was still his family's name: Benkert. However, if he wanted to represent a Hungarian case, he needed a Hungarian name, too. Therefore, he wrote home for a name change. The registration took place on the 23rd of September 1847 numbered 6613 and the permission arrived from the royal government on the 22nd of February 1848 numbered 8812 – Kertbeny (ca 1856), p. 121.

7 Kertbeny, K. (1868), *Levéltöredék 1868. május 6. [Letter fragment 1868 May 6].* Budapest: National Széchenyi Library, OSZK Kézirattár [Manuscript Archive] OctGerm 302/228, 1868.

8 Pál, G. (1927), *A homoszexuális probléma modern megvilágításban [The homosexual problem in a modern light].* Budapest: Mai Henrik és Fia Orvosi Könyvkiadó, Second Edition, III.

9 Urning is a reference to men who love other men, belonging to a transitional third gender. The term, being inspired by Plato's Symposium, was coined by the German jurist Karl Heinrich Ulrichs.

10 Pál (1927), p. 65.

11 Ibid.

12 Turcsányi, G. (ed.) (1929), *A modern bűnözés [Modern Criminality]*. Budapest: Rozsnyai Károly Kiadása, p. 133.

13 Nemes Nagy, Zoltán (1934), *Katasztrófák a szerelmi életben. Sexualpathologiai tanulmányok. II. kötet [Catastrophes in the love life. Sexualpathological studies. Volume II.]*. Budapest: Aesculap Kiadás, pp. 73–98.

14 Ibid., p. 73.

15 Ibid.

16 These included the Erzsébet square, where homosexuals gathered in groups on benches around the public toilet; bath houses with steam chambers such as in the Rác, the Király, the Lukács, the Kazinczy and previously the Császár Bath; public toilets at the Kálvin square, the corner of the Teréz boulevard and the Király street, the Emke corner, the little park at the Erzsébet bridge on the Buda side around the fountain and under the bridge, at the Keleti railway station on the departure side; and there used to be the Sasfészek, a homosexual restaurant in Buda, too. Ibid., pp. 75–9.

17 Lofland, Lyn H. (1973), *A World of Strangers: Order and Action in Urban Public Space*. New York: Basic Books.

18 Recently a document from 1942 was also recovered in a Hungarian archive, contributing to the still very scarce historical evidence that during World War II, homosexuals were also targets of life-threatening state control in Hungary: it is a list of 995 alleged homosexuals that was annexed to the correspondence between the State Security Centre and the Minister of Defence contemplating the possibility whether or not to use them as forced labourers within the wartime Labour Service System. This is the only known document that can provide a link between the history of homosexuality in Hungary and the Holocaust, and this link is not a very strong one, as at present, besides archive documents on perversion against nature court cases, there is no historical data available to find out what happened in Hungary during the 1940s to alleged homosexuals in general, and the 995 listed men from Budapest in particular. Source: Conscription of homosexual individuals to labour service, including a register of residents of the capital city (1942) HM 68763/Eln.1b. – 1942; Homoszexuális egyének bevonultatása munkaszolgálatra (benne névjegyzék a fővárosi lakosokról). Original archive document of the *Hadtörténelmi Levéltár* (Hungarian War Archive).

19 Instruction on criminal records (1958): Bűnügyi nyilvántartási utasítás. Ikt. szám 50-6/5-1958 ABTL. Original archive document of the Állambiztonsági Szolgálatok Történeti Levéltára (Historical Archives of the Hungarian State Security).

20 Takács, J. (2007a), *How to Put Equality into Practice? Anti-discrimination and Equal Treatment Policymaking and LGBT People*. Budapest: Új Mandátum Kiadó.

21 Zdravomyslova, E. and Temkina, A. (2005), 'Gendered citizenship in Soviet and post-Soviet societies', in V. Tolz and S. Booth (eds), *Nation and Gender in Contemporary Europe*. Manchester: Manchester University Press, pp. 96–113, p. 98.

22 Heleszta, S. and Rudas, J. (1978), *Munkásfiatalok és egyetemisták szexualitása. [Sexuality of young workers and university students]*. Budapest: Szociológiai Intézet.

23 Buda, B. (1972), *A szexualitás modern elmélete [Modern Theory of Sexuality]*. Budapest: Tankönyvkiadó, p. 70.

24 Bodnár, J. (2001), *Fin-de-Millénaire Budapest: Metamorphoses of Urban Life*. Minneapolis: University of Minnesota Press, p. 29.

25 Szelényi, I. (1996), 'Cities under socialism – and after', in G. Andrusz, M. Harloe and I. Szelenyi (eds), *Cities After Socialism: Urban and Regional Change and Conflict in Post-socialist Societies*. Cambridge, MA: Blackwell Publishers, pp. 286–317.

26 Borgos, A. (ed.) (2011), *Eltitkolt évek. Tizenhat leszbikus életút. [Secret Years. Sixteen lesbian life histories]*. Budapest: Labrisz Leszbikus Egyesület.

27 Ibid., p. 15.

28 Ibid., p. 80.

29 *Egymásra nézve [Another Way]*. dir. Károly Makk, 1 hr. 42 min., MAFILM DIALOG Filmstúdió – Meridian Films, 1982, DVD.

30 Borgos (2011), p. 49.

31 Ibid., p. 187.

32 Moss, K. and Simić, M. (2011), 'Post-communist lavender menace: Lesbians in mainstream East European film', *Journal of Lesbian Studies*, 15(3), 271–83.

33 Murai, A. and Tóth, E. Z. (2011), 'Női szerelmek a filmvásznon a rendszerváltás előtt és után [Female love stories on the screen before and after the system change]', in Judit Takács (ed.), *Homofóbia Magyarországon [Homophobia in Hungary]*. Budapest: L'Harmattan, pp. 69–79, pp. 74–5.

34 Földes, A. (1981), 'A törvényt teremteni kell [The law must be created]', *Kritika*, 3 April.

35 Erőss, L. (1984), *Furcsa párok. A homoszexuálisok titkai nyomában. [Strange Couples. Tracing the Secrets of Homosexuals]*. Budapest: Private edition of the author, p. 23.

36 Géczi, J. (1987), *Vadnarancsok II. Homosexuálisok vallomásai (1980-81) [Wild Oranges II. Homosexuals' Confessions (1980–81)]*. Budapest: Magvető, p. 5.

37 *Magyar Országos Levéltár* (National Archives of Hungary) M-KS 288.f.5/949.ő.e (1985.09.24.) 7R/124.

38 Vermes [no first name given]. 'A Minority at Risk', *Hungarian Digest*, April–June 1989, 54–6.

39 Láner, L. (2002), 'Romzi. Interjú Romsauer Lajossal [Interview with Lajos Romsauer]', *Mások*, 12(3), 12–15.

40 Ibid., p. 13.

41 Long, S. (1999), 'Gay and lesbian movements in Eastern Europe. Romania, Hungary, and the Czech Republic', in B. D. Adam, J. W. Duyvendak and A. Krouwel (eds), *The Global Emergence of Gay and Lesbian Politics: National Imprints of a Worldwide Movement*. Philadelphia Temple University Press, pp. 242–65, p. 251.

42 Láner (2002), p. 14.

43 The following cases are taken from my research interviews, which were conducted with elderly gay men having same-sex experiences also from the state socialist period in Budapest.

44 Bech, H. (1997), *When Men Meet*. Cambridge: Polity Press.

45 Hauer, Gudrun and Homosexuelle Initiative Wien (1984), *Rosa Liebe unterm roten Stern: Zur Lage der Lesben und Schwulen in Osteuropa*. Hamburg: Frühlings Erwachen.

46 Long (1999), p. 259.

47 Simon, J. (1996), 'A demokrácia értelmezése a posztkommunista országokban [Interpretation of Democracy in Post-Communist Countries]', *Szociológiai Szemle*, 1, 113–56.

48 Farkas, L. (2001), 'Nice on paper: The aborted liberalisation of gay rights in Hungary', in Robert Wintemute and M. Andenaes (eds), *Legal Recognition of Same-Sex Partnerships. A Study of National, European and International Law*. Oxford: Hart Publishing, pp. 563–74, p. 572.

49 However, it should be noted that in order to avoid registration problems the original name of this organisation was Háttér Support Society for Homosexuals, and it excluded people younger than 18 from its membership.

50 Borgos, A. (2007), 'Getting to know gays and lesbians in Hungary: Lessons from a gender-informed educational program', in Justyna Sempruch, Katharina Willems and Laura Shook (eds), *Multiple Marginalities: An Intercultural Dialogue on Gender in Education*. Königstein/Taunus: Ulrike Helmer Verlag, pp. 425–36.

51 As Helen Meller pointed out: 'The savage dismantling of the territory which had been Hungarian before World War I, reducing the country to a third of its former size, was to leave Budapest as a hydrocephalus, at least 15 times larger than the next largest Hungarian town'. – Meller, H. (2001), *European Cities 1890–1930s. History, Culture and the Built Environment*. Chichester: John Wiley & Sons, p. 102.

52 Knopp (2003).

53 Evans, D. T. (1993), *Sexual Citizenship: The Material Construction of Sexualities*. London: Routledge.

54 Research interview conducted by the author with László Mocsonaki in 2002.

55 Takács (2007a), pp. 13–16.

56 Herek, G. (2011), 'Anti-equality marriage amendments and sexual stigma', *Journal of Social Issues*, 67(2), 413–26.

57 The much smaller proportion of women among same-sex registered partners is influenced by the discriminatory nature of the Hungarian legislation on artificial insemination, denying access to treatment for lesbian women. Once a woman lives in a registered same-sex partnership, she has an official document showing that she is in a same-sex relationship, and is thus excluded from artificial insemination treatment.

58 KSH [Central Office of Statistics] (2012), 'Népmozgalom, 2011. január–december [Demography, 2011 January–December]', *Statisztikai Tükör*, 6(17), 1–6.

59 Bech (1997).

60 Takács, J. and Szalma, I. (2011), 'Homophobia and same-sex partnership legislation in Europe', *Equality, Diversity and Inclusion: An International Journal*, 30(5), 356–78.

61 Takács, J. (2007), '"It is only extra information . . ." – Social representation and value preferences of gay men in Hungary', in R. Kuhar and J. Takács (eds), *Beyond the Pink Curtain. Everyday Life of LGBT People in Eastern Europe*. Ljubljana: Mirovni Institut, pp. 185–97, pp. 186–90.

62 Hungarian research interviews conducted with gay identified MSM between 2007 and 2009 within the *HIV Prevention within High-Risk Social Networks – International Social Network Study II*. led by CAIR, MCW, USA.

63 Gruszczynska, A. (2007), 'Living "*la vida*" internet: Some notes on the cyberization of polish LGBT community', in R. Kuhar and J. Takács (eds), *Beyond the Pink Curtain. Everyday Life of LGBT People in Eastern Europe*. Ljubljana: Mirovni Institut, pp. 95–116, p. 101.

64 Young, I. M. (2011 [1990]), *Justice and the Politics of Difference*. Princeton: Princeton University Press.

65 Ipsos: *Meleg-felvonulás. Kutatási jelentés*, 5 September 2009 (Ipsos Gay Pride March report 2009) – I would like to thank Tamás Dombos for providing me with the data.

66 I would like to thank the Legal Aid Service of the Háttér Support Society for LGBT People for providing me with these pieces of information.

67 Renkin, H. Z. (2002), *Ambiguous Identities, Ambiguous Transitions: Lesbians, Gays, and the Sexual Politics of Citizenship in Postsocialist Hungary. Ph.D. dissertation*. Ann Arbor, MI: University of Michigan, p. 191.

68 Ibid., p. 178.

69 Ibid., p. 183.

70 Nora, P. (1989), 'Between memory and history: Les Lieux de Mémoire', *Representations*, 26, 7–25.

71 By 2011, activists involved in the Kertbeny ritual related collective memory-making project successfully achieved that the Hungarian National Committee of Reverence and Memorial Sites placed Kertbeny's gravesite under special protection by officially declaring that it belongs to the National Pantheon.

72 Young (2011 [1990]), p. 227.

73 Ibid.

Further reading

Borgos, A. (2007), 'Getting to know gays and lesbians in Hungary: Lessons from a gender-informed educational program', in J. Sempruch, K. Willems and L. Shook (eds), *Multiple Marginalities: An Intercultural Dialogue on Gender in Education*. Königstein/Taunus: Ulrike Helmer Verlag, pp. 425–36.

Borgos, A. (ed.) (2011), *Eltitkolt évek. Tizenhat leszbikus életút. [Secret Years. Sixteen lesbian life histories]*. Budapest: Labrisz Leszbikus Egyesület.

Farkas, L. (2001), 'Nice on paper: The aborted liberalisation of gay rights in Hungary', in R. Wintemute and M. Andenaes (eds), *Legal Recognition of Same-Sex Partnerships. A Study of National, European and International Law.* Oxford: Hart Publishing, pp. 563–74.

Kuhar, R. and J. Takács (eds) (2007), *Beyond the Pink Curtain. Everyday Life of LGBT People in Eastern Europe.* Ljubljana: Mirovni Institute, http://www. mirovni-institut.si/Publikacija/Detail/en/publikacija/Beyond-the-Pink-Curtain-Everyday-Life-of-LGBT-People-in-Eastern-Europe/.

Long, S. (1999), 'Gay and lesbian movements in Eastern Europe. Romania, Hungary, and the Czech Republic', in B. D. Adam, J. W. Duyvendak and A. Krouwel (eds), *The Global Emergence of Gay and Lesbian Politics: National Imprints of a Worldwide Movement.* Philadelphia Temple University Press, pp. 242–65.

Takács, J. (2004a), 'The double life of Kertbeny', in G. Hekma (ed.), *Past and Present of Radical Sexual Politics.* Amsterdam: UvA – Mosse Foundation, pp. 26–40.

—(2004b), *Homoszexualitás és társadalom [Homosexuality and Society]*, Új Mandátum Kiadó: Budapest, http://www.mek.oszk.hu/07000/07076/07076.pdf.

Takács, J. et al. (2012), 'Don't ask, don't tell, don't bother: Homophobia and the heteronorm in Hungary', in L. Trappolin, A. Gasparini and R. Wintemute (eds), *Confronting Homophobia in Europe. Social and Legal Perspectives.* Oxford: Hart Publishing, pp. 79–105.

11

Two cities of Helsinki?
One liberally gay and one
practically queer?[1]

Antu Sorainen

Helsinki is known today as one of the urban havens for queer people, the capital of a wealthy Nordic country with liberal legislation and an open atmosphere. Finland has recently been ranked as one of the countries with the happiest citizens; it has an extraordinarily stable economy compared to other EU countries and nations worldwide, and the capital, Helsinki, has been called as the world's most livable city, 'rich, happy and good at austerity' as the *Financial Times* put it sardonically in its special report in 2012.[2] Helsinki keeps pulsing with an active queer scene even during the current era, which David M. Halperin recently claimed is marked by 'the decline of the queer public sphere'. In Halperin's view, Western gay culture is dying out on the basis that straight people have bought up the houses of gay people after they died of AIDS in the 1980s and 1990s, and that the numbers of gay bars in major cities are on the decline from the peak years in the 1970s and 1980s. He blames the gentrification of those metropolitan areas that were populated by queer folks until the late 1990s and online hook-ups for the latter problem – which seems quite plausible as lesbians and gay men worldwide can now connect without the aid of commercial bars. In Helsinki, the number of centrally located bars, cafés and late-night clubs has, however, been quite steady since the 1990s – gay men in particular are well catered to. Lesbians and other queer people may be less visible in terms of the commercial bar scene, but they too continue to play an important role in the history of Helsinki's public sexual landscape.[3] Research has shown that it makes sense to lay out a suggestive distinction between 'practically queer' and 'liberally gay' Helsinki, insinuating that the two major queer districts of the city have been influenced by different political, economic, social-historical and gendered implications in terms of the openness and formations of queer life.[4] This gay/queer distinction can be detected between the 'respectable' gay and lesbian area in Punavuori in the South and the more 'rough' queer district of Kallio in the North-East of the city. In terms suggested by Samuel R. Delany in his study of gay urban transformations, Punavuori facilitates narrowing possibilities for inter-class connections and networking within an increasingly homogeneous social grouping, while Kallio is associated with less commercial queer visibility that actually serves to provide more inter-class contacts instead of identity- and class-based social grouping.[5] In this chapter, I will discuss the unique historical trajectory that led to these current practices, providing a useful way of discerning these intriguing analytical distinctions.

The assortment of public gay and queer bars and events in today's Helsinki is quite large given the city's small population, which consists of no more than about 500,000 inhabitants. This is somewhat extraordinary since it was only some 60 years ago, just after World War II, that Helsinki had neither an open nor a *public* queer life. It is noteworthy that the law decreed homosexual acts criminal for both women and men, with infractions carrying a maximum punishment of 2 years imprisonment. The law remained in force until 1971. Oppressive court cases on 'same-sex fornication' and 'fornication with a minor of the same sex' drastically increased at the beginning of the 1950s, but there were social groups, semi-public and private spaces, and cultural formations that allowed sexually dissident life to bloom with various queering effects for wider society, even before the concepts of gay (*homo*) or, particularly, lesbian (*lesbo*) were adopted into the Finnish lexicon. In the 1950s, sexology's terminology was occasionally used in academic, medical and legal contexts, but it was not yet at the level of a shared everyday language.[6] The figure and the concept of the male 'homosexual' became habitually known during the 1950s, but the concept 'lesbian' remained virtually unknown until the late 1970s – instead, homosexual women referred to themselves as 'different', 'like this' or 'like us'.[7] Even though the terminology was not coherent and homosexual acts were illegal until the early 1970s, we see queer life in the historical Helsinki nonetheless. Even during the era of criminalization, queer people found ways to socialize or fulfil their sexual desire in practical and innovative ways, often without claims to any fixed identity, whereas the more liberal era has seen an increase of the commercialization and the more narrow understanding of the 'decent' gay lifestyle, especially in the wealthy Punavuori.

Similarly, it is significant that the history of Finland's immigration policy differs from that of the other Northern European and Scandinavian national states: Helsinki is very white. This is reflected in the queer history of Helsinki in that racial issues have not been a substantial topic in queer cultures until very recently – not withstanding the fact that a prominent Finnish Roma has written stories of a lesbian coming of age based loosely on her experiences.[8] Queer emigration to Sweden and Denmark has, on the other hand, been an important phenomenon. In the 1960s and 1970s, because of the national economic crisis and late urbanization, the flow of immigrant workers was *from* Finland, specifically to Sweden, not into the country as in the other Nordic and Northern European countries. As a consequence of the late development of the welfare state and tight immigration politics in Finland compared to other Nordic countries, the number of immigrant workers, refugees and asylum seekers is still very low, even though there has been a slow increase. This contributes to a specific national discourse on 'Finnish' sexuality, which can be observed not only in public and parliamentary debates but also in research, that stresses the equality of sexes and liberal attitudes towards gays, lesbians and queer-identified people.[9] Recently, the 'liberalism' of Finnish society has been highlighted in the public response to the increasingly oppressive anti-gay legislation in its neighbouring country, Russia.

It is in this unique context that I situate the following questions: what were the important moments and social configurations, especially in the 1980s, that predated the current situation? And what role did the urban landscape play in shaping these experiences? I will argue that there are two cities of Helsinki, one liberally gay and one practically queer. This shows how queer sexualities entered into wider public discourse in Helsinki, and complicate the binary of pre- and post-queer history of the city by pointing to the complex intersections of same-sex desire and gender at work in the city itself.[10] I will discuss the queer history of Helsinki from the post-war criminalization period of same-sex sexual acts until the present day. Along the way, it is important to look at what kind of queer memories have gained publicity, and which are the ones that have remained more ephemeral: this enterprise helps us to reconsider the ways in which we claim to remember and know the urban queer past and so engage in the queer present.[11] One important element at work here is gender: as is often the case in queer European histories, gay men's lives, spaces and memories of Helsinki have been better documented than those of different kinds of trans people, lesbians and other sexually marginalized groups.

To help create a fuller picture, I will look at the city of Helsinki, in part, through my own experiences as a long-term queer lesbian resident of the city. I proceed from the assumption that my personal experience and narrative of queer Helsinki take a somewhat different look, first and foremost, from the dominant narrative, which claims that the 1980s was an oppressive era for sexual dissidents because of the societal panic caused by the discovery of AIDS.[12] Secondly, I will look at the period from 1990 onwards through my own history as an academic queer activist and inhabitant of one of the blossoming queer neighbourhoods of Helsinki, the multisexual district of *Kallio*.

War history and its impact on sexualities and gender in Finland

Finland differs from other Nordic countries not only in regard to language, culture and urban development but also in its political history. The cruel civil war of 1918 with its lethal concentration camps haunts the national narrative, and the construction and politics of its public memory.[13] This indicates the distinctiveness of Helsinki and of Finland in relation to some of the other cities and countries discussed in this collection. Moreover, recent Finnish research has emphasized that the specific construction of gender, sexuality, memory and myth was different than in the other Nordic countries as a result of the tenacious agrarian model.[14] The Finnish gender system was also somewhat different. Women had a rather active role in the political life of nation building in the nineteenth century, and unlike other European forms of jurisprudence surrounding the criminalization of same-sex sexuality, 'lesbian' acts were similarly punishable from 1889 to 1971.[15] The Finnish gender system was arguably less polarized and hierarchical when compared to the neighbouring countries. Perceived differences between women and men were not very tenacious in a Finnish society where the culture was still largely rural and agricultural, not urban or bourgeois.[16] In fact, the urbanization process only began in earnest from the late 1950s onward.[17] Furthermore, the national history of having been a part of both the Swedish and Russian empires, and the lost wars against the Soviets arguably brought their own specific problems for the construction of especially the male sexuality in Finland. On the one hand, there has existed among the population an understandably strong urge to ridicule Russian masculinities, while on the other, there remains a palpable inferiority complex in relation to the neighbouring Swedes. This dilemma has persisted in the cultural imagery since the nineteenth century. World War II only increased these national masculinity traumas.

Finland's role on the edge of Europe was a complicated one in the 1950s. World War II split apart the Scandinavian community as the Nordic countries were on different sides of the war. Finland was not only attacked by the Soviet Union in 1939 but it also attacked the Soviets themselves and fought on Germany's side in 1941–44. At the same time, Sweden remained neutral while Denmark and Norway were occupied by the Nazis, and Iceland, Greenland and the Faroese Islands were controlled by American and British troops. In actuality, Finland fought two wars against the Soviet Union, the first one referred to colloquially as the Winter War in 1939–40 and the second one called the Continuation War in 1941–44. The armistice agreement with the Soviet Union obliged Finland to break off relations with Germany, its former ally, and this led to a third escalation, culminating in the Lapland War between Finland and Germany from September 1944 to April 1945. Finland had to comply with harsh armistice demands. It ultimately lost 10 per cent of its territory with 12 per cent of its population displaced and resettled within the new borders of 1944–45.[18]

The lost wars and the sustained and bitter fight against the former ally had a strong impact on national sentiment, especially on popular visions of masculinity.[19] In large part, this was linked to a feeling of bitterness towards the Swedes who had managed to stay outside the war. Even though many Finnish soldiers had had homosexual experiences with members of the German troops during the war, derisive talk of Swedish men 'like that' – homosexual – increased after the war. Helsinki was one of the only European metropolitan cities in war, besides London, that was not occupied or tramped over by Nazis. During the war years, many gay men in Helsinki cruised both German and Russian soldiers: the creator of Tom of Finland, Touko Laaksonen, said that he had sexual contacts with German soldiers during curfew at the Esplanade in the heart of the city, and, after the war, with Russian soldiers at another centrally located park, Tähtitorninmäki.[20] German men, as former allies, were awkwardly close to Finnish ideals of masculinity, while Russian men were seen as profoundly other, so it seems only fitting that it was Swedish men who would become the target of repressed homosexual projections and fantasies and popularly labelled as 'wimps'. Their femininity was underscored by the thought that they had been unfit to fight, which was established as the measure of normative straight masculinity across the border in Finland.[21] Even in colloquial speech, the 'Swedish disease' [ruotsalainen tauti] served as a euphemism for homosexuality and its epidemic spread was greatly feared.[22]

Before gay and lesbian organization: 1950s

The war created new opportunities for same-sex socializing not only for gay men but also for lesbian women as gender roles had been defined anew, to some degree, under these crises circumstances. The wartime conditions demanded men to leave the domestic, mostly agrarian, sphere behind for the battlefield where men from all walks of life lived and fought together, and many young women worked in semi-military duties as members of Women's Auxiliary Services. In the 'home front', women had to take on such jobs and social tasks that were hitherto deemed men's duties and which made them more mobile in the social sphere, such as ambulance drivers or users of co-operative tractors and horses at farms.[23] This meant heightened opportunities for same-sex socializing. After the war, the state started a modernization process culminating in the 1960s. More and more young unmarried people moved to cities to look for new work in factories, civil service and trade. This widening out of the social space for queer encounters led, however, not directly to queer political organizing. One of the things that prevented the birth of a proper political gay movement in the 1950s and 1960s Helsinki was the fact that people were often not willing to expose their full names to each other in the small lesbian underground club or in gay men meeting places such as bars, parks and toilets. A code of anonymity was applied in queer social spaces and situations where queer life bloomed because of the fear of the police control. This could be partly a consequence of the harshening legislation and conservative post-war political climate. I suggest that it also reflected the fresh memories and the socially shared knowledge of the working methods of the undercover police in search of the underground members of the communist party before and during World War II.[24]

Even though there were some attempts to get organized around gay politics, without the use of real names it was hard to invite people to meetings or to sign manifestos or to address politicians.[25] For example, gay men's cruising culture seems to have embraced the idea of the lonely individual who only occasionally, even if practically every night, was led to parks and public toilets (known as bunkers) by his stubborn desire.[26] Further, Finland is geographically a large country with a sparse population and no metropolis – it was maybe difficult to find enough people, especially women, interested in organizing. Also, the influence of the English-language literature on homosexuality was minor, as only a few Finns could read English before the 1970s. Many books, most notably Havelock Ellis's *Sexual Inversion* (1897, with J. A. Symonds), Henry James's *The Bostonians* (1886), Radclyffe Hall's *The Well of Loneliness* (1928) and Alfred Kinsey Report on *Sexual Behavior in the Human Male* (1948)[27], important for identity politics in other European countries were simply not translated into Finnish. Only the Swedish-speaking Finns and members of the upper classes, such as the Moomin author Tove Jansson and her social circle, had access to this information, including the culture and networks of lesbian and gay organizations in Europe. Often these individuals had no meaningful political or intellectual contact with Finnish-speaking queer people from the 'lower classes', even if women from different class backgrounds might have had a chance to meet in philanthropic, bohemian or religious contexts. Cruising brought men from all walks of life together, but the parks and streets were no place for gathering political strength.[28] Modern lesbian or gay identity was thus not the basis of Helsinki queer life in the 1950s and 1960s.

Although gay men had the (relative) freedom to cruise public spaces in the city as they could meet in parks, bunkers and restaurants, this was not possible for lesbian women, who could not go to restaurants without a male companion until the late 1960s. While the regulation was officially aimed at curbing prostitution, it effectively prevented the development of lesbian bars in Helsinki.[29] Indeed, they only started to appear in the 1980s. The gender implications of the use of public space were also strong when it came to women's same-sex socializing on the streets and parks of Helsinki. It was not respectable for women to walk alone or together after the closing hours of theatres, cafes and soirees: they were easily taken to be prostitutes or vagrants unless they were factory workers returning from a nightshift.

Male homosexuality entered the nation's public discourse as a form of crime and illness, and the stories that were published in scandal papers and tabloids were invariably rather negative and stereotyped well into the 1970s, but they still granted the concept of male homosexuality public visibility. Men's homosexual deeds reportedly took place in easily accessible everyday environments. Furthermore, the tabloids assured that the idea of active male sexuality – even when directed towards other men – was culturally potent and multiply enforced when written or talked about. The constant exposure to the idea of male homosexuality habitually changed people's mental space to include the idea of men desiring other men sexually. While male homosexuality as an existing, although an undesired variation of human sexuality entered the public discourses, similar visibility did not apply to lesbians. The press had comparatively little to offer to women in search of validation for their same-sex feelings. It only managed to displace women's same-sex sexual activities as something rather exotic and unlikely to happen in average environments. The framing of the same-sex sexual deeds of women as a crime in the scandalous case of rural lesbians in court (The Herb Grove) did not take reference to older agrarian concepts such as being 'a woman-lover'. All this fostered ignorance about the idea of lesbian activity, and made it a rather unlikely concept for women to relate to. Instead of letting lesbians enter the public picture, the patriotic post-war period had taught young women to keep up their sexual morals as the most important contribution to the prosperity of the country. This respectable middle-class trajectory could hardly be seriously questioned, particularly since the presence of belittled war widows and 'excess spinsters' showed the consequences of falling outside of heterosexual normativity.[30]

Although the modern concept of 'lesbian' was not really available, proto-lesbian life was bubbling beneath the surface despite the regulation and cultural and social invisibility. Women with same-sex desires managed to find each other despite restaurant restrictions: working-class women came together in the factories, in shelters and in cafés. Middle- and upper-class women might meet in girls' gymnasiums and universities as teachers or as students, in private salons, philanthropic and other women's associations, as well as at dinner parties at home. Religious communities also formed an important site for the sociability of queer women.[31] However, these meetings took place by chance because of the lack of official or (semi)public meeting places or spaces for queer women in the city.

The rise of the welfare state and political organizing: 1960s–70s

The building of the Finnish social welfare state in the late 1960s and early 1970s and the rise of social democratic governments led to many important legal reforms, and to the organization of the proper gay movement. Even though the leftist movement's influence was growing during the 1960s, wider society was not always very friendly or hospitable for gays or lesbian feminists as they were seen by many Marxists as representing bourgeois excess.[32] For example, the squatting of the Helsinki Student House in 1968 became a huge generational experience for many leftist-radical Finnish young people of the time, but it did not offer a political space for lesbians and gays to 'step forward'. Similarly, Finland's first out-lesbian author, Pirkko Saisio, has vividly described (in fiction) how she faced problems with her sexuality in Marxist intellectual circles in Helsinki in the early 1970s as the ideology of the movement was strongly heteronormative.[33]

The first Finnish gay organizations were established in the late 1960s,[34] but the first demonstration for lesbian and gay rights took place only in 1974 in the Old Church Park in the Helsinki city centre near Punavuori – in the same park, interestingly, where the bodies of the Finnish and German *Whites* killed during the invasion of Helsinki 12 April 1918 are buried.[35] The first official national lesbian and gay organization, *Seta* (Sexual Equality), was founded in the same year, 1974, of the first public manifesto (a protest against the sacking of a church youth worker on the basis of his homosexuality).[36] A reading group gathered in its office in Helsinki and Dennis Altman's book *Homosexual: Oppression and Liberation* was studied. It seems that lesbian and gay activists learnt the term 'coming out' from Altman.[37] *Seta* started to organize Liberation Marches once a year in the city centre, attended by some hundred people.[38]

The early years of *Seta* were, according to many lesbians active in the organization, dominated by its male founders even though it had an equality policy. Most lesbian-feminists found it easier to get together at the premises of the women's movement (*Naisasialiitto Unioni*), in the old historical building near Punavuori, rather than at the male-dominated *Seta* office.[39] The first awakening of lesbian-feminism in Helsinki took place among Swedish-speaking intellectuals, who visited the feminist camp on *Femø* in Denmark in 1976. One of these women gave a talk on Shulamith Firestone's *The Dialectic of Sex* and Angela Davis in *Seta* meeting the same year, but gay men there were not happy: 'It became a war', this woman later recalled.[40] The first visible lesbian-feminist group in Helsinki was called Violet Hippies (*Liilat hämyt*), consisting of six to seven active members, but both the women's movement and *Seta* tended to ignore them.

Coming out in the modern sense was still not really possible.[41] In neighbouring Sweden, the concept used in the 1960s was to 'step forward/ to the front' (*stå fram/träda fram*), even though it was used not for homosexuality but by the leftist movement in the straight political context.[42] Finnish lesbians and gays started to 'come out' on a large scale only in the 1980s. One of the first public 'coming-outs' took place in 1979 on the part of a lesbian woman, Kersti Juva, a famous translator of children's fiction and a daughter of the then archbishop of the Lutheran Church, Mikko Juva. This political act had a profound effect on debates inside the Lutheran church as the father decided to take a stand for his daughter and for sexual equality itself in an article in 1982. Kersti Juva, a resident of Kallio, was a well-known figure in the closed circles of Helsinki high art lesbian scene but she also supported young anarchist queer women who had adopted a more in-your-face and take-it-to-streets politics from the United Kingdom, the United States and the Netherlands. In Juva's mixed gay-lib and lesbian feminist person,[43] a significant shift crystallized between the politics of the 1970s and that of the 1980s of the lesbian and gay residents of the city. Increasingly people emerged out from the privacy of their homes and from the city's anonymous cruising zones to semi-public official meetings and finally to public spaces with much higher visibility.

Proto-queering the city: 1980s

Even though the AIDS-related panic forced at least one queer club to move to another location, Helsinki still witnessed a vibrant liberalization of public sexual space in the early 1980s, partly as a resistance against the negative societal reaction to HIV+ patients, and partly for other reasons. Even though the first AIDS diagnosis in 1983 was followed by a media furore, the first openly lesbian and gay restaurant, *Gay Gambrini*, opened its doors in 1984, in the Punavuori district. It was indirectly owned by *Seta*, and activists renovated it with their own hands.[44] This meant an end of the era of Monday club nights in the premises of a straight restaurant *Botta* that had been organized by *Seta*. Botta was conveniently located near the railway station and next to the old gay cruising areas known as *Carousel and Museum Park*,[45] but still not quite in the actual city centre.

In Helsinki, the opening of *Gay Gambrini* marked the start of permanent public visibility for social categories of lesbian and gay. Further, the general opening up of Finnish culture in the 1980s meant that the whole city was in flux. As recent research on fantasies of metropolitan life and the making of permissive society has shown, there is an important relationship between consumerism and queer life.[46] In Helsinki, increased lesbian and gay visibility in Punavuori can be connected to the general narrowing of regulation and the 'birth' of a consumerist culture in the mid-1980s after the peak decade of the welfare state (1970s). For example, until the early 1980s there were only three TV channels and the national broadcaster's (*YLE*) radio channels, but now independent radio producers were given permission to go on air and MTV and other commercial broadcasting companies added to the narrow variety of television channels. *Radio City* was among the first to use this opportunity to create radio programmes that gave a voice to marginalized groups of the city, such as minority ethnic groups and non-heterosexual people. The Green Party was also gaining prominence, first as a part of other active new civil society movements, and later as a political party. Similarly, the art world was undergoing a process of transformation as young teachers who believed in mixed media, photography, video, performance art, and expressive visual visions of sexuality were hired at the Helsinki Fine Art Academy and other art schools to teach a new generation of students who had no personal connection to war or the Marxist movement. The 1960s and 1970s leftist/Marxist politics and social-democratic state rationality was now deemed by many to be nothing but a sombre dead end, and new individualized youth styles were invented, marketed and increasingly embraced.[47] All these added to the vibe of the city as a place where everything seemed possible. MTV accelerated the development of a range of visual public styles, and helped young people boost their English skills. For some years, Helsinki youths spoke English with a Dutch accent, as the first hosts of North-European MTV were from the Netherlands. A cosmopolitan activist sentiment gradually seeped into queer life.

My own personal memories of urban queer life in Helsinki start from the early 1980s when I moved into the city as a young and sexually ambitious but inexperienced university student from a small city of Pori where I had never met any lesbians. I remember every Monday evening walking past the nightclub where a lesbian and gay club of *Seta* organized and met. It was a Monday night because that was the quietest night of the week when the normally straight club rented out space for other uses so that the club owners could make some money out of queer patrons happy to acquire any night on offer.

It was 2 years before I started to participate in and even contribute to the queer life of Helsinki. During this period, I discovered a new life as a political 'dyke' and a lesbian sexual anarchist in Amsterdam. When I moved back to Helsinki in the summer of 1984, I was full of fresh ideas and sexual energy. I met another young woman who had been living in similar dyke squats in London and San Francisco. We soon realized that together we wanted to organize something new and distinctive in the Helsinki feminist and lesbian scene. We also wanted to address the media and art world because we had an interest in and talent for those fields, too. Above all, we wanted to be active and public – the more public, the better. To reach our aims to change the sexual culture of Helsinki for the better, we founded a proto-queer lesbian anarchist group, Extaasi. By 'proto-queerness'[48] I mean the specific gender politics and variety of sexualities in the group: the shared idea was social and sexual inclusivity, and feminism in a sex-adventurous way.

I have observed already that the Helsinki lesbian scene of the late 1970s and early 1980s suffered from some serious problems between men and feminist women in the national gay and lesbian organization, as noted above. Even though *Seta* had a parity principle concerning its chairs (50% women, 50% men), some of the activist lesbians were not happy with the gender politics of the organization. They visited the international lesbian conference organized by *Lesbiska Fronten* in Stockholm in 1976, and later also the feminist island, Femø, in Denmark – the place that was already visited by Swedish-speaking feminist pioneers. Upon their return, they brought back to Helsinki some strong lesbian-feminist ideas. As a consequence, they founded a women's only organization, Bad Seeds (*Akanat*), inside the general organization of *Seta*, and they also started to publish their own lesbian magazine, Odd Seed (*Torajyvä*). Further, the National League for Women published a feminist magazine, Women Folk (*Akkaväki*) (1975–96) that sporadically contained articles on lesbian issues, for example, the Finnish translation of Adrienne Rich's famous essay on compulsory heterosexuality and lesbian existence.[49] However, the organization was hampered by the fact that many lesbians had left the austere Helsinki in the late 1970s to live in what was deemed at the time to be the more liberal-minded and lesbian-friendly cities of Stockholm or Copenhagen.[50]

In queer history writing, it is often claimed that lesbians have been an underdog when it comes to cultural and political visibility. Kimberley O'Sullivan, for example, writes of Sydney that until the early 1990s, 'it was rare for a lesbian subject to make it into even the gay press. Intra-lesbian debates, furores and controversies of any kind, particularly about sexuality, remained unreported'.[51] However, the first publicly out 'acceptable' gay person in the Finnish media was a lesbian, the above noted Kersti Juva. After she had stepped into the public eye and after the queer anarchist group Extaasi came into being, the lesbian radicals also became visible in the mainstream media and in the social sphere of the city from 1984 onwards.[52] The invisibility of intra-queer debates in the gay press was true to some degree, though. For example, in 1993 the *Seta* magazine fired one of its lesbian editors for being too upfront on lesbian and trans issues, and on radical sexual politics such as s/m and cruising – matters that were not deemed respectable or important enough for 'official' gay politics.

Extaasi was a central part of new 'city' activism in the vibrant Helsinki of 1980s. The group wanted to move the discussion of women and lesbians towards cross-identifications and multiple subject positions. In the group, there were sexual anarchist dykes, feminist lesbians, transgendered people, bisexual women, straight butches and radical heterosexual men, lesbian mothers, and people with other sexual and gender identifications. The fact that the group was inclusive was different from many lesbian and gay communities that we then knew of in Europe and the United States. As Helsinki is a small city with a tiny queer population, inclusivity seemed to be the best (and only) option for any significant coalition. We had experienced the secluded lesbian communities in London, New York, San Francisco and Amsterdam, which seemed to restrict socializing to specifically categorized sexualities or genders. Extaasi was a broader church than the queer activist groups which came later in the United States and the United Kingdom and were more male dominated. Finally, the lesbian and gay scene of Helsinki has been rather mixed compared to many other metropolises of the western world.[53]

Extaasi organized events not only in Helsinki but also in London and Amsterdam. The club *Chain Reactions* was created: the first night took place in Amsterdam in 1985. After that, it became a long-term dyke club night in London. Del LaGrace Volcano displayed an image, from 'Bad Boys', taken in London's Chain Reactions in 1987, capturing four visitors to the club. According to LaGrace, an important actor in this image was the club itself – as a place in which queer subculture, queer sex and queer cultural production took place. 'Chain Reactions was everything I had dreamed of creating in San Francisco but hadn't managed. It was political, collective and full of hot dykes willing to take their politics out of the bedroom into the streets'.[54] The cross-national mobility of some Extaasi members was made possible by the Finnish social welfare system: I remember many occasions receiving generous social benefit money in Helsinki and hitch-hiking immediately to London or Amsterdam to live on it there for some months. As we lived in squats and took our electricity for free, everyday living costs were really low. Many of the contemporary queer youths from Helsinki are now leading a rather similar life in Berlin squats. However, they also need to work or claim student status, because social benefits are now much more vigorously regulated in the EU than they were in the heyday of the Finnish Welfare State. The formation of proto-queer activism and organizing has thus been closely tied to the developments of the state ideology and European economic system.

   In Helsinki, Extaasi deliberately wanted to avoid locational stability by organizing events in various places: in a leftist book café in Kallio, in a photography gallery in Punavuori, and more permanently, in the New Student House at the very heart of the city centre. It organized squats, art happenings, performances, club nights and public talks. One regular lesbian client later observed how she had been impressed in a debate on journalism and gender organized by Extaasi about seeing how one of the lesbians brought her underage daughter with her to the event. An intra-community and extra-community perspective then was that lesbians could not have children or families.[55] Further, she wrote about how in Extaasi parties 'the atmosphere was wild and weird, and the most common interior design element consisted of black garbage bags'.[56] There was also an all-female punk band called *Extaasi*. The group published a queer zine *Of the Lust to Rats* (*Himosta Rottiin*) and a book *Obscene Women* (*Julmia Naisia*) documenting its activities with a popular publishing house. The book contains interviews, literary essays, art photography and drawings, comic strips, media clips, manuals and translations of some important texts such as excerpts from *Coming to Power*.[57] The motivation to publish the book *Julmia Naisia* was to contribute to the lesbian archive and the documentation of sexual anarchism with some artistic aspiration, and it quickly sold out. In the introduction to the book, Extaasi members helpfully listed public spaces in Helsinki where one could hang out with these women: for example, the university café and women-only evenings at a public swimming pool.[58]

   Events were advertised in Helsinki evening papers and in *Helsingin Sanomat*, the biggest national newspaper. The activities of Extaasi were eagerly reported by the Finnish media. There were several TV documentaries, talk shows and panels involving its members, and a number of newspaper articles were published about Extaasi events. The police also followed *Extaasi* – in particular after a lesbian-feminist graffiti action on the steps of the Parliament house. The move angered police but further raised interest in the group. Members co-operated closely with male punk scene leaders – something that also interested police. Extaasi flats acted sometimes as public performance spaces or art galleries – the events were advertised in newspapers and everyone could attend. Eventually, there was one court case where the male landlord of the Extaasi commune accused the group of keeping an SM-bordello as well as an international youth hostel. The liberal-minded Helsinki district court judge laughed off these claims. Some of the 1970s generation lesbians active in *Seta* were afraid of Extaasi experiments[59] – but they also occasionally took part in the events or in the anarchist activities, for example by lending their cars for night-time happenings such as graffiti actions.

Towards the late 1980s and early 1990s, many things in Helsinki changed. Members of Extaasi matured, too: some had children or started their art career, while some entered university or emigrated from Finland permanently. I was one of the members that started MA studies at the University of Helsinki. We soon founded a queer reading group, in 1991, and read texts from Monique Wittig's *On the Social Contract* (1989) to Judith Butler's *Gender Trouble* (1990) and David Halperin's *Saint Foucault* (1995). Queer-themed courses were organized by lesbian, gay, transgender and queer research activists. We took our degrees and went on towards PhDs and got more professional in outlook.[60] We had the feeling from the very beginning of our academic careers that we had been protoqueers in various ways for a long time before we had read Foucault and Butler or learnt about the US movement *ACT UP!*. This gave us a strong motive and basis to criticise Anglo-centric formations in queer theory,[61] in addition to the queer/gay formations of the city we lived in. As we ourselves had been an active part of the amalgamation of the 1970s social-democratic welfare state and the 1980s new consumerist culture that put stress on individual freedom and expression, it becomes self-evident that an analysis of the gay and queer distinction in the more contemporary Helsinki is meaningful.

Gay gentrification of Punavuori: 1990s

Finland joined the EU in the mid-1990s and the effects of this were soon to be witnessed in Helsinki queer life. As one indirect consequence of the EU membership, massive criminal law reform took place in 1999, and the infamous 'propaganda for homosexuality' clause that had regulated broadcasting and school teaching on lesbian and gay topics after decriminalization in 1971 was finally removed from the law. The discriminatory clauses on the age of consent (18 years for homosexual and 16 years for heterosexual acts) were also adjusted.[62] The traffic and trade between Finland and other European countries were made easier, as the Schengen Agreement, which Finland signed in 1996, allowed free individual travel between Norway, Iceland and Switzerland and the EU member countries – excluding the United Kingdom and Ireland. Helsinki was no longer the exotic distant out-post it had once seemed to be until the break up of the Soviet Union. The city opened up to non-normative sexualities and visible lesbian and gay styles, and many new queer bars and club nights opened their doors, including a lesbian dominated *Nalle Pub* in the working-class Kallio, and the biggest gay club in Nordic counties, *DTM*, in the trendy Punavuori.

Punavuori used to be home to a rich variety of queer people as well as other kinds of urban underworlds in 1950s–80s, but after its upscaling in the mid-1980s the sexually and otherwise morally dubious urban citizenry has been moving to the *Kallio* district. This history marks a sort of gay gentrification in Helsinki; thus, it makes sense to sketch out a brief layout of this urban transformation. Punavuori and its surroundings constitute a kind of *perverse archive* of Helsinki.[63] The district is located near the Helsinki harbour, making the district popular among the visiting sailors. Until the 1970s, it had a dangerous reputation for its underclass population, with many bordellos, seedy bars and tea rooms (or 'cottages') for men looking for sex with other men. From the point of view of the bourgeoisie, it represented the unknown and feared periphery of the city: stupidity, indecency and drinking were located there in the middle class imagination.[64] It was also home to criminals: bootlegging, hardcore pornography and the drug scene.[65]

Many of these criminals went to prison or moved to Stockholm in the 1970s, and towards the mid-1980s young and rich yuppies alike – homosexual as well as straight – invested lots of money in the Punavuori area and invented a new urban mentality they called *the city culture*. As expensive cars and design boutiques appeared in the streets, the sense of spectacle and transgression receded from view as its history and reputation as an untamed and dangerous urban district was gradually erased. Just as gentrification sanitized Punavuori of its underclass, criminals and eccentricity, it did the same for attitudes.[66] Gay men in particular have been seen to play the pivotal role in queer gentrification in an Anglo-American context (for example *Boys Town* in Chicago)[67]; this probably plays a part in Punavuori, too, as gay men now own and populate the gay bars in the area; poor queers, lesbians and transgendered people are consequently left in margins.

Homosexuality has become liberated, tolerated and respectable in Punavuori; gay in the middle class and the commercialized sense of the word, at the same time as the shadier forms of sexuality – what I call here practically queer – has also moved into Kallio district. In Kallio, the simultaneous impact of various social factors such as class, age, ethnicity, nationality, gender, economical and citizenship status and age are visible in complex mixtures, providing a positive record of the productive interactions of and resistance to such institutional and cultural factors as poverty, racism, homophobia, philanthropic movements, Christian and state social work. From this perspective, sexuality in the 'Kallio sense' cannot be properly examined in isolation: these other social and cultural institutions have shaped and been shaped by the history of sexual life and gender identifications of the area.

When queer sexuality moved to Kallio: From 2000 onwards

The social history of Kallio is part of the working-class political history of Helsinki. It has also acted as a laboratory for Finnish social policy, social work, and philanthropy networks and organizations: Finnish Deaconry, the Salvation Army, Settlement Movement,[68] children's care and social welfare all have their roots or headquarters there.[69] Many of these efforts are part of queer history, too, albeit in complex ways. For example, the first Finnish kindergarten, *Ebeneser* (1908) was founded in Kallio by a lesbian couple, Elisabeth Alander and Hanna Rothman.[70] Also the first abortion clinics, motherhood advice clinics, and other social hygienic or governmental attempts to control working class women's fertility and sexualities were first tried out there.[71]

In a geographical sense too, the area has historically been divided from the bourgeois downtown (surrounded by the sea in the south) by the famous Long Bridge (*Pitkäsilta*) that leads to the north. The flats in Kallio are small, typically one room with a kitchenette and less than about 30 square meters of living space. Until the 1960s, these small flats were usually inhabited by more than one family, with lots of children and tenants sleeping on the floor at nights. More than half of the flats had no bathroom or toilet. Language has also divided the area from the south parts of the city: when the district started to grow in the early twentieth century, it also meant a growth of the Finnish-speaking population in Helsinki. Residents of the southern parts of the city were predominantly Swedish-speaking, but the working-class people moving to Kallio only knew Finnish.[72] This language divide is still noticeable in the everyday life in Kallio (predominantly Finnish-speaking people) and Punavuori (with its more Swedish-speaking residents).

The memoirs of police officers and research on sex offenders often focus on the construction of men and masculine sexualities from the point of view of violence and criminality.[73] However, Kallio has always had an exceptionally strong presence of women, which helps usher forth a different narrative of sexual formations. Before 1917, the year when Finland claimed independence, men were almost erased from this urban milieu. They were forced to look for work outside of city as builders of the rail route system from Finland to Russia. Also in 1918, when a red light was lit in the tower of the Labor House in Kallio marking the beginning of the Civil War, working-class women had to wait for their fathers, brothers and husbands to return from the War – even though many women in *Reds* (the working-class and rural workers uprising in the civil war) also took part in gunfights and other war practices.[74] After the war, when the *Whites* (the landowners and members of upper classes in the war, assisted by German troops) built massive concentration camps, one in the fortress island Suomenlinna in Helsinki, and others around the country, almost half of the men of the *Reds* never returned. They died of hunger, cruelty and disease, or were executed for 'war crimes'. A remarkable number of working-class women – most of them under 25 years old – were also executed as *Red* rebel soldiers after the Civil War.[75] Kallio streets were suddenly populated with Red widows with their children.

This crisis was augmented by the deteriorating state of the economy, which between the 1917 and 1922, went into rapid decline. The brunt of its impact was heavily felt in Kallio, as the state focused strict control of the minimum number of tenants in small flats. Furthermore, working-class men started to return from the prison camps, one by one. This meant that the flats and streets that had once been inhabited by women became crowded with limping, ill, broken men. Alongside the war veterans were teams of young men from the countryside searching out jobs in factories. As new tenants, they increased the adult male visibility in the small flats and narrow streets, together with those men who had returned alive from the concentration camps. However, in 1939, men of a certain age (18–50) disappeared again, this time due to World War II. Once more Kallio became an almost all-female district. But soon after the cessation of fighting, war refugees from Carelia were settled by the thousands in the area. As a result of this, in the late 1940s, the number of inhabitants was higher than ever before (or ever again). However, despite the flow of war refugees and other immigrants, new flats were not built. When the men came back from the war, as in other countries similarly battling issues of space, labour and reintegration, a baby boom followed and in the 1950s, the tiny flats became more crowded than ever. In 1955, there were about 1.8 inhabitants for every room in Kallio.[76] Men were more visible in the streets and everyday life than they ever had been.

The possible implications of this area being a predominantly female working-class community for long periods at a stretch pose a question of whether this history indicates an intense comradely and emotional bond between women. Indeed, a social democrat MP Martta Salmela-Järvinen, in her memoirs about life in Kallio in the beginning of twentieth century, recalls how working-class women supported each other when their men were working on the railroad, drinking or in the prison camps. The lack of privacy in homes and proper education effected also in negative ways the construction of young girls' lives; queer female sexuality especially had no space in the working-class or social-democratic imagination. Working-class mothers were sometimes really harsh on their daughters, and prostitution and problems with alcohol were a reality in many homes. Social anonymity was not possible for girls growing up in the district.[77] 'Decency' understood as a strictly (hetero)normative morality was an implicit part of the ideology in left-wing women's political organizations, and it was a commonly shared thought that it was women's duty to keep up the respectable working-class community. Many socialist women were active in building women's shelters, senior homes and maids' organizations.[78] However, the neighbourhood saw greater tolerance towards single mothers and other 'wayward' women than the bourgeois community in the city centre.[79] Accordingly, until the 1970s, representations of working-class lives in Kallio were predominantly heterosexual. The reproductive capacity of this social-democratic neighbourhood was marked in 1950s when the biggest comprehensive mixed-gender school in Europe of the time was built in the area.

The pace of the everyday life took a new course in Kallio in the 1960s. Until the 1950s, agrarian Finland, with its kin-owned farmhouses, had been the nutritional and economic resource for working-class mothers and single women living in cities. In the 1960s and 1970s, the traditional kinship and family ties that connected rural Finland with urban Helsinki were broken. A quick and thorough structural change took place in Finnish society. The government decided to switch course from promoting an agrarian society to investing in an urban one. Because of this profound and drastic change in national politics, a new wave of migrants from poor rural areas found their way into the cheap rented flats of Kallio, in search of paid work and social security in the growing capital city of the post-war society.[80] Along with this economic migration came a host of new sexual cultures. From the late 1980s on, the underclass district image of Kallio slowly began to change as working-class families moved to bigger flats in suburbs, and students and "single" people started to move in – rents became higher and living costs more expensive, and many marginalized people such as alcoholics and petty criminals had to move to more remote areas of the city.[81]

Even though there were fears that the upscaling of the neighbourhood would expose Kallio to the same kind of capitalist fate and gentrification as Punavuori, its development took a somewhat different course. While Punavuori lost its rough queer appeal towards the end of the 1990s and, arguably, its excitement because of an increase in investment and gentrification, the collective fantasy of untamed urban sexualities shifted into Kallio. New social groups arrived, and new sexual cultures became visible, while capitalist cooptation was more or less kept at bay – partly because of the strong heritage of the workers movement. The headquarters of the Social-Democrat Party and the trade union, as well as the library, archives and many active organizations of the workers movement are located in Kallio area. The social-democrat ex-president, Tarja Halonen, was born in Kallio and lived there. She is also active in the Settlement House management. However, during the last 3 years or so there has been increased pressure on Kallio to gentrify along with the arrival of young wealthy professionals looking for gritty urbanity. The gentrification of Kallio has thus started, but it is uncertain what this will mean for queer life in the future. The neighbourhood is somehow more "authentic" in many peoples' minds than the central district, as one can meet more foreigners and tourists in Punavuori gay bars, but in Kallio one still meets predominantly Finnish people and a specific regional culture in queer bars and cafes. The 'authentic' sphere also means less commercialized in terms of sexual lives and practices – thus 'practically queer' in terms of housing experiments, heterogeneous social groupings and more critical political attitudes than in the liberally gay Punavuori district.

By the early 2000s, in the collective imaginary of Helsinki at least, uncontrollable and unstable sexuality had moved to Kallio. However, in the fantasies of the elite and middle classes, 'sex' had actually already been there, since working-class sexuality had always been perceived as dangerous, something that constituted a potential danger to the stability of the reproduction of the nation as in other urban European contexts.[82] These fears were explicitly expressed, for example, in the parliamentary debates on child care in the 1920s and castration, sterilization and abortion laws in late 1940s: it was the working-class girls who needed protection from the dangerous working-class men's sexualities, and the young nation needed to control the wild reproduction of its under class women – in the minds of the upper and middle class MPs.[83]

Today, there are multiple heterosexual cultures visible in all their resplendent diversity in Kallio. Interestingly, these coexist rather peaceably with different ethnic and queer cultures. From men who have sex with men in gay saunas to strong and self-reliant retired working-class women in the public pool, African boys in bars owned by Asian women, asylum seekers from Tunis and ethnic shop-keepers from Pakistan and Turkey, street sex workers and numerous Thai massage parlours, all are as much a part of the everyday scene as the lesbian mothers pushing their prams around the neighbourhood. Some of these folks meet in the Bear Park Café, a small meeting spot tended by a group of middle-aged gay men in the heart of Kallio, open since 2002. Next to it was the predominantly lesbian Nalle (aka Little Bear) Pub, with its darkened windows, open from 1992 until 2013.

Helsinki today: Two cities – one recently queer, one liberally gay

The impact that the history and demographics of Kallio and Punavuori had in creating diverse queer cultures are multifaceted. For example, both have a history with the sex trade, Punavuori with its historical bordellos and contemporary Kallio with its many Thai massage parlours. Arguably, this can be attached to queer cultures as a specific form of queer economics: one of the Kallio S/M-studios in the 1990s was run by a Finnish woman who hired lesbians to work with her straight male customers, and two famous porn shops in Punavuori were run by queer women. If there might be a queer and feminist sex radicalism to this, the sex work here can also be seen by some as capitalist and a further form of repression of women and queer people.

Lesbians, sexually dissident transgendered people, anti-scene gay men and others identifying as queer in Helsinki are still not in a position to enjoy many public places inclusive enough or specifically catering to them, and these social places, bars and clubs tend to be less visible or less entrepreneurial than the commercial gay venues in the city centre populated mostly by white gay men, with additional young lesbians and an increasing number of heterosexuals. Helsinki is surrounded by the sea, and there are a number of beaches and parks that are known as lesbian or gay spaces in the summer time.[84] Public venues regarded as 'queer' tend to be activist spaces, geographically located in Kallio or in its surroundings, whereas the mainstream gay hot spots are in Punavuori or in the city centre. Helsinki Queer Pride gathers people together at the centre from all city districts, and it has become increasingly popular among straight progressives after a neo-nazi gas attack after the 2011 Pride March and the 2013 Heteropride raised awareness. Liberal legislation and attitudes have made this carnevalesque representation of queer sexualities a part of the city centre landscape. A big Pride women's party attended by thousands has been organized in Punavuori in recent years. Such gender-specific events have a broad appeal precisely because they trade on this notion of queer sociability, attracting many women beyond the city.

In other ways too, the two public queer areas of Helsinki are quite separate in peoples' minds and everyday lives. Younger queer men and women from Kallio often went for drinks in the Nalle Pub[85] before taking a taxi to Punavuori for a party the same night. Rarely does this happen the other way around, and those living a more precarious existence in Kallio (poor people, non-hipster queers and lesbian mothers) do not tend to socialize in Punavuori commercial spaces because of the high prices and different clientele. This social and sexual geography is fluid, however, as there are some interesting events and bars in Kallio that attract Punavuori people, and some places in the city centre can be regarded as not-trendy, like the gay karaoke bar *Mann's Street* or are not permanent, like the occasional club nights of the Granny Valley, a society for elderly lesbians.

The reaffirmation of regional identities seems to be on the increase, fed by resurgent notions of the 'city village' among middle and upper class residents of Helsinki, and it causes simultaneously alienating and engaging feelings among queer residents of the city. With two queer capitals, as it were, the gentrification of queer Helsinki has taken two distinctly different paths. On the one hand, there is Kallio, the former workers district, with its contemporary queer politics of inclusiveness, which grows more and more alluring for people interested in radical social city politics, locally owned stories, regional culture and diversity. On the other hand, there is Punavuori, which tends to attract white Finns with *liberal views on gay and lesbian sexuality* but more conservative views and/or lack of awareness on class stratification – they are openly gay or officially gay-friendly, but they do not aim for social change with the same vigour as many of the queer residents of Kallio. This vigour is a conscious politics that resists domestication by rights discourse and promises of upscaling. Instead, many queer residents of Kallio are deeply aware of the dangers created by such neo-liberal promises – the danger being that new exclusions will be created in the process and queer people will be divided into first- and second-class citizens in their own city. Kallio's inclusive public politics is visible in its central area, Bear Park (*Karhupuisto*), which impacts on the everyday life of many people. In the summer time, there is an outdoor gay café and a drag queen race alongside other open-access queer events. Students sit in the same park drinking, and the senior citizens of the district take care of the flowers. Lots of people pass through the park from the tram station on their way to home. Publicly and *practically queer* areas like these have an important influence on the changing everyday practices of Helsinki's citizens – this expands queerness as the straight people living in Kallio become, by chance, active participants of queer events and spaces because they are (or have been, hitherto) the most public and popular in the area.[86] Consequently, the more visible various queer lives have become in these two districts, the more courageous queer people have become in general in terms of no longer accepting invisibility and silence surrounding how they live out their lives and desires.

Provocatively public queer wedding ceremonies provide a good case in point. The first public same-sex wedding took place in the city centre (Esplanade) in 1992, 10 years before the law on registered partnerships. Twenty years later, in 2012, a lesbian couple was blessed into matrimony by a Lutheran priest – even though the law still excludes gender-neutral marriage – in the Senate Square in front of the Dom Church, next to Esplanade and the University main building and the government headquarters. With this act, a connection was made between state politics, legislation, religion, queer theory, gay history and the geography of the city. Public areas have thus been queered through not only public events such as Queer Pride but also through politically significant individual acts such as commitment rituals in well-known places in the city. This individual activism brings queerness in the city out from the premises of queer organizations, commercial bars or private homes to the public view. The city of Helsinki has thus emerged as the crucible through which an overt lesbian, gay and queer politics can be forged.[87]

Helsinki: A queer repository of struggle and symbiosis

The distinctiveness of categories in use in Anglo-Saxon queer theory and history occludes some of the ways in which indigenous queer cultures came into being and flourished. The city of Helsinki houses multiple memories of queer sexualities, and literally functions as a repository of stories of conflict and struggle, certainly, but also of symbiosis and success.[88] When we consider personal accounts alongside official and semi-official discourse, we see that there are multiple and overlapping queer Helsinkis. As I have sought to demonstrate here, queer cultures evolved in Helsinki via a process that complicated and contested the binaries between gay and queer in the past and ongoing history of the city.

'Queer' as a concept has not become an everyday term or an argument familiar in Finnish politics, unlike in Sweden where its use has spread from the academy into the media and political mainstream.[89] Instead, in Finland, a richly textured variation of non-normative, semi-visible sexual lives has been floating under the heteronormative radar; often with less firmly fixed identities than those we now associate with gay and lesbian lexicon.[90] In Helsinki, lesbian anarchism flourished in various public locations in the 1980s (Extaasi); this proto-queer story adds to the dominant narrative of the gay and lesbian movement (*Seta*) and also to the tragic but somewhat repressive narrative of the AIDS panic. On the one hand, contemporary Helsinki offers possibilities to engage with the city in an individualistic manner, especially in Punavuori's *liberal but commodified mainstream gay scene*. This relates closely to the metropolitan impulse to inscribe a personal mapping of the city as part of the quest for a distinctive sense of self. The working and lower middle class district of Kallio, on the other hand, the central location for urban resistance and protest,[91] has offered cheap rents and cross-class and cross-gendered feelings *of practical queer comradeship not only for the radically political but also for the closeted, poor or non-trendy queer people.*[92] However, both areas have been crucial to the genesis of ideas of lesbian, gay and transgender identities in the city, in promoting the assumption that there is something to see, and in making people aware of the non-heterosexual history and present of Helsinki.[93]

Notes

1   I am in a great debt to *Kati Mustola*, the pioneering researcher of lesbian and gay history of Helsinki. I would also like to thank Jennifer Evans, Matt Cook, Elsi Hyttinen, Tuula Juvonen and Alisa Zhabenko for their invaluable comments on the draft.

2   *Financial Times 30 May 2012*. World Economic Forum Global Competitiveness Report 2012–2013 ranked Finland in third position of national competitiveness worldwide (www.weforum.org/issues/global-competitiveness). About happiness and 'livability' of Helsinki, see: http://www.guardian.co.uk/commentisfree/2012/apr/04/unhappy-in-britain?fb=native&CMP=FBCNETTXT9038 and http://www.helsinkibeyonddreams.com/.

3 Sorainen, A. and A. Kallioniemi (2006), 'Multisexual Kallio: A queer social history of one neighbourhood in Helsinki', *Yearbook for the Finnish Society of Social Pedagogy*, 9, 105–14.

4 Mustola, K. (2007), 'Finland 1889-1999: A turbulent past', in K. Mustola and J. Rydström (eds), *Criminally Queer: Homosexuality and Criminal Law in Scandinavia 1842-1999*. Amsterdam: Aksant, pp. 215–50.

5 Delany, S. R. (1999), 'Three, two, one, contact . . . Times Square Red, 1998', in J. Copjec and M. Sorkin (eds), *Giving Ground: The Politics of Propinquity*. London: Verso, pp. 19–85.

6 The concept 'sexual crime' was introduced in the legislation only in 1950 and it took almost 50 years more before it actually replaced the older *Sittlichkeit* (decency)–terminology in the Finnish sexual criminal law in 1999. See Sorainen, A. (2011a), 'Siveellisyys ja seksuaalisuus Suomen rikosoikeustieteessä' [Decency and sexuality in the Finnish criminal law science], in T. Pulkkinen and A. Sorainen (eds), *Siveellisyydestä seksuaalisuuteen – poliittisen käsitteen historia* [From Decency to Sexuality – History of a Political Concept]. Helsinki: Finnish Literature Society, pp. 192–239.

7 Hirvonen, E. and Sorainen, A. (1994), 'Forbidden deeds: A case study of fornication between two women in Finland in the 1950's, in S. Hänninen (ed.), *Silence, Discourse and Deprivation*. Jyväskylä: National Research and Development Centre for Welfare and Health, p. 78, n. 9.

8 Kiba Lumberg wrote the first woman-authored Finnish Roma novels titled the *Memesa* – trilogy (Turku: Sammakko, 2011). The trilogy tells about a queer girl who grows up in the Finnish Roma culture but escapes from its misogyny and homophobia into the art world.

9 However, the danger of queer rights has recently been compared to the dangerous increase in the Muslim population, which many people see as leading to a rise in indecent, violent or excessive sexual habits and customs. See the Parliament of Finland debate on equal marriage law (21 March 2012): http://www.goodmoodtv.com/internettv/application/eduskunta/system/Eduskunta.html.

10 Cook, M. (2003), *London and the Culture of Homosexuality, 1885–1914* Cambridge: Cambridge University Press; Cook, M. (ed.) (2007), *A Gay History of Britain: Love and Sex Between Men since the Middle Ages*. Oxford: Greenwood; Monk, D. (2012), 'E M Forster's will: An overlooked posthumous publication', *Journal of Legal Studies*, DOI: 10.1111/j.1748-121X.2012.00264.x, pp. 1–26.

11 Munoz, J. (2009), *Cruising Utopia: The Then and There of Queer Futurity*. New York and London: New York University Press, p. 127.

12 Stålström, O. (2009), Ollin oppivuodet [Olli's Education]. http://www.ranneliike.net/blogi.

13 Peltonen, U. (2003), *Muistin paikat: Vuoden 1918 sisällissodan muistamisesta ja unohtamisesta* [Memory Sites: Of Forgetting and Recalling the Civil War of 1918]. Helsinki: Finnish Literature Society, pp. 9–24.

14 Juvonen, T. (2002), *Varjoelämää ja julkisia salaisuuksia* [Shadow Lives and Public Secrets]. Tampere: Vastapaino; Löfström, J. (ed.) (1998), *Scandinavian*

Homosexualities: Essays on Gay and Lesbian Studies. New York: The Haworth Press; Löfström, J. (1999), *Sukupuoliero agraarikulttuurissa* [Sexual Difference in the Agrarian Culture]. Helsinki: Finnish Literature Society; Mustola, K. (2007), *Criminally Queer*, pp. 215–50; Rydström, J. (2007), 'Introduction', in K. Mustola and J. Rydström (eds), *Criminally Queer*, pp. 13–40; Sorainen, A. (2006), 'Productive trials: English and Finnish legislation and conceptualizations of same-sex sexualities in course of trials of Oscar Wilde, Maud Allan, Radclyffe Hall and Herb Grove, from 1889 to 1957', *SQS – Journal of Queer Studies in Finland*, 1(1), 17–38.

15 Sorainen, A. (2012), 'Cross-generational lesbian relationships before 'the lesbian': Conceptualisations of women's same-sex sexuality in 1950s rural Finland', in H. Bauer and M. Cook (eds), *Queer 1950s: Rethinking Sexuality in the Postwar Years*. London: Palgrave MacMillan, pp. 77–94.

16 Löfström (1999), pp. 163–95.

17 Mustola (2007), pp. 215–50; Rydström (2007), pp. 13–40.

18 Mustola (2007), p. 216; Rydström (2007), pp. 13–40.

19 See on gay male sexualities during and after the war in fiction, Holappa, P. (1998), *Ystävän muotokuva* [A Portrait of A Friend]. Helsinki: WSOY; Hilvo, S. (2010), *Viinakortti* [The Booze Card]. Helsinki: Tammi.

20 Kalha, H. (2012), *Tom of Finland – taidetta seksin vuoksi* [Tom of Finland – Art for Sex's Sake]. Helsinki: Finnish Literature Society, p. 191.

21 Mustola (2007), pp. 215–50.

22 Juvonen (2002), pp. 153–6.

23 Kalha (2012), p. 191; Sorainen (2012), pp. 77–94.

24 The fear of the law and the police was of course not the only reason for the lack of organisation but these other reasons need further study. There were actual court cases where the full revelation of one's identity did prove dangerous: for example, in one case in the Helsinki district court in 1957 a woman reported herself and her ex-lover for the police – obviously the relationship had ended in a conflict about money: as a result, both women were convicted for same-sex fornication. Hirvonen, E., *Virallinen syyttäjä vs. Alina ja Silja – oikeustapaustutkimuksia naisten välisestä haureuden harjoittamisesta 1950-luvun Suomessa* ['General prosecutor vs Alina and Silja – court cases on same-sex fornication between women in the 1950s Finland']. BA thesis (Law), University of Helsinki, 2010, p. 19.

25 Mustola (2007), pp. 215–250; Melanko, V. (2012), *Puistohomot: Raportti Helsingin 1960-luvun homokulttuurista* [Cruising Gays: A Report from the 1960s Gay Culture in Helsinki]. Helsinki: Finnish Literature Society, pp. 101–2; Stålström, O. (2009), *Ollin oppivuodet*.

26 Melanko, V. (2011), On the 'lonely pervert', see Munoz (2009), p. 119.

27 Mustola, K. (1996), 'Syöjättärestä naapurintytöksi – naisia rakastavia naisia ennen vuotta 1971 suomeksi julkaistussa kaunokirjallisuudessa' [From women-seducer to a girl from neighbour: Woman-loving-women in the translated fiction before 1971 in Finland], in P. Hekanaho, K. Mustola, A. Lassila and M. Suhonen (eds), *Uusin silmin: lesbinen katse kulttuuriin* [With New Eyes: A Lesbian Gaze to Culture]. Helsinki: Gaudeamus, pp. 67–113.

28 Melanko (2012), pp. 99–102.

29 Mustola (2007), pp. 215–50.

30 Juvonen, T. (2006), 'Shadow lives and public secrets: Queering gendered spaces in 1950s and 60s Tampere', *SQS – Journal of Queer Studies in Finland*, 1(1), 49–70; Sorainen (2012), pp. 77–94.

31 Sorainen (2012), pp. 77–94.

32 Ingström, P. (2007), 'Lesbofeministejä?' [Lesbian feminists?], in P. Ingström (ed.), *Lentävä feministi ja muita muistoja 70-luvulta* [The Flying Feminist and Other Memories from the 1970s]. Helsinki: Schildts, pp. 126–7, 198, 242–9.

33 Saisio, P. (2003), *Punainen erokirja* [The Red Divorce Book]. Helsinki: WSOY.

34 Mustola (2007), pp. 215–50.

35 Saarinen, T. (ed.) (1994), *Alussa oli kellari – viisi helsinkiläistä lesbotarinaa* [In the Beginning There Was the Basement – Five Lesbian Stories from Helsinki]. Helsinki: Seta, p. 2; Suolahti, E. (1972), *Helsingin neljä vuosisataa* [The Four Centuries of Helsinki]. Helsinki: Otava, p. 265.

36 *Seta* promptly started to publish official magazine. Nowadays *Seta* is an expert organization on the LGBT rights in Finland, recognized by the government, and it hosts a number of local members associations around the country, manages social work and counselling for queer people and promotes sexual education.

37 Oral note from Olli Stålström, one of the founding members of *Seta*, 19.2. 2012; Altman, D. (1971), *Homosexual: Oppression and Liberation*. New York: Outerbridge & Dienstfrey.

38 Later, the name of the event was changed into Pride. See Stålström, O. (2009), *Ollin oppivuodet*.

39 Ingström (2007), pp. 242–9.

40 Ingström (2007), pp. 242–6; Firestone, S. (1970), *The Dialectic of Sex: The Case for Feminist Revolution*. New York: Morrow.

41 Until 1981, homosexuality was listed as a mental disorder in the classification of mental illnesses, and, what is more, the legal ban to public 'encouragement of homosexuality' remained in force from 1971 until 1999.

42 The term 'coming out' was only used from the 1970s onwards in Sweden. See Hallgren, H. (2008), *När lesbiska blev kvinnor. Lesbiskfeministiska kvinnors diskursproduktion rörande kropp, kön, sexualitet och identitet under 1970– och 1980–talen i Sverige* [When Lesbians Became Women. The Discoursive Production of Lesbian–Feminist Women Regarding Body, Gender, Sexuality and Identity in the 1970s–1980s Sweden]. Göteborg: Kabusa Böcker, p. 204.

43 Personal discussion with Kersti Juva, 13.9.2012.

44 Stålström (2009).

45 Melanko (2012), pp. 22–40.

46 Mort, F. (1996), *Cultures of Consumption: Masculinity and Social Space in Twentieth-Century Britain*. London: Routledge; Mort, F. (2010), *Capital Affairs: London and The Making of the Permissive Society*. New York: Yale University Press.

47 Flinck, J. and Minkkinen, P. (1987), *Räikeitä sanomia* [Flashy Messages]. Helsinki: Gaudeamus.

48 See for a definition of 'proto-queerness', Rubin, G. (2011), 'Blood under the bridge: Reflections on "Thinking Sex"', *GLQ – A Journal of Lesbian and Gay Studies*, 17(1), 415–48.

49 Rich, A. (1985), Heteroseksuaalisuuden pakko ja lesbon olemassaolo [Compulsory Heterosexuality and Lesbian Existence] (transl. Kaija Anttonen). *Akkaväki* 3/1985, Naistutkimus – ja teorialiite [Women's Studies research and theory attachment]. Helsinki: Naisten kulttuuriyhdistys.

50 Ingström (2007), pp. 242–9; Saarinen (1994), pp. 11–12; Manner, I. (2002), *Ennen näkymättömät. Naisaktivistien toimintakokemuksia Setan alkuajoilta* [Invisibles. Experiences of Activist Women from the Early Years of Seta]. MA thesis (Social Sciences), Joensuu University: Department of Social Politics, pp. 5, 33–53; Oksanen, P. P. (2012), *Extaasi*. Helsinki: an unpublished draft (in the possession of the author); Vallinharju, R. (2012), *Lesbian Lives in the 1970s–80s Helsinki*. Helsinki: an unpublished draft (in the possession of the author).

51 O'Sullivan, K. (1997), 'Dangerous desire: Lesbianism as sex or politics', in J. J. Matthews (ed.), *Sex in Public: Australian Sexual Cultures*. Sydney: Allen & Unwin, p. 114.

52 The name of the group did not refer to the drug but to the deep liberating feeling according to which everything we wanted to do in the public seemed possible and do-able.

53 This coalitional practice was reflected also in the close relationship of gay and lesbian studies and queer studies with the inception of Women's Studies at the University of Helsinki in the latter part of the 1980s and early 1990s.

54 http://www.normallove.de/htm/engl_artists.html.

55 See on lesbian intra- and extra-community perspectives in the 1980s, Green, S. F. (1997), *Urban Amazons – Lesbian Feminism and Beyond in the Gender, Sexuality and Identity Battles of London*. London: MacMillan, p. 96.

56 Pakkanen, J. (2010), 'Outo koti, oma kaupunki' [Queer home, home city], in A. Biström, R. Paqvalén and H. Rask (eds), *Naisten Helsinki: Kulttuurihistoriallinen opas* [Women's Helsinki: A Cultural History Guide]. Helsinki: Schildts, pp. 190–5.

57 Samois (1982), *Coming to Power. Writings and Graphics on Lesbian S/M*. San Francisco: SAMOIS.

58 Extaasi (1989), *Julmia naisia: Sadomasokistinaiset kertovat* [Obscene Women: Sadomasochist Women Speak Out]. Helsinki: Odessa, p. 1.

59 Personal discussion with Kersti Juva, 6.4.2012.

60 The Society for Queer Studies in Finland was founded in 2006 at the University of Helsinki, and the society started to publish a peer reviewed open-access journal, *SQS*, in the same year.

61 See on this critic also Mizielinska, J. and R. Kulpa (2011), 'Introduction', in R. Kulpa and J. Mizielinska (eds), *De-Centring Western Sexualities: Central and Eastern European Perspectives*. Farnham: Ashgate, pp. 1–9.

62   Sorainen, A. (2011a), *Siveellisyydestä seksuaalisuuteen*, p. 229.

63   Nostalgic memoirs of the underworlds of the past Punavuori have recently started to be published (for example, Nykänen, H. and J. Sjöberg (2010) (*Rööperi*), and also a movie reflecting the district's criminal background was screened in 2009 (*Rööperi*).

64   Pedersen, A. T. (2010), 'Punavuoren Ruth' [Ruth from Punavuori], in A. Biström, R. Paqvalen and H. Rask (eds), *Naisten Helsinki: Kulttuurihistoriallinen opas* [Women's Helsinki: A Cultural History Guide]. Helsinki: Schildts, p. 134.

65   Nykänen, H. and T. Sjöberg (2010), *Rööperi – rikoksen vuodet 1955–2005* [Punavuori – Years of Crime 1955–2005]. Helsinki: Johnny Kniga.

66   See on the effects of gentrification Schulman, S. (2012), *The Gentrification of Mind: Witness to a Lost Imagination*. Berkeley: University of California Press.

67   Butler, T. and G. Robson (2001), 'Social change, gentrification and neighbourhood change in London: A comparison of three areas of South London', *Urban Studies*, 38, 2145–62, 2156; Glass, R. (1964), *London: Aspects of Change*. London: MacGibbon & Kee; Hamnett, C. (2003), 'Gentrification and the middle-class remaking of inner London, 1961–2001', *Urban Studies*, 40, 2401–26; www.originalplumbing.com (27 August 2012).

68   Settlement Movement is a reformist social movement, beginning in the 1870–80s in London. Its main object was the establishment of 'settlement houses' in poor urban areas, in which volunteer middle-class settlement workers would live, with the goal of getting the rich and the poor of the society to live more closely together in an interdependent community. See Blank, B. T. (1998), 'Settlement houses: Old idea in new form builds communities', *The New Social Worker*, 5(3), 4–7. The first Settlement House in Finland was built in Kallio in 1919. See Peltola, J. (2009), *Yksilö, yhteisö ja yhteiskunta: Kalliolan settlementti 1919-2009* [Individual, community and society: Kalliola Settlement House 1919–2009]. Helsinki: Kalliola Settlement Publications, p. 3.

69   Heiskanen, O. and M. Santakari (2004), *Asuuko neiti Töölössä? Elämää elokuvien Helsingissä* [Does the Lady Live in Tölö? – Life in the Helsinki of Movies]. Helsinki: Teos, pp. 122–5.

70   Rothman followed the ideas of the English Settlement movement already in 1888 when she founded her first day-care centre in the area. The house where Ebeneser was located was designed by Wivi Lönn, the first Finnish woman architect, who herself lived with her female partner in another townhouse she had designed for YWCA, near Punavuori. This building is now known as *Helka Hotel*. Peltola (2009), pp. 15–19; Paqvalen, R. (2010), 'Arkkitehdin katse. Varhaiset naisarkkitehdit Suomessa' [The Gaze of the architect. Early women architects in Finland] in A. Biström et al. (eds), *Naisten Helsinki: Kulttuurihistoriallinen opas* [Women's Helsinki: A Cultural History Guide]. Helsinki: Schildts, pp. 35–6; http://www.tarinoidenhelsinki.fi/paikka/ebeneser-talo.

71   Sorainen and Kallioniemi (2006); Sorainen, A. (2007), 'Moral panic! The figure of the paedophile and sexual politics of fear in Finland', in S. V. Knudsen, L. Löfgren-Mårtenson and S. Månsson (eds), *Generation P? Youth, Gender and Pornography*. Copenhagen: Danish University of Education Press, pp. 189–203.

72 Suolahti (1972), pp. 222–3.

73 Anttila, I. (1956), *Alaikäisiin kohdistuneet siveellisyysrikokset ja niiden tekijät* [Indecent crimes against minors and about the offenders]. Helsinki: Finnish Lawyers' Association, A-series No: 50; Hietaniemi, T. (1992), *Lain vartiossa: poliisi Suomen politiikassa 1917–1948* [Guarding the Law: Police in the Finnish Politics 1917–1948]. Helsinki: Finnish Historical Society; Lauhakangas, O. and T. Vuoristo (1991), *Napit vastakkain: Suomalaiset poliisit kertovat* [At Odds: Finnish Police Tells]. Helsinki: Finnish Literature Society.

74 See on the life of a 'red wife' in Kallio before and during the Civil War: memoirs of the early social-democrat woman MP M. Salmela-Järvinen (1965), *Kun se parasta on ollut* [When It Was at Its Best]. Porvoo: WSOY; and (1966), *Alas lyötiin vanha maailma* [Down with the Old Regime]. Porvoo, Helsinki: WSOY.

75 Peltonen (2009), p. 144.

76 Heiskanen and Santakari (2004), p. 119.

77 Salmela-Järvinen (1965); Salmela-Järvinen (1966); Salmela-Järvinen, M. (1967), *Taipui vaan ei taittunut* [Bended But Not Broken]. Porvoo, Helsinki: WSOY; Salmela-Järvinen, M. (1968), *Kaikissa meissä vikaa on* [No One Is Innocent]. Porvoo, Helsinki: WSOY; Saisio, P. (1975), *Elämänmeno* [The Tenor of One's Life]. Helsinki: Kirjayhtymä. See also Lassi Sinkkonen's novel *Solveigin laulu* [Solveig's Song], Porvoo: Söderström, 1971 about growing up as a working-class girl in 1950s Kallio.

78 Leivo-Larsson, T. (1970), *Elämässä tapaa ja tapahtuu* [Events and People]. Helsinki: Weilin + Göös, pp. 12, 100–1.

79 Kilpi, S. (1965), *Sörnäisten tytön vaellusvuodet* [The Gallavaganting Years of a Sörnäis Girl]. Helsinki: Tammi, pp. 135–6.

80 Tani, S. (1997), 'Maineen ja muistojen Vaasankatua [Vaasankatu – a Kallio street full of reputation and memories], in M. Koskijoki (ed.), *Kotikaduilla – kaupunkilaiselämää 1970–luvun Helsingissä* [Home Streets – Urban Life in 1970s Helsinki]. Helsinki: Edita, pp. 234–7.

81 For example, 10 years ago some of my middle class colleagues at the University of Helsinki, residents of the more posh city districts, told me that they had never visited Kallio after working hours and found the idea frightening.

82 See on how wealthy and middle class people have portrayed the poor, Koven, S. (2004), *Slumming: Sexual and Social Politics in Victorian London*. Princeton: Princeton University Press.

83 Sorainen, A. (2007), pp. 194–5; Sorainen, A. (2011b), 'Suomalainen keskustelu pedofiliasta' [Finnish debate on paedophilia], in M. Satka, L. Alanen, T. Harrikari and E. Pekkarinen (eds), *Lapset, nuoret ja muuttuva hallinta* [Children, Adolescents and the Changing Practices of Regulation]. Tampere: Vastapaino, pp. 351–89. See also how Nordic child welfare worked not only as social defence against crime but also as social defence against female sexuality among the poor: Ericsson, K. (2005), 'Child Welfare as social defense against sexuality: A Norwegian example', in E. Bernstein and L. Schaffner (eds), *Regulating Sex. The Politics of Intimacy and Identity*. New York and London: Routledge, p. 130.

84 The city is currently looking to transform a nude beach with segregated areas for women and men, popular among lesbians and gays, to a mixed-gender 'family beach'.

85 Nalle Pub is a sports bar now. There was a "funeral night" 11 November 2013, attended by lots of queer regular clients, including me.

86 Peltonen (2003), p. 10.

87 Cook (2003), p. 142.

88 For a view of the city as an archive of sexualities Evans, J. (2011), *Life Among the Ruins: Cityscape and Sexuality in Cold War Berlin*. London: Palgrave MacMillan.

89 Kulick, D. (2005), 'Inledning', in D. Kulick (ed.), *Queersverige* [Queersweden]. Stockholm: Natur och Kultur, pp. 8–22.

90 See, for example, Kalha (2012); Melanko (2012); Saarinen (1994); Sorainen (2012).

91 Finnish working class created its own public in the early twentieth century; its own media, printing houses and theatres, and thus resisted in a concrete way the privilege of the bourgeois and middle class to define what constitutes the public. Many of the locations of the contra-public were in Kallio district. See Hyttinen, E. (2012), *Kovaa työtä ja kohtalon oikkuja: Elvira Willmanin kamppailu työläiskirjallisuuden tekijyydestä vuosisadanvaihteen Suomessa* [Hard Work and Twists of Fate: Elvira Willman's Struggle for Working-Class Authorship]. Turku: Uniprint Turku, p. 31.

92 One recent example of semi-visible queer economics in Kallio is a pub owned by a lesbian businesswoman and her gay friend: the pub is popular among the straight middle-class cultural clientele but it also offers a safe space for lesbians and gays. It is hard to recognize the queer policy from an external perspective as the pub 'looks' straight, but if one is familiar with the local lesbian and gay scene the queer clientele of the pub becomes obvious.

93 Cook (2003), pp. 12, 148–9.

Further reading

Altman, D. (1971), *Homosexual: Oppression and Liberation*. New York: Outerbridge & Dienstfrey.

Berlant, L. and M. Warner (1998), 'Sex in Public', *Critical Inquiry* 24(2) (Winter), 547–66.

Dahl, U. (2011), 'Queer in Nordic region', in L. Downing and R. Gillett (eds), *Queer in Europe*. London: Ashgate, pp. 143–58.

Extaasi Group (1989), *Julmia naisia: Sadomasokistinaiset kertovat* [Obscene Women: Sadomasochist Women Speak Out]. Helsinki: Odessa.

Firestone, S. (1970), *The Dialectic of Sex: The Case for Feminist Revolution*. New York: Morrow.

Gerodetti, N. (2005), *Modernising Sexualities: Towards a Socio-Historical Understanding of Sexualities in the Swiss Nation*. Bern: Peter Lang.

Hallgren, H. (2008), *När lesbiska blev kvinnor. Lesbiskfeministiska kvinnors diskursproduktion rörande kropp, kön, sexualitet och identitet under 1970- och*

1980-talen I Sverige [When Lesbians Became Women. The Discoursive Production of Lesbian-feminist Women Regarding Body, Gender, Sexuality and Identity in the 1970s–1980s Sweden]. Göteborg: Kabusa Böcker.

Hirvonen, E. and A. Sorainen (1994), 'Forbidden deeds: A case study of fornication between two women in Finland in the 1950's, in S. Hänninen (ed.), *Silence, Discourse and Deprivation*. Jyväskylä: National Research and Development Centre for Welfare and Health, pp. 58–80.

Juvonen, T. (2006), 'Introduction: Queering the Hegemonies of LGBT historiography', *SQS – Suomen Queer-tutkimuksen Seuran Lehti – Tidskrift för Queerforskning i Finland – Journal of Queer Studies in Finland*, 1(1), 7–16.

Juvonen, T. (2006), 'Shadow lives and public secrets: Queering gendered spaces in 1950s and 60s tampere', *SQS – Suomen Queer-tutkimuksen Seuran Lehti – Tidskrift för Queerforskning i Finland – Journal of Queer Studies in Finland*, 1(1), 49–70.

Kulick, D. (ed.) (2005), *Queersverige* [Queersweden]. Stockholm: Natur och Kultur.

Löfström, J. (2000), 'Reflecting why Sweden is more progressive than Finland in gay and lesbian formal rights', in L. Tedebrand (ed.), *Sex, state and society*. Stockholm: Almqvist & Wiksell, pp. 111–25.

—(2007), 'Sexual cultures in Scandinavia', *The Blackwell Encyclopedia of Sociology*, 4th edn. Malden, MA: Blackwell, pp. 4227–30.

Mizielinska, J. and R. Kulpa (eds) (2011), *De-Centring Western Sexualities: Central and Eastern European perspectives*. London: Ashgate.

Newton, E. (1993), *Cherry Grove, Fire Island: Sixty Years in America's First Gay and Lesbian Town*. Boston: Beacon Press.

Matthews, J. J. (ed.) (1997), *Sex in Public: Australian Sexual Cultures*. Sydney: Allen & Unwin.

Peltonen, U. (2003), *Muistin paikat. Vuoden 1918 sisällissodan muistamisesta ja unohtamisesta* [Places of Memory. On the remembering and forgetting of the Civil War 1918]. Helsinki: Finnish Literature Society.

Rubin, G. (1984), 'Thinking sex. Notes for a radical theory of the politics of sexuality', in C. S. Vance (ed.), *Pleasure and Danger: Exploring Female Sexuality*. Boston: Routledge and Kegan Paul, pp. 267–319.

Rydström, J. (2003), *Sinners and Citizens. Bestiality and Homosexuality in Sweden, 1880–1950*. Chicago and London: The University of Chicago Press.

Rydström, J. and K. Mustola (eds) (2007), *Criminally Queer: Homosexuality and Criminal Law in Scandinavia 1842–1999*. Amsterdam: Aksant.

Samois (1982), *Coming to Power. Writings and Graphics on Lesbian S/M*. San Francisco: SAMOIS.

Satka, M. and T. Harrikari (2008), 'The present Finnish Formation of Child Welfare and history', *British Journal of Social Work*, 38(4), 645–61.

Schulman, S. (2012), *The Gentrification of Mind: Witness to a Lost Imagination*. University of California Press.

Stychin, Carl F. (2002), 'A queer nation by rights: European integration, sexual identity politics, and the discourse of rights', in K. Chedgzoy and F. Pitt (eds), *Queer Place. Sexuality and Belonging in British and European Context*. London: Ashgate, pp. 207–23.

12

Paris: 'Resting on its Laurels'?

Florence Tamagne

Since the nineteenth century, Paris has been described as a 'queer' metropolis, achieving an almost mythical status in the minds of many men and women, who hoped to find, in the capital of pleasures, the possibility to live a life true to their desires. In the first part of the twentieth century, the visibility of such well-known figures as Natalie Barney or André Gide, as well as the flamboyance of meeting places in Montmartre or Pigalle, helped to construct the image of Paris as a 'queer' capital, even though Berlin, London or Amsterdam provided a larger choice of organizations and places to meet and socialize. After 1945, this image lived on, but was reshaped along new lines. Although many provincial cities now host LGBT associations and several organize their own pride parade, France is still a very centralized country. Paris is the only French city with an organized gay quarter, and various sources report that 46 per cent of France's gay men lived in Paris in the 1990s.[1] If the '*Gaité parisienne*' (Benoît Duteurtre) remains unchallenged nationwide, with 140 LGBT commercial locations (bars, clubs but also shops, hotels, restaurants . . .) in 2004, Paris competes with Berlin for the title of LGBT capital of Europe, and ranks only second behind New York for the title of LGBT capital of the world.[2] However, in terms of activism and even nightlife – despite the number of venues, Paris is not the trendiest LGBT city – Paris cannot compare with cities like San Francisco, New York or Sydney, or even its nearer former rivals London and Berlin.[3]

In order to understand the gap that exists between lasting images of the city and its new self, four aspects of Paris' queer lives and cultures will be examined: homophobia, activism, sexual geographies and identities. Two methodological problems need to be addressed at the outset. First, as several authors have noted, 'the republican tradition of universalism and integration' has shaped language to the extent that French gays and lesbians 'express their sexuality more forcefully in terms of a non specified "difference"'.[4] The citizen is an abstract being, the nation is 'one and indivisible'. Identity politics are therefore seen as an expression of 'communautarism' or 'American multiculturalism' and are deeply divisive. 'Gay', as an adjective or a noun referring to same-sex practices, wasn't used in France before the 1970s, and it remained for a long time associated with American gay politics; 'queer' is not used in France except by activists and academics, and mostly in reference to queer theory; the acronym LGBT, used since the 1990s, although now well known within the community, remains obscure to a large part of the population. I have tried, as much as possible, not to use terms that would be considered anachronisms in the French context. I chose to use 'queer' whenever I wanted to stress a flexible identity and/or behaviours that would appear at the time as challenging traditional sex and gender norms. Except for the last 10 years, when some people have identified as 'queer', I don't intend it to describe a distinct identity. Secondly, even though queer studies in France are on the rise, studies about queer France, and more specifically queer Paris after World War II, remain few and far between. Most of these studies focus on gay men, and the risk is therefore to offer a rather biased and limited view of queer Paris, but a view that also coincides with the relative (in)visibility of many LGBT groups within the city. I have, though, tried to counter this tendency by providing, whenever possible, alternative narratives.

'Things could have been worse'?[5] repression and homophobia in 'Gai Paris'

The migration of queer people to metropolises where the intermingling of people made casual encounters easier and in some ways less dangerous – in terms of reputation in particular – is in no way peculiar to Paris. However, in the first part of the twentieth century, Paris enjoyed a reputation of sexual freedom which remained largely unchallenged. France had been the first country to decriminalize sodomy in 1791 and, for many years, Paris would be seen as a refuge for sexual outcasts.[6] However, even though France, and especially its capital city, enjoyed a reputation of licentiousness and was famous for its gay and lesbian bars, dance halls and even bordellos, public space had always been strictly regulated. Indecent exposure as well as indecent assault remained liable to prosecution, in the case of homo- or heterosexual relations. The vice squad organized unofficial surveillance of the main areas of soliciting and carefully watched homosexual cruising grounds, such as the Seine banks, public parks, theatre galleries, the arcades of the Palais Royal and the Champs-Elysées, as well as bathing houses and male urinals, called *tasses* in queer argot. Montmartre, Pigalle, Montparnasse and Bastille gathered most of the queer bars, where customers would rub shoulders with artistic bohemia and a *demi-monde* of tricksters, queens and thieves.[7]

The 1950s and 1960s experienced a strengthening of police surveillance. On 6 August 1942, the Vichy regime, in response to concerns about 'demoralization' in the Navy and 'youth corruption', passed a law which stated that same-sex relations between men or between women were liable to a prison sentence and/or a fine, in the case that one of the partners, at least, was under 21. This measure was confirmed at the Liberation by the ordinance of 8 February 1945.[8] 'Back to normalcy' implied the reaffirmation of traditional values and the denunciation of deviancies, an agenda supported both by the Christian-democrats of the MRP (*Mouvement Républicain Populaire*) and the Communist Party. On 1 February 1949, a police ordinance forbade men, in Paris, to put on drag or to dance together in public places. On 18 July 1960, the Mirguet amendment, which defined homosexuality as a 'social plague', resulted in the aggravation of sentences for 'indecent exposure' in the case of same-sex relations between men or between women. Other discriminatory measures were also directed at queer people. For example, the Statute of the Civil Servants, the Labour Code or the Renting Law all included a 'morality' commitment, which compelled men and women to secrecy in their professional as well as private life. The law of 16 July 1949 on youth publications was also used to ban homophile magazines, such as *Futur* (1952–56), a provocative journal created by Jean Thibault. In March 1953, its exposure to public view, outside or inside shops or kiosks was forbidden; in 1956, it was condemned for affront to public decency along with homophile journal *Arcadie,* which was also forbidden to minors. Of course, one may consider that, in regard to what happened in other countries, 'things could have been worse' and that, thanks to the French republican legal system which limited the actions of lawmakers, French homosexuals were 'spared more extreme forms of legal repression'.[9]

As a matter of fact, although the police perceived the homosexual *milieu* as criminal,[10] same-sex relations were tolerated as long as they remained discreet. The real danger was queer visibility in public spaces. In the 1950s and 1960s, the geography of gay and lesbian meeting places was very similar to that of the 1930s. Queer people still shared with other marginalized (in particular youth, migrant and criminal) subcultures the same territories, a cause for competition, but also interrelation between groups often thought of as separate. Paris was then the western capital of transgender culture, with cabarets like the Carrousel (1947), or Madame Arthur (1946), which welcomed the most famous transvestite artists and enjoyed an international reputation. Because transvestism was forbidden by the police, the artists, who used to be men wearing drag for the show, were slowly replaced by transsexuals, who took hormones and identified as women, therefore cunningly subverting the law.[11]

Some new queer areas also emerged, like rue Sainte-Anne, where private gay clubs like Le Vagabond (1956) or Le César (1959) had settled, and above all Saint-Germain-des-Prés, which became in the 1950s the major meeting place for gays and lesbians.[12] The centre of existentialism and bohemia, Saint-Germain-des-Prés was famous for its cafés *chics*, like Café de Flore, where Jean-Paul Sartre and Simone de Beauvoir could be spotted, and its jazz caves where young people danced and listened to swing orchestra. Famous homosexual artists like Jean Genet, Jean Cocteau and Jean Marais were regulars at the Flore, Le Royal Saint-Germain or La Pergola. Le Fiacre was the most famous homosexual hangout, also frequented by foreign gay visitors such as Christopher Isherwood. Young prostitutes paced up and down the boulevard and picked up tricks in street urinals, causing discontent among residents. Popular newspapers, like *France-Soir*, and also homophile journals looked critically at what they saw as a criminal phenomenon. Although *Futur* denounced police harassment in Saint-Germain-des-Prés, and held the MRP, especially MP Pierre-Henri Teitgen responsible for the new morality stance, *Arcadie* and *Juventus* (May–November 1959), a gay journal that promoted a virile image of homosexuality, both asked for a reinforcement of prosecutions against tricksters and prostitutes. Several times, Parisian local councillors complained about the 'growing number of inverts – most of them very young men – who indulged in disgraceful and shameless practices with impunity in several Parisian districts, especially at the Champs-Elysées roundabout'. According to socialist councillor Coutrot, speaking in October 1966, such 'flaunting' was 'shocking for honest citizens and harmful for the reputation of the City of Lights, notably regarding the tourists'. He wondered why these men who had gone 'astray, who do not even have the decency to hide' were not 'ruthlessly hunted down or even prosecuted'. In May 1967, conservative councillor Edouard Frédéric-Dupont asked the police to heighten surveillance between boulevard Raspail and Saint-Germain-des-Prés square. According to the Prefect of Police, controls had already been strengthened in the evening and at night. In January 1967, 528 people were questioned by the police, and of these 412 were taken to the police station.[13] Throughout the 1950s and 1960s, gay bars were raided, sometimes with the owner's complicity.

Lesbians were less liable to police harassment. Most of them preferred to meet discreetly within private circles of close friends, and they rarely visited bars. Since it was thought both dangerous and compromising to wander the streets alone, they would not cruise in places such as parks, especially at night. Intimate gestures between women, such as holding hands, hugging or kissing were considered harmless. They were therefore seldom worried by the police, except in cases such as those involving a fight between prostitutes, a murder, a lesbian 'gang', which robbed tourists in bars or a marriage between women.[14] According to criminal statistics, between one and 12 women were convicted of 'homosexuality' each year between 1953 and 1978. The majority were between 20 and 30 years old and generally came from a modest background (12% were unskilled workers, 11% were office workers). The 37 per cent who were unemployed were probably housewives. Indeed, while 56 per cent of the women convicted were single, 23 per cent were married, 15 per cent divorced and 2 per cent widows. Fifty per cent had at least one child.[15]

If prosecutions were relatively low, it is impossible to assess the number of lesbians who were the victims of verbal or physical aggression, especially those who went out as a couple, or whose 'masculine' appearance made them an easy target. These 'masculine' lesbians were victims of a backlash, not only from the heterosexual world, but from other lesbians too. In the 1950s and 1960s, the question of butch [*Jules*]/fem[*femme*] roles was a subject of debate among lesbians, as was the question of effeminacy among gay men. At the root of this tension was a generation gap. Many young women refused to identify as butch or fem, and found these distinctions outdated, a travesty of love between women.[16] They also did not bear well the rituals associated with lesbian meeting places, where '*femmes*' and '*Jules*' were supposed to act according to their position, and where the simplest gestures – to buy a girl a drink, to ask a girl to dance – were subject to complex subcultural regulation. '*Jules*', often compared with pimps, were especially rejected as they seemed to embody the very aggressive and dominating masculinity most girls wanted to escape.[17] Class distinctions were also at stake. Bars were popular mainly with working-class women, who did not fear for their reputation. According to Elula Perrin, the owner of the most famous lesbian nightclub of the 1960s, few women could afford, or wanted to support a girlfriend; many were looking for lovers in their own class.[18] Even if some women appreciated intermingling, many more, especially from the middle-class, loathed 'exhibitionism', and didn't hide their disgust in front of drunken women in flashy clothes.[19] Prejudice against homosexuality was deeply internalized by some lesbians, especially as they had difficulties finding positive references either in popular culture, (mostly male) homophile groups or the feminist movement. In 1971, the radical feminist journal *Le torchon brûle* was still the stage for a theoretical struggle between young activists who denounced the 'chauvinistic' and 'reactionary' tendencies of *Jules*, and others who condemned this 'tendency to divide women' by making them feel guilty.[20]

Trouble in Arcadia: Sexual politics and activism in France's capital city

The abolition of discriminatory laws and the destruction of police files on queer people would be one of the main purposes of the revolutionary gay and lesbian movements of the 1970s. However, Arcadie's role and influence should not be underestimated or misinterpreted.[21] As a journal that lasted from 1954 to 1982, and a club which opened in Paris in 1957 but which claimed, in 1975, 11 provincial off-shoots, Arcadie shaped the lives of many gay men – and a few lesbians – in the capital and the provinces.

Until the 1970s, all French gay and lesbian movements were born in Paris. Revolutionary activist Jean Le Bitoux remembers Arcadie as a very centralized Parisian association,[22] whose activities strongly depended on its creator, André Baudry, a catholic and former seminarist. If the Club was a mostly Parisian affair, the journal proved particularly attractive to provincial readers, who often led an isolated life. In 1974, half of its readership lived in the provinces. A reformist and assimilationist body, Arcadie wanted to enlighten the general public about homosexuality, and to help 'homophile' men and women to live their life fully. Club Arcadie would be the place where they could safely meet and, until the end of the 1960s, the only place in Paris where men could dance together, although Baudry insisted they behave 'decently' to avoid police investigation. Arcadie rejected promiscuity and looked critically at any flashy behaviour, especially effeminacy that was seen as reinforcing prejudices against gay men. Above all, it wanted to distinguish homosexuality from prostitution and paedophilia.

A self-proclaimed apolitical association, Arcadie was at odds with the 1968 movement. Strongly criticized by the new revolutionary gay and lesbian organizations, abandoned by some of its former members, notably many lesbians who considered it had never given them real attention, it did not however lose influence, quite to the contrary. Baudry became a public figure, fought against discriminatory laws and even considered demanding the legalization of gay and lesbian adoption, a question that was still being debated as late as 2013.[23] In May 1979, for its 25th anniversary, Arcadie gathered more than 900 people in Paris, among them Michel Foucault. It finally disappeared in 1982, at a time when most of discriminatory laws had been abolished, and the thriving gay subculture rendered its club rather outdated. By that time, its memory had been almost erased by the gay and lesbian movement, born in the aftermath of May 1968.

In 1968, Guy Chevalier, a literature student, had drafted with a friend the CAPR (*Comité d'action pédérastique révolutionnaire*: Committee of Revolutionary Pederastic Action) manifesto and stuck it on the wall of a Sorbonne lecture hall. Although the posters were soon torn down by far-left groups, who feared that homosexuals would sully the revolution, they went on handing out flyers near the Odeon Theatre and the Place Maubert urinal. Much more important was the foundation of the MLF (*Mouvement de Libération des Femmes*; the Women's Liberation Movement), and of the FHAR (*Front Homosexuel d'Action Révolutionnaire*; Homosexual Front for Revolutionary Action), in 1970 and 1971. Created by lesbians, feminists and gay activists, influenced by Trotskyism and situationism, the FHAR urged gay men and women to 'stop keeping a low profile', and condemned the assimilationist stance of Arcadie, although some of its founding members used to be part of the association. Claiming the 'right to difference', it favoured spectacular actions and inflammatory slogans. Inside the FHAR, the Gazolines, a group of provocative transgender activists, were particularly vocal in their criticism of heterosexism, and urged queer people to 'leave their province full of yokels and come to Paris!'[24] Indeed, although it soon had sections in other cities, the FHAR was a Parisian creation, and it gathered on Thursday evenings at the Ecole des Beaux-Arts (National School of Fine Arts), in the 6th arrondissement. For Jean Le Bitoux, then aged 22 and living in Nice, it was an eye-opener. He recalled living in various Parisian gay communes in the 1970s and 1980s and taking part in the first meetings of the GLH (*Groupe de libération homosexuel*; Homosexual Liberation Group) after the split of the FHAR into various groups.[25] Lesbians, such as Marie-Jo Bonnet, who had decided to leave the FHAR because of reigning male chauvinism, created informal groups, such as the *Gouines Rouges* (Red Dykes), and/or joined the MLF, where they played a very active role. Remarkably, the GLH was born in Lyon, not in Paris. Several lesbian associations were also created in the provinces, notably in Toulouse. They tried to propose alternative strategies to the Parisian agenda, which often ignored the problems experienced by queer people living outside the metropolis. The GLH, however, soon split into several groups, with the mostly Parisian and far-left GLH-PQ (*Politique et Quotidien*; Politics and everyday life) section gaining the majority.

Radical groups were unsuccessful in pressing for legal change. In 1979, the CUARH (*Comité d'Urgence Anti-Répression Homosexuelle*: Anti-Repression Homosexual Urgency Committee), founded by Jan-Paul Pouliquen, centralized provincial and Parisian LGBT movements. Its aims were the suppression of discriminating laws, especially those on sexual majority, as well as the declassification of homosexuality as an illness, thanks to a strategy of compromise and accommodation. It tried to ally with the MRAP (*Mouvement contre le Racisme et pour l'Amitié entre les Peuples*: Movement Against Racism and for Friendship between Peoples), after the homophobic murder of a gay man in the Tuileries garden. A march was organized in Paris on 27 February 1981. Finally, in 1982 and 1985, most discriminatory laws were lifted by President François Mitterrand. Nevertheless, still in 1984, several backroom bars, like Le Sling or Le BH, were closed by the *Préfecture de Police* for 'security reasons' or 'breach of the peace at night', although the main reason was that they refused to light their backroom or to forbid sexual activity.

The beginning of the 1980s saw the rapid growth of a gay and lesbian community, based on businesses and cultural associations, many centred in Paris – gay and lesbian radio stations Radio Mauve (1978) and Fréquence Gaie (1981), for example. Most gay and lesbian magazines such as *Gai Pied* (co-founded in 1979 by Jean Le Bitoux and other activists) also had their head office in Paris. According to a survey published in the December 1980 issue, 33 per cent of its readership was located in Paris and 14 per cent in Ile-de-France. *Lesbia*, the major French lesbian magazine, was also launched in Paris in 1982 by Christiane Jouve and Catherine Marjollet. In April 1977, the first homosexual film festival took place in Paris at the Olympic cinema, owned by Frédéric Mitterrand.[26] Whereas cultural initiatives were on the rise, political movements were on the decline. The AIDS epidemic came as a shock in a largely demobilized community. At first sceptical of what they saw as a new example of 'moral panic', the leaders of gay associations as well as the gay press did not assess the scale of the crisis until 1984. Voluntary AIDS organizations such as Aides (created in 1984 by Daniel Defert), or ACT-Up Paris (created in 1989 by Didier Lestrade, Pascal Loubet and Luc Coulavin), were all founded in Paris. Whereas Aides favoured an integrationist strategy, gathering supports well beyond gays and lesbians, ACT-Up Paris privileged the notion of 'community', in order to fight the isolation produced by AIDS. By 1989, AIDS had become the leading cause of death among Parisian men aged 25–44 years, but there was still no community centre for LGBT people, until the opening of the MdH (*Maison des Homosexualités*: House of Homosexuality) in the Marais in 1989. Now called Centre LGBT Paris-Ile de France, it has relocated in the 3rd arrondissement.

During the 1990s, AIDS remained a central issue within the community, while at the same time structuring militancy around contradictory notions of 'universalism', understood as compatible with the French republican model, and 'communautarism', often criticized as an Anglo-American import.[27] These tensions were at the core of the debate on same-sex unions and adoption that emerged at the time. The project to create a civil union, although originally intended for same-sex couples, was rejected several times by parliament before being redrafted to be less exclusive. In 1999, after years of legal struggle, culminating in a huge march in Paris the 17 October 1998, the PACS (*Pacte civil de solidarité*: civil solidarity pact), a civil union between two adults of the same-sex or of the opposite-sex, was voted in. Ninety-five per cent of the PACS are currently contracted by straight couples in an example of the way changes affecting LGBT lifestyles have also altered straight lifestyles, providing new ways of imagining family and social relations. Despite strong opposition, mostly from right-wing parties and catholic associations, a bill legalizing same-sex marriage and adoption was promulgated on 18 May 2013, with the support of left-wing President François Hollande.[28] By then a law prohibiting discrimination against transgender people had been voted in (July 2012), completing the 2004 amendment to the anti-discrimination law which made homophobic comments illegal. Changes regarding transsexual people have nevertheless been very slow. In the 1950s and 1960s, Coccinelle, a transsexual artist who had worked in several Parisian cabarets, became a celebrity after she publicized her sex reassignment.[29] Her marriage in 1962 was the first transsexual union to be legally recognized in France. Sex change, nevertheless, remained illegal in France until 1975, and many transsexuals went to Morocco for their operations. It was almost impossible for transsexuals to change their legal gender until 1992 and transsexualism remained classified as an illness until 2010. Founded in Paris in 1976 by Joseph Doucé, a Baptist pastor, the CCL (*Centre du Christ Libérateur*; Liberation Christian Centre), was the first French association to welcome transsexuals, as well as other sexual minorities. The collective Existrans has organized a march of transsexual and transgender people in Paris since 1997.

Although political and strategic issues continue to divide and fracture the Parisian LGBT community, the 2000s have seen some real advances in terms of LGBT rights and visibility. Mixed associations have been created. Sometimes known as *'transpédégouine'* [transqueerdyke], they are particularly appreciated by the younger generation and have been influenced by queer theory. LGBT student associations have been created in many Parisian universities and *grandes écoles*, some of them offering courses in gay and lesbian studies as well as queer theory. Despite a series of crises, a LGBT Archives Centre is currently being set up, with the support of the city council of Paris, whose left-wing mayor, Bertrand Delanoe, elected in 2001, came out on French television in 1998. The inter-LGBT, the umbrella for more than 60 associations, also organizes the Paris pride parade, which attracts between 500 and 800,000 people and is the highlight of the year.[30] In 2011, the European White Paper, *Combating Homophobia*, ranked Paris among the first fifth European cities in terms of local policies against homophobia.[31] Described as one of the most LGBT friendly cities in the world, Paris has been chosen to host the Gay Games in 2018. One should not forget, however, that homophobia is still a reality in Paris – as demonstrated by the huge anti-gay marriage demonstrations, as well as by the unexpected rise of homophobic violence during the same period. In April 2013, for example, Wilfred de Bruijn was attacked with his boyfriend in the 19th arrondissement because they were gay.

'Je sors ce soir'[32] [I'm going out tonight]: Parisian sexual geographies

Writing in 1984, Jan-Paul Pouliquen remarked that Parisian gay nightlife had changed a lot in 5 years. Even though, according to him, the French gay 'scene' remained 'terribly timorous' compared to other western countries, the capital city was less 'hung-up' than before.[33] At the beginning of the 1970s, a ghetto culture operated in the area between Palais Royal and Opera, especially rue Sainte-Anne. With its strictly guarded private clubs, invisible in the daytime, it catered for a rather wealthy clientele, though it also attracted a crowd of gigolos and young prostitutes. Gerald Nanty, the founder of Le Colony (1972) and the Bronx (1973), the first backroom bar, and Fabrice Emaer, the founder of Le Pimm's Bar (1964), Le Sept (1968) and Le Palace (1978) were the main figures of the period. Famous for its outrageousness, crazy parties and unbelievable décor, Le Palace, copying Studio 54 in New York, attracted an improbable crowd of underground punks, artists, models, celebrities and billionaires. Welcoming queer people, it also organized, each Sunday afternoon, a free gay Tea Dance, which soon became the symbol of the gay revolution. Paquita Paquin, a former Gazoline, Jenny Bel'Air, a transvestite, Edwige, the 'queen of punks' and Farida Khelfa, a supermodel, daughter of Algerian migrants, were among the gatekeepers.

If Emaer was the king of the gay night, Elula Perrin, who opened Le Katmandou, Le Privilege or Le Rive Gauche, was the queen of the lesbian night. Lesbian subculture was still much less visible. According to Perrin, only 2,000 lesbians, most of them under 30, went out on a regular basis. Single women who had to work went out only on weekend nights. Women's purchasing power was lower than men's, although women's clubs charged less than gay clubs. Many women also loathed cruising in places they found both squalid and depressing. Clubs like Le Monocle, Chez Moune, Elle et Lui or New Moon, which put on drag acts and sometimes lesbian SM shows, attracted more tourists and voyeurs than women who loved women. From 1968 until 1989, however, Le Katmandou succeeded in building up a reputation both in the lesbian *milieu* and in *le Tout-Paris*, despite its strict women-only policy. There was no equivalent in provincial France, where lesbians and gay men often shared the same places, aside from the Riviera, during the summer.[34]

The beginning of the 1980s saw a major change in Parisian sexual geographies. David Girard, a former prostitute and one of the leading gay businessmen of the 1970s and 1980s, played a major role in the moving of the gay commercial subculture from the 2nd arrondissement to the Marais, in the 3rd and 4th arrondissement. In 1983, he opened a disco, the Haute Tension, two saunas and a restaurant, and launched two magazines. In 1987, he also opened the biggest French gay club in Barbès, Le Mégatown. Girard was severely criticized by activists like Le Bitoux, who held him responsible for the depoliticization of the gay community, and what they saw as the 'selling out' of the gay press. The Parisian gay district, although it attracted only a minority of homosexuals, proved popular. Inspired by the West Village in Manhattan or the Castro in San Francisco, the Marais was situated in the very heart of the city. The new bars, which tried to attract 'clones' with Americanized names like the Central or the Sling, were no longer reserved for the elite. Their addresses were publicized in the new gay and lesbian press and they were cheap. The first gay bar, Le Village, opened there in 1978, at a time when the area remained populous and real estate prices were still low. Les Mots à la Bouche, the oldest gay and lesbian bookshop in Paris, which opened in 1980 in the 18th arrondissement, soon relocated to rue Sainte-Croix-de-la-Bretonnerie, in the Marais. In fact, rue Sainte-Croix-de-la-Bretonnerie, rue des Archive, rue du Temple, and rue Vieille-du-Temple concentrate most of the Marais LGBT venues, which mostly apply a gay-only policy. Well-known bars such as Le Banana Café (ex Broad Side), Le Quetzal, the Open Café or the Cox are listed in gay guides, referred to in conversations, and name-dropped in cult novels such as Renaud Camus's

Tricks (1981) or Guillaume Dustan's *Dans ma chambre* (1996). Many places cater for a specific clientele, identified by codes and dress styles. These last years have seen the opening of 'bear clubs', such as Bear's Den, though the first leather bars go back to the 1980s.

According to Stéphane Leroy, 70 per cent of LGBT commercial locations (bars, clubs, but also restaurants and shops) are today situated in the four first arrondissements, located in the centre of Paris, on the Right Bank. Forty per cent of all LGBT commercial locations are located in the Marais.[35] This may be the result of strategies by proprietors aimed at maximising profits by grouping similar enterprises together and therefore reducing distances for potential consumers.[36] It also shows how locales have spread from a central area across the neighbourhood following the main arteries. Though the Marais shares with many American-style gay neighbourhoods an emphasis on 'commercialism, gay pride and coming-out of the closet',[37] it also differs in many ways from its Anglo-American counterparts. The Marais is less a 'village' where one lives and works than an entrance to a pleasure area[38] – though most saunas, cruising bars and sex-clubs equipped with backrooms, such as Le Transfert, the Keller's (both leather bars) and above all Le Dépôt, the biggest cruising bar in Europe, are located on the periphery of Le Marais, or in other popular gay areas. Nightclubs and discos like Le Scorp and the Boy's (both now closed) or the Queen, are also located outside the Marais, off the Grands Boulevards or on the Champs Elysées, though the Broad, very popular in the 1980s but now closed, was situated in Les Halles. Popular parties such as 'Scream' or the 'Follivores' are also held in theatre venues outside the Marais.

Since the 1980s, the Marais has offered the opportunity to live one's sexuality in the open. For maybe the first time, a gay and (to a lesser extent) lesbian area was loosely delimited and identifiable even by outsiders to the LGBT community. In the evening, customers of gay bars, recognizable by their rainbow flags, tend to spill out onto the pavement in the busiest streets, giving the area a unique atmosphere but also stirring up complaints from neighbours. Despite the talk of the ghetto the Marais remains indeed a socially mixed neighbourhood, popular with tourists, but also home to a strong residential and commercial Jewish community, centred on rue des Rosiers. One of the most striking features of this 'reterritorialisation' of the city[39] by queer people, is what Colin Giraud calls 'gaytrification', that is the gentrification of a whole area by mostly gay and lesbian people, a phenomenon that is not specific to Paris. In the 1950s and 1960s, the Marais was indeed a rather derelict area, mostly inhabited by employees, craftsmen and working-class people. From the middle of the 1960s, as a result of an urban renovation plan, the Marais experienced a profound transformation. Today, it is one of the wealthiest parts of the city, and more than 45 per cent of its inhabitants belong to the upper middle class. In the absence of detailed statistics, it is impossible to know whether these persons are queer or not, but one finds here a majority of 'DINKS' (double income no kids) and of persons living alone. However, Colin Giraud remarks that, even for gay men, living in the Marais does not necessarily mean enjoying a gay lifestyle. Since it often represents an achievement in terms of social status, the gay men who inhabit the Marais are often inclined to avoid what they sometimes see as the 'ghetto' – deemed too fashionable, popular or normalized – and tend to favour more upscale venues in other parts of the city.[40] Most queer people *do not* live in the Marais, which remains, for obvious economic reasons, a leisure more than a residential area. Nevertheless, several studies, which mostly focus on gay men and typically leave the situation of lesbians unclear, have shown that gay men are overrepresented on the Right Bank, in the centre and the North-East of the capital, especially the 1st, 2nd and 3rd arrondissements, closely followed by the 4th, 10th and 11th.[41] Because of real estate prices, the (relatively) more affordable North-East, which is a continuation of the Marais, is becoming more and more attractive and is itself undergoing gentrification. Former homosexual centres, such as Saint-Germain-des Prés, nowadays a posh, dull and overpriced area, have simply disappeared from the queer map, although in the 1980s, the café Mabillon was still famous for its 'clones' and BDSM customers.[42]

Other changes are currently taking place. Sexual geographies have been thoroughly reshaped by electronic media. As early as 1995, a survey led by Marie-Ange Schiltz revealed that 43 per cent of gay men used messaging services and 33 per cent virtual social networks to meet sexual partners.[43] Today, location-based mobile phone apps like Grindr enable you to constantly reconfigure the queer map of the city according to your desires, making cruising almost redundant. The development of the internet has encouraged the dematerialization of social relations, and virtual social networks are probably the first meeting place for young LGBT people today. Young gays and lesbians, especially from the middle-class, are also more inclined to socialize outside the LGBT community. Their lifestyle seems to be less structured by their sexual orientation. Although they frequent the Marais, sometimes at an earlier age than before, they often find it too 'commercial' or 'vulgar', and they prefer to meet in gay-friendly bars and discos or at parties, an attitude that is not always well understood by their elders, for whom the Marais was both a refuge and a symbol of the gay liberation.[44] Straight young men and women, especially those involved in alternative subcultures, such as electronic music fans, seem also more inclined to share their own spaces with LGBT people. The permeation of straight locations like the Rex Club by queer men and women, but also the heterosexualization of queer places, such as Le Queen – which marked the beginning of its decline – show that the Parisian landscape should not be thought of in terms of closed spaces and definite identities, but demands a multilayered approach.

'Nous transportons chacun notre ghetto avec nous' ['We all carry our ghetto with us'][45] or how queer is the city?

From the 1990s, sexual and identity politics have been the subject of heated debates in France. Ambivalence towards the American model of the gay and lesbian liberation had been noticeable within the French LGBT community since the 1970s. Claude Lejeune dismissed the 'clone' as an American import, Frank Arnal deplored the disappearance of the last *tasses*, whereas 'the very American backrooms flourish', while Guy Hocquenghem regretted the loss of old figures of French queer subculture such as the 'Arab queen' or the 'fat Mediterranean fairy.[46] For Scott Gunther: 'In exchange for successful assimilation, the less palatable elements of the early '70s movements – particularly the pedophilic, pederastic, sadomasochistic, transsexual, transvestite, promiscuous, and public-sex elements – had to be excluded or at least ignored by those occupying the new gay spaces of the '80s'.[47] The Marais was the symbol of the new visibility – and respectability – of the French gay and lesbian community.

Although the commodification of gay and lesbian lives, the rationalization of sexual practices,[48] the cult of youth and beauty have all been criticized by LGBT activists, the new gay media, such as *Gai Pied*, soon abandoned opinion pages dealing with provocative issues for articles about sex and fashion and other mainstream topics.[49] Nevertheless, although the sexual landscape has been partly remodelled along communal and commercial locations, it doesn't mean that everybody chooses to conform to what many see as a homogenized and alienating way of life. Phrases like 'out of the ghetto' or 'straight looking guy' have been the staple of gay personal ads since the 1970s. Married men, who identify as straight, but who have sex with men, are among those who favour less obvious cruising places than the Marais, such as parks, RER and railway stations or wastelands, places which require anonymity, are spread across the city, and are also used by homeless people or drug addicts.[50] If some, such as derelict warehouses, are used opportunistically and for a limited period of time, others, like the Quais des Tuileries (nicknamed 'Tata Beach' or 'Fags Beach') or the Père Lachaise cemetery, are traditional cruising places, deeply ingrained in homosexual memory. Former central gay and lesbian areas, such as Pigalle and Montmartre, with their old movie theatres and sex shops, as well as popular and mixed-race neighbourhoods, such as Strasbourg-Saint-Denis, Jaurès and Barbès still remain attractive for many queer people, especially those who don't feel welcome in the Marais. Gay and transgender prostitutes also favour less central locations, such as the Bois de Boulogne, the Boulevards des Maréchaux and Porte Dauphine, also frequented by women prostitutes and swingers. Despite and/or because of their unattractiveness, filth or dangerousness, these spaces are valued and fetishized. They bear testimonies to the secret homosexualization of the city, a personalized and collective process, shaped by years of sexual misery, 'shameful' desires and social constraints, but also the longing for interracial and inter-class relationships, impersonal encounters and hard sex.[51] The fact that such places also attract straight men makes them especially valuable for men who are looking for this kind of sexual partner.

Here the notion of a queer city, without fixed shape and borders, as opposed to the gay ghetto, comes into view. For Guy Hocquenghem, who recalled Le Louxor, an old-fashioned movie theatre in Barbès which served as a refuge for all kinds of queer men, white and Arab, old and young, rich and poor, 'my ghetto is not a portion, a fraction, a member of the city. It is spread everywhere'.[52] Although the FHAR activists, who considered that homosexuals and migrants were both oppressed minorities, asserted their solidarity with Arab men, migrants and/or persons of colour were denied admittance to most gay clubs until the 1990s and they are still not numerous in LGBT associations.[53] Some ethnic LGBT associations do however exist, such as Kelma, created in 1997 and dedicated to Arab gay men. Black and Arab men often find themselves ill at ease in the Marais, a mostly white area, either because they resent the racism still present in the community, or because they feel objectified in the bars, where they can attract a lot of attention. They often prefer areas such as Pigalle or Barbès, which are not purposely dedicated to gay sex.[54] *'Black, Blanc, Beur'* [Black, White, Arab] parties, hosted in the 2000s by the Folie's Pigalle, are particularly popular because of their interracial policy. Bars, saunas, sex-clubs do also organize nights aimed at particular ethnic groups and there are also websites which are similarly demarcated. Raï, R'n'B, hip-hop and reggae are played at these themed parties, and there might also be dance from the Middle East and mint tea available alongside other drinks.[55]

Relationships between black, white and Arab men within the gay community remain ambiguous to say the least, notably because many white gay men see black and Arab men as virile, well-hung and mostly straight sexual partners (*lascars*), who can dominate, or even humiliate them – roles that do not necessarily appeal.[56] The fetish for the Arab or black thug, mythologized by Jean Genet in his essays and novels, has been revisited with a twist by pornographic film studios like Citébeur, while the colonial fantasy of the pliant Arab boy in the tradition of André Gide has also remained popular, as exemplified by Jean-Daniel Cadinot porn movies (for example, *Harem* 1984). Black and Arab men and women meanwhile often have to face a strong homophobia in their own neighbourhoods, especially in the impoverished *banlieue* where virility is defined in opposition to homosexuality and female homosexuality remains mostly unfathomable. As the sociologist Sébastien Barraud has shown, although some Arab or Berber people do identify as gay, lesbian, bi or trans, religious prejudices as well as familial expectations can prevent many men and women from coming out or associating with the LGBT community through fear of rejection or even aggression (including insults, confinement, forced return to Maghreb, physical assault by the father or/and the brothers, and sometimes rape).[57] Some Arab, Berber or Black men (and others) who have sexual relations with other men identify as straight because they assume an exclusively active role during sexual intercourse. Many associations, clubs or bars dedicated to lesbians of colour are meanwhile made almost totally invisible, especially for those aimed at the *beurettes* – Muslim girls born in France but whose parents emigrated from North Africa. According to Christelle Hamel, there weren't any associations, clubs or bars dedicated to lesbian Arab women in Paris before 2002.[58]

The problem is not limited to the suburbs. In many ways, Paris remains a contradictory city, which segregates as well as integrates social and ethnic diversity. It can still be daring, even dangerous today for two men – and sometimes two women – to walk in the city holding hands, at least beyond the Marais and its periphery. In February 2011, a poll for gay magazine *Têtu* revealed that physical assaults against gay, lesbian and bisexual people were more frequent in Paris and its region (22%) than in provincial France (12%). The situation is even grimmer for transgender people. In many ways, Paris remains a heteronormative space, where sexual and gender transgression is frowned upon and must be kept hidden outside a few tightly delimited areas. Above all, Parisian nightlife remains a mostly masculine affair. According to Stéphane Leroy, 97 per cent of LGBT locations in Paris cater only for gay men,[59] a striking example of the male domination of the 'queer city', something that has been denounced by many lesbian and queer activists, notably Marie-Jo Bonnet and Marie-Hélène Bourcier. Lesbian theme-parties have been on the rise these last 10 years, but the number of lesbian-friendly locations remains rather limited, although the situation is often much direr in the provinces. By way of explanation, many bar and club-owners complain that it is much more difficult to build a steady lesbian clientele than a gay one: women go out less often, and they drink less.[60] As a matter of fact, because they are women, they often still earn less than men, and would find it more difficult to buy or rent property in the centre of Paris. Even though Le Marais is also frequented by lesbians, especially younger ones, lesbians often meet in less central areas, such as Montreuil, where many women-only associations are located, notably the main one, the CLF (*Coordination Lesbienne en France*: Lesbian Coordination in France), or Thermopyles-rue Raymonde Losserand, in the 14th arrondissement.[61] As a whole, a map of lesbian Paris would appear sparser and much more dispersed than a map of gay Paris[62] and more organized around lesbian and feminist associations than commercial places.[63]

In line with the feminist movement, women-only places flourished in the 1970s and 1980s. In 1984, radical lesbians Les Diabol'Amantes gathered in La Clef. In 1986, a large lesbian centre, *La Mutinerie*, opened in the 20th arrondissement. From 1999 to 2007 La Barbare functioned as a lesbian feminist women-only self-run association. Workshops dealing with sexual and gender issues were also created, many, such as the MIEL (*Mouvement d'Information et d'Echanges Lesbiens*; Lesbian Information and Exchanges Movement), being regrouped within the Maison des Femmes, now located in the 12th arrondissement. It still houses the lesbian archives, founded in 1983. In 1989, the first lesbian publishing house was opened by Geneviève Pastre, while the International Festival of Lesbian and Feminist Film, today the biggest and oldest French lesbian gathering, was launched by the association Cineffable. Violette and Co (11th arrondissement), a lesbian and feminist bookshop opened in 2004. There is also a network of women-only non-political convivial associations, centred on leisure, sport and cultural activities, as well as numerous commercial hangouts, like La Champmeslé (2nd arrondissement), the oldest lesbian bar in Paris which opened in 1979. In the 1980s, lesbians were welcome in saunas, like Gaia Club (17th arrondissement) and Evohé (6th arrondissement) at certain hours. Some clubs, like Le Lolita (14th) practised an exclusive policy. *Lesbia* claimed that its owner, a gay man, was exploiting women, and encouraged its readers to boycott it. Men were not the only ones to enforce discriminatory policies. Patricia, the owner of lesbian restaurant L'Etrier (18th), refused women who looked too 'masculine', arguing that they would give a bad reputation to her venue.[64] The Pulp, the most famous lesbian nightclub of the 2000s, with great electro and rock DJ-sets, closed in 2007. Although many clubs and bars today welcome a mixed crowd of gay, lesbian and gay-friendly customers, some lesbians do still prefer women-only places, where they feel more at ease and where they have more freedom.[65]

Conclusion

Ever since I'd been a child, an imaginary Paris had been the bright planet pushing at the heart of my mental star map, but the one time I'd gone to Paris I had been dressed in a horrible shiny blazer and everyone in the cafes had laughed at me. I said to a French acquaintance as we left the Flore, "I know I'm being paranoid", but he said matter-of-factly, "No they are laughing at you".[66]

The sexual geography of Paris was, and probably still is, mostly an imagined geography, a map of love and desire decipherable only by those in the know, the place of the 'homosexual drift' (Guy Hocquenghem), whose experience has been made universal by movies and literature. For foreigners, but also for those who came up from the provinces to the 'city of love', Paris was a fantasy born from and nourished by too many cult names and references. For many LGBT tourists around the world, Paris remains today an attractive place. Stéphane Leroy recalls that in the British series *Queer as Folk*, most characters dream of living in Paris.[67]

French people have always been more doubtful: in the 1920s, they found Berlin much wilder than Paris; in the 1970s, French queens flew to

San Francisco; in the 1990s, they turned to London for good music and hard sex. In 1997, in an article for *Têtu*, Didier Lestrade and Thomas Doustaly wondered, in echo of other media, if Paris had been resting on its laurels. The reputation of Parisian nightlife appeared to them grossly overrated.[68] In 2002, the situation remained dire: 'Let's be honest: American or Italian gay tourists do not come to Paris for the clubs. The city of light is today the world capital of backrooms with at least 50 bordellos. It is a fuckpad [*baisodrome*], where it is much easier to get fucked in the ass than to find a decent dance floor'.[69] A rather harsh judgement, born of frustration and too many expectations, although one could agree that, in many ways, Paris has been living on its past charm and glory. However, and despite its flaws, Denis Provencher is certainly right when he argues that Paris still occupies a central place in gay and lesbian imaginary, and that the Marais 'serves as a canonical reference or '*lieu de mémoire*' [realm of memory] for many of France's homosexual citizens'.[70]

Notes

1   Sibalis, M. (1999), 'Paris', in D. Higgs (ed.), *Queer Sites. Gay Urban Histories Since 1600*. New York, Routledge, p. 33. In 2009, there were more than 2.2M inhabitants in Paris, 11.7 in Ile de France (Paris and its region). The second largest city, Marseille had about 850,000 inhabitants, and the third, Lyon, 484,000.

2   Leroy, S. (Juin 2005), 'Le Paris Gay. Eléments pour une géographie de l'homosexualité', *Annales de géographie*, 646, 585.

3   On 1 December 2009, daily newspaper *Le Monde* nicknamed Paris 'the European capital of boredom'.

4   Provencher, Denis M. (2007), *Queer French. Globalization, Language and Sexual Citizenship in France*. Aldershot: Ashgate, p. 193 and Gunther, S. (2009), *The Elastic Closet. A History of Homosexuality in France, 1942-present*. Basingstoke, Palgrave-Macmillan, pp. 120–6.

5   Gunther (2009), p. 38.

6   See Tamagne, F. (2006), *A History of Homosexuality in Europe. Berlin, London, Paris. 1919-1939*. London, Algora Pub.

7   See Tamagne (2006); Revenin, R. (2005), *Homosexualité et prostitution masculines à Paris (1870-1918)*. Paris, L'Harmattan.

8   The age of consent for heterosexual acts was fixed at 13 in 1942, 15 in 1945.

9   Gunther (2009), p. 38.

10   Fernet, M. (janvier 1959), 'L'homosexualité et son influence sur la délinquance', *Revue internationale de police criminelle*, 124, 14–20.

11   Foerster, M. (2006), *Histoire des transsexuels en France*. Béziers: H&O, pp. 87–108.

12   Sidéris, G. (2000), 'Des folles de Saint-Germain-des-Prés au "Fléau Social". Le discours homophile contre l'efféminement dans les années 1950: une

expression de la haine de soi?', in E. Benbassa and J-C. Attias (eds), *La haine de soi: difficiles identités*. Paris: Stock, pp. 121–42.

13 *Bulletin Municipal Officiel de la Ville de Paris*, n. 221, septembre–décembre 1966, 94 and 118, mai-août 1967.

14 See magazine *Détective* between 1960 and 1962.

15 I've compiled the statistics for the years 1953–78 (there are no statistics available relating to female homosexuality before 1953). 'Homosexuality' is mentioned as a separate entry in the judiciary statistics from 1945; it referred until 1960 to offences committed under Article 331 and also, from 1960, Article 330–2. Unfortunately, the details given vary greatly depending on the year. See for each year *Compte général de la justice criminelle* published by the Ministère de la Justice under different names.

16 See See G., born 1946, quoted by Lesselier C., *Aspects de l'expérience lesbienne en France 1930–1968*, Mémoire pour le DEA en sociologie sous la direction de Robert Castel, Université de Paris IX, novembre 1987, p. 66. She conducted, between October 1985 and May 1987, 20 interviews with lesbian women.

17 Perrin E. (1977), *Les femmes préfèrent les femmes*. Paris: Ramsay, J'ai Lu, p. 113.

18 Ibid., pp. 109–11.

19 See also the novel by Mallet-Jorris, F. (1951), *Le rempart des béguines*. Paris, René Julliard, pp. 134–9. The young Hélène, led by her older lover Tamara, was horrified when she entered for the first time the Lucy's bar. The very long scene echoed, in its squalor, the one that took place at the Narcisse in Radcliffe Hall's *The Well of loneliness*.

20 'La révolte féminine ça commence dans un "garçon manqué", ça commence dans une sale "gouine" aussi', *Le torchon brûle*, n. 2, juillet 1971 and 'Révolte. Garçon manquée. Subversion', *Le torchon brûle*, n. 5, nd, [1972?].

21 Jackson, J. (2009), *Arcadie. La vie homosexuelle en France, de l'après-guerre à la dépénalisation*. Paris: Autrement.

22 Le Bitoux, J. (2003), *Citoyen de seconde zone*. Paris, Hachette Littératures.

23 Jackson (2009), p. 256.

24 Le Bitoux (2003), p. 89.

25 Ibid., pp. 125–32, 158–61.

26 Frédéric Mitterrand is the nephew of President François Mitterrand. He became Minister of Culture and Communication from 2009 to 2012, under President Nicolas Sarkozy.

27 See Martel, F. (2000), *The Pink and the Black. Homosexuals in France since 1968*. Stanford: Stanford University Press.

28 One should note that 11 nationalities are excluded from the law, because of former bilateral agreements. For the time being, same-sex couples consisting of a French and a Moroccan, an Algerian, a Tunisian, a Cambodian, a Laotian, a Slovenian, a Bosnia-Herzegovinan, a Serbian, an inhabitant of Montenegro, a Kosovian or a Pole still cannot get married.

29 Foerster (2006).

30 From 1971 to 1978, queer people used to march on 1 May with trade-unions and far-left groups, also they were not always welcomed.

31 *Combating Homophobia. Local Policies for Equality on the grounds of Sexual Orientation and Gender Identity. A European White Paper*, AHEAD (Against Homophobia, European Local Administration Devices), Ajuntament de Barcelona, 2011. The municipality's investment in the fight against HIV/AIDS, support to the LGBT Center, as well as the creation of a free LGBT map of Paris, were notably mentioned.

32 Dustan, G. (1997), *Je sors ce soir*. Paris: POL.

33 *Gai Pied Hebdo*, n. 103, 21–27 janvier 1984, pp. 24–6.

34 Perrin (1977), pp. 82–3.

35 The Marais, a historic district, is spread across parts of the 3rd and 4th arrondissements. It is notably delimited by the Pompidou Centre on the west side and the Boulevard Beaumarchais (near Bastille) on the east side.

36 Leroy (Juin 2005), p. 588.

37 Provencher (2007), p. 156.

38 Leroy (Juin 2005), p. 595.

39 Ibid., p. 582.

40 Giraud, C. (2007), 'Habiter les quartiers gays', in Michel Lussault, Thierry Paquot, Chris Younès (dir.), *Habiter, le propre de l'humain*. Paris: La Découverte, pp. 295–312.

41 Giraud, C., 'Enquête sur les lieux de résidence des homosexuels masculins à Paris', *Sociétés contemporaines*, n. 81, mars 2011, pp. 151–65.

42 *Têtu*, n. 32, mars 1999, pp. 64–73.

43 Quoted by Blidon, M. (février 2008), 'Jalons pour une géographie des homosexualités', *L'espace géographique*, tome 37, 181.

44 Giraud, C. (janvier 2012), 'Quartiers gays et jeunesses homosexuelles à Paris et à Montréal', *Agora débats/jeunesses*, 60, 79–92.

45 Hocquenghem, G. (1980), *Le Gay voyage. Guide et regard homosexuels sur les grandes métropoles*. Paris: Albin Michel, p. 10.

46 *Gai Pied*, n. 14, mai 1980, pp. 12–13 and n. 35, février 1982, p. 56; Bory J.-L. and G. Hocquenghem (1977), *Comment nous appelez-vous déjà? Ces hommes que l'on dit homosexuels*. Paris: Calmann-Levy, pp. 161, 210.

47 Gunther (2009), p. 68.

48 Pollak, M. (1982), 'L'homosexualité masculine, ou le bonheur dans le ghetto?', *Communication*, 35, 37–55.

49 Le Bitoux (2003) and Gunther (2009), p. 76.

50 Proth, B. (2002), *Lieux de drague. Scènes et coulisses d'une sexualité masculine*. Paris, Octarès éditions, p. 129.

51 Ibid., pp. 191–3.

52 Hocquenghem, G., *op. cit.*, 10 and 135.

53 For multiracial gay clubs, see *Têtu*, n. 9, décembre 1996, pp. 25–32.

54 Many testimonies can be found in the online magazine babyboy.fr.

55 Barraud S. (2005), *Etre un homme homosexuel et d'origine maghrébine à Paris et en région parisienne: stratégies psychosociales, identités intersectionnelles et modernité*, Mémoire de DEA sous la direction de François Vourc'h, Université de Paris VII, p. 15.

56 See for example, Welzer-Lang, D. (août 2005), 'La place du Beur dans le porno gay', *Les Inrockuptibles*, n. 504, p. 61.

57 Barraud (2005), p. 10.

58 Hamel, C. (janvier 2012), 'Devenir lesbienne: le parcours de jeunes femmes d'origine maghrébine', Agora débats/jeunesses, 60, 93–105; Chaumont, F. (2009), *Homo-ghetto. Gay et lesbiennes dans les cités. Les clandestins de la République*. Paris: Le Cherche-Midi.

59 Leroy (Juin 2005), p. 582.

60 Vives, M., 'Loin de Paris, le clubbing lesbien peine à décoller', *tetu.com*, 3 janvier 2011. http://www.tetu.com/actualites/france/loin-de-paris-le-clubbing-lesbien-peine-a-decoller-18555.

61 Blidon (février 2008), p. 183.

62 Provencher (2007), pp. 169–75.

63 Chetcuti, N. (2010), *Se dire lesbienne. Vie de couple, sexualité, représentation de soi*. Paris: Payot.

64 *Lesbia*, n. 14, février 1984, n. 19, juillet 1984, n. 20, septembre 1984.

65 Chetcuti (2010), p. 49.

66 White, E. (1997), *The Farewell Symphony: A Novel*. New York: A. A. Knopf, p. 4.

67 Leroy (Juin 2005), p. 585.

68 *Têtu*, n. 14, mai 1997, p. 41.

69 *Têtu*, n. 64, 2002, p. 18.

70 Provencher (2007), pp. 152–3.

Further reading

Chetcuti N. (2010), *Se dire lesbienne. Vie de couple, sexualité, représentation de soi*. Paris: Payot.
Foerster M. (2006), *Histoire des transsexuels en France*. Béziers: H&O.
Gunther S. (2009), *The Elastic Closet. A History of Homosexuality in France, 1942-present*. Basingstoke: Palgrave-Macmillan.
Jackson J. (2009), *Living in Arcadia: Homosexuality, Politics, and Morality in France from the Liberation to AIDS*. Chicago: University of Chicago Press.
Le Bitoux, J. (2003), *Citoyen de seconde zone. Trente ans de lutte pour la reconnaissance de l'homosexualité en France (1971-2002)*. Paris: Hachette Littératures.
McCaffrey E. (2005), *The Gay Republic. Sexuality, Citizenship and Subversion in France*. Aldershot: Ashgate.
Martel F. (2000), *The Pink and the Black. Homosexuals in France since 1968*. Stanford: Stanford University Press.
Proth B. (2002), *Lieux de drague. Scènes et coulisses d'une sexualité masculine*, Paris: Octarès éditions.

Provencher D. M. (2007), *Queer French. Globalization, Language and Sexual Citizenship in France*. Aldershot: Ashgate.

Rees-Robert N. (2008), *French Queer Cinema*. Edinburgh: Edinburgh University Press.

Revenin R. (2005), *Homosexualité et prostitution masculines à Paris (1870–1918)*. Paris: L'Harmattan.

Sibalis, M. (1999), 'Paris', in D. Higgs (ed.), *Queer Sites. Gay Urban Histories since 1600*. New York: Routledge, 1999.

Tamagne F. (2006), *A History of Homosexuality in Europe en Europe. Berlin, London, Paris. 1919–1939*. London: Algora Pub.

Closing Reflections

13

'Gays Who Cannot Properly be Gay'. Queer Muslims in the neo-liberal European city[1]

Fatima El-Tayeb

Introduction

The twenty-first century European city seems almost necessarily queer; that is, openly queer communities and neighbourhoods are not only tolerated but cherished parts of nearly every metropole, reflecting the continent's unique ability to constantly evolve ('Europe's self-generating capacity to produce, like a silk-worm, the circumstances of her own evolution from within her own body', as Stuart Hall put it with mild sarcasm in 1991)[2] to always be where the avant-garde is. Europe, after all, is not only a geographical location or an economic union, but the home of enlightened humanism. Consequently, its inclusivity of queers is one of the things that sets Europe apart from the rest of the world – from the US American ally, more powerful, but less mature and refined and certainly less secular than Europe, and more than that from the non-West, increasingly represented by Islam. Islam has had a key role in twenty-first century politics (or at least in mainstream discourses about these politics), and is also seen to pose a threat not only to global peace but also to Europe's internal stability, in the shape of several million Muslim 'immigrants', whose values with regard to almost everything, but certainly gender and sexuality, violently clash with European practices. These culture clashes take place primarily in urban landscapes. Or so the story goes.

In this chapter, I hope to offer a critical investigation into the Muslim/European dichotomy as well as into the supposedly harmonious relationship between 'queer' and 'Europe', which, I argue, needs to be qualified: queerness becomes tolerable if and when it is perceived as being compatible with neo-liberal demands. The resulting depoliticizing of queerness in turn becomes complicit with a neo-liberal project that produces new forms of exclusion. In the current European context, Muslims, including queer Muslims, emerge as a primary target, metonymically representing racialized Others.[3] Thus, I posit that the externalization of Muslims and other racialized groups is a European phenomenon, which, in fact, the Europeanization of the continent's nation-states is in no small part manifest in a shared Islamophobia and a framing of immigration as the main threat to the continental union. In what follows, I therefore first sketch these intersecting discourses as they play out across Europe. Then, I will look closer at Amsterdam as exemplifying not only the European city as a site of 'homophile Islamophobia', but also as paradigmatic for the strategies of resistance developed by groups whose presence is virtually erased through these discourses, namely queer Muslims.[4]

(Post)multicultural Europe and its racialized minorities

Since the fall of the Soviet empire more than 20 years ago, the uniting Europe has struggled to create a post-national system of governance able to address the challenges posed by an increasingly interconnected twenty-first century world. Ironically though, while the continent frequently defines itself around shared values of humanism, equality and tolerance, there is an increasingly intolerant and repressive attitude towards migrants and racialized minorities – justified by their supposed threat to exactly these values, especially when they are identified as Muslim.[5] The growing centrality of the (second generation, Muslim) migrant as internal menace to Europe can also be read, however, as being caused by and at the same time hiding an important change: the continent-wide shift to a 'migrant' population that is largely minoritarian, that is, consisting of the so-called 2nd and 3rd generation, born and raised in their countries of residence, which in effect have become multi-ethnic and multi-religious.[6] This shift (and its political, social and economic consequences) nevertheless continues to be largely denied in policy debates and public discourses.

Until the 1980s, West European perceptions of labour migration were shaped by the belief that the vast majority of migrants and their children would simply 'return home', once they were not needed anymore. This same rhetoric rings increasingly hollow when referencing a population whose only home *is* Europe, their experiences if not passports making them part of the continental community. Rather than acknowledging this reality, however, policy and media debates seem stuck in assessing how exactly racialized minorities will have to assimilate before they can conditionally be considered European. Meanwhile, their socio-economic marginalization remains unaddressed as it is seen as merely an indication of their failure to adept.[7] Accordingly, their perceived Otherness is primarily framed as one of fundamental *cultural* opposition to everything Europe stands for. Thus, while there is a reluctant and belated admittance that (West) European states have become 'immigration nations', the increasingly popular claim of 'the failure of multiculturalism' still manages to position racialized minorities outside of the space of 'proper' Europeanness.[8]

The undeniable presence of minoritarian Europeans is thus reframed as a threat to the continent's foundations that needs to be contained through new forms of spatial governance: while borders within Europe became increasingly diffused with the progressing unification, the internal divide between 'Europeans' and 'non-Europeans' is reinforced along lines of race and religion. One of the most striking examples of this is the role of gender and sexuality in discourses around the continent's Muslim communities.[9] The latter's construction as static and repressive, preventing its members from moving – literally in case of women or intellectually in case of men – goes hand in hand with and hides legal, political and economic restrictions imposed on racialized communities, limiting their ability to move across borders between and within nations, often even within cities.[10]

While the delegitimizing difference of visible minorities is still most obvious in rural areas, their presence is most contested in urban spaces, which they are frequently accused of polluting or taking over.[11] Thus, when addressing the interplay of discourses around queer and Muslim Europeanness, my focus is on issues of containment and mobility in particular in cities. I am less interested here in explicit forms of state violence and racial profiling than in the policing of urban spaces through a neo-liberal discourse bent on controlling the public through privatization and through framing the city as a site of consumption. The result is spatial politics, in which marginalized groups are not completely expelled from the city/nation, but remain excluded and contained through their failure to achieve consumer-citizen status. This failure in turn is linked back to the discourse of a cultural deficit of Muslim/migrant communities.

Urban mobility in borderless Europe

The link becomes especially relevant in the neo-liberal city where (white, middle-class, male) gay consumer-citizens represent the successful integration of minorities into the mainstream.[12] Urban metropoles, the 'global' and 'creative' cities, become increasingly central to neoliberalism as the nation state – with its promise of stability, reliable and permanent borders, unambiguous group and class identities, and normative life-paths – loses importance to global capitalism. The apparent dissolution of binaries that have characterized modernity is visible in conceptualizations of the city that move away from a functional model, in which urban spaces figure largely as containers into which different populations are sorted. In line with a post-national, 'borderless' Europe, the former instead prioritizes the flexible, mobile consumer-citizen, equally at home everywhere, unconcerned with limiting national or personal loyalties and thus achieving ultimate freedom from twentieth-century constraints. The relationship between cities and their inhabitants appears as dynamic, both constantly shaping each other, adapting to conditions produced by a global economy and its translocal citizens.

A closer look at this (not so) new model shows however that neoliberalism's diffusion of old binaries and borders merely reconfigures rather than destabilizes familiar forms of domination. Not all kinds of mobility are equally desirable: while the transnational entrepreneur and global bohemian exemplify the proper cosmopolitan subject, the capital-less labour migrant embodies its opposite. And this undesirability is extended to the descendants of migrants, even if their mobility is simultaneously curtailed: while post-war industrial metropoles had been in need of unskilled migrant labour, contemporary post-industrial centres have moved to the service sector, which draws from an entirely different pool of potential employees. As a result, a working migrant population, frequently concentrated in poor neighbourhoods directly adjacent to factories, has been replaced by a largely unemployed multi-ethnic underclass, stuck in these increasingly deteriorating spaces. Responsibility for this process is transferred onto racialized communities through the trope of 'self-segregation' and 'self-ghettoization', supposedly caused by their fundamentally different and inferior culture, increasingly identified with Islam.[13] In other words, the visible presence of racialized populations, whose concentrated presence implies a threatening violation of the 'normal,' makes the city the primary battleground for the culture wars between Muslim invaders, threatening to destroy 'European values' and those defending them – the latter an ever-growing coalition of neoliberals, progressive white queer activists, conservatives, feminists, homonationalists and white supremacists.

What they have in common is an understanding of Islam as not a religion, practiced in a variety of forms, but as an all-encompassing ideology, stripping its adherents of all individuality. The content of this ideology in turn is determined not so much by Muslims themselves but by European experts. This, of course, is in line with a long Orientalist tradition, in which Muslims appear as lacking individuality and agency, their collective actions determined by an archaic religion/culture dictating their every move.[14] Aggressor and victim at the same time, unable to make the necessary transition into modernity on their own, Muslim societies need Western intervention, in the form of (neo)colonialist 'humanitarian missions'. Through the process of civilizing the East, the West defines itself, creating an internal coherence impossible to achieve without the external Other. Part of this process is the appropriation of groups whose status within the nation is contested but whose conditional inclusion serves both to assure their loyalty and to affirm the West's superior ability to tolerate difference. The role of feminists and more recently gays and lesbians in the mobilization of the nation around the (neo)colonial civilizing mission has been extensively analysed.[15] Critical deconstructions of contemporary versions of this 'strategic humanism' tend to focus on the United States however, as the dominant military power and self-declared leader in the 'war on terror'. Less attention is paid to the ways in which Europe exerts economic control over formerly colonized spaces. The latter, less obvious system of domination is firmly situated within human rights discourses that tend to hide rather than address economic violence by drawing on the larger framework of civilizing West/underdeveloped Global South.[16] This dynamic plays out not only in international relations, but also in the neo-liberal restructuring of European cities, in which class is replaced by notions of culture that deeply racialize urban hierarchies.

The far (Human) Right(s) versus European Muslims

The exclusion of Muslim Europeans through the claim of Islam being incompatible with a commitment to human rights that is deeply European thus builds on a larger tradition, but its specifics have led to a transformation of the continent's political landscape. Europe's far right over the last decade became an increasingly important factor in electoral politics across the continent, either through direct government participation or by justifying 'moderate' parties' move to explicitly Islamophobic and anti-immigrant positions.[17] In turn, groups like the Belgian Vlaamse Belang, the Dutch Partij voor de Vrijheid or the British National Party have moved away from a traditional right-wing anti-urbanism to claim the city as a site of the fight against an 'Islamization' of Europe and in defence of values such as gender equality and LGBT rights that they have not been traditionally known to care much about. But positing homophobia and sexism as defining characteristics of Muslim communities to the point that they have become *the* shorthand for the supposed incompatibility of 'Islam' and 'Europe' requires at least a rhetorical commitment to the threatened values by Europe's defenders, even if their actual investment in them is more than doubtful.[18]

Thus the reference to the status of women in the introductory quote from the charter of 'Cities against Islamisation', a translocal network founded in 2008 in Antwerp by right-wing parties from across Europe – Belgium, the Netherlands, Germany, Austria, France and Spain.[19] Since the participating organizations are explicitly nationalist and anti-European, their choice to create a continent-wide, city-based network in order to combat 'Islamization' is significant. It reflects not only the growing internationalization of white supremacist organizations, but also the importance of the urban space for anti-Muslim activism: it is here that the trope of a continent overrun by foreigners can be bolstered by the presence of 'ghettos'. In addition, the question as to whether Muslim communities should be allowed to build publicly identifiable mosques has become an extremely successful site for Islamophobic mobilization. The result is a consensus that the presence of minarets in European cities indicates that multiculturalism has indeed gone too far (since it would establish the presence of Muslims as permanent rather than preliminary).[20] A protest against the construction of a mosque in the Belgian Lier, organized by 'Cities against Islamisation' sums it up: 'With the coming of the mosque that district and the whole of Lier are going to Islamise in a fast way. Big mosques attracts [sic] new Muslims. As you well know a mosque is not only a house of prayer but also a cultural centre'.[21]

This characterization of Islam as a culture rather than a religion is another central element in the de-Europeanizing of Muslims. According to the CAI charter 'Islam is more of a social order rather than a religion. This social order . . . is at odds with the entirety of values and standards, which are part of our European society'.[22] The framing of Islam not only as a 'social order' dictating every aspect of the life of every Muslim, but also as an order incompatible with, if not actively opposing, 'European values' of tolerance and democracy has been thoroughly mainstreamed. The hijab and then 'honour killings' have become symbols of a social order that violently and necessarily oppresses women. More recently, hate crimes by Muslim youths against gay men have become another seeming proof of Islam's inherently and uncontrollably violent nature.[23] And while white supremacist groups are still somewhat hesitant to embrace gay rights, there is a segment represented among others by the Dutch Lijst Pim Fortuijn and Geert Wilders' Partij voor de Vrijheid, both quite successful in national elections, that does embrace gay rights. More importantly though, with the rise of the creative city hype, affluent gay men have become a valuable constituency for cities struggling with weak economies. Erasing class as a relevant factor in the violence produced by the gentrification of urban spaces, the increasing pitting of (implicitly white) gay community against (implicitly straight) Muslim community posits the former as a victim of the latter, creating common ground between neoliberal and white supremacist interests: a discourse on culturally motivated 'hate crimes' targeting white gay men allows for the implementation of punishment, re-education and control towards not only individuals but also the communities producing them.[24] At the same time, they justify the neo-liberal reordering of the city, interpolating the mainstream gay community as successful subjects of the 'creative city', which in turn justifies their full inclusion into the (post)nation.

Neo-liberal cityscapes: Homonormative versus queer

Reacting to the crisis of the industrial metropole that began in the 1970s, a crisis that produced forms of situated resistance like the squatter and Hip-Hop movements, authors such as Richard Florida appropriated and tamed the subversive impulses produced within these movements into a neo-liberal market model of the city, postulating a creative class as the new driving force behind the resurrection of urban spaces. Florida's (pseudo)quantitative creative city model offers ethnic diversity, patent applications per head and the number of gay (male) residents as the three main indicators of an urban community's desirability within the new 'creative' economy.[25] This index seemingly legitimizes the presence of sexual as well as racial minorities, thus presenting a move beyond earlier models aimed at pushing non-normative populations outside the city limits. However, there is a difference not only between types of culture but also between those embodying creativity, the 'gay residents', and those representing 'ethnic diversity' – with the former defined along the lines of a rather tired stereotype: the wealthy, artistic, (white) gay man, favouring the aesthetic over the political, consumption over activism, and participation in the status quo over change. This stereotype gained new credibility and positive value with the discovery of the gay market in the 1990s.[26] As cultural sociologist Andreas Reckwitz and others have shown however, this postmodern model, while superficially celebrating a dynamic mode of living opposed to the static restrictions of the modern age, in fact contains and constrains the shifts taking place in late twentieth-century city life and integrates them into a new binary, whose Other is quite familiar, namely 'the non-Cultural, that is, the sphere of that which does not see itself as cultural or is not (initially) accessible to culturation',[27] in other words: the ethnic.

Operating through interpellation as much as exclusion, the creative city makes use of what Lisa Duggan termed homonormativity[28]: a mainstreamed gay discourse that attempts to expand rather than dismantle heteronormativity by internalizing a conceptualization of LGBT identity that constructs legitimacy and rights along established lines, challenging neither the exclusion of those who do not or cannot play by the rules nor a system whose very existence depends on such exclusions. In the Western European context, homonormative queers are offered protection through an Islamophobic consensus that frames the policing of poor, racialized communities as a protection of human rights.[29] As a result, despite the stated openness of the creative city, white, middle-class and male once again seems to constitute the unquestioned norm and certain groups occupy similar marginal positions in hetero- and homonormative discourses, among them the Muslim community – including queer Muslims – which provides colour, exotic food and sexual objects, but also stands for restrictive morality, crime and poverty.

The city is not only a site of gay consumption however, but also of queer activism. As Halberstam and others have argued, the urban space long held the promise of allowing for a radically anti-assimilationist queer identity rejecting the spatio-temporal foundations of the nation state: 'Queer subcultures produce alternative temporalities by allowing their participants to believe that their futures can be imagined according to logics that lie outside of those paradigmatic markers of life experience – namely, birth, marriage, reproduction, and death'.[30] But while those markers – marriage, childrearing, military service – have moved to the centre of mainstream gay and lesbian activism, progressive queer conceptions of space and time, rejecting notions of mainstreamed LGBT normalcy and respectability, are not necessarily in opposition to neo-liberal demands. Despite being critical of the effects of homo- and heteronormativity, white queer organizations fail to develop a new political language and practice adequate to the changed structures of global domination.[31] Instead, the old arsenal of anti-establishment political rhetoric can be kept useful by directing it towards a new target: Islam. The Muslim community stands for an outmoded form of heterosexuality – intolerant of difference, violent towards women and gays, oppressive, static and unwilling to go with the times – in the eyes of radical queers (and feminists) as much as in those of liberals, conservatives and right-wingers. Embodying the failed essentialism of identity politics, religious fundamentalism, political correctness, and the doomed industrial class system of twentieth-century capitalism, Muslims are positioned in opposition to the new values of diversity, tolerance and mobility. Identifying homophobia and misogyny as main characteristics of the global and European Muslim cultural practice allows white feminist and queer activists to remain within an analytic developed in response to forms of repression that seem to have vanished from Western European societies – except in its Muslim enclaves. Muslim minorities as the source of gays and lesbians' victimization finally validate the latter as it can be recognized by the majority, which becomes the protector, rather than the oppressor of the LGBT minority.

Gay rescue missions: Saving queer Muslims from their culture

This binary discursive formation extends to the queer community, where white (West) Europeans play the part of civilizer, while queer Muslims have nothing to offer, as they, like all Muslims, are cast as products of a culture that is fundamentally inferior to the secular West. This logic is exemplified in this quote from a 2003 report on 'Homosexuality and Citizenship' in the Netherlands:

> The many personal stories of gays of color are to a certain extent comparable. A *coming-out* like the one experienced by many Dutch gays is not (yet) seen as a necessary step by the majority and is not common. Many migrant/minority gays and lesbians live a double live and do not see any chance of living openly as gay, because, according to them, that would bring shame for their families within the community.

Published by *Forum*, independent Dutch 'Institute for Multicultural Affairs', this assessment reflects dominant perceptions of a normative, healthy and desirable LGBT identity, centred around 'coming out' and represented by the white, Western gay subject. This norm is complimented by its underdeveloped Other, embodied by racialized queers, held back from achieving the former's liberated state by their homophobic culture of origin. Emancipation thus can only be achieved by assimilating into dominant culture.

Absent from this discourse is a progressive queer critique that applies intersectionality in order to analyse the effects of race and class on this seeming clash between progressive, tolerant, dynamic European society and traditional, intolerant, static Muslim community. Instead, as the Dutch queer of colour collective Strange Fruit observed as early as 1997, it is 'assumed that all minorities have psycho-social problems', expressed in a pathologized deviance that threatens the nation's core values and thus needs to be cured through a mixture of (forced) assimilation, punishment and (re)education. That is, both queer and straight Muslims appear as misfits within twenty-first century models of identity: while the former, still culturally stuck in the age of shame, are incapable of embracing a modern queer identity manifest in particular in the normative coming out process, the latter cling to a repressive model of heterosexuality, out of synch with the age of neo-liberal consumer citizens, offering participation to anyone willing and able to pay the price, including those formerly excluded, such as women and queers. Thus, while the European Muslim community as a whole is judged to present the 'wrong', that is, misogynist, homophobic, type of heterosexuality, feminist and queer Muslims too are confronted with the demand to take sides in the imaginary clash of cultures in which 'the West' stands for liberal and progressive cosmopolitanism.

This legible and thus acceptable image of the victimized queer Muslim saved by Western humanitarianism (often via white queer organizations)[32] is directly opposed to the position expressed in the quote by Amsterdam-based Strange Fruit introducing this chapter. The collective, whose name simultaneously references queer positionalities and African diasporic traditions, almost perfectly represents the subaltern of contemporary European discourses around race, religion and migration in their implied impact on gender and sexuality. Active from 1989 to 2002, the group was founded by queer youths of Muslim and Afro-Caribbean background, for the most part welfare recipients and/or sex workers, who came together intending to challenge their marginalization within both their ethnic communities and the Dutch gay scene. Committed to a non-hierarchical self-help approach, the activists offered an insider's perspective to other queer youths of colour, rather than that of aid workers delivering 'expert knowledge'. Instead, they used the expertise present even within the community in order to counter authoritative discourses such as the one producing the Forum report, thus questioning the assumption of a deficiency of non-white/non-Western queerness and identifying racism and Islamophobia as intrinsically linked to dominant models of gay liberation.

It is likely no coincidence that a Dutch queer of colour group was among the first observing the pinkwashing of post-1989 Europe. Over the past two decades, the Netherlands in many ways have become the paradigmatic site of the Othering of racialized Europeans via a discourse that presents Islamophobia as the logical, in fact necessary, response to Islam's homophobia.[33] Cracks in the idealized narrative of Dutch liberal tolerance have largely been defined as caused by the nation's growing Muslim population, unwilling and unable to partake in the 'live and let live' mentality that for centuries managed to maintain a delicate equilibrium between diverse populations.[34] Several studies devoted to the issue of Islam and homosexuality in the Netherlands produced results that seemed to confirm the adverse relationship between the two. One of the first, a survey of local high schools published in 1996 by the City of Amsterdam, identified rampant homophobia among minority youths, especially Muslims.[35] This claim gained wide attention in part by feeding into an ongoing larger debate on 'senseless violence' supposedly originating in migrant communities, in part by tying into growing concerns about the rise of 'black schools', that is, schools with a high number of students of colour, and the negative effect of this trend on white Dutch students.[36] The study's findings were complimented by the 2003 *Forum* report mentioned earlier, exploring the status of non-white queers. The publication presents the familiar dichotomy of stories of oppression representative for queers of colour and narratives of liberation exemplifying Dutch queer identity (with 'Dutch' and 'minority' being conceived of as mutually exclusive); thus queers of colour appear as 'not there yet,' as trying to catch up with white society, victims not of Dutch racism but of an oppressive, archaic ethnic culture:

> The risk of expulsion from family and/or community is real. Thus, these are reasons to avoid a confrontation with cultural and/or religious traditions and to hide their sexual preference from family and community. For gays of color it is often already a big step – towards self-realization – to use the meeting places created by migrant/minority gays. Initiatives such as Strange Fruit and Secret Garden of the Amsterdam COC and the Melting Pot of the Hague's COC. These initiatives have diverse aims: from help and support to the organizing of informal meeting nights.[37]

The model character of the 'autochthon' gay Dutch community and the usefulness of the linear coming out binary as indicator of a successful 'self-realization' remain unquestioned. By focusing on minority queers' inability to come out and live openly, the Forum report puts them firmly on the wrong side of the oppressed/liberated dichotomy. Consequently, it presents the step of approaching one of the minority LGBT organizations working under the umbrella of larger Dutch queer organizations, namely the COC, as the only way to cross over to the right side, out of the (cultural) closet.[38]

The dichotomy between pre- and post-pride gay identity as Marlon Ross, Hiram Perez and others have argued, posits the closet as 'ground zero in the project of articulating an "epistemology" of sexuality'.[39] Strikingly reflected in the *Forum* report, this understanding of the closet 'narrativizes gay and lesbian identity in a manner that violently excludes or includes the subjects it names according to their access to specific kinds of privacy, property, and mobility'.[40] The link between linear mobility and progress ties the normative coming out story to the larger discourse around racialized minorities in the neo-liberal European city as both present communities of colour as spaces of oppression that need to be permanently left in order to enter the domain of the liberated consumer-citizen. At the same time, 'being out' becomes increasingly manifest in forms of commercialized mobility that neatly tie into creative city models, in which race and class are the true signifiers of who can be properly gay: 'Needless to say, the mobility that modern gay identity requires is not universally available. Here we encounter trouble in the form of noncanonical bodies (not surprisingly, also quite often brown bodies) nonetheless interpellated as gay. Gays who cannot properly be gay'.[41]

The city as site of resistance: Queer of colour activism in Amsterdam

The enactment of this clash between mobile modern gay identity and those who cannot properly be gay is particularly evident in a city like Amsterdam. It in many ways exemplifies the neo-liberal creative city, with its mixture of quaint architecture and edgy metrosexual culture, idyllic canals and multicultural markets, liberal drug laws and its own version of the low income neighbourhoods, meant to temporarily house labour migrants, that can be found in most European cities. These neighbourhoods, such as the (mostly black) Bijlmer and (mostly Muslim) Slotervaart, have become permanent home to an increasingly segregated, criminalized and policed multi-ethnic population of colour, disproportionally poor and young[42] – out of sight of the millions of visitors who come to the city each year, but at the same time available when needed to mobilize fears around a foreign, fanatical, violent Other or to provide an accessible, exotic and titillatingly dangerous site for the more daring traveller, straight or gay, local or international. It is exactly this combination that made the city one of Europe's most popular tourist destinations and the prime site of what Hiram Perez calls gay cosmopolitan tourism.[43] This is a tourism that affirms a particular gay identity as normative by tying liberation to specific types of mobility. Gay cosmopolitan tourism thus requires, and produces, the same kind of seemingly fluid but in fact, strictly hierarchical urban spaces provided by the neoliberal creative city, including poor communities of colour in its landscape, but containing and isolating them to ensure that movement takes place only in one direction, conceiving of them primarily as a resource – of labour, food, sex and other commodities valued by the consumer-citizen. These racialized communities are thus both defined as lacking the individualized and commercialized mobility of the (homo- and heteronormative) Western subject, while they are at the same time forever reduced to a hypermobile, uprooted state, whose presence is a marketable touristic commodity exactly because it is perceived to exist outside of the normative. It thus includes an element of danger, of the excessive exotic within the confines of the civilized city, a permanent potential threat to the humanist consensus of post-national Europe.

This characterization aligns with Strange Fruit's assessment of why minority queers are ambiguous about white organizations like the COC, namely the fact that '[i]t is hardly ever discussed what problems these minority youths encounter within the Dutch society/the Dutch education system, in gay and lesbian organizations, subcultures, in contacts, friendships, relationships with Dutch peers/adults, hardly ever is there room for survival strategies, statements by the youths themselves or for the insights of black/ migrant experts'.[44] Instead, coming out becomes a decontextualized fetish around which the familiar superiority of Western individuality is built, while queers of colour are expected to catch up, to overcome their inherent cultural disadvantage. Racialized queers and in particular queer Muslims are forced to negotiate an incredibly complicated terrain, constantly confronted with silencing, appropriation, exclusion and the overwhelming demand to adept their reality to ideologies proclaiming them an oxymoron. Challenging as this is, queer activists of colour have managed to successfully circumvent this pressure, resisting the divisions imposed on them by minority and majority communities through a politicized creolization of traditions and identities. This creolization, which I have called a queering of ethnicity, acknowledges the fact that supposedly incompatible cultures and histories have already merged in European practices and uses the 'improper', 'inauthentic' and impossible positionality of racialized Europeans as the starting point for situated, specifically European strategies of resistance.[45] I will end this piece by briefly exploring how Strange Fruit exemplifies this intersectional queer of colour politics resisting racism and Islamophobia.

Although the possibility of a queer Muslim identity beyond homonormative Western models and heteronormative interpretations of Islam was from the beginning a central concern for the activists, it was however never the only one.[46] The group included members from a variety of backgrounds: North African, Caribbean, Middle Eastern, Afro-Dutch, Asian and Asian-Dutch. What they shared was the experience of being racialized within Dutch society and the very heterogeneity of the group allowed the activists to explore the common patterns of this racialization. Strange Fruit's strategies reacted to the process of Othering directed at European migrant and minority communities by speaking from the position of racialized subjects, emphasizing exactly this Othering rather than accepting it as reflecting an essential truth, thus engaging in the queering of ethnicity by claiming autonomy without authenticity.

Throughout its roughly 13-year existence, Strange Fruit organized a wide variety of activities, from weekly radio programmes and safer sex education workshops to a monthly club night and refugee support groups.[47] The collective went against dominant notions of progressive queer identity by drawing on non-Western traditions, persistently seeking contact with community organizations and elders while maintaining explicitly queer positions thus challenging the dominant Dutch (and European) gay and lesbian consensus of the mainstream white community as normative, as the model of emancipation to which migrants and minorities from less enlightened backgrounds necessarily aspire to. Instead, they creolized various traditions in order to adapt them for their own purposes. Building for example on the presence of oral tradition in Afro-Caribbean and Muslim cultures, they subverted the linear Western coming out narrative through the use of Toris, a Surinamese storytelling tradition whose collective and non-linear structure more adequately reflected the experience of negotiating same-sex desire among queers of colours, emphasizing the complex and ongoing dynamic between them and their communities, which can be and often are both safe havens and sites of oppression.[48]

Strange Fruit persistently explored this tension, as well as others buried under the LGBT moniker: transgendered members were a small but vocal presence from the beginning and while most of its original members had been men, the group soon included an equal number of women. For more than a decade, the group was able to maintain an intersectional practice in which identities and discourses were eclectically appropriated, rearranged, and transformed without a single model of ethnic, gender or sexual definitions becoming normative.

Conclusion

Rejecting culturalist categorizations, the Strange Fruit activists resist divide and conquer policies that not only pit 'gay' against 'migrant' communities but also separate the latter into assimilable Christians and unassimilable Muslims. Instead, they applied an understanding of cross-communal solidarity that allows for alliances without denying differences, practicing a form of resistance rooted in women of colour feminism's intersectional analytical framework. As Grace Hong observed:

> While 1960s and 1970s black feminism's intersectional analytic was, as it is often narrativized, a critique of the sexism within black nationalist movements or of racism within white feminism, we must also understand the larger implications of intersectionality: it was a complete critique of the epistemological formation of the white supremacist moment of global capital organized around colonial capitalism.[49]

I believe that a queer of colour analysis, drawing on intersectionality and on the practice of groups like Strange Fruit can offer a similarly complete critique of neoliberal capitalism. And while I certainly could not provide it in the space of this chapter, I did hopefully show that contemporary Europe is a promising site for such a critique. European minority queers' attempts at self-articulation are routinely stifled by seemingly antagonistic groups with supposedly opposing aims who are however united in their claim to authenticity, be it authentically queer or authentically Muslim values, allowing them to 'speak for' rather than with, not to mention listen to, queers of colour who are primarily defined through their lack of authentic claims to either identity or culture. This accusation of inauthenticity links minoritarian queers back to the larger group of racialized communities who are neither perceived as proper Europeans by the majority nor properly fit the definition of 'migrant' attributed to them, their supposed 'in-between-state' justifying their silencing and exclusion. The unambiguous identity that frequently is uncritically posited as normative and desirable in this discourse in turn is not merely a reflection of reality but a narrative in whose production considerable energy is invested and on whose internalization by those it targets the system of exclusion fundamentally depends: it remains stable as long as the structure as a whole is left unquestioned and the 'failure' is instead located within those who exceed the boundaries of normative identifications – such as queer Muslims. The framing of the inability to belong as an individual/cultural failure rather than as the outcome of structural exclusions works to disempower and alienate groups who threaten the binary identifications on which Europeanness continues to be built. The ongoing purging of Europe's internal racial Others, black, Muslim, Jewish, Roma, from the continent's history keeps alive a narrative that presents Europe as eternally untouched by any form of hybridity or creolization. The European city emerges as the primary site for an implementation of the discursively produced binaries, but with its intersection of communities, it also provides the source for activist strategies of creolization (as opposed to the assimilation demanded by white society). A queer of colour critique allows us to theorize these creolized positionalities, deemed impossible in dominant identity formations, making them the source of a new discourse rather than attempting to enter the existing one as legitimate subjects. This inter-minority counterdiscourse embracing inauthenticity in turn might be among the most important developments in Europe after 1989, offering an interpretation of a post-national and 'postethnic' continent that is radically different from the model celebrated in official narratives and far more promising for exactly this reason.

Notes

1   An earlier version of this essay was published in *European Journal of Women's Studies*, February 2012, 19(1), 79–95.
2   Hall (1991), p. 18.

3   This notwithstanding, according to a 2005 BBC study, based largely on
    government estimates, in most European nations (with a few exceptions like
    Albania and Bosnia-Herzegovina) Muslims make up no more than 3–7 per cent
    of the population. See: http://news.bbc.co.uk/2/hi/europe/4385768.stm.

4   To be clear: my topic here is not whether Muslim communities are
    homophobic, but the discursive use of this proclaimed homophobia for an
    entirely different purpose, namely the justification of the social and economic
    marginalization of these communities. I argue that the discourse around
    'Muslim homophobia' does nothing to counter anti-queer attitudes among
    Muslims, that it in fact disempowers groups effectively combating intersecting
    oppressions within as well as towards minority communities, such as the Safra
    project in the United Kingdom, SUSPECT in Germany or the Dutch Strange
    Fruit, whose work I will address briefly in this article.

5   'Identified as Muslim', since this ascription is less a matter of religious practice
    or self-identification than of culturalist assignments that assume the existence
    of a homogeneous version of Islam shaping the cultural (rather than religious)
    identity of all members of communities originating in majority Muslim
    nations.

6   That is not to say that this is a new phenomenon: the long presence of Roma,
    Jews and Muslims among others is testament both to the traditionally multi-
    ethnic and multi-religious composition of European societies and to the
    continuous attempt to erase this diversity. See El-Tayeb, F. (2011), *European
    Others. Queering Ethnicity in Postnational Europe*. Minneapolis: University of
    Minnesota Press.

7   See e.g. the short-term recognition of economic segregation and discrimination
    in response to the 2005 French uprisings – and the subsequent failure to put
    any of the measures deemed necessary into practice. See: Coleman, Y. (2006),
    The French Riots: Dancing with the Wolves, 1 January, available at: www.
    solidarity-us.org/node/33.

8   While German chancellor Merkel's statement to this effect in October 2010
    made international headlines, 'the failure of multiculturalism' as the failure
    of Muslims to become 'European' is largely treated as a fact in mainstream
    debates now. See: Conolly, K. (2010), 'Angela Merkel declares death of German
    multiculturalism', *The Guardian*, 18 October, 10.

9   See in particular the expanding anti-hijab legislation. The hijab serves as key
    symbol of Muslim difference, representing parallel societies that are shaped by
    ancient and primitive rather than modern Western structures and need to be
    forcibly 'integrated' for their own (and Europe's) good.

10 People born within the European Union whose parents do not possess EU
    citizenship face larger hurdles on the way towards naturalization and often
    grow up without access to many of the services and privileges available to
    EU members. As Seyla Benhabib observed, 'a two-tiered status of foreignness
    is thus evolving: on the one hand there are third-country national foreign
    residents of European countries, some of whom have been born and raised in
    these countries and who know of no other homeland; on the other hand are
    those who may be near-total strangers to the language, customs, and history of
    their host country but who enjoy special status and privilege by virtue of being

nationals of states which are EU members'. (Benhabib, S. (2002), *The Claims of Culture. Equality and Diversity in the Global Era*. Princeton, NJ: Princeton University Press, p. 158). The situation is further complicated by a two-tiered EU membership which grants Eastern European states lesser influence in the Union.

11 See e.g. the 'Cities against Islamisation' network discussed below.

12 See Manalansan, M. (2005), 'Race, violence, and neoliberal spatial politics in the global city', *Social Text*, 84–5 (23), 141–56; Haritaworn, J., T. Tauquir and E. Erdem (2008), 'Gay imperialism: Gender and sexuality discourse in the "War on Terror"', in A. Kuntsman and Esperanza Miyake (eds), *Out of Place: Interrogating Silences in Queerness/Raciality*. York: Raw Nerve Books.

13 The accusation of migrants' self-segregation is a staple of the recent Europe-wide consensus on the 'failure of multiculturalism', which is taken to mean the failure of minorities to assimilate into majority culture (leaving unexplored the question how such an assimilation into a culture that is explicitly racist and Islamophobic might work). See: El-Tayeb (2011).

14 Said, E. (1979), *Orientalism*. New York: Vintage.

15 Spivak, G. C. (1988), 'Can the subaltern speak?', in C. Nelson and L. Grossberg (eds), *Marxism and the Interpretation of Culture*. Chicago: University of Illinois Press, pp. 271–313; Puar, J. (2007), *Terrorist Assemblages: Homonationalism in Queer Times*. Durham: Duke University Press.

16 See Williams, R. (2010), *The Divided World: Human Rights and Its Violence*. Minneapolis: University of Minnesota Press.

17 Interestingly, far-right parties fare better in European Parliament than national elections. See: http://www.spiegel.de/international/europe/0,1518,629142,00.html.

18 In the Netherlands, these debates are tied to the rise of openly gay and racist politician Pim Fortuijn (who was assassinated in 2002 by a white Dutch environmentalist), the murder of Theo van Gogh by a Dutch-Moroccan Muslim in 2003 and the continuing success of Gert Wilders' Islamophobic but 'pro-gay' Party for Freedom. See: Buruma, I. (2006), *Murder in Amsterdam*. London: Penguin Books; Jivraj, S. and A. de Jong (2011), 'The Dutch homo-emancipation policy and its silencing effects on queer muslims', *Feminist Legal Studies*. Special Issue: 'Liabilities of Queer Antiracist Critique'.

19 See: 'Cities against Islamization', 20 January 2008, http://gatesofvienna.blogspot.com/2008/01/cities-against-islamization.html.

20 According to José Casonova, '[a]s liberal democratic systems, all European societies respect the private exercise of religion, including Islam, as an individual human right. It is the public and collective free exercise of Islam as an immigrant religion that most European societies find difficult to tolerate precisely on the grounds that Islam is perceived as an "un–European" religion'. Casanova, J. (2004), 'Religion, European secular identities, and European integration', *Eurozine*, 29 July, available at: http://www.eurozine.com/articles/2004-07-29-casanova-en.html (last accessed 13 February 2010), p. 7.

21 'Cities against Islamization', http://www.citiesagainstislamisation.com/En/2/.

22 Ibid.

23   See Bernhardt, M. (2007), 'Rassistische Hetze im rosa Gewand. Berliner Schwulenprojekt bläst erneut zur Hatz auf Migranten', *Junge Welt*, 30 June, p. 5; Wolter, S. and K. Yılmaz-Günay (2009), 'Muslimische Jugendliche und Homophobie – braucht es eine zielgrup- penspezifische Pädagogik?', in Bundschuh/Jagusch/Mai (eds), *Facebook, Fun und Ramadan*. Düsseldorf: Informations- und Dokumentationszentrums für Antirassismusarbeit e.V., available at: www.gladt.de.

24   See Haritaworn, J. (2010), 'Queer injuries: The racial politics of "homophobic hate crime" in Germany', *Social Justice*, 37(1), 69–85.

25   See Florida, R. (2002), 'Bohemia and economic Geography', *Journal of Economic Geography*, 2, 55–71.

26   As Alexandra Chasin has shown, the research behind early 1990s studies claiming above-average income for gay men and lesbians was deeply flawed, focusing disproportionally on white, middle-class men (Chasin, A. (2000), *Selling Out. The Gay and Lesbian Movement Goes to Market*. New York: Palgrave, p. 36). Thus, while the discovery of the 'gay market' was clearly a symptom of the larger developments described here and an important step towards the ideology of homonormativity, which sees the interpellation of gay men, and to a much lesser extend lesbians, as consumers as a sign of integration and integration in turn as symptomatic of equality, this discursive shift is not reflective of actual economic gains.

27   Reckwitz, A. (2009), 'Die Selbstkulturalisierung der Stadt', *Eurozine*, 20 May, 1–23, available at: http://www.eurozine.com/articles/2009-05-20-reckwitz-de. html, p. 18.

28   See Duggan, L. (2002), 'The new homonormativity: The sexual politics of neoliberalism', in R. Castronovo and D. D. Nelson (eds), *Materializing Democracy*. Durham, NC: Duke University Press, pp. 173–94.

29   See for example the controversy around the 2010 'East End Pride', targeting a largely Muslim London neighbourhood for its 'rampant homophobia.' The march was cancelled after protests from a coalition of Muslim, queer of colour and progressive organizations and once the organizers' connection to right wing groups was revealed. See: http://www.decolonizequeer.org/?p=60.

30   Halberstam (2005), p. 2.

31   This is true for the European Left in general, which has been slow in letting go of class as the sole marker of oppression, in favour of more intersectional approaches. And while gender and sexuality have been included to a certain extent, race as an analytical category (rather than a biological 'fact') and intersectionality as a methodology arc still largely absent from European Marxist analysis (see e.g. Bourdieu, P. and L. Wacquant (1999), 'On the cunning of imperialist reason', *Theory, Culture & Society*, 16(1), 41–58).

32   See Haritaworn et al. (2008).

33   The focus on homophobia rather than sexism is in part due to the centrality of 'homo-emancipation' to the liberal Dutch self-image (Jivraj and de Jong [2011]). But while this sets the country apart from other European nations, it is important to note that in the Netherlands, too, gender was the first site of conflict. See the pioneering role of Ayaan Hirsi Ali in the Europe-wide rising popularity of 'escape narratives' by (ex)Muslims (El-Tayeb [2011]).

34	Fittingly, the Netherlands' first ever 'anti-radicalization' task force was established in Amsterdam Slotervaart in 2008, targeting Muslim youths and thus confirming that it is this group, and this group alone, that embodies a radicalism threatening the nation (Amsterdam-Slotervaart City Council. Slotervaart (2007), *Action Plan: Countering Radicalisation*, available at: http://www.nuansa.nl/documentatie/beleidsstukken/countering-radicalisation; Slotervaart (2008), *Progress Report Slotervaart Action Plan: Countering Radicalisation*, available at: http://www.nuansa.nl/documentatie/beleidsstukken/progress-report-slotervaart-action-plan.

35	See Strange Fruit (1997), *Strange Fruit Files 1992-1996*. Amsterdam, p. 25.

36	See Arts, H. and A. Nabha (2001), 'Education in the Netherlands: Segregation in a "Tolerant" society', New York: *Humanity in Action Research Report*.

37	Forum, Instituut voor Multiculturele Ontwikkeling (2003), *Homoseksualiteit en gedeeld burgerschap*. Utrecht: Forum, p. 11.

38	The COC, short for Cultuur en Ontspanningscentrum (Center for Culture and Leisure) was founded in 1946, making it the oldest surviving LGBT organization in Europe. Today, it functions as an umbrella group, with a national board focusing on lobbying and about 20 local centres, organizing a variety of activities (see http://www.coc.nl).

39	Ross, M. (2005), 'Beyond the closet as raceless paradigm', in E. P. Johnson and M. G. Henderson (eds), *Black Queer Studies. A Critical Anthology*. Durham: Duke University Press, pp. 161–89, p. 162.

40	Perez, H. (2005), 'You can have my brown body and eat it, too!', *Social Text*, 84–5(23/3–4), 171–92, 177.

41	Ibid.

42	See Open Society Institute (2008), *At Home in Europe Project Muslims in Europe—A Report on 11 EU Cities Findings and Recommendation*, available at: http://www.soros.org/initiatives/home/articles_publications/publications/muslims-europe-20091215 and Amsterdam-Slotervaart City Council (2007) and (2008).

43	Perez (2005).

44	Strange Fruit (1997), p. 23.

45	See El-Tayeb (2011).

46	Strange Fruit went through a number of transformations, including the splitting off of activists who felt the group needed to specifically address the concerns of queer Muslims (Strange Fruit, 1997). Reconstituting themselves as *Secret Garden*, the latter are still active as a COC workgroup.

47	For more details see El-Tayeb (2011).

48	The first of these toris was held in 1994 at the Cosmic theatre in Amsterdam, the centre of Dutch black theater; it had two Surinamese men, an Antillian boy and a Moroccan girl talk about their identities and understanding of queerness (Strange Fruit [1997], p. 10).

49	Grace Hong (2008), p. 101.

Further reading

Bernhardt, M. (2007), 'Rassistische Hetze im rosa Gewand. Berliner Schwulenprojekt bläst erneut zur Hatz auf Migranten', *Junge Welt*, 30 June.

Casanova, J. (2004), 'Religion, European secular identities, and European integration', *Eurozine*, 29 July, available at: http://www.eurozine.com/articles/2004-07-29-casanova-en.html (last accessed 13 February 2010).

Chasin, A. (2000), *Selling Out. The Gay and Lesbian Movement Goes to Market*. New York: Palgrave.

Duggan, L. (2002), 'The new homonormativity: The sexual politics of neoliberalism', in R. Castronovo and D. D. Nelson (eds), *Materializing Democracy*. Durham, NC: Duke University Press, pp. 173–94.

El-Tayeb, F. (2011), *European Others. Queering Ethnicity in Postnational Europe*. Minneapolis: University of Minnesota Press.

—(February 2012), 'Gays who cannot properly be gay': Queer muslims in the neoliberal European city', *European Journal of Women's Studies*, 19(1), 79–95.

Haritaworn, J. (2010), 'Queer injuries: The racial politics of "homophobic hate crime" in Germany', *Social Justice*, 37(1), 69–85.

Haritaworn, J., T. Tauquir and E. Erdem (2008), 'Gay imperialism: Gender and sexuality discourse in the "War on Terror"', in A. Kuntsman and E. Miyake (eds), *Out of Place: Interrogating Silences in Queerness/Raciality*. York: Raw Nerve Books.

Jivraj, S. and A. de Jong (2011), 'The Dutch homo-emancipation policy and its silencing effects on queer muslims', *Feminist Legal Studies*, Special Issue: 'Liabilities of Queer Antiracist Critique'.

Manalansan, M. (2005), 'Race, violence, and neoliberal spatial politics in the global city', *Social Text*, 84–5(23), 141–56.

Puar, J. (2007), *Terrorist Assemblages: Homonationalism in Queer Times*. Durham: Duke University Press.

Perez, H. (2005), 'You can have my brown body and eat it, too!', *Social Text*, 84–5(23/3–4), 171–92, 177.

Ross, M. (2005), 'Beyond the closet as raceless paradigm', in E. P. Johnson and M. G. Henderson (eds), *Black Queer Studies. A Critical Anthology*. Durham: Duke University Press, pp. 161–89.

Wolter, S. and K. Yılmaz-Günay (2009), 'Muslimische Jugendliche und Homophobie – braucht es eine zielgrup- penspezifische Pädagogik?', in Bundschuh/Jagusch/Mai (eds), *Facebook, Fun und Ramadan*. Düsseldorf: Informations- und Dokumentationszentrums für Antirassismusarbeit e.V., available at: www.gladt.de.

14

Seeing like a queer city

Tom Boellstorff

Introduction

It would be impossible to summarize the 12 core chapters making up this volume; along with the introduction and first postscript, they address a staggering array of topics regarding queer cities. I instead extend some key themes, building on three aspects of my own history. First, I have been involved in queer urban activism at various points in my life. This includes involvement in the events during the 1991 coup attempt in Moscow described by Dan Healey in Chapter 5 – some of which took place in my apartment at the time.[1] Second, I have conducted research on *gay* and *lesbi* Indonesians, focusing on cities in that archipelago.[2] Third, I have conducted research on internet sociality.[3]

Reflecting on the varied insights provided by the contributors to this volume in light of these intellectual and activist experiences, I see five key themes of value for future work. First, the contributions to this volume demonstrate the limits of 'neoliberalism' as a conceptual framework. Second, they suggest how work in urban theory that highlights the partial, emergent and contradictory aspects of city governance has much to offer a queer perspective. I will weave the work of Mariana Valverde into the discussion to illustrate this point. Third, while the contributions to this volume take European cities as their foci, they suggest comparative lines of inquiry beyond what I might term a queer Hanseatic League. Fourth, the chapters in diverse ways all insist on attention to the historicity of sexuality and the urban. Finally, the authors of these chapters point towards the growing relevance of digital sociality in queer urbanity.

All told, then, in what follows I reflect on themes of law and governance, norms and practices, history and change. It is through such a contextual and processual approach to queer urbanity that we can best appreciate the contributions to this volume and their import for future research.

Beyond 'Neoliberalism' and normativity

We have reached a point where 'neoliberalism' has lost analytical purchase save when carefully deployed in reference to the use of market models in governance.[4] In many debates within queer studies, the term is used in a much more diffused manner, even acting as a synonym for 'capitalism'. The danger here is a functionalist analytic treatment of an anthropomorphized 'neoliberalism' as knowing what it wants – as possessing a unified set of interests that 'it' pursues through the coherent and consistent exploitation, abjection and exclusion of those who are not white, male, heterosexual, citizens, middle class, abled and so on. The 'good guys' and 'bad guys' are clear – the politics comfortable and known at the outset. That these exclusions and exploitations are very real should not blind us to the limitations of this 'neoliberal' analysis. This recalls Stuart Hall's classic critique of the idea that 'Of course, the right represents the ruling class in power. It represents the occupancy, by capital, of the state which is nothing but its instrument. . . . This is Marxism as a theory of the obvious. The question delivers no new knowledge, only the answer we already knew'.[5]

Construals of state power being self-aware and seamless can backfire in that they ascribe great efficacy to such power, making it hard to see how social change could occur. As Gibson-Graham and many others have long noted, this elides the diverse and often contradictory forms of capitalist and non-capitalist economic practice occurring on an everyday basis.[6] It dehistoricizes capitalism, making it hard to see how this particular hegemony, despite its often violent power, is nonetheless a project that must be constantly renewed and is thus constantly vulnerable to reconfiguration.

This brings us to the question of normativity. In many ways, the critique of heteronormativity has linked a broad range of work falling in some fashion under the rubric of queer studies.[7] Challenging heteronormativity, the view that heterosexual relationships and practices are more natural, holy or proper, is valuable not least because it allows us to differentiate and relate questions of law and social belonging to questions of emotion and affect. This, for instance, provides conceptual tools for distinguishing heterosexism from homophobia, which is vital for understanding and countering differential forms of oppression.[8]

Queer studies scholars have for some time now developed critiques of homonormativity, which occurs when certain forms of homosexuality get ranked over others and marked for preferential inclusion by the state (in particular, the legally sanctioned couple, the white gay man, the middle class lesbian, etc.).[9] What remains deemphasized in this body of analysis is a discussion of queernormativity: often its very existence is ignored or denied.

Yet any discursive formation, any cultural logic, can have normalizing effects linked to political economic dynamics, and the figure of the 'queer' is not exempt. This insight was at the heart of Foucault's preference for a notion of 'reverse discourse' that allowed us to better understand how 'homosexuality began to speak on its own behalf, to demand that its legitimacy or "naturality" be acknowledged, often in the same vocabulary, using the same categories by which it was medically disqualified'.[10]

The point Foucault makes here – a top candidate for the foundational conceptual intervention of queer theory itself – is that we are shaped by the historical dynamics of power that constitute the cultural lifeworlds we in turn change. Foucault's dissatisfaction with the notion of 'liberation' was shaped by its implication that one could begin from a tabula rasa, stepping outside society and context, particularly the idea that such an impossible standpoint of absolute purity was necessary for political efficacy and cultural authenticity. This notion of being within the that which one critiques is at the heart of the notion of 'queer': transforming that which dominates. This implies complicities, contaminations, intimacies. It is a set of insights shared with many allied fields of inquiry like post-colonial theory, and it means recognizing that discursive fields represented as oppositional are not immune to the possibility of producing normativities of their own.

Legal nonconforming and nuisances of queer urbanity

Moving beyond the languages of neoliberalism and normativity as self-evident constructs permits us to advance a more nuanced analysis of queer urbanity. To demonstrate this in the most succinct manner possible, I will turn to the work of Mariana Valverde. The title of this chapter pays homage to her article 'Seeing Like a City: The Dialectic of Modern and Premodern Ways of Seeing in Urban Governance'.[11] Valverde advances the claim that the 'seeing like a state' rubric associated with James Scott, while of value in many contexts, cannot be simply extrapolated to questions of the urban.[12] Forms of urban power are notable for their conjunctural character – city council districts, fire districts and police districts may not overlap, indeed may use different data sets and modes of governance, and thus have difficulty communicating with each other. Valverde challenges the 'methodological tendency to regard legal and governance inventions . . . as tools chosen to implement a fixed political project'.[13] This is quite a queer point. Given the emphasis on history that we find in most chapters in this volume, it is relevant that Valverde underscores how 'the relationship between modern and premodern modes of urban power/knowledge . . . is not captured by narratives in which one mode of power/knowledge replaces the other in Weberian fashion. Neither is the relationship reducible to the hegemony-versus-resistance paradigm'.[14]

In regard to intersections of the queer and urban, two aspects of Valverde's analysis are of particular interest. The first is Valverde's concept of 'structural contingency', which provides one way to avoid totalizing narratives of neoliberalism.[15] Valverde charts the history of the fascinating concept of the 'legal nonconforming' building or social formation in urban law, through what I might term the routinization of exception:

> The fundamental role played by the exception-granting mechanism in contemporary planning is well known to practitioners, but it is not reflected in planning textbooks or in official law. The fact is that in many cities today, legal nonconforming uses are everywhere. There are condominium buildings that are twice as tall as the zoning regulations theoretically allow, many low-income people continue to live above workshops and stores despite the zoning rules, and there are numerous businesses that are not supposed to be located where they actually are.[16]

What is striking here is that 'legal nonconforming use' is 'the category that installs exceptionality, indeed illegality, at the very heart of modernist planning law'.[17] Note this is very different from the 'state of exception' discussed in the work of Agamben and linked to the figure of the concentration camp.[18] The notion of 'legal nonconforming use' queers the city by instilling exceptionality within its heart, not at its margins. It both geographically and legally incorporates the Other in the tension of the nonconforming. Surely there is great potential for a queer reading of Valverde's analysis that would permit advancing a notion of 'queer nonconforming' that is included through exception. Such an analytical approach would generate research questions and theoretical insights that could significantly advance the narratives of queer communities in European cities presented in the volume.

A second issue raised by Valverde with relevance to the analysis of queer urbanity is 'the category of nuisance'.[19] Emphasizing that 'the capacious and rather fuzzy category of nuisance enables a significant amount of legal governance', Valverde shows how this category is linked to a category of 'enjoyment' – if you prevent someone from enjoying their urban environment, you are making a nuisance.[20] Thus 'nuisance is an inherently relational and thus embodied category'.[21] As a result, 'since microcommunities, in the context of urban governance, are always assumed to share certain local norms and tastes . . . nuisance and related legal disputes play a constitutive role in the construction of culturally specific collective subjectivities'.[22]

As with the notion of 'legal nonconforming' discussed earlier, the category of nuisance has rich potential for advancing queer urban analysis. Historically, queer persons have often been targeted for 'nuisance abatement' – seen not so much as an existential threat to the city, but endangering others' 'enjoyment' of the urban context. Furthermore, as Valverde notes, the notion of nuisance is powerfully intersubjective and embodied.

Tracking, for instance, how a gay pride march is sometimes construed as a nuisance and in other cases as an asset might thus have much to offer future investigations into queer urbanity.

Beyond the queer Hanseatic League

Valverde developed her analysis regarding the specificities of urban governance, of 'seeing like a city', with regard to North America and particularly Canada. Yet I do not think this makes her insights any less valuable for the contexts discussed in this volume. This is not only because city governments worldwide often share ideas and copy policies first implemented elsewhere. In addition, the insights discussed above are valuable because they help push us into a more comparative and less Eurocentric frame.

To be clear: my point is not to find fault with the fact that the chapters in this volume discuss Europe. No one book can do everything; focus is important, and in any case the range of cities and issues discussed is impressive indeed. My point is rather that the studies in this volume can now be situated in a more global perspective. For instance, in my own work in Indonesia I have seen *gay* and *lesbi* Indonesians engage in what de Certeau referred to as 'tactics' of place-making in urban environments, from parks to apartments and salons.[23] Given that Indonesia is the fourth-most populous nation (after China, India and the United States) and home to more Muslims than any other country, the questions of Islam and belonging that haunt discussions of contemporary European cities can be usefully placed in dialogue with urban contexts where Islam is the majority religion.[24] Similarly, forms of queer urbanity elsewhere in Asia, in Latin America, in Africa and beyond can provide fascinating comparative material to extend the insights of these chapters.

History, event, movement

A common theme of the chapters in this volume, which largely take the form of linear chronological narratives, is an attention to history. The World Wars loom in the background as transformative disruptions in urban life and national identity, and attention is paid to activism and organizing. In terms of this overall interest in the historicity of queer urbanity and also the concerns with queernormativity discussed earlier, it is worth asking how European urban and national histories shape not just forms of exclusion, but forms of inclusion as well.

For instance, in his book *Symptoms of Modernity: Jews and Queers in Late-Twentieth-Century Vienna*, Matti Bunzl explores over a century of relationships between Jews, queers and national belonging in Austria.

He notes that 'through the modern twin discourses of anti-Semitism and homophobia, these groups were mobilized and fortified as the constitutive outsides of respectable Germanness, thereby allowing the retrospective fixing of the nation-state as a fantasized public space of ethnic and sexual purity'.[25] Of particular interest is his conclusion that:

> [T]he emergence of Jews and queers into Vienna's public sphere should be read as a signpost of postmodernity. This is meant literally, in that the unprecedented prominence of these groups within the city's urban landscape signals a genuine departure from the modern logic of Jews' and homosexuals' foundational abjection. In a globalizing world, the principal Others of the modern nation-state no longer figure as constitutive outsides. On the contrary, they have been incorporated as fundamental elements of a diversified public sphere.[26]

The significance of this insight cannot be underestimated. Recalling my earlier discussion of inclusion through 'legal nonconforming', Bunzl here gestures towards a contemporary dynamic of contested belonging in the European city worth additional investigation. The attention paid by queer scholars to inequality and exclusion is critical to that intellectual project, but as several contributors to this volume note, that project loses comprehensive force if we disavow or downplay the forms of social justice and inclusion that, however, incomplete and unequally distributed, must be brought into the analytical frame in a manner that resists both triumphalism and teleology.

An important emphasis in Bunzl's analysis, shared by nearly every chapter in this volume, is the role of events in urban queer subject and community formation – from Berlin to Ljubljana. Unlike a community or an enclave, 'events' in my formulation here are delimited geographically and temporally. When the geographical delimitation is highlighted, they are often termed 'memorials'; when the temporal delimitation is highlighted, they are often termed 'marches' or 'protests'. It is unusual for such events to take place in the countryside or even the suburb; rather, people typically hold them in a place seen as the city's heart.

Forms of movement are also a common theme in analyses of queer urbanity. While of course, many queer people are born in cities, cities are also the prototypical destination for queer persons in Europe and beyond (i.e. for instance, very much the case in Indonesia). The 'coming out' narrative, in whatever form it takes in varied cultural contexts, often includes not just a personal coming-to-consciousness, but a physical movement away from the family home to an urban context. In the United States, this narrative has been transformed by many persons, particularly but not exclusively queer persons of colour, for whom separation from the family is undesirable for affective, economic and social reasons. In Indonesia as well, persons often live in the parental home until married: many *gay* and *lesbi* Indonesians use the excuse of a job opportunity (almost always a major city) as a reason to move from the family home, but still keep in close contact.

As several contributions to this volume note, movement between cities is also a feature of many queer urban lives, ranging from brief visits for a pride parade or to visit friends, to longer-term migrations (for instance, from Helsinki to Sweden or Denmark). In Europe as in many other parts of the world, international forms of migration are often to cities, and these migrations continue to transform queer urban experiences.

Digital queer urbanity

As an anthropologist, I always hesitate to make universalizing claims, but it may not be hyperbole to assert that we have already reached a point in human history where there is no such thing as a queer selfhood that does not have a digital component. In particular, the rapid global spread of mobile devices, even to persons living in poverty, means that forms of 'digital divide' are in flux. However, while internet technologies are reshaping diverse domains of human existence, we must not let the technology sector's affinity for hype-filled narratives to occlude historical legacies and continuities.

The impact of online sociality on queer urbanity is so vast that I will here simply note three forms this impact can take that are worthy of empirical and theoretical attention. First are the globalizing aspects of digital technologies. Because historically queer life is rarely learnt from one's 'tradition' or family, queer persons have long engaged with translocal narratives in forging subjectivities and communities that are influenced by, but not reducible to, that translocality. In my own work, I have used the notion of 'dubbing culture' to discuss how queer persons reconfigure translocal narratives in the context of technology, in a manner analogous to a 'dubbed' film where the moving lips of the actors and the voice rendered in another language do not match up.[27] In contemporary urban contexts, internet technologies allow for important forms of communication and interaction between cities, between cities and their countrysides, and international organizations. Simply because someone who suspects they may not be heterosexual lives in a city does not mean they will know how to access information and community in their environs. Often, important connections will be with distant others through forms of digital intimacy ranging from Facebook posts to informational websites.

Second, one of the biggest developments in the digital realm since the mid-2000s has been the rise of mobile devices like smartphones and tablets. The prominence of these devices has shaped a growing use of the internet for localizing as well as globalizing connection. As the internet increasingly moves with us in real time, queer urban identity, community and practice is simultaneously online and offline, and this overlay between the digital and the physical is certain to reshape cities. For instance, the experience of public transportation is vastly different now that riding a bus or train typically means engaging with mobile devices at the same time. This means being in a state of privatized online connection– using a personal device rather than watching a shared monitor – even while in a public vehicle moving through an urban environment.

Third, the digital does not simply play a derivative or secondary role compared to the physical. The growing omnipresence of internet engagement means that the offline is gradually becoming experienced as the state of being temporally not online. There can thus emerge forms of online sociality that have their own logics, norms and even digital places that cannot be reduced to any one physical-world place or social context. From virtual worlds to online games and some social network sites and other browser-based venues, we find urban denizens engaging in forms of digital placemaking – even participating in virtual cities that exist only online.

Needless to say, these three impacts of the digital on urban experience are not exhaustive. They simply point towards some of the many ways that online socialities will continue to transform urban experience. As with any other technological disruption, these effects of the online could be exclusionary or inclusive, corporatized or community-based, in service of social justice or contributing to forms of discrimination. It depends on what we do with these technologies, and for that reason alone continuing research on them is desperately needed.

Conclusion

While there is, of course, no singular way that queer cities 'see', in this discussion I have sought to track key intersections of queer sexualities and urbanisms. Worldwide, the trend towards greater urbanization continues apace, particularly in non-Western contexts. Our cities of the future could be dystopian slums of despair, utopian metropolises of progress, or both at once, zoned into uneasy coexistence.

Given that queer communities have been central to the development of the modern city in Europe and beyond, attention to the place of sexuality in urban life could provide pathways towards a better understanding of how urban life might contribute more powerfully to human flourishing. If we try seeing like a queer city, just for a little while, what new vistas might emerge?

Notes

1   See Boellstorff, T. (2007a), *A Coincidence of Desires: Anthropology, Queer Studies, Indonesia*. Durham: Duke University Press, pp. 9–10; Boellstorff, T. (2012), 'The politics of similitude: Global sexuality activism, ethnography, and the western subject', *Trans-Scripts*, 2, 22–39, p. 25; Gessen, M. (1991), 'Soviet queers fight coup: Gay newspaper became printing plant for Russian resistance', *The Advocate*, 24 September, p. 50.

2 See Boellstorff, T. (2005a), *The Gay Archipelago: Sexuality and Nation in Indonesia.* Princeton: Princeton University Press; Boellstorff, T. (2005b), 'Between religion and desire: Being Muslim and *Gay* in Indonesia', *American Anthropologist*, 107(4), 575–85; Boellstorff (2007a).

3 Boellstorff, T. (2008), *Coming of Age in Second Life: An Anthropologist Explores the Virtually Human.* Princeton: Princeton University Press; Boellstorff, T., B. Nardi, C. Pearce and T. L. Tylor (2012), *Ethnography and Virtual Worlds: A Handbook of Method.* Princeton: Princeton University Press.

4 Ong, A. (2006), *Neoliberalism as Exception: Mutations in Citizenship and Sovereignty.* Durham: Duke University Press.

5 Hall, S. (1988), *The Hard Road to Renewal: Thatcherism and the Crisis of the Left.* London: Verso, p. 165.

6 Gibson-Graham, J. K. (1996), *The End of Capitalism (As We Knew It): A Feminist Critique of Political Economy.* Minneapolis: University of Minnesota Press; Gibson-Graham, J. K. (2006), *A Postcapitalist Politics.* Minneapolis: University of Minnesota Press.

7 Wiegman, R. (2012), *Object Lessons.* Durham: Duke University Press.

8 Boellstorff, T. (2004), 'The emergence of political homophobia in Indonesia: Masculinity and national belonging', *Ethnos*, 69(4), 465–86.

9 For example: Duggan, L. (2003), *The Twilight of Equality? Neoliberalism, Cultural Politics, and the Attack on Democracy.* Boston: Beacon Press.

10 Foucault, M. (1978), *The History of Sexuality, Volume 1: An Introduction.* New York: Vintage Books, p. 101. For further discussion: Boellstorff, T. (2007b), 'When marriage falls: Queer coincidences in straight time', *GLQ: A Journal of Gay and Lesbian Studies*, 13(2/3), 227–48; Boellstorff, T. (2011), 'But do not identify as gay: A proleptic genealogy of the MSM category', *Cultural Anthropology*, 26(2), 287–312.

11 Valverde, M. (2011), 'Seeing like a city: The dialectic of modern and premodern ways of seeing in urban governance', *Law & Society Review*, 45(2), 277–312.

12 Scott, J. (1998), *Seeing Like a State: How Certain Schemes to Improve the Human Condition Have Failed.* New Haven: Yale University Press.

13 Valverde (2011), p. 280.

14 Ibid.

15 Ibid., p. 289.

16 Ibid., p. 290.

17 Ibid., p. 291.

18 Agamben, G. (1998), *Homo Sacer: Sovereign Power and Bare Life.* Stanford: Stanford University Press.

19 Valverde (2011), p. 291.

20 Ibid., p. 292.

21 Ibid., p. 294.

22 Ibid., p. 295.

23 Boellstorff (2005a), p. 129.

24 Boellstorff (2005b).

25 Bunzl, M. (2002), *Symptoms of Modernity: Jews and Queers in Late-Twentieth-Century Vienna*. Berkeley: University of California Press, p. ix.

26 Bunzl (2004), p. x.

27 See Boellstorff (2005a) for a detailed discussion.

Further reading

Agamben, G. (1998), *Homo Sacer: Sovereign Power and Bare Life*. Stanford: Stanford University Press.

Boellstorff, T. (2004), 'The emergence of political homophobia in Indonesia: Masculinity and national belonging', *Ethnos*, 69(4), 465–86.

—(2005a), *The Gay Archipelago: Sexuality and Nation in Indonesia*. Princeton: Princeton University Press.

—(2005b), 'Between religion and desire: Being Muslim and *Gay* in Indonesia', *American Anthropologist*, 107(4), 575–85.

—(2007a), *A Coincidence of Desires: Anthropology, Queer Studies, Indonesia*. Durham: Duke University Press.

—(2007b), 'When marriage falls: Queer coincidences in straight time', *GLQ: A Journal of Gay and Lesbian Studies*, 13(2/3), 227–48.

—(2008), *Coming of Age in Second Life: An Anthropologist Explores the Virtually Human*. Princeton: Princeton University Press.

—(2011), 'But do not identify as gay: A proleptic genealogy of the MSM category', *Cultural Anthropology*, 26(2), 287–312.

—(2012), 'The politics of similitude: Global sexuality activism, ethnography, and the western subject', *Trans-Scripts*, 2, 22–39.

Bunzl, M. (2002), *Symptoms of Modernity: Jews and Queers in Late-Twentieth-Century Vienna*. Berkeley: University of California Press.

Duggan, L. (2003), *The Twilight of Equality? Neoliberalism, Cultural Politics, and the Attack on Democracy*. Boston: Beacon Press.

Foucault, M. (1978), *The History of Sexuality, Volume 1: An Introduction*. New York: Vintage Books.

Gessen, M. (1991), 'Soviet queers fight coup: Gay newspaper became printing plant for Russian resistance', *The Advocate*, 24 September, p. 50.

Gibson-Graham, J. K. (1996), *The End Of Capitalism (As We Knew It): A Feminist Critique of Political Economy*. Minneapolis: University of Minnesota Press.

—(2006), *A Postcapitalist Politics*. Minneapolis: University of Minnesota Press.

Hall, S. (1988), *The Hard Road to Renewal: Thatcherism and the Crisis of the Left*. London: Verso.

Ong, A. (2006), *Neoliberalism as Exception: Mutations in Citizenship and Sovereignty*. Durham: Duke University Press.

Scott, J. (1998), *Seeing Like a State: How Certain Schemes to Improve the Human Condition Have Failed*. New Haven: Yale University Press.

Valverde, M. (2011), 'Seeing like a city: The dialectic of modern and premodern ways of seeing in urban governance', *Law & Society Review*, 45(2), 277–312.

Wiegman, R. (2012), *Object Lessons*. Durham: Duke University Press.

INDEX